for
the
people

▲Addison-Wesley

Publishing Company
Reading, Massachusetts · Menlo Park, California
London · Amsterdam · Don Mills, Ontario · Sydney

for the people

A Consumer Action Handbook

Joanne Manning Anderson

introduction by
Ralph Nader

ISBN 0-201-00200-0
ABCDEFGHIJ-DO-7987

TO JIM

introduction

The informed consumer asks questions about what to buy or not to buy. The active consumer does something about what is sold. This collection of consumer action project guides gives the active consumer some effective tools to take on consumer injustice and make a difference. In the process of using these guides, citizens will develop their own strategies and their own pathways to greater effectiveness. Indeed, much of what is in this volume by Joanne Manning Anderson reflects both the experience and insights of citizens who grappled with the same problems in their community that so many other people around the country are complaining about in frustration.

Being an astute consumer and backing up your grievances with constructive action to tame corporate derelictions and other commercial abuses is not something usually learned in formal education. If it is to be learned, self-education is the most likely way. This self-education can be fun as well as useful in improving one's money's worth in the marketplace. It is always a stretching of one's development as a human being helping other human beings.

As you absorb and apply these materials, you will come across references to additional consumer materials distributed by Public Citizen and other consumer groups which are marking the advent of a new literature for developing life skills. These skills are civic, not occupational, in nature. They relate more to ends, not the means, of what an economy should be about. They speak toward the quality of economic activity which should be the good life in broad dimensions. Better health, more efficient energy, safer, more nutritious food and the development of civic skills do not register the conventional inputs of the gross national product. They simply make for a better standard of living.

Your comments and suggestions will help in the periodic refinement of these and other consumer action projects. We would like to hear from you as you discover new and better ways to achieve your goals. Please send your ideas to Public Citizen, P.O. Box 19404, Washington, D.C., 20036. Your progress will hearten other Americans who are committing themselves to similar efforts.

Washington, D.C.   Ralph Nader
May 1977

acknowledgments

The many talented and dedicated people who worked with me on various aspects of this book deserve more credit and thanks than these acknowledgments can express.

Public Citizen's Health Research Group provided many of the ideas and materials for Chapters 1 and 2, "How to Develop a Consumers' Directory of Doctors," and "How to Stop the Rx Ripoff." Keith Johnson offered most helpful technical assistance on "How to Stop the Rx Ripoff." Patricia Powers and Elma Grissel advised me as I waded through the volumes of materials and project ideas regarding nursing homes.

Martin Rogol, Director of the National Public Interest Research Group (PIRG) and the staff members of the Vermont PIRG developed the ideas and initial materials on the projects discussed in Chapter 5, "Fighting for Lower Utility Bills." Martin Rogol also did most of the work on Chapter 1, "Working Effectively with the Media."

The Connecticut Citizen Action Group (CCAG) developed Chapter 12, "Changing the Laws." Ruth Fort and Faith Keating provided invaluable assistance with editing and Gaylord Bourne, Jan Elvin, Mary Alice McKean, and Elizabeth Hatch all contributed much needed administrative support.

The many student interns who worked with me provided research assistance as well as enthusiasm and good humor that added an immeasurable dimension to our working environment. I thank them all: Stuart Allen, Richard Hirsch, Seth Kovens, Susan Mudd, Larry Platt, Bunny Wagner, Doug Woodham, and Kathy Wyotech.

Washington, D.C.   J.M.A.
May 1977

contents

PART 2 ENERGY PROJECTS 89

PART 3 GROCERY PROJECTS 133

4

PART **4** THE MEDIA AND EFFECTING LEGISLATION   205

PART 1
health care projects

The health of the people is really the foundation upon which all their happiness and all their powers as a state depend.

Benjamin Disraeli
Speech, July 24, 1877

INTRODUCTION

Health care costs in the United States are spiraling; in 1960, $25.9 billion was spent on health care, but by 1975 the amount had more than quadrupled to reach an estimated $115 billion.[1] That figure represents 8 percent of our Gross National Product. For the one out of every ten Americans who have no form of health insurance, these costs can be devastating. Even those with health insurance find, on the average, that only 30 percent of health care costs are covered. Physicians fees alone cost Americans about $20 billion annually, drug costs have reached $10 billion, and nursing home care, $7.5 billion.

Despite the enormous amounts of money that flow into our health care system and the fact that the industry employs over 3 million people, it does not offer all Americans satisfactory health care. In fact, unnecessary surgery, misprescribing of drugs, unnecessary hospitalization, and other dangerous and expensive excesses in the health care system are thought to be among the leading causes of preventable death in the United States.

Unless the health care industry is made accountable to those it serves, we will continue to receive inadequate health care at astronomical prices. Citizens must become aware of their rights as patients, exercise those rights, and work to lower costs and improve care. The action projects in Part One provide guidelines for change in some of the most problematic areas: prescription drug prices, availability of information about physician costs and services, and the care and rights of nursing home residents.

Chapter 1, "How to Stop the Rx Ripoff," outlines why prescription drug costs are unnecessarily high and unavailable to consumers for comparative shopping. The project details action citizens can take to make those prices available, competitive, and, therefore, lower.

Chapter 2, "Compiling a Consumers' Directory of Doctors," is a step-by-step guide to publishing the kind of basic information about doctors—training, services and fees—that are now unavailable but needed by consumers before making the important decision about which doctor to visit.

In Chapter 3, "Nursing Homes—A First Step to Change," two investigative surveys are presented that can lead to reform of this abuse-ridden industry. The first—a review of the licenses and inspection reports of nursing homes—will provide consumers and reform groups with information about nursing homes which are not in compliance with regulations but which continue to operate. The second survey is a review of the policies and practices of homes to determine whether they are complying with federal regulations which guarantee patients in nursing homes certain basic rights.

The projects are not untried; citizen groups across the country have proved them workable and worthwhile. In Michigan, Vermont, and Connecticut, these prescription drug projects resulted in new laws which lower the costs of prescription drugs by allowing generic substitution or mandating in-store price posting. Consumers in parts of Maryland, Massachusetts, Michigan, New York and other states can make more informed choices when selecting physicians because consumer groups in those states

---

[1]All numbered references will be found at the back of the book under References.

3

have followed the guide presented in Chapter 2 and published Doctors' Directories. California's nursing home residents now have an ombudsman monitoring the industry because citizens discovered that nursing homes were improperly licensed and inspected.

Citizen action programs like these are a necessity to improve health care and make the medical community more responsive to consumers. Only if more and more citizens take action on health care problems will the industry undertake reforms to make America a nation where money invested in health care prevents illness and increases the quality of life.

CHAPTER 1

how to stop the R℞ ripoff

WHY IS PRESCRIPTION DRUG PRICE DISCLOSURE NECESSARY?

The cost of prescription drugs affects everyone and for some it is a continuous expense. Most consumers take prescriptions to the nearest drug store and unquestioningly pay the bill. Some never return for their medicine after being quoted a price they cannot afford.

What these consumers don't know about drug pricing hurts them economically and sometimes medically. What they don't know is that they might have purchased the same brand name drug for two-thirds the price at another store. Or, if their doctor had prescribed generically, they might have purchased a chemically equivalent drug under its generic name* in the same store at even greater savings. In a survey conducted by the Missouri PIRG, prices for the brand drug Equanil ranged from $4.15 to $7.20 while meprobamate, the generic name for Equanil, sold for as little as $1.50! Surveys by dozens of other PIRGs and consumer groups have shown equally extreme price differences among stores.

Furthermore, a pharmacy may inadvertently or deliberately charge customers different prices for the same drug. A District of Columbia PIRG study in 1975 re-

---

*A generic name is that given to all drugs with the same active ingredients. For example, acetaminophen is a generic name; Tylenol is a brand name. All drugs have generic names.

5

vealed that out of 28 pharmacies surveyed three times each for the price of the same drug, only ten charged the same price on all three occasions. Fourteen of the stores had discrepancies between prices of as much as 80 cents.

Consumers can conveniently compare price differences for almost every other commodity they purchase, so why not for prescription drugs? When releasing the results of a pricing survey, the Director of the Connecticut Citizen Action Group said:

> It is outrageous that the same drug is selling for more than three times as much in stores on the same block and yet there is no way for the public to know this.

This project suggests citizen action aimed at educating consumers about prescription drugs and lowering drug prices—action that has proven successful for citizen groups in Vermont, Michigan, Connecticut, California, and many other states. Two surveys are suggested. One, for use in states without price disclosure laws, will provide prescription drug price information useful to area consumers and supportive of such laws. The second, designed for use in states with disclosure laws, enables groups to evaluate the laws and determine whether pharmacies are in compliance.

WHY ARE PRESCRIPTION DRUG PRICES HIGH AND DIFFICULT TO COMPARE?

Prescription drug prices have risen steadily over the last 15 years. The burden of rising costs falls most heavily on those who can least afford the increased expenses—the elderly, those with low incomes, and the chronically ill. The blame for unnecessarily high costs and consumer abuse rests with pharmaceutical companies, pharmacists, physicians, and the government.

The pharmaceutical industry has led most United States industries in profit rates for the last ten years,[1] with worldwide sales soaring from $3 million in 1960 to $14 billion in 1976.[2] Within the industry the prescription drug market is dominated by large manufacturers; in 1975 the 21 largest firms accounted for 83.5 percent of the total United States market[3] and the largest pharmaceutical company represented 7.5 percent of that market.[4] The growth of the drug industry and the dominance of large companies is due, in large part, to their expensive and successful promotional campaigns and to government patent laws which promote price monopolies on drugs.

In the late 1960s and early 1970s, the industry spent about $1 billion on the promotion and advertising of drugs, or about 20 cents out of every sales dollar. At the same time, the industry expended only 2.5 cents of the sales dollar on quality control research.[5]

The situation today remains virtually the same. Donald Rucker, formerly of the Department of Health, Education, and Welfare, has stated that about 85 percent of the money spent on promotion and advertising can be classified as "economic waste" because the campaigns, which are aimed at physicians, have little to do with the actual value of one drug over another.[6] The large manufacturers promote their brand name drugs, claiming higher quality than either generic drugs or the brand name drugs of smaller companies.

Due to drug patent laws and market manipulation by manufacturers, only about 25 percent of drugs on the market at any given time are available under their generic name; the other 75 percent are available under one or several brand names.

Most drugs are first marketed under a brand name which is protected by a trademark and patent for ten years. During that time no other manufacturer may produce the drug under another brand name or the generic name. Of the 200 most frequently prescribed drugs in the United States, approximately one-half are protected by a patent and, therefore, are available only from that company. Even when the patent expires, other manufacturers often choose not to produce the drug because physicians have been deluged with promotional materials about the original drug and have become used to prescribing by the brand name. Furthermore, manufacturers are inclined to allow each other to corner the market on a particular drug and avoid price competition.

If manufacturers do produce the drug under another brand name or the generic name, they fight an uphill battle to convince physicians that their drug is not inferior to the well-known brand names, despite overwhelming evidence in support of their contention. The Food and Drug Administration reviews and assesses test data presented by manufacturers on all new drugs before they can be marketed. They have found, with few exceptions, that generic and lesser known brand name drugs are chemically and therapeutically equivalent to the original brand name product. A former director of FDA's Bureau of Drugs[7] writes:

> On the basis of the data we have accrued to date, we cannot conclude there is a significant difference in quality between the generic and brand name tested. . . . Some professionals seem to mistakenly equate "big manufacturer" or "generic" with bad. This impression is not borne out by the facts.

Other supporters of the bioequivalency of the majority of generic drugs include a nine-person task force, headed by Dr. Richard W. Berliner, Dean of the Yale University School of Medicine. The task force developed a 78-page report on the subject for the Office of Technology Assessment of the United States Congress. Physicians, however, generally continue to prescribe by the well-known brand name, unaware of or unconcerned about the fact that their patients are needlessly paying more for these prescriptions. The bonus gifts physicians are offered along with the brand name drug by many drug company salespersons have "convinced" some physicians; other physicians simply do not take the time to compare the composition of drugs and fall prey to the high-powered and sometimes exaggerated claims of large manufacturers.

Manufacturers and physicians are not solely responsible for the high and varying costs that consumers pay for prescription drugs. Pharmacies, which set prices for prescription drugs, share the blame insofar as they charge excess markups, vary prices from customer to customer, or fail to substitute low-cost generic drugs when allowed by law. Due to the efforts of pharmacies and their trade associations, in most states antiadvertising laws or regulations protect pharmacies from competitive pricing. Antisubstitution laws prohibit substitution of generic or lower cost brand names for the brand designated in the prescription.

Antiadvertising Laws

As of late 1974, antiadvertising laws or pharmacy board regulations prohibited the disclosure of prescription drug prices in all but sixteen states and the District of

Columbia.* The laws vary from state to state, with some prohibiting all types of price disclosure and others prohibiting only certain types of disclosure. A chart summarizing all state statutes regarding disclosure of prescription drug prices appears in Resource 1.1. The chart was compiled in early 1975, and the law in your state may have changed, so check the current status with the state pharmacy board or the clerk of the state legislature.

Disclosure of prices can take several different forms:

☐   in-store, verbal disclosure to persons with or without a prescription;

☐   telephone disclosure to persons with or without a prescription;

☐   in-store price posters;

☐   in-store booklets listing prices;

☐   price lists available for consumers to take home; and

☐   media advertising of prices.

Even in those states where disclosure is not prohibited, there is no guarantee that consumers can compare drug prices. The state pharmacy board may consider advertising unethical, or pharmacists may simply choose not to disclose prices. Of the 17 jurisdictions without antiadvertising laws, only one—New Hampshire—has a statute requiring in-store posting of prescription prices. Only two—Nevada and Washington—require verbal in-store and telephone disclosure of drug prices.[8]

Consumer surveys in the states without antiadvertising laws that do not have price disclosure legislation, demonstrate the difficulty of determining prescription prices. Even persistent citizens who can invest a great deal of time have often been unable to make complete and accurate comparisons because not all pharmacists cooperate with their efforts. For example, in 1975 the North Carolina PIRG conducted a telephone pricing survey in six cities and found that the percentage of pharmacies refusing to disclose prices varied considerably from city to city and was as high as 43 percent.

Repeal of antiadvertising statutes will not ensure price disclosure and must be coupled with enactment of new legislation making some forms of drug price disclosure mandatory and setting guidelines for price advertising.

The Supreme Court's decision in *Virginia State Board of Pharmacy v. Virginia Citizens Consumer Council*† has paved the way for consumers to obtain price information from pharmacists. The case struck down the Virginia law which prohibited pharmacists from advertising prescription drug price information, holding that such laws unconstitutionally interfered with the First Amendment right of consumers to receive such information. Moreover, the following week, in *Terry v. California State Board of Pharmacy,*‡ the Supreme Court struck down a California statute prohibiting media advertising of drug prices.

---

*States which allow, but do not necessarily require, price disclosure include: Delaware, Idaho, Kentucky, Montana, Nevada, New Hampshire, North Carolina, Oregon, South Carolina, Tennessee, Utah, Vermont, Virginia, Washington, Wisconsin, and Wyoming.

†No. 75-895, 44 U.S.L.W. 4686 (May 24, 1976).

‡395 F. Supp. 94 (N.D. Calif., 1975) (three-judge court), affd., No. 75-336, 44 U.S.L.W. (June 7, 1976).

Statutes in other states which prohibit drug price advertising may vary from the Virginia and California statutes but, as a practical matter, it is very unlikely that any such statutes can now survive constitutional scrutiny. You should consult with local attorneys to gauge the impact that the recent Supreme Court cases will have on the laws in your state. If those laws appear to be invalid, consumer groups should begin to work for passage of legislation mandating price disclosure and setting guidelines for advertising (See the Model Substitution Statute, in Resource 1.2). Publicize the Supreme Court decisions, obtain official statements from state attorneys general indicating that the statutes will not be enforced, and conduct pricing surveys to provide legislatures with data to support your claims that price discrepancies are extreme. If there is some question concerning the constitutionality of your state statute, consider litigation challenging the constitutionality of the statute.

The Federal Trade Commission, after reviewing reams of information, including prescription drug pricing surveys done by eleven PIRGs and many other consumer groups, proposed two regulations relating to prescription drug price disclosure (see Resource 1.3). The proposed regulations would preempt state antiadvertising statutes and pharmacy board regulations or ethical codes by allowing, but not making mandatory, disclosure of drug prices. The regulations also specify the information that must be included with price disclosure. Final action has been postponed pending evaluation of the impact of the Supreme Court decision.

Antisubstitution Laws

Until the 1950s, antisubstitution laws were meant to protect consumers from pharmacist substitution of a drug chemically different from that prescribed. However, at the behest of large drug companies and with considerable lobbying by the National Pharmaceutical Council (an organization of large manufacturers), states broadened the meaning of the laws to protect drug companies, not consumers. Antisubstitution laws now prohibit a pharmacist from filling a prescription with any other brand of the same drug or with the generic equivalent even if a considerably cheaper and chemically and therapeutically equivalent drug is available. If the physician has prescribed the drug by its generic name, the pharmacist may fill the prescription with any drug bearing that generic name—a brand name drug, or a lower cost generic drug.

Substitution is prohibited by law or pharmacy board codes of ethics in all states except Connecticut, Maryland, Michigan, and Kentucky. The District of Columbia also does not prohibit substitution.

The repeal of antisubstitution laws is imperative to guarantee equitable availability and pricing of prescription drugs However, price posting laws must precede such action, to ensure that pharmacists fill prescriptions with low cost generic drugs and pass the savings along to customers. The Texas PIRG pointed out the need for this precaution in their pricing survey:

Our survey showed that when pharmacists were presented with prescriptions for tetracycline [a generic name] over one-third of the pharmacists quoted a price for one of the most expensive brand names of tetracycline.

LIST OF DRUGS

In top 200				Not in top 200			
Acute		Chronic		Acute		Chronic	
Generic	Brand name	Generic	Brand name	Generic	Brand name	Generic	Brand name
Ampicillin 250 mg No. 40	Polycillin 250 mg No. 40	Meprobamate 400 mg No. 50	Equanil 400 mg No. 50	Chloral Hydrate 500 mg No. 20	Noctec 500 mg No. 20	P.E.T.N. 10 mg No. 100	Peritrate** 10 mg No. 100
Tetracycline 250 mg No. 40	Achromycin V 250 mg No. 40	Estrogens Conjugated* 1.25 mg No. 63	Premarin* 1.25 mg No. 63	Cyproheptadine	Periactin 4 mg No. 36	Nylidrine***	Arlidin** 6 mg No. 50
Indomethacin***	Indocin 25 mg No. 100	Methyldopa***	Aldomet** 250 mg			Allopurinol ***	Zyloprim** 100 mg No. 100
Propoxyphene Cpd-65 No. 36	Darvon Cpd-65 No. 36	[Hydrochlorothiazide] No. 100	HydroDiuril** 50 mg				

*Generally prescribed for older females.

**Generally prescribed for older population.

***Currently not available under the generic name because manufacturer patent is still in effect.

These following drugs might be prescribed at the same time, and thus surveyors can price any pair at the same time: Aldomat-HydroDiuril (high blood pressure), Indocine-Chloral Hydrate (infection/pain), Tetracycline-Darvon Cpd-65 (infection/pain), Peritrate-Equanil (cardiac).

Fig. 1.1   List of drugs to include in a pricing survey. Developed by Public Citizens' Health Research. For those groups who choose not to use this list of drugs, a list of the 20 drugs most prescribed nationwide in 1976 is included in Fig. 1.2.

WHY DO A PRICING SURVEY?

If prescription prices are not public information in your state, a drug pricing survey can serve as the first step toward lowering prices and making price disclosure mandatory.

Many PIRGs and citizen action groups have undertaken prescription drug price surveys, the purposes and results varying with their resources and expertise. Some choose simply to make the prices public in order to inform consumers about prescription drug costs and to alert them to the lower costs of generic drugs. In Connecticut, Vermont, Massachusetts, Michigan, and California, PIRGs and citizen groups used the survey data to lobby successfully for the repeal of antiadvertising laws and the enactment of price disclosure laws, and several PIRGs are still working toward such legislation. Still others, the Connecticut Citizen Action Group and the Michigan PIRG, also presented their data to state legislators who in turn repealed antisubstitution laws. In states, such as Minnesota, that have prescription price disclosure laws, citizen groups have tested pharmacy compliance with the law.

Whatever the purpose of the survey, the first step is the same: gathering accurate and useful survey data. The survey outlines presented here will help you do just that. The first was developed for use in states that do not have a law mandating the disclosure of prescription drug prices and the second for use in states that do have such a law. Suggestions on action to take after completion of the surveys and examples of "model" price posting and substitution legislation follow the survey outlines.

SURVEY FOR USE IN STATES WHERE PRICE DISCLOSURE IS NOT MANDATORY

If your sole purpose in doing this project is to provide consumers with a guide to prescription drug prices, the survey may include any geographic area, from one neighborhood to the entire city. However, if your purpose is to provide data supporting repeal of a state antiadvertising law and the passage of legislation mandating drug price disclosure or allowing substitution, the data would be more persuasive if they included surveys of several large cities and a representative sampling from smaller cities and towns.

After determining the geographic areas to be surveyed, consult the Yellow Pages for a list of all the pharmacies in those areas. Surveying a random sampling of these stores is adequate for this study, but the data will be more relevant if they differentiate between chain and independent stores, city and suburban stores, stores in low and high socioeconomic areas, or stores serving different racial neighborhoods. If such comparisons are intended, classify pharmacies according to type and choose stores randomly from each group.

The Colorado PIRG classified stores according to income areas served and found that the average price for all drugs included in the survey was as much as 25 percent higher in low- and middle-income areas than in upper-income areas. Missouri PIRG found average prices *within the same chains* were as much as 14 percent higher in city stores than in suburban stores.

Figure 1.1 shows a list of prescription drugs recommended for your survey. It includes generic and brand name medications so your survey data will reflect the substantial differences in price between the two, and because certain stores may not pass savings from generic drugs on to consumers. The list includes medications for acute and chronic conditions. (An acute condition is one that comes on quickly and is cleared up in a relatively short period of time, and a chronic condition is one of long duration). Stores may charge higher rates for acute medications than for chronic medications, as these patients have less time and incentive to comparison shop. The list also includes "slow-moving" versus "fast-moving" medications because stores may charge disproportionately higher rates for slow-moving items—those not among the top 100 most frequently prescribed drugs. The consumer must be able to assess all of these situations. Surveying drugs from each of these categories will expose pharmacy pricing strategies and provide the most accurate pricing comparisons. A list of the 20 drugs most frequently prescribed nationwide in 1976 is shown in Fig. 1.2.

The more drug prices you include, the more helpful the information will be to consumers and the more credible the results will be in showing pricing patterns between stores and chains.

Before beginning the survey, weigh the following considerations to decide whether pharmacists will be told about your study. If the state antiadvertising law prohibits

Drug	Manufacturer	Most common strength	Common amount prescribed
Valium	Roche	5 mg	100
Ampicillin	Unspecified*	65 mg	36
Lasix	Hoechst-Roussel	10 mg	100
Tetracycline HCl	Unspecified*	125 mg	63
Aldomet	MSD	250 mg	40
HydroDiuril	Unspecified*	50 mg	50
Premarin	Ayerst	250 mg	40
Librium	Roche	40 mg	50
Dimetapp	Robins	tablets	100
Lanoxin	Burroughs-Welcon	tablets	36
Tylenol/codeine	McNeil	½ gr codeine	13
Empirin Cmpd/Codeine	B-W	#3 (½ gr codeine)	24
Actifed	B-W	0.25 mg	100
Motrin	Upjohn	400 mg	60
Darvon Compound-65	Lilly	250 mg	40
Dyazide	SA & F	—	100
V-Cillin K	Lilly	—	1 month's supply
Darvoset-N	Lilly	100 mg	40
Dalmane	Roche	30 mg	30
Inderal	Ayerst	40 mg	100

*Generic drugs

Fig. 1.2 Twenty drugs most frequently prescribed nationwide in 1976. Source of first three columns: *Pharmacy Times*, April 1977, Source of right-hand column: Keith Johnson, formerly with Public Citizens' Health Research Group.

PRESCRIPTION DRUG PRICING SURVEY

Name of pharmacy_____

Address_____

Telephone number_____

This store is: Independent___, Part of a local chain ____
   Part of a national chain____.

Survey conducted: By phone____, In person____

Name of surveyor, phone number, and address_____

_____

Brand name and dosage	Amount	Price	Generic name	Amount	Price
1.					

Fig. 1.3 Prescription drug pricing survey form. All the information on this form (except the name of the surveyor and the price of the drug) should be filled in in advance by the project coordinator before the forms are distributed to surveyors. This will eliminate the possibility of surveyors pricing the same drugs or the same drug stores.

any type of price disclosure, you may have to tell pharmacists or use surveyors with prescriptions. However, certain pharmacies may respond with prices that are not representative of their true pricing structure if surveyors identify themselves as part of a study.

It is important to complete the study as quickly as possible because some prices change from week to week and comparisons spread over a long period of time may be out of date and unfair to stores surveyed later than others.

Outlined below are three methods of surveying prescription drug prices and a discussion of the advantages and disadvantages of each. Choose one of these methods and conduct the price survey (Fig. 1.3) followed by the pharmacy services survey (Fig. 1.4).

Surveying by Telephone

A telephone survey requires fewer surveyors and less time than does surveying in person. In some states, however, antiadvertising regulations or pharmacy board codes of ethics make it illegal for pharmacists to quote prices over the phone. Check with the state pharmacy board for the most recent information about the antiadvertising law in your state. Even in states where telephone dissemination of this information is legal, groups have found some pharmacists uncooperative. Furthermore, surveyors have

Pharmacy Services Survey

Name of pharmacy_____

Address_____

Telephone number_____ Date and time of survey

_____

This store is: Independent ___ , Part of a local chain___ ,

Part of a national chain___ .

Name of surveyor, phone number, and address_____

_____

1. What hours is the store open?_____

2. a) Does it have provisions for 24-hour emergency
service?_____
   b) Is there a charge for emergency service?_____
   c) Is there an emergency number listed in the phone
book?_____

3. a) Does the store deliver?   yes( ) no ( )
   b) If yes, is delivery free?   yes( ) no ( )
   c) If there is a charge, what is it?_____

4. Does the store keep patient profiles?*yes( ) no ( )

5. Will it tabulate records of prescription drug
purchases by a customer for health insurance or tax
purposes? yes( ) no ( )

6. Does it offer consultations? yes ( ) no ( )

7. Does it extend informal credit to your customers?
      yes ( ) no ( )

8. a) Does it accept credit cards? yes( ) no ( )
   b) If "yes", which ones? Bank Americard ( )
American Express ( ) Master Charge ( ) others_____

_____

9. Does the store give discounts?_____
   If yes, to whom and how much?_____

_____

10. a) Does the store service Medicaid and other Welfare programs?_____

    b) List programs not serviced_____

11. Does the store post prescription drug prices?_____

12. What other services does it offer?_____

_____

_____

*A patient profile is an updated record of all prescriptions filled for a patient. If used correctly, it should be referred to every time the pharmacist fills a prescription for that patient, allowing him or her to spot potentially harmful drug combinations, overprescribing, etc. The use of profiles is particularly helpful for patients who visit several doctors who may not be aware of other medications prescribed for that patient. Obviously, unless pharmacists refer to the profiles consistently, the fact that they are kept is meaningless. Consumers should be educated as to the usefulness of such records and encouraged to find out whether the drug store they use keeps profiles and uses them effectively.

Fig. 1.4 Pharmacy services survey.

found that drug prices quoted over the phone are sometimes different from prices actually charged.

When the District of Columbia PIRG surveyed pharmacies by telephone in early 1975, 73 percent of the stores contacted either would not disclose prices or quoted prices as much as one dollar lower than prices quoted to surveyors in the store for the same drug.

Despite these problems, a telephone survey can save time and legwork and may be a good way to begin the survey. The pricing survey form (Fig. 1.3) can be used to record prices obtained from telephone surveys as well as from in-store surveys, but be sure to indicate those prices which were quoted over the phone.

If pharmacists are not being informed about the survey, the most efficient way to obtain prices is to have each surveyor call all pharmacies for the price of one particular drug. This method minimizes inter-store variations caused by different surveyors' techniques and eliminates the problem of pharmacists recognizing a surveyor calling for the prices of several drugs. Questions about pharmacy services can easily be asked of a store in a single phone call made after all pricing surveys have been completed.

If pharmacists have been informed of the survey, surveyors may request pricing information about all drugs and at the same time inquire about customer services.

Survey in person all stores that did not provide price information over the phone.

NR=no response
NS=not in stock

St. Louis

Store	Terracycline HCl (250mg/40)	Achromycin V (250mg/40)	Erythromycin (250mg/60)	Erythrocin (250mg/60)	Propoxyphene Cpd-65 (16)	Darvon Cpd-65 (36)	Meprobamate (400mg/50)	Equanil (400mg/50)	Valium (5mg/100)	Ovulen-21 (One Month)	Indocin (25mg/100)	Chloral Hydrate (500mg/20)	Noctec (500mg/20)	P.E.T.N. (10mg/100)	Peritrate (10mg/100)	Ovacon-21 (One Month)	Diabinese (250mg/100)	Gantrisin (6 ounces)
KNIGHT PHARMACY, 2821 N. Ballas Rd.	4.20	4.70	10.70	15.80	3.50	4.65	2.95	4.50	9.80	2.80	18.80	2.40	3.40	NS	4.75	2.90	13.85	4.90
KNIGHT PHARMACY, 141 N. Meramec	5.00	5.00	12.75	15.80	3.50	4.95	3.35	6.25	11.20	3.10	20.25	2.60	2.75	NR	NR	2.60	16.25	4.90
SHUMATE PRESCRIPTION SHOP, 114 E. Lockwood	6.00	6.00	10.75	12.95	3.20	4.75	4.20	7.20	8.95	2.49	11.50	NS	2.30	4.50	4.50	2.49	13.95	4.25
FRANK WESTLAKE PRESCRIPTIONS, 7520 Natural Bridge	NR	NR	NR	NR	NR	NR	NR	NR	NR	NR	NR	NR	NR	NR	NR	NR	NR	NR
VILLAGE PHARMACY, 921 Airport Rd.	NR	NR	NR	NR	3.75	3.75	NR	NR	2.25	2.25	12.50	NS	NR	NR	5.00	2.50	NR	NR
CRESTWOOD PRESCRIPTION SHOP, 9730 E. Watson	4.00	4.00	12.00	21.00	2.16	5.40	3.25	6.25	12.00	2.50	12.50	NS	3.00	5.00	4.25	2.25	17.00	4.50
CYTRON PHARMACY, 6353 N. Rosebury	2.25	8.45	8.45	12.00	2.60	3.95	2.25	4.50	11.50	2.25	9.90	1.75	2.75	NS	4.25	2.25	10.50	4.40
DEERING PHARMACY, 1699 S. Brentwood Blvd.	2.25	2.95	5.70	7.35	3.10	4.65	1.60	4.95	8.95	2.00	9.45	2.95	2.25	2.95	5.80	1.95	12.05	4.65
WINKELMANN SONS DRUG CO., 3300 Meramec	NR	NR	7.50	8.70	3.85	5.25	NR	5.75	8.75	2.75	8.90	2.25	NS	2.25	4.90	2.85	11.75	4.50
LLOYD H. HERRING PHARMACY, 6811 Gravois	2.75	2.95	6.20	15.30	2.95	3.95	3.25	NR	10.95	2.65	NR	1.75	3.00	3.50	4.85	2.65	14.50	4.80
GASLIGHT DRUGS, 4901 Martin Luther King	NR	NR	8.25	21.00	4.50	4.50	1.50	4.15	8.25	2.87	NR	2.50	3.50	NS	2.75	2.75	NR	4.75
MEDI-MARK PHARMACY, 7540 Hampton	2.30	2.30	6.95	11.95	2.20	3.05	1.50	4.15	8.25	1.95	8.85	1.10	1.00	1.00	3.40	1.95	11.60	3.35
MEDI-MARK PHARMACY, Lindbergh & Highway 66	2.30	2.30	6.95	11.95	2.20	3.05	1.50	4.15	8.25	1.95	8.85	1.10	3.00	3.49	3.49	1.99	12.19	3.37
WALGREENS, 500 N. Grand	2.09	2.88	6.00	10.80	2.10	3.28	1.84	5.65	8.49	1.99	8.79	1.25	NS	1.90	3.49	1.99	12.19	3.37
WALGREENS, 675 Northwest Plaza	2.09	2.89	6.00	10.80	2.65	3.19	1.99	4.49	8.49	1.99	8.79	1.09	1.90	3.49	3.89	1.89	12.49	3.79
SKAGGS DRUG CENTER, 441 N. Kirkwood	1.91	5.39	9.69	10.99	NS	4.65	2.59	4.99	10.89	1.89	11.69	1.95	1.95	3.89	4.59	2.19	11.99	3.49
SKAGGS DRUG CENTER, 6150 Natural Bridge	1.91	9.69	10.99	10.99	3.75	3.75	2.49	6.49	8.45	2.19	9.69	1.05	1.95	3.90	3.90	1.99	11.99	3.00
TARGET PHARMACY, 5252 S. Lindbergh	2.80	2.80	7.85	8.45	2.65	3.60	2.25	4.50	7.50	1.99	7.55	1.05	1.85	4.45	4.45	1.99	9.95	3.05
TARGET PHARMACY, 8020 Olive Street Road	2.45	2.90	7.00	12.10	2.60	3.15	2.25	4.40	7.50	1.99	7.55	NS	1.85	4.45	4.45	1.99	9.95	3.05
VENTURE PHARMACY, 4930 Christy	2.30	2.90	7.69	11.28	2.17	3.17	1.82	4.45	8.19	1.89	8.33	NS	2.64	3.64	3.64	1.89	10.15	3.39
VENTURE PHARMACY, 1225 S. Kirkwood	3.18	2.89	7.24	11.29	NS	3.17	1.82	4.44	8.19	1.99	8.33	NS	1.81	3.64	3.64	1.89	10.15	3.06
LADUE REXALL PHARMACY, 9832 Clayton Rd.	NR	NR	9.00	NS	NR	4.00	NR	NR	11.00	2.45	NR	NR	2.00	3.90	2.45	2.45	NR	NR
LIEBERMAN DRUGS, 2400 N. Grand	3.75	3.75	5.80	11.75	2.84	4.32	NR	4.73	9.10	2.45	9.75	2.00	1.95	4.53	4.53	2.25	NR	3.65
KARE DRUGS, 4127 N. Grand	2.25	3.29	6.10	9.75	2.59	3.72	1.90	5.00	8.19	2.00	8.69	1.93	2.90	4.73	4.73	1.90	11.75	2.75
KARE DRUGS, 7017 S. Lindbergh	4.00	4.00	11.40	13.50	2.55	4.40	2.00	4.28	9.33	2.00	9.87	NS	1.95	3.52	3.52	1.95	13.34	2.83
GLASER DRUGS, 1119 S. Big Bend	4.00	4.00	10.67	12.40	NS	3.75	NR	5.25	10.50	2.00	9.87	NR	NR	3.60	3.60	1.95	12.60	2.83
GLASER DRUGS, 40 N. Euclid	3.00	3.39	9.22	12.25	3.28	3.65	NS	5.65	8.59	1.99	10.63	1.88	2.70	5.73	5.73	1.99	13.23	4.45
GASEN DRUGS, 44 N. Florissant	3.00	3.39	8.10	13.50	NS	3.85	NR	5.55	8.99	2.29	10.63	1.84	2.51	5.53	5.53	2.29	10.49	4.35
GASEN DRUGS, 4049 Lindell	2.40	2.40	5.35	12.25	3.15	3.15	1.60	4.20	8.50	2.00	8.33	.95	1.55	3.64	3.64	1.95	11.75	3.40
MEDICARE PHARMACY, 6331 Delmar	2.40	2.40	5.35	12.25	3.15	3.15	1.60	4.20	8.50	2.00	8.33	.95	1.05	3.64	3.64	1.95	11.75	3.40
MEDICARE PHARMACY, 623 N. Grand	2.40	2.40	8.60	12.25	3.15	3.15	1.60	4.20	8.50	2.00	8.33	1.15	NS	3.64	3.64	1.95	11.75	3.40
WILLIAMS PHARMACY, 7010 Pershing	NR	NR	NR	NR	NR	4.20	NR	5.50	10.00	NR	11.45	2.50	2.90	5.50	5.50	2.75	12.00	4.25
WILLOWBROOK PHARMACY, 10483 Old Olive Street Rd.	3.50	5.95	NS	7.50	2.00	3.25	2.00	4.35	8.50	2.00	9.90	1.90	1.80	3.60	3.60	2.00	12.90	3.50
METROPOLITAN PHARMACY, 3658 West Pine	NR	NR	NR	NR	NR	3.95	NR	NR	NR	NR	NR	NR	NR	NR	NR	NR	NR	NR
CREVE COEUR PHARMACY, 11252 Olive St. Rd.	2.00	2.50	5.95	7.00	2.25	3.95	2.00	5.00	8.50	2.20	8.90	1.50	2.00	4.00	4.00	2.20	11.95	NS
Average	2.99	3.38	8.04	12.16	2.75	3.90	2.30	5.03	9.20	2.22	10.22	1.77	2.25	2.13	4.27	2.21	12.28	3.80
High	6.00	6.00	12.75	21.00	3.85	5.40	4.20	7.20	12.00	3.10	20.25	2.95	3.40	5.80	5.80	2.90	17.00	4.90
Low	1.91	1.91	5.35	7.35	2.00	3.05	1.50	4.15	7.50	1.89	7.55	.95	1.00	3.40	3.40	1.89	9.95	2.75

Table 1.1 Comparative drug prices in St. Louis.

Surveying in Person—Without Prescriptions

If pharmacists are not being informed about your study, survey only one drug at a time per store. Be careful to coordinate the assignment of drugs to survey and stores to visit to ensure that only a few visits are made to each store on the same day. If surveyors approach the counter at a time when there are a few other customers, the pharmacist or clerk may not notice the influx of prescriptionless customers. If the pharmacist or clerk is very busy, wait a few minutes before making your request. An otherwise cooperative pharmacist may not respond if he or she is very busy. Complete a pricing survey form for each store with data handed in by all surveyors who priced a drug at that store.

Surveying in Person—With "Dummy" Prescriptions

Because pharmacists in many states will not disclose prices to customers without prescriptions, it may be necessary to get "dummy" prescriptions from cooperating physicians. Prescriptions written for other than a valid medical need are called dummy prescriptions.

This method is very effective, but may be impossible to implement because physicians who write prescriptions for persons without a valid medical need may be accused by the local Medical Association of a breach in professional ethics. Therefore, check with several sympathetic physicians and an attorney with a forensic law practice before using this survey technique.

Compiling Pricing Survey Results

Make up a chart like the one in Table 1.1, listing the prices charged for each drug at each pharmacy. Mark the lowest and highest price for each drug and then determine the average (mean) price for the drug by dividing the sum of all prices by the number of prices. Then rank the stores by total costs for all drugs surveyed.

Another useful figure to calculate is the variation factor for each drug; the difference between the highest and lowest price. A very complete statistical analysis of prices could also include the *standard deviation in price* for each drug, but this is not a necessary component of survey results. Instructions for determining standard deviation are given in Resource 1.4.

Several important pricing comparisons should be made. One is the comparative cost of generic and brand name drugs. Based on the average cost of each drug, determine how much more (what percentage) the brand name costs than the generic drug by subtracting the cost of the generic drug from the cost of the brand name drug and dividing the difference by the cost of the generic drug. See Table 1.2 for sample format for presenting this information.

Compare the differences between the average total cost of drugs in city versus suburban stores; between stores serving high versus low economic areas; or between stores serving predominately white versus minority areas. These comparisons are most effective if they illustrate the pricing variances in stores of the same chains. Add up the store total for prices of all drugs. This will give you an average cost which can be compared from store to store. The format used by the Missouri PIRG in presenting this kind of comparison is shown in Table 1.3.

Format for Presenting
the Comparative Cost of
Generic and Brand Name Drugs

Columbia

Darvon Cpd-65	38% more than	Propoxyphene Cpd-65
Achromycin V	29% more than	Tetracycline HCl
Erythrocin	52% more than	Erythromycin
Equanil	98% more than	Meprobamate
Noctec	18% more than	Chloral Hydrate
Peritrate	181% more than	P.E.T.N.

Kansas City

Darvon Cpd-65	34% more than	Propoxyphene Cpd-65
Achromycin V	25% more than	Tetracycline HCl
Erythrocin	25% more than	Erythromycin
Equanil	111% more than	Meprobamate
Noctec	9% more than	Chloral Hydrate
Peritrate	36% more than	P.E.T.N.

St. Louis

Darvon Cpd-65	42% more than	Propoxyphene Cpd-65
Achromycin V	12% more than	Tetracycline HCl
Erythrocin	51% more than	Erythromycin
Equanil	119% more than	Meprobamate
Noctec	27% more than	Chloral Hydrate
Peritrate	100% more than	P.E.T.N.

Note: The figures in Table 1.2 are based on the average cost of the drugs in question at all stores surveyed in the three cities.

Table 1.2 Twenty drugs most frequently prescribed nationwide in 1975. From the *Pharmacy Times*, April 1976.

Finally, look at prices to see whether any chain shows patterns of consistently higher or lower prices than the average, and whether chains or independent stores have consistently higher or lower prices. Compile a chart comparing the services available at each store surveyed, referring to the sample in Fig. 1.5. In writing your final report or brochure, include information from the pharmacy services survey which may be helpful to consumers in choosing a pharmacy.

Also, consider including information on how to read a prescription like that reprinted in Fig. 1.6.

Action to Take after Completing the Pricing Survey

After survey results have been compiled, make the information public through a news release or a news conference. Refer to the sample news release in Fig. 1.7. Send a copy

Average Prescription Prices of
Chain Stores in St. Louis City and County

Chain	City Store-- Price Average	Country Store-- Price Average
Medicare Pharmacies	623 N. Grand-- $4.59	University City-- $4.22
Gasen Drugs	4049 Lindel-- $5.78	Florissant-- $5.75
Glaser Drugs	40 N. Euclid-- $6.42	Richmond Hts.-- $5.68
Kare Drugs	4127 N. Grand-- $5.30	Mehlville-- $4.67
*Venture Pharmacy	4930 Christy-- $4.56	Kirkwood-- $4.87
Skaggs Drug Centers	6150 Natural Bridge--$5.70	Kirkwood-- $5.51
Walgreens	500 N. Grand-- $4.66	Northwest Plaza-- $4.55

* Venture is the only chain with lower average prices in
its city store than in its county store.

Table 1.3 Prescription drug pricing survey form. All the Information on this form (except the name of the surveyor and the price of the drug) should be filled in in advance by the project coordinator before the forms are distributed to surveyors. This will eliminate the possibility of surveyors pricing the same drugs or the same drug stores.

of your report to the state pharmacy board, the Governor's office and the appropriate committee of the state legislature.

In some states, antiadvertising statutes prohibit individuals and consumer groups, as well as pharmacists, from publicizing pharmacy names along with prices. The state Attorney General's Office can provide you with an interpretation of the law in your state. If the law prohibits release of pharmacy names and drug prices, publicize only the prices obtained and price comparisons discussed above, without mentioning pharmacy names.

Budget permitting, print flyers summarizing survey results, background information about generic drugs, and legislation affecting prescription drug prices and see that they are widely distributed, particularly to consumer and senior citizen groups.

Attach to the news release and to flyers: the pricing chart, the list of stores with the highest and lowest overall prices, and the chart of stores' customer services.

The drug pricing survey data can serve as the basis for efforts to enact drug price disclosure legislation and substitution legislation. If your group does not have the time or expertise for lobbying, make sure your survey results are sent to groups that may be interested in working for appropriate legislation.

Model bills, incorporating all elements essential to price disclosure legislation and substitution legislation are found in Resource 1.5. Refer to Chapter 12 for a guide to lobbying.

Pharmacy Services Chart

Names and Addresses of Stores									
Store hours									
24 hr. emerg. service									
Charge for service									
Emerg. no. listed									
Delivery Free or Charge									
Patient profiles									
Tabulate purchase records									
Consul-tations									
Informal Credit									
Credit cards accepted									
Discounts									
Accept Medicaid									
Post Prices									
Other Services Offered									

Fig. 1.5   Pharmacy services chart. Make up a code for other services offered and list full name and codes on the bottom.

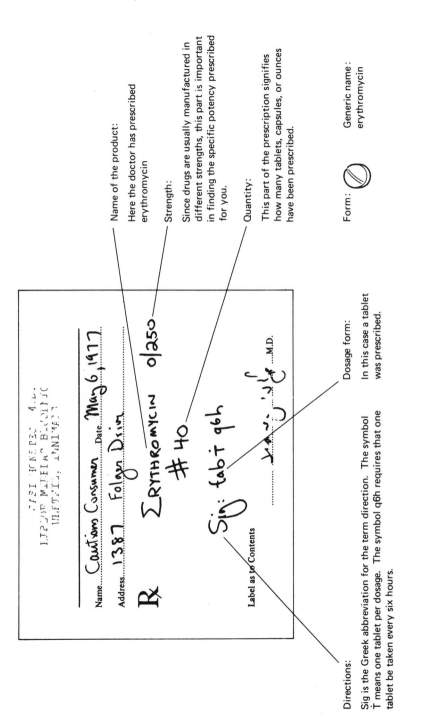

Fig. 1.6 How to read a prescription. From OSCO Drug Prescription Price Booklet, Copyright 1976, OSCO Drug, Inc., Oakbrook, Ill. Reprinted with permission.

Name of the product:

Here the doctor has prescribed erythromycin

Strength:

Since drugs are usually manufactured in different strengths, this part is important in finding the specific potency prescribed for you.

Quantity:

This part of the prescription signifies how many tablets, capsules, or ounces have been prescribed.

Form:

Generic name : erythromycin

Dosage form:

In this case a tablet was prescribed.

Directions:

Sig is the Greek abbreviation for the term direction. The symbol T̄ means one tablet per dosage. The symbol q6h requires that one tablet be taken every six hours.

Label as to Contents

MoPIRG

Missouri Public Interest Research Group
P.O. Box 8276
St. Louis, Mo. 63156
314 361-5200

PRESS RELEASE

For Release: 10:00 a.m.. Thursday, June 12, 1975

Contact: Steve Graham -- 361-5200
                         367-6925

CONSUMER GROUP ASSAILS

PRESCRIPTION DRUG PRICING SYSTEM

The Missouri Public Interest Research Group charged today that drug manufacturers and Missouri retail pharmacies are engaged in a systematic effort to inflate drug prices through noncompetitive marketing and pricing policies. The charges include an indictment of the Food and Drug Administration and the Missouri State Board of Pharmacy for failing to fulfill their regulatory responsibilities in regard to drug pricing. The medical and pharmacy professions were also criticized for their role in maintaining inflated drug prices.

The Research Group charges were issued in a study entitled "Prescription Drug Pricing: The Politics of Pills and Profits," which is the product of a six-month research project on the manufacture and sale of prescription drugs. The study includes a survey of prescription drug prices charged by 70 retail pharmacies in Kansas City, Columbia, and St. Louis.

The survey indicates large price differences for the same prescription in area pharmacies. According to the MoPIRG study, prices vary as much as 300%. In addition, the survey documents that consumers can save as much as 400% by purchasing drugs under their chemical name rather than under their brand name, providing they can persuade their doctors to write prescriptions by chemical name.

Such price discrepancies reflect the efforts of drug manufacturers and retailers to maintain high prices by controlling the market for prescription drug products.

The large drug chains in St. Louis all claim to charge the lowest prices for prescription drugs, but our survey clearly shows that there are substantial price differences for any prescription a consumer buys. Pharmacies do everything they can to hide the enormity of these differences, because

22

they're afraid that consumers will start to shop comparatively for their prescriptions.

Six of the seven St. Louis retail chains surveyed were found to charge higher prices in their city stores than in their county outlets. In fact, the study shows a general pattern of higher prices being charged in predominantly black neighborhoods than in the largely white St. Louis County suburbs.

The study recommends broad changes in state and federal law and administrative policy to challenge the drug monopoly and to encourage greater competition in the production and marketing of prescription drugs.

These recommendations include the enactment of Missouri state laws which would:
1. require pharmacists to post prices and distribute price lists of the 100 most widely prescribed drugs;

2. modify the current statute which prohibits pharmacists from substituting chemically equivalent drugs for brand name products prescribed by physicians; and

3. add public members to the Missouri Board of Pharmacy.

On the federal level, the study calls for:

1. reduction of drug patent rights from seventeen to five years;

2. stiffening of conflict of interest regulations in the Food and Drug Administration;

3. adoption of the Maximum Allowable Cost Program which would establish limits for the cost of prescriptions filled for government agencies and programs; and

4. increased labeling requirements to include the suggested retail price and the chemical name of the drug prescribed on all prescriptions.

The study is available from the Missouri Public Interest Research Group, P.O. Box 8276, St. Louis, Missouri 63156 at $1.50 for individuals and $5.00 for institutions.

Fig. 1.7 Sample news release in states lacking price disclosure laws.

SURVEY FOR STATES WHERE
PRESCRIPTION DRUG PRICE DISCLOSURE IS MANDATORY

Review the law to find out what must be disclosed. If in-store price posting is mandatory, what are the specific requirements for poster sign format, size, and location and what drugs are to be listed on the posters? Design a survey form like the one in Fig. 1.8, with a backup sheet listing information about all drugs to be surveyed. Surveyors will record whether the store is complying with all aspects of the law.

Compile a list of all area drug stores and break the list into categories—chain store branches in the city, chain store branches in the suburbs, independent stores, stores serving both high and low socioeconomic areas and stores serving different racial neighborhoods. Then choose a representative sample from each category to be surveyed. Combine your compliance survey with a pricing survey using whatever method from the previous section is most appropriate given your state law. If prices must be posted in the store, survey the store in person; if the law provides for price disclosure by phone, conduct a telephone survey of pharmacies.

In compiling survey results, list stores by name, and if the law was violated, specify those sections with which the store did not comply and send the report to the state pharmacy board and the state's Attorney General, Bureau of Consumer Protection. Refer to the directions in Fig. 1.3 for calculating price comparisons.

Make your results public, referring to the press release in Fig. 1.9. Consider distributing flyers which cover in more detail the survey results and your demands for corrective action against stores that violated the disclosure law and recommendations about changes in the law. The Vermont PIRG flyer in Fig. 1.10 is a good example. Include pricing data with the press release and flyer as discussed earlier.

When the Vermont PIRG surveyed pharmacies to determine whether they were complying with the state price posting law they charged several pharmacies with failing to place posters in "conspicuous locations" and charged two with refusing to allow surveyors to record prices from price posters. As a result, both the State Board of Pharmacy and the Consumer Protection Bureau of the State Attorney General's Office investigated the charges and the stores involved received considerable adverse publicity in the local press.

SURVEY FOR USE IN STATES WHERE PRICE DISCLOSURE IS MANDATORY

Name of store_____

Address_____

Date and time of survey_____

Name and phone number of surveyor_____

_____

A. Price posting

1. Is there a prescription drug price
posting sign in the store?   ___yes ___ no

2. Is it posted conspicuously at the
prescription counter (or wherever your
law requires)?   ___yes ___no

3. Is the sign 2 feet wide by 3 feet
high (or whatever your law requires)?   ___yes ___ no

4. Is the print at least 1/2 inch high
(or whatever your law requires)?   ___yes ___no

5. Is the sign orange (or whatever
color is designated by your law)?   ___yes ___no

6. Does the sign include information
about the services offered by the store
(if this is required by your law)?   ___yes ___no

7. Does the sign list all of the drugs
listed on the attached sheet? (The sheet
will list all drugs that must be included
on the sign. Surveyors can simply circle
the drugs on the backup sheet and fill in
this section later.)   ___yes ___no

_____ _____ _____

_____ _____ _____

8. a) Does the posted sign include all of
       the information about the drugs that
       law requires and which are listed on
       the attached sheet?   ___yes ___no

Fig. 1.8 **Survey for use in states in which price disclosure is mandatory.**

25

b) If no, what type(s) of information are not included?

_____

_____

9. a) Is any information included on the pricing poster that is not required by law? ___yes ___no

   b) If yes, please describe exactly what type of information is extraneously included and whether or not it is included for all drugs.

_____

_____

10. If you encountered any problems with the pharmacist while surveying, please explain.

_____

_____

_____

B. In-Store Booklets or Leaflets for Consumers to Take Home

		Yes	No
1.	Booklets/Flyers in right location?	___	___
2.	Booklets/Flyers in reasonable condition?	___	___
3.	Flyers in sufficient quantity?	___	___
4.	Contain info on all drugs required by law? (Surveyors will have backup sheet with the requirements of the law)	___	___
5.	Observe customers at pharmacy counter. Do they appear to be aware of booklets/flyers?	___	___
6.	If no, ask if they know booklets/flyers are available and record response.	___	___

_____

_____

Fig. 1.8 *Continued*

C. Telephone Disclosure

Name and address of Pharmacy	Date and time called	Name, Dosage and amount of drug priced	Price quoted	Refused to quote price

Fig. 1.8 *Continued*

CALPIRG

CALIFORNIA PUBLIC INTEREST RESEARCH GROUP, INC.

334 Kalmia Street
San Diego, California 92101
(714) 236-1509

FOR RELEASE: 2 February 1976
CONTACT: Susan Sayler, 714-236-1509

At least a quarter, and perhaps as many as a half of all pharmacies in San Diego are violating the provisions of the State's prescription drug price posting law. This was the result of a survey of 165 pharmacies in the metropolitan area by the California Public Interest Research Group (CALPIRG). The study examined compliance with the drug price posting law, as well as compiled drug prices from pharmacies. The study revealed that while most pharmacy prices fall within a fairly narrow range, the differences between some of the low and high priced pharmacies is as much as 400-600%.

"The drug price posting law went into effect just two years ago. It requires pharmacies to post a list of the one hundred most commonly prescribed drugs in the State," explained Susan Sayler, project coordinator. "The law says that pharmacies must post the retail price actually charged for each drug. Yet we found many pharmacies openly admitting that they posted their maximum price for drugs, and offering to give us the real prices they charged. These prices were usually substantially less than the posted price. This practice is illegal and misleading. It makes comparisons between pharmacies impossible. Some pharmacies were even listing, '$99 or less' for all drug prices."

Besides inaccurate prices being placed on the posters, CALPIRG discovered that it's often difficult to find or read the posters. "We found many pharmacies would put the price poster in some out of the way corner. Others would place it so far behind a counter that you'd have to ask to step behind the counter in order to read the poster," commented Steve Colman, another project coordinator from UCSD.

The CALPIRG study also notes that an important provision of the price posting law requires that price information be given by pharmacists, no matter how the request is communicated. "This means con-

28

sumers are entitled to an accurate answer to their queries on drug prices, whether made over the phone or in the pharmacy. As a matter of fact, we specifically recommend people not merely rely on the price information in our study, but call pharmacies for current prices," said Mr. Colman. Mr. Colman also recommended that consumers compare different services as well as prices. "Some of the lower-priced pharmacies do not offer as many services as others, or as long hours. If you have special needs, you should consider this."

"Not enough advertising of drug prices is taking place," according to Ms. Sayler, "We only found two pharmacies distributing flyers giving drug price information. A ruling by California Courts last year made it legal for pharmacies to advertise drug prices, but few have done so yet. Advertising is the best way to communicate drug price information, if properly used. I have enough faith in pharmacies to know they won't go in for advertisements announcing, 'Big New Shipment of Valium.' But there also need to be some guidelines set forth requiring the ads to contain information which will make comparison shopping possible. The Federal Trade Commission has already moved in this direction, by requiring that certain information be listed in all advertisements."

The Drug Price Posting Study concludes that the poster idea, for all its present faults, is not a bad one, but that it needs major reforms to make it useful to consumers. The study also points out that advertising is a better solution to the problem of inadequate consumer information on prescription drugs, since use of the price posters requires consumers to actually be present at the pharmacy to use.

"In this age of technology and mass production, it sometimes means a lot to deal with people who are a little more congenial and concerned than the average person," noted Ms. Sayler. "CALPIRG is interested in giving consumers information about how to get the most for their dollars, but we do not discount the importance of good relations and trust between pharmacist and consumer."

More information, and copies of the forty page Drug Price Posting Study, are available from CALPIRG, 334 Kalmia Street, San Diego, CA. 92101. Price is $1.00, plus $.50 for postage and handling.

Fig. 1.9   Sample press release.

1974 PRESCRIPTION DRUG SURVEY

Published by

Vermont Public Interest Research Group, Inc.

In February, 1974, VPIRG conducted its second statewide prescription drug survey. The results give conclusive evidence that great price fluctuations still exist all across the state for the same drugs at different stores. By shopping around, smart consumers can reduce their family's drug bill by 33%

Before examining the results of the survey however, the consumer must be aware of its limitations: the prices on this survey are valid only for the specific strengths and quantities that are listed for each drug.

HOW THE SURVEY WAS CONDUCTED

Vermont law requires pharmacies to post a price list of 100 commonly prescribed drugs selected by the state. This list must be clearly written and conspicuously displayed in every pharmacy in the state.

VPIRG selected 50 of these drugs, and recorded the price as it appeared on the posted list. Blank spaces in the survey columns indicate that the pharmacy does not carry that medication. At the bottom of each column we have indicated whether the store has higher-than-average prices (high) or whether the store has lower-than-average prices (low) when compared to posted prices of other stores in the region. Although this only refers to 50 items, it can be used as an overall indication of that store's pricing policy.

In addition, VPIRG has boxed in the highest price and circled the lowest price charged for each drug in the region. The prices can also be compared to the regional averages which appear in the extreme right-hand column.

The drugs are followed by numbers referring to their strengths and to the quantity asked for. You should notice that next to four of the drugs is the word "generic". This means that the drug is made by more than one company and it is therefore subject to price competition.

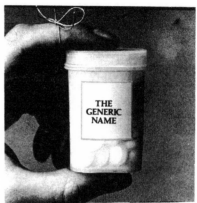

THE GENERIC NAME

Last year's survey included information about services offered, such as patient profiles and credit. Except for free delivery, these services have been deleted from this survey because additional research has found that simple "yes" or "no" answers do not accurately indicate the extent to which these services are actually offered.

RESULTS

Once again VPIRG found large variations in price - this time up to 413%. If all 50 drugs were purchased in Vermont the market basket prices would range from $196.76 to $295.15.

1. Regional Differences Of all the regions surveyed, the Burlington region had the lowest price averages. VPIRG feels this can be attributed to the competitive situation that Burlington consumers enjoy by having a large number of drug stores in a small area.

2. Differences among long term medications Hypertension (high-blood pressure) often requires life-long medication with a drug such as Aldomet, which according to our survey, can vary in price from $6.49 to $12.50 per 100 tablets. This represents a difference of $66 per year. For someone using it over a long period of time, this can mean a greater than $1000 difference between the two pharmacies.

3. Year-to-year differences The effects of competition are apparent when we compare last year's survey results to this year's results. The period of time following the release of the 1973 survey has been one of the most competitive periods in the field of retail

pharmacy in Vermont. Fourteen of the fifty drugs surveyed correspond exactly with last year's survey. The average cost for these 14 items last year was $72.45, while the average cost this year is $69.44. This is a 4.2% decrease in cost in a year that has experienced a 10% increase in the cost of living.

4. Differences among generic products: The 4 drugs that are available generically show some of the highest variations in prices, since some pharmacies use highly advertised name brands while others use generic products for the price list. For example, Prednisone sells for $.98 at one store and $4.05 at another—a 413% variation. The other generic products show the same kind of variations in price:

Ampicillin----397%
Erythromycin--333%
Tetracycline--382%

GAMES PHARMACIES PLAY

Consumers should be aware that the fact that a pharmacy is low-priced on a number of the surveyed drugs does not necessarily mean that it is low-priced on all items it sells. VPIRG suspects that some pharmacies may have lowered their prices on posted drugs while prices on other drugs remain at higher levels.

For example, two Burlington pharmacies, City Drug and Grandway, are close competitors. On VPIRG's 1973 survey, Grandway was the low priced store in its region for the majority of drugs and had lower prices than City Drug on all but one of the fifty drugs surveyed. However, this year's survey shows City Drug with lower prices than Grandway on forty-three of the fifty drugs surveyed.

In order to learn more about this surprising turnabout, a VPIRG researcher visited these two stores with a list of seven drugs WHICH ARE NOT ON THE LIST, but which are commonly prescribed. City Drug had higher prices on all seven items. In fact, the seven drugs would have cost $56.41 at City Drug and only $42.18 across the street at Grandway.

While this suggests that the prise posting law is having the desired effect in encouraging healthy price competition on commonly prescribed drugs, it demonstrates that consumers should not automatically assume that

a store doing well on this survey is the lowest priced store for other drugs.

RECOMMENDATIONS

1. Generic Drug Law - The most effective means of lowering prescription drug prices in Vermont would be passage of a controlled substitution law. Such a law would allow a pharmacist to substitute a lower priced generic drug for costly name brand drugs, where the generic drug is chemically, biologically and clinically equivalent.

Such a bill, S. 150, was introduced in the legislature this year by Senator Robert Daniels, but failed to come to a vote in the Senate, largely because of delaying tactics by Senator Madeline Harwood, Chairperson of the Health and Welfare Committee. However, the legislation will undoubtedly be introduced again and all Vermonters concerned about lowering drug prices should give it their active support.

2. State Purchasing - Great savings would result if the State Purchasing Department were able to act on behalf of pharmacies and consumers and order bulk quantities of drugs on a bid basis. Such aggressive state purchasing could save the state millions of dollars, both in the costs of institutional care and in the out-of-pocket expenditures of consumers. In fact, Vermont presently does do some purchasing, but its activities are limited to a few items, primarily for patients at Waterbury State Hospital and for persons involved in a special program for heart illness.

3. Price Posting - VPIRG recommends that lists of prescription drugs be posted in pharmacy doors or windows on 8" x 11" printed sheets. This would give consumers far better access to price information than the present signs which are sometimes on a back wall, sometimes near the ceiling, and often hidden by counter displays. It would also enable pharmacies to make corrections more often (our surveyors found many errors on posted signs throughout the state) and keep their lists up to date.

-Michael LaBella
-Lenny Fieber
-Jay Breines

Fig. 1.10 Sample Vermont PIRG flyer.

BIBLIOGRAPHY

A consumer's guide to the Colorado prescription drug industry. Colorado Public Interest Research Group, April 22, 1974.

An outline for consumer action. Report by Public Citizen's Health Research Group, 1973.

Drug pricing and the Rx police states. Consumer Reports **37**, 3, March, 1972: 136–140.

Everything you always wanted to know about prescription drug prices but were afraid to ask. Oregon Student Public Interest Research Group, October, 1973.

New York's other drug law. New York Public Interest Research Group, 1972.

Pharmacy in Washington, D.C.: not quite what the doctor ordered. District of Columbia Public Interest Research Group, 1973.

Prescription drug prices. A Report by Public Citizen's Health Research Group, 1973.

Prescription drug prices in Iowa, or ... how can you let your fingers do the walking when your druggist won't give you a hand? Iowa Student Public Interest Research Group, February 11, 1974.

Prescription drug pricing. A report by the Consumer Federation of America, September, 1972.

Prescription drug pricing survey. Indiana Public Interest Research Group.

Prescription drug pricing, the politics of pills and profits. Missouri Public Interest Research Group, May, 1975.

The prescription drug project. Western Massachusetts Public Interest Research Group.

Price comparison of prescription drugs in Virginia. A Joint Study by the Virginia Citizens Consumer Council and the Citizen Action Group, May 21, 1973.

The real cost of prescription drugs—a study of prescription drug prices in North Carolina. North Carolina Public Interest Research Group, June 1, 1973.

The real cost of prescription drugs. Texas Public Interest Research Group, 1972.

Winter, Ruth, *How to reduce your medical bills,* New York: Crown, 1970.

U.S. Department of Health, Education and Welfare, *Prescription drug data summary,* 1971.

CHAPTER 2.

compiling a consumer's directory of doctors

Most people can find out more about a car they plan to buy than they can about a doctor who may hold their life in his hands.

A Consumer's Directory of Prince
George's County Doctors
Public Citizen's Health Research Group

Not all the practices of doctors are alike. Some doctors will accept Medicaid and Medicare, others will not. Some prescribe drugs by their generic names, others do not. Some doctors will try to see unscheduled patients, others will see them only in emergencies. Fees for the same services vary tremendously from doctor to doctor. Consumers have little access to this kind of information and, relying on general referrals from friends or other doctors, must conduct lengthy phone interviews or trust to fate that the doctor they visit will provide the services needed at prices they can afford.

One of the purposes of a doctors' directory is to provide consumers with basic information—information about education, availability, fees, and services—that will enable them to make a more informed choice when selecting a doctor. In addition, a doctors' directory can help demystify the medical profession in the minds of consumers by arousing consumer consciousness about questions to ask doctors. A directory provides a first step towards a more open relationship between doctor and patient, and the willingness or reluctance of doctors to cooperate may indicate their attitude towards such a relationship. The directory outlined in this project should not be viewed as an attempt to evaluate the medical competence of doctors.

Doctors' Directories developed by PIRGs and citizen groups have met with overwhelmingly positive responses by consumers, many physicians, and the press. *Newsweek* magazine, the *Boston Globe, Newsday/The Long Island Newspaper,* and *New York Medicine* are a few of the publications that have informed consumers about the availability and usefulness of Doctors' Directories.

These excerpts from letters exemplify the responses of consumers and physicians to Directories.

How much better to have firsthand statistics than to have to rely on gossip and hearsay in choosing a physician.
Congratulations on a fine attempt to keep the public informed.

Consumer's letter to the
Massachusetts PIRG

Would you please send me a copy of the directory for Western Mass? Enclosed is a check for $5.00 which is my contribution.
I support your goal of making information about physicians more available to the consumer.

Physician's letter to the
Massachusetts PIRG

Developing a directory of doctors involves several stages:

☐ Checking the *physician antiadvertising statute* in your state for restrictions against physicians cooperating with your efforts to compile information.

☐ Deciding whether to *inform the local medical society* in advance about the directory.

☐ Deciding *what size directory* you can compile.

☐ Doing *preliminary research* to gather as much information as possible about individual doctors through the use of the Yellow Pages and medical directories.

☐ Using a *questionnaire* to interview doctors and their assistants over the phone for further information.

☐ *Verifying* all information by mailing copies of the completed questionnaires to each doctor for corrections, additions, and final approval to publish.

☐ *Publishing* the directory and offering it for sale to consumers at *cost* (can include salaries, facilities as well as materials and production costs).

WHY IS INFORMATION ABOUT DOCTORS DIFFICULT TO FIND?

Laws prohibiting physicians from advertising have been in effect in most states for many years. When these laws were originally enacted, they were meant to protect the public from the fraudulent claims of quacks and charlatans. Today, these laws, which are enforced by state commissions on medical discipline and state and county medical societies, protect doctors from public scrutiny. Doctors in most states are prohibited from publicizing even such basic information as availability, services offered, and fees. However, physicians are allowed to place listings in the Yellow Pages of the telephone book. Although many of those listed are not even licensed physicians, medical societies, as a rule, do not check Yellow Page listings against their medical directories and inform neither the phone company nor the public about nonphysicians who advertise. At the same time medical societies remain silent while consumers are treated by nonphysicians; they hide behind antiadvertising laws to avoid providing consumers with information about practicing, licensed physicians.

State antiadvertising statutes usually prohibit *physicians*, not consumers, from publishing information about services and fees. Most do not specifically prohibit consumers from publishing, on a nonprofit basis, nonprejudicial information about doctors when no qualitative judgments are made.

Check the law in your state (Resource 2.1) before publishing a Doctors' Directory. If the law appears to prohibit either consumers from publishing a directory or doctors from cooperating with your efforts to collect information, contact Public Citizens' Litigation Group, 2000 P Street, N.W., Washington, D.C.   20036.

WILL YOU INFORM THE MEDICAL SOCIETY?

Decide at the outset whether to inform the local medical society in advance about your plan to develop a directory. This important decision should be made on the basis of whether you think the medical society will assist or hinder your efforts. By no means do you have to obtain medical society permission to gather information and publish a directory.

The American Medical Society, whose *Principles of Medical Ethics* form the basis of state laws and medical society rules on physicians' conduct, changed the *Principles* in December, 1974, to permit doctors to cooperate in consumer-sponsored doctor directories. The AMA ruling reads as follows:

Community Professional Directories

It is not unethical for a physician to authorize the listing of his name and practice in a directory for professional or lay use which is intended to list all physicians in the community on a uniform and nondiscriminatory basis. The listing shall not include any self-aggrandizing statements or qualitative judgment regarding the physician's skills or competence. The American Medical Directory provides an example of the kind of information that may be properly listed in the national as well as community directories for health service personnel. Likewise, specialties or specialty practices used in the American Medical Directory should set the pattern for specialty designations.

The directories that the AMA refers to do not include information about fees or services offered, but concentrate on credentials. They should not be viewed as a guide to what can and should be included in a directory for consumers. The important point in the AMA Resolution is that community directories of doctors are gaining acceptance although the inclusion of fee information remains a point of contention.

But be wary. The state and local societies are apt to be conservative in their views. Inform them about the project only if you have good reason to believe they will encourage doctors to cooperate with your efforts. In many states where consumer groups have prepared directories, the medical society, upon hearing about the project, either advised physicians that they did not have to cooperate or stated that physicians should not give out information for the directory. This action considerably lowered the number of doctors who agreed to be included in the directories.

Neither the Public Citizens' Health Research Group nor the Massachusetts PIRG informed their local medical societies before beginning this project. They argue that the desired information should be available to the public without medical society permission. When the Massachusetts Medical Society learned about the Massachusetts PIRG project, they issued the following statement:[1]

> *All members of the Society are advised that the consumer's directory is a project of Mass PIRG and not a cooperative effort with the Massachusetts Medical Society. The Committee on Ethics and Discipline, however, is of the opinion that making appropriate information concerning physicians available to consumers can be helpful in providing good medical care to the citizens of the Commonwealth.*

On the other hand, the New York State Education Department, which licenses physicians, contended that consumer directories constitute illegal advertising. Upon learning about New York PIRG's efforts to compile a doctors' directory, they warned that doctors may be acting unethically and illegally if they cooperate with groups compiling such directories.[2]

WHAT SIZE DIRECTORY CAN YOU COMPILE?

The directory can serve as a guide to physicians in a county, a city, a particular area of a city, or a suburb. If the area to be covered by the directory is very large, it may be difficult for residents, particularly newcomers, to identify doctors' office locations. In this case, follow the Health Research Group's example and include a map of the area divided into several sections, with each section numbered or identified by name. Doctors can then be listed according to location.

Compiling a directory will probably take from two to six months of intermittent effort, depending on the number of physicians contacted, how many people work on the directory, and how frequently they work. If you do not have enough surveyors to initially contact all area physicians within a month or two, consider limiting the directory to specific types of doctors. Information about "Family physicians," (general practitioners or specialists in internal medicine), pediatricians and obstetricians–gynecologists will prove useful to the largest numbers of consumers.

Funds are needed to cover stationery, duplicating, printing and mailing costs.

PRELIMINARY RESEARCH

First check with Public Citizen, P.O. Box 19404, Washington, D.C., 20036, to find out if any group in your area has already developed a doctors' directory. Then choose a coordinator to be responsible for the administrative aspects of the project.

Begin your compilation of a list of licensed, practicing physicians by referring to the Yellow Pages of the telephone directory. Although surveys in New York City and Washington, D.C., showed that as many as five percent of all persons listed as "physicians" are not licensed to practice medicine, and some doctors choose not to be listed, the Yellow Pages will provide a basic list of doctors. Verify and add to your initial list by checking such sources as:

- [ ] local and state medical societies
- [ ] the state medical licensure board
- [ ] local and state health departments (Medicaid information)
- [ ] local libraries and medical libraries
- [ ] local comprehensive health planning agency
- [ ] commercial professional health care directories available to doctors and hospitals
- [ ] the local Social Security Office (Medicare information)
- [ ] local hospitals
- [ ] office of the state legislator from area being surveyed (State legislators may keep lists of constituents broken down by profession.)

THE QUESTIONNAIRE

The information about doctors most appropriate for a consumers' directory is included in the *Doctors' Directory General Questionnaire* (Fig. 2.1).

Some groups have preferred to use a shortened version of the questionnaire, concentrating on fees, office hours and basic services provided. New York PIRG at Queens shortened the questionnaire and their version appears in Fig. 2.2. While reviewing the questionnaire (Fig. 2.1), refer to the Glossary at the end of this chapter.

Fill out as much of the questionnaire as possible from information provided in professional medical directories. Consult *The Directory of Medical Specialists*; Marquis *Who's Who* (15th ed., Chicago: 1972); the *American Medical Directory*, the American Medical Association (26th ed., Chicago: 1974); and medical directories published by each state and local medical societies, to gather the following information about each physician:

- [ ] date of birth
- [ ] medical education—where and when received M.D.
- [ ] date of license
- [ ] certifying agency and year certified
- [ ] type of practice
- [ ] teaching positions

(Continued on page 42)

Doctors' Directory General Questionnaire

*Name of doctor _____

Date of birth _____

Name of interviewer _____

Phone interview information: Date_____ Hour_____

Name and position of person interviewed _____

---

*1. Are you a practicing physician? _____ Yes _____ No
(if 'no', terminate interview)

What is your specialty?_____

2. What type of practice are you engaged in?
_____ solo practice   _____ group practice

_____ other   a) How many are there in
      (please specify)   the group?
                               _____
_____   b) What are their
                                  specialties?
_____ refused to answer
                               _____

_____ Prepaid group practice _____
                               _____

*3. Do you have any other positions such as teaching,
hospital staff, staff appointments, or research?

_____ Yes _____ No _____ refused to answer

What are the positions?_____

*4. a) From what medical school did you graduate and in
what year?

_____
_____ refused to answer

b) Where did you take your internship?

_____

c) If you took a residency, where did you take it and
in what specialty?

_____

* Questions for which you should be able to find information in medical directories.

Fig. 2.1 Doctors' directory general questionnaire.

d) Have you taken any other special training?

_____ Yes _____ No _____ refused to
answer

If yes, of what type? _____

Where? _____ Number of years _____

*5. Are you Board-certified?

_____ Yes _____ No _____ refused to
answer

If no, are you Board-eligible?

_____ Yes _____ No _____ refused to
answer

*6. With what hospitals do you have admittance privileges?

_____

_____

7. What are the office hours at each of your offices?

days   hours   office address   phone number

_____

_____

8. What is your after-hours coverage for: _____ refused
to answer
none   answering   can be reached   other   doctors cover-
service   at home   ing

Weekends _____ _____ _____ _____

After
closing _____ _____ _____ _____

Vacations _____ _____ _____ _____

9. How many of the following support personnel do you
have in your office?
_____ refused to answer
_____ registered nurse   _____ licensed practical
_____ laboratory technicians   nurses
_____ other (specify)   _____ secretary and book-
keepers

_____

10. Do you make house calls? _____ Yes _____ No
_____ refused to answer
If only for older patients, etc., please specify.

_____ ( ) emergencies only

Fig. 2.1 *Continued*

39

11. Will you accept new patients?_____ Yes _____ No
_____ refused to answer

12. What is the average waiting time for nonemergency
appointments?
_____
_____ refused to answer

13. How much time do you schedule for each patient,
assuming you are not seeing the patient for the first
time and are not doing a complete physical?
_____
_____ refused to answer

14. Do you see unscheduled walk-in patients?
_____ Yes _____ No
_____ refused to answer
_____ only in emergencies
_____ only if patient of the doctor

15. Can you take care of non-English speaking patients in
their own language? _____ Yes _____ No

list languages_____

16. a) Do you accept: ___ Yes ___ No ___ refused to
answer
Medicaid patients__   ___   ___
Medicare patients__   ___   ___
If yes, to Medicare:
b) Do you accept Medicare fee schedule as payments
in full? ___ Yes ___ No ___ depends on patient's
economic status

___ refused to answer

c) Does your office submit claims for patients?
___ Yes ___ No ___ refused to answer

17. What is your standard fee for:
variable | refused to answer

initial office visit $_____   _____   _____
routine office visit $_____   _____   _____
routine hospital visit $_____   _____   _____

18. Do you take samples in your office for the following:

Test	Yes	No	Fee	refused to answer	not appli-cable
Urinalysis	___	___	___	___	___
Complete blood count SMA-12	___	___	___	___	___
If no, blood sugar	___	___	___	___	___
Throat culture	___	___	___	___	___
Pap smear	___	___	___	___	___

Fig. 2.1 *Continued*

19. a) Do you require patients to pay your fee at the time of the appointment?
    ___ Yes ___ No ___ refused to answer
    b) How do you bill?
    ___ following each visit
    ___ monthly ___ refused to answer

20. Do you routinely give the following immunizations?

	Yes	No	Fee	no extra charge	refused to answer	not applicable
series of 3 polio shots	___	___	___	___	___	___
4 shot series, DPT	___	___	___	___	___	___
tetanus diphtheria boosters	___	___	___	___	___	___

21. Do you customarily adjust your fees to the patient's ability to pay?
    ___ Yes ___ No ___ refused to answer

22. Do you accept time deferred payments?
    ___ Yes ___ No ___ refused to answer

23. Do you prescribe contraceptives? (IUD, diaphragm, pills) ___ Yes ___ No ___ refused to answer

24. Do you routinely test for lead poisoning? (This question is not relevant in all areas.)
    ___ Yes ___ No ___ refused to answer

25. Do you routinely test for venereal disease?
    ___ Yes ___ No ___ refused to answer

26. Do you routinely prescribe drugs by generic name if available?
    ___ Yes ___ No ___ refused to answer

27. Do you customarily allow patients who so request to see their medical records?
    ___ Yes ___ No ___ refused to answer

28. Thank the interviewee.

Fig. 2.1 *Continued*

☐   associations, affiliations, research positions, and appointments

☐   specialty

☐   hospital(s) primarily used.

These directories are available in medical libraries or good public libraries. Some medical libraries do not admit the public, so call to find out whether you can use the library, and whether you need authorization from a doctor, a member of the library staff, or a university professor.

This information should be typed or printed on the questionnaire form. Using the partially completed questionnaires, interview doctors or their staff over the telephone. A phone survey is preferable to a mail survey because physicians and their staff receive volumes of mail and are much more likely to respond positively to a personal request for information. Data from the American Medical Association show that a compilation of the *American Medical Directory* usually requires seven separate mailings for an 80 percent response rate from physicians.

Some doctors or their staff may indicate that they do not have the time to answer your questions over the telephone. In those cases, offer to call at a more convenient time. If they refuse to answer your questions during a second or third phone call, offer to send the questionnaire by mail. In-person interviews are time-consuming, but may prove necessary with doctors who refuse to answer questions over the telephone or by mail.

Doctors will want information about your group and the purpose of the directory. The *Telephone Response Sheet*, Fig. 2.3, includes a sample explanation. All surveyors should become familiar with the *Telephone Instructions*, Fig. 2.4, and list of *Key Questions Doctors May Ask*, Fig. 2.5. Provide each surveyor with a list of doctors to contact, and questionnaires partially filled in with information gathered from medical directories.

VERIFICATION

All information gathered over the phone must be verified to ensure that no misrepresentations occur. The publishing of unverified information could lead to a libel suit. Information gathered from official medical directories can be published without doctors' verifications, but be sure to document the source.

Mail a copy of the completed questionnaire to each doctor with a covering letter explaining who is compiling the directory, its purpose, costs, and (if you choose) figures on the percentage of doctors who have thus far responded favorably. Include a date by which the verified questionnaire must be returned. Mail a blank copy of the questionniare to all doctors who refused to cooperate, giving them another opportunity to respond. Send the questionnaires in an envelope with a stamp rather than a stamp meter marking. Many professionals just throw away any envelope marked by a stamp meter because they receive so much "junk" mail with that kind of postage.

If you do not receive a timely response from some doctors, additional phone calls or letters may be necessary to urge them to return verified questionnaires.

PHYSICIANS QUESTIONNAIRE

NEW YORK PUBLIC INTEREST RESEARCH GROUP - QUEENS

Name of doctor_____

Name of interviewer_____

Contacts: Date_____ Hour_____ Name of person contacted

_____ _____ _____

1. Are you a practicing physician? yes___ no___

2. What type of practice are you engaged in?

   solo_____ group_____ other_____

3. What are your office hours?

   day_____ hour_____

4. What is you after-hour coverage for:

	none	answering service	can be reached at home	other doctor covering
Weekends				
After closing				
Vacations				

5. Which hospitals do you primarily use?_____

   _____

6. Do you make housecalls? yes___ no___

7. Do you accept:
   Medicare patients: yes___ no___ would not answer___
   Medicaid patients: yes___ no___ would not answer___

8. Do you require patients to pay your fee at the time of their appointment? yes___ no___ would not answer___

Fig. 2.2 Physician's questionnaire, New York PIRG, Queens.

9. What is your standard fee for:

An initial office visit_____ would not answer___

A routine office visit _____ would not answer___

10. Do you give the following tests in your office?

TEST	yes	no	fee	would not answer
complete blood count				
urinalysis				

11. Do you routinely give immunizations

to adults? yes___ No___ would not answer___

to children? yes___ no___ would not answer?___

If yes, what kind of immunizations?

_____

_____

_____

_____

Fig. 2.2 *Continued*

TELEPHONE RESPONSE SHEET

Interviewer's name_____Date_____

Doctor's name_____

  Specialty_____Phone number_____

SURVEYOR'S INTRODUCTORY STATEMENT

    Good morning (afternoon, etc.). This is __(your name)__.
I am working with the_____ Group. We're a
nonprofit organization doing research in areas of consumer interest. We are putting together a directory of
doctors which we hope to make available to consumers so
that they will have additional information to use when
selecting a doctor. And I'd like to ask Dr. _____
a few questions. Is he/she available? (If not, ask the
receptionist if he or she or another member of the office
staff can answer the questions. If not, arrange a time
to call back. Mention that a copy of the questionnaire
will be sent to the doctor for verification prior to
publication.)

    (If cooperation is refused, tell the person that this
is a consumer effort and--if your group has decided on
this approach--that their refusal to cooperate will be
made public when the directory is published.)

First call: _____ questionnaire completed
           _____ call back on __(day)_ at _(time)_
           _____ no cooperation; flat refusal
           _____ Doctor's office will return call on
              (day) at _(time)_.

Second call:_____ questionnaire completed
           _____ call back on __(day)_ at _(time)_.
           _____ no cooperation; flat refusal
           _____ Doctor's office will return call on
              (day) at __(time)_.

Third call: _____ questionnaire completed
           _____ call back on _(day)_ at _(time)_
           _____ no cooperation; flat refusal
           _____ Doctor's office will return call on
              (day) at _(time)_.

Please make comments and notes especially on any irregularities or refusals on this sheet. Try to get direct
quotes from doctors on their reaction, both positive and
negative, to the idea of the directory.

Mark their responses accordingly on the telephone response
sheet and remember to thank the person to whom you are
talking.

Fig. 2.3 Telephone response sheet.

TELEPHONE INSTRUCTIONS

☐ Review the *Questionnaire* and use the *Glossary* at the end of the chapter to help you become familiar with terminology used in the questionnaire. Keep the *Glossary* and the list of *Key Questions* near your telephone.

☐ Write down (print) information as accurately as you can without slowing up the delivery of your questions. Keep it moving. Don't pause between a response and the next question. After each interview, review what you've written down and fill in any details.

☐ You may speak with someone who is very curt and impolite. If someone says, "Go to hell," step back from the situation for a minute and do not take the comment personally. Stress that this is a consumer-directed project. Be polite, but firm. If you don't get anywhere, acknowledge the doctor's right to refuse. If the doctor or any of the staff threatens to sue, say thank you and make your next call.

☐ If the doctor is too busy or the secretary simply doesn't have the time to answer questions, ask if later in the day or tomorrow would be a more convenient time to call. If yes, find out when and note on the telephone response sheet. If no, ask if it would be possible to phone the doctor at home in the evening. If no one will agree to speak with you, stress that this is a consumer project, etc. Ask if they will respond to a mailed questionnaire or to a personal interview.

☐ If you speak with someone other than the doctor and that person does not know the answer to a question and must consult the doctor for the answer, make a note on the questionnaire and move on *immediately* to the next question. At the end of the questioning, ask when the best time would be to call the doctor for that information. Don't leave it up to the doctor's office to call you. Note on the *Telephone Response Sheet* what time you are to return the call.

☐ If you are asked a question that you cannot answer, explain that you will speak with the project coordinator and call back with the answer. But, if possible, complete the rest of the questionnaire right away. If someone insists on speaking to the coordinator, state that you will see that the person receives such a call. Then call the coordinator and explain the problem.

☐ Remember to thank the person you've spoken to for his or her time.

☐ Fill out a *Telephone Response Sheet* for each doctor you call. In addition to noting any irregularities or comments that accompany a refusal to cooperate, please make any comments that you feel are significant about your conversation. Note physicians that were particularly supportive of the project.

☐ Should any difficulty arise call the project coordinator. Be sure that the coordinator knows how to reach you and when to expect you to return with your forms.

☐ Return *Telephone Response Sheets, Questionnaires,* and list of doctors after you've contacted every doctor on your list. Completed questionnaires should be returned to the project coordinator immediately so a typed version can be sent as soon as possible to the doctor for verification.

☐ Don't worry if your first phone call or two is somewhat awkward. You'll find that you become better and more confident with each call.

☐ Remember to ask each physician every question and put the appropriate response where needed. If a question is left blank by you, the project coordinator won't know whether the doctor (or staff) refused to answer, was unable to answer, or that the question, for some reason, was not asked.

Fig. 2.4 Telephone instructions. Developed by Massachusetts PIRG.

Key Questions Doctors May Ask and How to Answer Them

We have attempted to anticipate some important questions that may arise during the interview. The following questions, answers, and suggestions will help prepare you for a potentially awkward situation. Please review these pages and familiarize yourself with them. Use language that you feel comfortable with, but do not change the substance of the responses as stated here.

1. **Q.** I don't believe that what you're doing is legal. After all, doctors are not allowed to advertise. Aren't you aware of this?

   A. Fill in the answer after finding out what type of antiadvertising statute your state has and after referring to Resource 2.1, *State Physician Antiadvertising Laws: A State-by-State Survey.*

2. **Q.** I support what you are doing; it is necessary, and it's about time people knew more about their doctors. What you don't seem to understand is that the medical society has rules and regulations. If I were to answer your questions, I might lose my license. What more can I say?

   A. It's unlikely that the society could have a license revoked. We are expecting a favorable response. Directories have been developed in eight states and in (name of city in your state if Citizen Action Group so indicated.) Doctors like yourself who support this directory realize that they are not alone. You're obviously concerned with your patients, and by providing consumers with information about your practice you will better the understanding between patient and doctor.

3. **Q.** I don't object to telling you where I went to school, which hospitals I admit patients to, or whether or not I accept Medicaid patients. Of course people should know this information. But questions about fees are entirely different. How can I tell in advance how much it will cost to treat someone for an illness I have not yet diagnosed? It's a matter of professional judgment.

   A. We're asking for the average or standard fee, not a set rate. We understand that there might be complications that would change the fee.

4. **Q.** What does this directory offer physicians? Why is it in my interest to answer these questions?

   A. Physicians will find this directory useful for referrals. Physicians will learn more about their peers. Most important, by being open about his or her practice, the individual doctor will benefit by knowing that he or she is contributing to a better understanding between doctor and patient.

Fig. 2.5. Key questions doctors may ask and how to answer them. Developed by Massachusetts PIRG.

PUBLISHING THE DIRECTORY

In order to make your Doctors' Directory most useful to consumers, present the information in a way that makes comparisons between physicians easy for the reader. One way of simplifying the directory is to list doctors by geographic area and by specialty group within those areas. Present statistics (especially information on fees) in short form for easy reference. Review the Sample Directory Format in Fig. 2.6.

If some doctors refused to provide information for your survey, do one of the following:

1. List all doctors' names under whichever of these headings is appropriate:

    No cooperation—doctors who refused to respond to the questionnaire or responded but later refused to allow the information to be published.

    No response—doctors who refused to answer the questionnaire over the phone, asked that it be mailed, but never returned the questionnaire.

    Unconfirmed—doctors who responded to the questionnaire but never returned the copy of the questionnaire sent to office for verification.

    Unavailable—doctors on vacation, out of town.

    Not reached—telephone disconnected, nonpracticing, retired, etc.

2. List doctors' names along with information gathered from preliminary research with or without mentioning their lack of cooperation.

3. Do not list doctors who would not cooperate or respond.

A glossary similar to the one at the end of this chapter should be contained in the appendix of every directory. Consider including the following articles as well: "A Family Guide to Immunizations" and "How to Judge a Hospital," both copyrighted in 1974 by Consumers Union of United States, Inc., and printed in the August 1974 and September 1974 issues of *Consumer Reports*. Reprints of the articles may be obtained from Consumers Union, Reprint Department, Orangeburg, New York 10962, (1 copy, $.35, 10 copies $3.00, 100 copies, $25.00). Other useful additions are: "How to Read a Prescription," and "Prescription Abbreviations," from the Osco Prescription Price Book, copyright 1974 by Osco Drugs, Inc., 1818 Swift Dr., Oakbrook, Illinois 60521.

The directories ought to be made available to consumers at cost. Check state anti-advertising statutes to see if profits from such a directory are prohibited.

For examples of attractive and utilitarian consumer guides, review the Doctor Directories developed by Massachusetts PIRG, 120 Boylston St., Room 320, Boston, Mass. 02216 and by New York PIRG, 5 Beekman Street, New York 10038.

As with any project, it is important to publicize your results through a news conference or news release. A reprint of a Massachusetts news release is shown in Fig. 2.7. Good media coverage and broad distribution are important to ensure that the directory makes a real impact in the community. Groups that might be interested in buying the directory or distributing it for you include the League of Women Voters, Welcome Wagon, and senior citizen groups.

Consider compiling a second directory eight months to a year after completion of the initial one. The response rate from doctors will probably improve dramatically, as doctors will have seen or heard about the initial directory and its popularity with consumers.

Sample Directory Format
Area (I)
(Type of practice)

Name of physician _____

Office address and phone _____

Medical school _____

Year graduated _____

Internship _____

Residency _____

Special training _____

Positions _____

Hospital affiliations _____

Continuing education _____

Board-certified or eligible _____

Office Information

Hours _____

After-hours coverage _____

Makes house-calls _____

Average waiting time for an appointment is _____

Fees

Initial visit _____

Routine visit _____

Payment required at time of appointment? Does or does not customarily adjust fees? Does or does not accept time-deferred payments? Does or does not accept Medicaid or Medicare?

Practice Information
Solo/group/prepaid group/other _____

Office staff: _____

Fig. 2.6 Sample directory format.

Tests: types available and costs _____

_____

Lead poisoning test_____

Venereal disease test_____

Birth control_____

Drugs: Customarily does/does not prescribe generically

Immunizations available (List) _____

_____

Routine scheduling per appointment_____minutes

On request patient may/may not see record.

Consultant if patient requests_____

Complaints? How handled _____

Languages spoken _____

Fig. 2.6 *Continued*

North Shore Health Planning Council   FOR RELEASE: Immediate
10 First Avenue
Peabody, Massachusetts 01960   CONTACT: Mary Ellen O'Shea
   593-0246   593-0246

                    DOCTOR DIRECTORY PUBLISHED

A health care directory for the Eastern Middlesex and Tri-Cities
area has been published by the Eastern Middlesex Sub-Area Health Planning Council, the local branch of the North Shore Health Planning Council. The Eastern Middlesex Sub-Area Council serves the eight communities of North Reading, Reading, Melrose, Wakefield, Stoneham, Malden,
Medford, and Everett.

The name, address, telephone number, and specialty of most of
the general practitioners, internists, pediatricians, obstetricians-
gynecologists, osteopaths, and general surgeons in the area are
listed in the directory. Information on which hospitals the doctors
admit patients to, what languages other than English are spoken in
their offices, whether they do or do not accept new patients and
Medicaid patients, and what their office hours are is also included
in the directory.

A list of other health resources in the area, such as hospital
outpatient services, home health agencies, and ambulance services,
is in the health care directory.

This directory is the result of several months of work and
careful preparation by the Bus-Area Council's Primary Care Committee,
chaired by Louise Duggan of Everett.

In November questionnaires were sent to each family care physician
in the Eastern Middlesex/Tri-Cities area. The list of physicians was
obtained from "Datawell's 1972-73 Medical Directory of Massachusetts,"
the yellow pages of the telephone book, and the 1975 staff lists of
four of the five area hospitals.

Fig. 2.7 Sample news release.

A large percentage of the physicians who did not return a questionnaire were contacted by a member of the Sub-Area Council. Doctors also received copies of their responses, as they would appear in the directory, for verification before the final printing.

Out of 173 family care physicians currently practicing in the Eastern Middlesex/Tri-Cities area, 116 responses for the directory were received. Seventeen physicians did not want to be included in the directory. Their names, addresses, phone numbers, and specialties appear in the directory.

Commenting on the directory, Sub-Area Council Chairperson Helen McCabe of Wakefield said, "We see this directory primarily as an aid to new people in the area and to people who do not have a family doctor. The directory contains some basic information on doctors and other health resources in the area. It encourages people to seek out information on their own and to select a source of health care before they become sick."

People who live in Malden, Medford, or Everett, and who are interested in having a copy of the directory may pick up a free one at the following locations: the city clerk's office in Malden, Malden Hospital, Malden Public Library, Lawrence Memorial Hospital, the city clerk's office in Medford, the Medford Public Library, Whidden Memorial Hospital, Everett City Hall at the switchboard, and Parlin Memorial and Shute Memorial Libraries in Everett.

Other members of the Primary Care Committee were Agnes Commito of Stoneham, Denise Healy of Stoneham, Sanford Monsein, O.D., of Malden, and Mildred Schweiger of Stoneham.

7/23/76

Fig. 2.7 *Continued*

GLOSSARY

The medical profession has a vocabulary unto itself. This glossary will help consumers develop an understanding of this "foreign language." Below are words and phrases that appear on the questionnaire or that may be in a response. The numbers in parentheses refer to the question number in which the word or phrase appears.

PRACTICING engaged in seeing and treating patients; an example of a non-practicing physician is a doctor who is a hospital administrator or a doctor who is engaged exclusively in research.(1.a)

SPECIALTY a branch of medicine concerned with particular body functions, organs, or systems. This list does not cover all the medical specialties, but rather covers primary care physicians—general practice, pediatrics, internal medicine, ophthalmology, etc.—and the more common internal medicine subspecialties—allergy, gastroenterology, rheumatology, etc.(1.b)

Allergy
Dermatology-skin disorders
Family Practice
Gastroenterology-gastrointestinal tract
General Practice
Geriatrics-older people
Gynecology-female reproductive system
Internal Medicine
Obstetrics-pre- and post-childbirth
Obstetrics and gynecology
Ophthalmology-eye
Otorhinolaryngology-ear, nose, throat
Pediatrics-children
Rheumatology-arthritis
Surgery, General
Surgery, Orthopedic-Corrective

Group practice several physicians who practice together, sharing office space, facilities, and, sometimes, personnel. A group practice may have physicians in one or several specialties.(2)

Solo practice a physician who practices alone.(2)

Prepaid group practice a type of practice in which an individual or a family "enroll" by paying a flat annual or monthly rate for comprehensive health care. In a prepaid group practice there is usually a closed panel of physicians performing services. Under certain specified conditions, such as accident emergencies, a prepaid group practice *may* cover the expenses for services performed by physicians other than those on the panel. However, customarily, under prepaid group practices if an "enrollee" has routine services performed by a physician who is not on the panel, then the enrollee must pay out of his or her own pocket. (2)

Staff appointment a formal hospital affiliation. Commonly there are four appointment levels: consulting, active, associate and courtesy. Each level has certain privileges and limitations. (3)

Internship   a one-year period of hospital training following graduation from medical school.(4.b)

Residency   a hospital training period of two or more years for physicians who become specialists; taken after an internship. (4.c)

Board certification and **Board eligibility**   Board certification status is granted by medical specialty boards, each of which establishes training requirements and qualifications and administers examinations for its particular specialty area. There are 22 such boards in existence today. The first board was established in the specialty of ophthalmology in 1917 and the most recent was established in the specialty of generalists—family practice—in 1970.

A *Board-certified* physician is a physician who has been granted certification by the American Board within his or her specialty area. He or she has completed a formal residency training followed by at least two years in full time specialty practice and has passed oral, written, and practical examinations within a specialty area.(5)

Board eligible means that a physician has completed specialty training but has not taken the certification exams.(5)

While it is often the case that specialists seeking positions in prestigious universities or hospitals need to be board certified, neither board certification nor board eligibility is required for a physician to practice medicine in any specialty he or she chooses. However, all physicians must be licensed by the state board of medical examiners in their respective states before they can legally practice medicine.

A physician may also be a fellow of a "college," an honorary association with certain qualifications for membership, concerned with continuing education within a specialty. Examples are: American College of Surgeons (FACS); American College of Obstetrics and Gynecology (FACOG); American Academy of Pediatrics (FAAP); American Academy of Family Physicians (AAFP).

Hospital admittance rights   a physician may admit patients only to hospitals with which he or she is affiliated.(6) (See **Staff appointment.**)

Nurse Practitioner   a registered nurse with additional training enabling him or her to diagnose and treat common illnesses, such as strep throat, cystitis, and upper respiratory infection and to undertake the long-term management of chronic illnesses such as diabetes and hypertension. He or she is also trained to take a patient's medical and social history and to conduct routine physical examinations. A nurse practitioner always works under the direction and supervision of a physician. (9)

Medicaid   a health care assistance program for low-income and needy people, funded by the state and federal government. Medicaid is administered by the Public Welfare Dept.(16)

Medicare   a health insurance program for people 65 and over. Under Medicare the major portion of hospital and medical costs are paid for by the federal government. The remainder is paid for by the subscriber. The monthly premium for subscribers is now $6.70. This monthly premium can be paid by Medicaid if eligible. Medicare is administered by Social Security.(16)

Physicians fees under Medicare: A physician who *accepts assignment* is one who agrees to bill the intermediary—Medicare—and accepts Medicare's assigned payment (the "usual and customary" rate determined by Medicare fee schedules) as payment in full. If a physician does not accept assignment and his or her bill is higher than Medicare's assigned payment, the patient must pay the difference. Physicians can alternate between accepting or not accepting assignment for Medicare payments.(16)

Initial office visit more extensive than a *routine visit;* usually including complete history and diagnostic procedures—physical exam and laboratory tests.(17)

Urinalysis examination of urine for evidence of abnormalities or conditions such as diabetes, kidney or bladder infection, kidney stones, urinary tract infections or poorly functioning kidneys.(18)

Complete blood count (CBC) an analysis of the number of red and white blood cells and other aspects of the blood such as hemoglobin, varying percentages of white cells, and the like. (18)

Throat culture test for bacterial infection such as streptococcus.(18)

SMA-12 a routine diagnostic screening test which measures basic body metabolism: liver, kidney, parathyroid functions, and blood sugar.(18)

Blood sugar measurement of the level of sugar in blood; used to detect diabetes and other disorders.(18)

Pap smear a sample of cells usually taken from the cervix used to detect cancer and other abnormalities.(18)

Immunizations protections or inoculations against diseases such as: small pox, whooping cough, diphtheria, measles, polio, typhoid, tetanus, flu, etc.(20)

Lead poisoning systemic poisoning due to a high level of lead; most common in children. Can be severely damaging. (24)

Venereal diseases bacterial infections that are almost always transmitted through sexual intercourse, the most common being syphilis and gonorrhea. (22b)

Generic name the name given to all drugs with the same chemical composition. For example, aspirin is a generic name and Bayer is a brand name. Generic drugs cost considerably less than brand name drugs and, with few exceptions, have been found to be chemically and therapeutically equivalent. (26)

BIBLIOGRAPHY

A consumer's directory of doctors with select health care guides. Massachusetts Public Interest Research Group, Inc., 1975.

A consumer's directory of Prince George's County doctors. Public Citizen's Health Research Group, Washington, D.C., 1974.

Consumer's guide to Onondaga physicians. New York Public Interest Research Group, 1974.

Consumer's guide to Queens doctors. New York Public Interest Research Group, 1974.

Health Maintenance Organization sourcebook, The Health Law Center, Aspen Systems Corporation, Rockville, Md., 1973.

CHAPTER 3

nursing homes- a first step to change

INTRODUCTION

And so from hour to hour we ripe and ripe
And then from hour to hour we rot and rot
And thereby hangs a tale

Shakespeare: *As You Like It*

Shakespeare describes a morbid view of aging indeed, but his description would not seem exaggerated to many of the elderly Americans who are passing their waning years in nursing homes. Numerous investigations have revealed illegal, unethical, and inhuman conditions in nursing homes across the country. Criticisms leveled at the nursing home industry range from deliberate physical abuse of patients to unsafe and unsanitary facilities; from lack of adequate medical and nursing care to untrained and poorly paid support staff; from disregard of the legal rights of patients to lack of rehabilitative programs.

Twenty-two million people in the United States—10 percent of the population—are 65 years or older, and their numbers grow each year. One in every five of these older Americans will spend some time in a nursing home.[1] With few exceptions they look forward to that experience with fear—fear of poor care, loneliness, abuse, or loss of dignity. Currently these institutions house more than one million people. At a time when they most need and deserve good care and companionship, many of these nursing home residents live a less than human existence and wait for death to release them from their misery.

The government, faced with a tightly organized industry lobbying force and an almost silent citizenry, has left the nursing home industry virtually unchecked to administer to the elderly. The historical development of the nursing home industry in the United States shows an increased governmental awareness of the financial plight of the elderly, but also demonstrates that assistance programs primarily benefit the nursing home industry, not the patients.

Before 1935, most homes for the aged were either state-supported poorhouses and almshouses, or homes operated by churches or social groups on a nonprofit basis for use by members only. A few small nursing homes were run for profit, usually as a family enterprise.

During the Depression the number of older Americans having no means of financial support increased, and state money for old-age assistance become scarce. In 1935, Congress responded to that situation by passing the Social Security Act, which made federal money available both to individuals over the age of 65 residing in private institutions and directly to nursing homes. This availability of public money fostered the beginning of the nursing home industry as we know it today.

In 1954, the Hill-Burton Act, which provided federal grant assistance to states for the construction of hospitals, was amended to include assistance for construction of public and nonprofit, long-term care institutions, including nursing homes.

The Social Security Act Amendments of 1965, Titles XVIII and XIX, provide substantial financial coverage for nursing home care through the Medicare and Medicaid programs. With this new influx of public money to nursing homes and the growing number of citizens 65 and over, the industry expanded from 9582 nursing homes and related facilities in 1960, to 23,000 in 1974. Of these facilities, 77 percent are run for profit, 15 percent are nonprofit, and 8 percent are operated by the government. Estimates of the average cost of nursing home care vary considerably, but the most generally accepted figure is $600 per patient per month.[2]

Federal and state subsidies to nursing homes have grown annually since 1965, becoming the financial backbone of the industry. The total expenditure for nursing home care in the United States rose from $555 million in 1960 to $7.5 billion in 1974. Of that total, federal and state payments made through the Medicaid program accounted for more than 50 percent, or $3.7 billion, and federal Medicaid payments provided another 3 percent, or $225 million. Private patients spent $3.5 billion on nursing home care in 1974, but Social Security or Veterans Assistance checks accounted for a sizeable portion of those private payments.[3]

Over the past ten years, increased public awareness of fraud and abuses in the nursing home industry has created a rising impetus directed toward reform. Newpaper exposés and organized citizen action have resulted in nursing home investigations by private groups and special state commissions or legislative committees. In 1976, the Subcommittee on Long-Term Care of the Senate Special Committee on Aging, which has been investigating nursing homes for several years, issued reports and recommended federal legislation aimed at correcting some of the abuses within the nursing home industry. Similar measures are underway in many states. Now, more than ever before, citizen action can result in meaningful reform. Timely input from knowledgeable individuals and citizen groups around the country may ensure that pending legislation is adequately drafted and, most importantly, properly enforced.

The project guides which follow have been prepared to aid citizens in monitoring certain aspects of the nursing home industry. They do not encompass all the possibilities for action, and should be viewed as a first step to change.[4] These projects focus on: (1) a review of the licensing and inspection reports of nursing homes and; (2) investigating nursing home compliance with federal patients' rights regulations.

HOW ARE NURSING HOMES REGULATED, AND WHY ISN'T THE SYSTEM WORKING?

Despite the fact that the federal government and most states have regulations governing nursing homes, patients in the majority of homes apparently receive inadequate health care. Many facilities continue to be substandard, and their administrators and owners defraud patients, their families, and the government.

The Subcommittee on Long-Term Care of the Special Senate Committee on Aging concluded in December 1974, on the basis of 15 years of research, that "at least 50 percent of nursing homes in the United States are substandard with one or more life-threatening condition[s]."[5] Basing their report on newspaper investigations and reports by "official investigatory bodies," the committee drew up this appalling list[6] of the most common abuses by nursing homes:

Lack of human dignity; lack of activities; untrained and inadequate numbers of staff; ineffective inspections and enforcement; profiteering; lack of control on drugs; poor care; unsanitary conditions; poor food; poor fire protection and other hazards to life; excessive charges in addition to the daily rate; unnecessary or unauthorized use of restraints; negligence leading to death or injury; theft; lack of psychiatric care; untrained administrators; discrimination against minority groups; reprisals against those who complain; lack of dental care; advance notice of state inspections; false advertising.

In some cases these abuses have not been corrected because of inadequate regulations; in the majority of cases, abuses continue because of loose licensing and enforcement systems at the federal, state and local levels.

In all states, nursing homes must be licensed (certified) by the state in order to operate legally. States have regulations setting standards for health, fire, and safety conditions with which nursing homes must comply. Usually it is the Department or Board of Health that is authorized to license and inspect facilities for compliance with state regulations relating to health. The state Fire Marshall is authorized to license and inspect facilities for compliance with state regulations relating to fire and safety.

However, the state often authorizes county or local agencies to conduct the inspections and grant licenses.

According to state regulations, a full license indicates that the facility was inspected and found to meet all the standards. A conditional or temporary license indicates that the facility was inspected, did not meet all standards, but has agreed to make the necessary improvements within a given time period. But these licenses are not always accurate indicators of nursing home conditions, because actual licensing procedures may be much less stringent than those called for in the regulations. Regulations, inspection procedures, and the conditions under which facilities are given conditional licenses vary from state to state and must be carefully studied. In some states, homes are licensed at different levels, such as A-1, A-2, etc., which indicate the number of deficiencies found, or the general level of care offered. Be sure you understand any such rating systems used in your state.

Nursing homes which receive federal money through the Medicare and/or Medicaid programs must also meet standards set in federal regulations. Because a majority of homes receive more than 50 percent of their income through these programs, it is important to understand exactly how Medicare and Medicaid work.

MEDICARE

The Medicare program, (established under Title XVIII of the Social Security Act) is a 100 percent federally financed health care insurance program available to anyone 65 years of age or older who is eligible for social security payments or railroad worker's insurance. Medicare provides payments for most types of health care, including up to 100 days of care in nursing homes which qualify as Skilled Nursing Facilities under federal regulations.

Although the Medicare program is financed and administered by the Social Security Administration, insurance companies act as the fiscal intermediaries between patients, Skilled Nursing Facilities, and the government. Using Social Security Administration guidelines, insurance companies determine the rights of patients to Medicare benefits. The facilities are paid on a "cost-plus" basis. That is, for costs plus a reasonable profit. A state agency, usually the Department of Health, determines the rate of payment for each Skilled Nursing Facility in the state.

The regional offices of the Social Security Administration have final authority for the enforcement of federal standards in facilities receiving Medicare payments. However, they may authorize a state agency, usually the State Department of Health, to do the inspection and licensing of participating facilities. Homes that do not meet the federal requirements continue to receive federal money, but have cancellation clauses in their agreements which may be applied if they do not make necessary changes. In some cases, the state department authorizes county or city agencies to handle inspections and licensing.

Many nursing homes dropped out of the program in 1969, when the Social Security Administration adopted more stringent Medicare guidelines, and chose instead to participate in the Medicaid program. Thus, the Medicaid program, with its weaker regulations, became the financial mainstay of the industry.

MEDICAID

The Medicaid program (established under Title XIX of the Social Security Act) is a medical care payment system for the "medically indigent." Medicaid operates as a matching state and federal program with the amount of federal assistance based on the per capita income of each state and ranging from 50 percent to 75 percent.

Medicaid payments for nursing home care are made to those Skilled Nursing Facilities and Intermediate Care Facilities which qualify as nursing care facilities for the aged or infirm under the federal regulations. The $3.7 billion in Medicaid funds paid to nursing homes in 1974 covered twenty million recipients. Of that figure, $2.0 billion was federal money and $1.7 billion was state money.

The Department of Health, Education, and Welfare (HEW) administers the Medicaid program and sets the standards for participating facilities. But HEW has delegated most of the regulatory power of the program to the states, including responsibility for determining who is eligible for Medicaid payments and the amount of money to be paid to facilities for each patient. Generally the state Welfare Department makes these determinations and the Department of Health, under contract with HEW, licenses and inspects facilities for compliances with the federal regulations and standards.

Because Skilled Nursing Facilities may receive both Medicare and Medicaid funds, the standards and procedures for inspecting and certifying these facilities for both programs were unified in January 1974. The federal regulations covering Skilled Nursing Facilities and Intermediate Care Facilities participating in Medicare and/or Medicaid are available from Social Security Administration offices. Summaries of the major points in those regulations appear in Resources 3.1 and 3.2.

WHAT CAN CITIZENS DO TO EFFECT CHANGE?

Focusing on a review of nursing homes' licenses and federal inspection reports is the logical first step in working toward nursing home reform. In order to recommend effective and valid changes in state regulations and enforcement systems, it is necessary to support your demands with evidence that many nursing homes providing inadequate care continue to operate under present regulations and enforcement systems.

The California PIRG surveyed nursing homes in 1975 and revealed that nearly one half of the homes for which inspection reports were reviewed had the same violations in the last two inspection reports. Of the repeated violations, 37 percent fell into the crucial areas of adequate medical records and nursing care.

Similarly, Oregon PIRG revealed that in 119 nursing homes for which follow-up inspections were done to check on previous deficiencies, 44 percent of the violations went uncorrected.

Moreover, consumers cannot make intelligent choices among nursing homes unless they have information about nursing homes that do not meet all federal and state standards. In most states this information is not readily available. Publication of the license status and inspection report findings will provide an invaluable service to the public.

Where to Start

The state Department of Health will most likely have responsibility for health-related licensing and inspections, as well as information on where to find records of the current licensing status of nursing homes and copies of state regulations covering licensing and inspection. If the department will not provide this information, make a "freedom of information"* request and send a copy to the state Attorney General's Office. See Resource 3.3.

The department should have a current list of nursing homes in the state; if not, contact the state Nursing Home Association and check in telephone books. Local Social Security offices have names of nursing homes that participate in Medicare and local Welfare offices have names of homes participating in Medicaid.

This project will take at least three months to complete. Before deciding the geographic areas to cover and the number and types of homes to be included, determine the number of volunteers available, their locations, and how much time they can devote to the study.

Reviewing and summarizing one full Medicare or Medicaid inspection report will probably take five or six hours. The time required to review state inspection reports and licenses will vary with the cooperativeness of department employees and the condition of their files. Unfortunately, few states allow public access to state inspection reports. State licenses are open to review in all states. Getting access to the reports and files will probably take one to two weeks. Reviewing one state inspection report may take a researcher three hours. Two researchers spending four hours scanning licensing records should find the licenses of at least 15 nursing homes.

If you don't have the time to review both federal and state inspection reports and the state licensing status of all nursing homes in your area, limit the study in one of the following ways: concentrate solely on surveying the federal inspection reports and state licensing status of those homes that receive Medicare or Medicaid payments; or review only the current licensing status of nursing homes.

WHAT TYPES OF NURSING HOMES WILL YOU INVESTIGATE?

Skilled nursing facilities and intermediate care facilities that participate in Medicare and/or Medicaid programs Approximately one half of the nursing homes in the United States participate in one or both of these programs and the number grows annually. For that reason, your report will not be complete without data on Skilled Nursing Facilities which participate in Medicare and/or Medicaid and Intermediate Care Facilities which participate in Medicaid. These homes are also licensed under state law, so review their licenses as well.

Nursing homes that offer nursing care but which do not participate in either the Medicare or Medicaid programs These homes may have chosen not to participate in Medi-

---

*Freedom of Information Laws, mandating that most types of government records, reports, etc. must be made available to the public, are in effect in most states. Any letter requesting information or documents under the Freedom of Information Act must be answered by the receiving agency. Unless the information requested is exempted from the law, it must be made available to you, although there may be charges for reproduction. If you are met with unwarranted resistance, contact the Freedom of Information Clearinghouse, Box 19367, Washington, D.C. 20036.

care or Medicaid, or may not have met the standards necessary for certification as participating facilities. Called Skilled Nursing Facilities, Intermediate Care Facilities, Basic Care Facilities, or other names designated by state law, these homes must be licensed by the state and will comprise an important part of your investigation of licenses.

Nursing homes that provide custodial care, but no nursing care These types of homes are licensed and inspected in most states and may be called custodial homes, personal care homes, boarding homes, adult foster care homes, or other names designated by state law. If they must be licensed in your state, review their licenses only if your group has time to do so without excluding the types mentioned above.

WHERE WILL YOU FIND THE INFORMATION?

Medicaid and Medicare reports In 1972, the United States Congress mandated public disclosure of Medicare and Medicaid inspection reports no later than 90 days after completion of the inspections. There are two types of Medicare/Medicaid reports, one for Intermediate Care Facilities (Medicaid) and one for Skilled Nursing Facilities (Medicare and Medicaid). Medicare inspection reports are available through the regional and district offices of the Social Security Administration. Medicaid inspection reports are available through local Welfare offices.

The Social Security Administration (SSA) district offices and local Welfare offices only make available part of the inspection reports—a statement of deficiencies found by investigators. These statements include information about major deficiencies, corrective action taken, and some positive features of the nursing home, but do not provide a complete picture of how the homes operate. Consequently, it is perferable to review full inspection reports which list ownership, numbers and types of personnel, services available and inspectors' comments on a wide range of conditions. The full inspection reports are available from SSA regional offices. Citizens can obtain those reports by making a written request to the district Social Security office. It may take as long as a month before the district office receives the reports from the regional office. (Figure 3.1 is a list of SSA regional offices.)

The reports may be reviewed at the district office at no charge. However, if you wish to take the report with you there is a charge for reproduction costs—usually 15 to 25 cents a page. As the reports are about 60 pages long, most groups will choose to do their reviewing at the district office.

If you are located in one of the eleven cities where there is a regional office you may prefer to approach them directly, thus eliminating the time lag involved in transferring the reports from office to office. But be prepared for some resistance, as these offices are not used to dealing directly with the public.

The personnel at local and district offices are often unaware of the public disclosure law. The Connecticut PIRG experience illustrates the difficulties you may encounter in obtaining access to Medicare and Medicaid inspection reports. Prior to their requests, only one other individual had requested copies of the reports—and he was a prospective purchaser of a home!

Connecticut PIRG called six Welfare offices requesting Medicaid reports and reported that "all of them were skeptical about the public's right to view the reports."

BOSTON
John Fitzgerald Kennedy Bldg.
Room 1109, Government Center
Boston, Massachusetts 02203

NEW YORK
Room 737, 26 Federal Plaza
New York, New York 10007

PHILADELPHIA
P.O. Box 8788
3535 Market St.
Philadelphia, Pennsylvania 19101

ATLANTA
Room 129
50 Seventh St., N.E.
Atlanta, Georgia 30323

CHICAGO
300 S. Wacker Dr.
Chicago, Illinois 60606

CLEVELAND
6th Floor
14600 Detroit Ave.
Cleveland, Ohio 44107

KANSAS CITY
Federal Bldg.
601 East Twelfth St.
Kansas City, Missouri 64106

DALLAS
1200 Main Tower
21st Floor
1200 Commerce St.
Dallas, Texas 75202

DENVER
Room 9017
Federal Office Bldg.
19th & Stout Sts.
Denver, Colorado 80202

SAN FRANCISCO
100 Van Ness Ave.
San Francisco, California 94102

SEATTLE
Mail Stop 615
Arcade Plaza Bldg.
1321 Second Ave.
Seattle, Washington 98101

Fig. 3.1 Social Security Administration regional offices addresses.

Furthermore, five of the offices stated that the Health Department, not Welfare offices, kept such records. Four of ten Social Security Offices they contacted for copies of Medicare reports were not sure that the public had access to the reports and referred the surveyors to the Health Department. With perserverance you, like Conn PIRG, can obtain access through the Social Security and Welfare offices.

Make your initial request in the form of a freedom of information request, and include a copy of the disclosure law (see Resource 3.3). If you are not allowed access to summaries of full reports within a month, lodge a written complaint with the regional Social Security Office, and send copies to the Office of the General Counsel, Social Security Administration, Woodlawn, Maryland 21235.

State (or Local) Licenses and Inspection Reports

Check with the state Health Department or Board of Health for licenses and inspection reports covering state health standards and with the state or local Fire Marshal's office for state fire safety licenses and inspection reports.

Information on the current licenses of homes is available to the public in all states, but may be difficult to obtain. If you are denied access to license information, contact the Attorney General's Office or seek legal assistance.

Obtain from state or local officials their definition of "full" and "conditional" license status and information on conditions and deficiencies that result in "conditional" licensing. Compare the license status of each home for at least the last two inspection periods. Under a general classification system it is impossible to distinguish major from minor deficiencies. Homes with deficiencies in relatively minor areas (usually easier to correct) should have achieved full status in a following inspection. Therefore it is more equitable to record and make public two or three consecutive license ratings and include specific information about deficiencies cited.

If you have been informed that state inspection reports, under state law, are not available to the public, check the state statute referred to, or call the Attorney General's Office for verification.

Lobbying for public access to these reports is an important aspect of regulatory reform and should be incorporated into your efforts toward reform of the nursing home industry.

WHAT TO LOOK FOR IN INSPECTION REPORTS

A sample summary form for use when reviewing the Medicare/Medicaid reports appears in Fig. 3.2. If you have not purchased full reports but intend to review them at the district office, purchase copies of a completed inspection report for a Skilled Nursing Facility (Medicare) and an Intermediate Care Facility (Medicaid) for use in surveyor training sessions. If you can't afford two completed reports, ask for copies of blank ones. Hold training sessions for all surveyors for familiarization with the report formats and with the summary form. The study will be valid and valuable to consumers only if all surveyors record the same data from inspection reports.

If state inspection reports are available, and depending on the length and content of those reports, you may choose to have surveyors record all the information or develop a summary form similar to the one for Medicare/Medicaid homes.

MAKE YOUR STUDY PUBLIC AND READILY AVAILABLE TO CONSUMERS

Prepare a *final report* containing survey data and your recommendations for reform, and make it available to others working for nursing home reform, to the press, and to legislators and state agency officials. Although useful to some consumers, a lengthy report will not provide an easy guide to comparing homes and should not serve as a substitute for a shorter consumer guide.

Prepare a "Consumer's Guide to Area Nursing Homes" in a *flyer* or *pamphlet* form. Include the health and fire license status for at least the last two inspections and information about homes will also be useful, including: whether they accept and are certified for Medicare and/or Medicaid patients; costs; number of beds; and whether skilled and/or intermediate nursing care is available. If you include many homes, list in separate sections the homes that provide nursing care and those that do not.

If you reviewed Medicare and Medicaid inspection reports, include in your brochure summary information on: medical services, nursing services, deficiencies in

Sample Format for Summary of Official Medicare
and Medicaid Inspection Reports

Facility_____

Address_____

Telephone_____ Date of Survey_____

Bed capacity _____

Survey for Medicare/Medicaid (Circle one or both)

Responsible Officials: _____

Nonprofit_____ Profit_____

Owners _____

Administrator _____

Director of nursing_____

Medical director or advisory physicians _____

_____

1. Medical Services

    a) Deficiencies cited_____

    _____

    b) Major comments provided_____

    _____

2. Nursing Services

    a) Registered nurse on all shifts? yes___ no___

    b) If no, which shifts not covered by registered
    nurse? day___ evening___ night___ weekend___

    c) Registered nurse hours per day_____
       Licensed practical nurse hours per day_____
       Aide/orderly hours per day_____
       Total hours per day_____
       Total hours per day per patient_____
       (divide total average hours per day by bed capacity)
       (recommended absolute minimum: 2.25 hours/day)

Fig. 3.2 Sample format for summary of official Medicare and Medicaid inspection reports, prepared by the National Consumers' League, Washington, D.C.

d) Deficiencies cited_____

e) Major comments provided_____

3.   Type of Patient Mix   Skilled   Intermediate   Domi-
                                        Care   ciliary

	Skilled	Intermediate Care	Domiciliary
Bedfast			
Ambulatory			
Need assistance to walk			
Need assistance to eat			
Incontinent			
With deubit(skin ulcers)			
Disoriented or confused			

4.   Nutrition

a) Deficiencies cited_____

b) Comments provided_____

c) Professional dietician in charge full time?
      yes___ no___

d) If no, is there regular consultation with one?
      yes___ no___

e) Number of patients on modified diets_____

f) Inservice training given to kitchen staff?_____

g) Mealtimes (and snack times)
      breakfast___ lunch___ dinner___
      snacks at ____ and ____

5.   Therapists

a) Physical therapist available? yes___ no___

b) How paid? Fee for service by patient___ Other___

c) Other therapists available:
   Speech   yes___ no___ hours/month___
   Occupational   yes___ no___ hours/month___
   Other (specify) yes___ no___ hours/month___

6.   Advisory Dentist/Ophthalmologist

a) Dentist available yes___ no___

b) Ophthalmologist available yes___ no___

7.   Patient Activities and Social Services

a) Is there a social service person? yes___ no___

Fig. 3.2 *Continued*

b) Complete social services?   yes____ no____

c) Is there a patient-activity leader? yes____ no____

d) If yes, for how many hours?_____

e) Comments provided_____

_____

8. Environment and Fire Safety

a) Are there deficiencies? _____ Date corrected_____

b) List major uncorrected deficiencies, if any_____

_____

c) Major comments provided_____

_____

9. Transfer-to-hospital Agreement

List hospitals to which patient may be transferred in
an emergency_____

10. Miscellaneous
Any comments given by surveyor but not incorporated
above_____

_____

Fig. 3.2 *Continued*

nutrition and dietetic services, types of therapy available and costs, dental and ophthalmology services and costs, safety conditions, patient activities, and patient information, such as the percentage of residents in the home that are not disoriented or confused, percentage that are ambulatory, percentage that do not need assistance to walk and to eat.

Groups located in metropolitan areas who want to perform a consumer service might consider setting up a *Consumer Information Center.* Such a center can provide an excellent vehicle for expanding community awareness and interest in nursing home reform. The National Consumer League established such a consumer center in Washington, D.C., and consumer response was overwhelming.

The center would have files on every home in the area containing: (1) the licensing status of the home; (2) a summary of the full inspection report; (3) a copy of the deficiency summary prepared by surveyors; (4) full inspection reports (if you can afford the charges); (5) summaries of state inspection reports (if available) for homes that do not participate in Medicare or Medicaid.

Because Medicare and Medicaid inspections are announced to facilities prior to the inspection and the same procedure is followed in many states before state inspection, it will be important to add other information to the files, including: (1) reports made after your surveyors have visited nursing homes, including comments from patients; (2) letters and comments solicited from consumers in the area who either visit a patient in a home or have visited homes; letters and comments solicited from physicians, welfare case workers (who decide what home a welfare patient will reside in) and other professionals or state and local employees familiar with nursing homes; (3) comments received from nursing home administrators or owners, and (4) any other reports or investigations done on area nursing homes.

HOW CAN PATIENTS IN NURSING HOMES BE ASSURED THEIR RIGHTS?

Admittance to a nursing home should not mean forfeiture of one's rights as an individual or as a citizen. But nursing home patients are often systematically stripped of basic rights: the right to be treated with consideration and to be free from physical and mental abuse; the right to refuse to work for the facility; the right to receive visitors and telephone calls and to receive and send mail; the right to refuse medication not prescribed by a physician, the right to retain and use personal possessions.

Connecticut PIRG investigators personally visited area nursing homes and "discovered that there is practically no protection for a resident of a nursing home from personal or financial abuse."

To prevent the occurrence of such abuses, patients who may not know their rights or are afraid to demand them need protection—protection from homes that deny these rights in order to make the care of residents as uniform, easy, and inexpensive as possible.

The government must define and guarantee under law the rights of nursing home patients and ensure that strict enforcement follows. Patients and their relatives must be informed about patients' rights and the procedure for reporting violations.

The federal government has taken action to define and regulate the basic rights of nursing home patients. Regulations formulated by the Department of Health, Education and Welfare guarantee not only the patients' well-recognized constitutional rights, but other basic rights as well. A separate set of regulations covers Skilled Nursing Facilities (Resource 3.4) and Intermediate Care Facilities (Resource 3.5) that participate in the Medicare/Medicaid programs. Facilities that do not comply with the regulations can and *should* lose their federal funding. However, enforcement of the regulations is poor, with responsibilities for oversight being passed on to the states.

The two patients' rights surveys presented here are designed to test for compliance by facilities with the federal regulations. A summary of those regulations appears in Fig. 3.3 and is followed by the survey information.

§ 405.1121(k) Standard: Patients' rights.   These patients' rights policies and procedures ensure that, at least, each patient admitted to the facility:

1) Is fully informed, as evidenced by the patients' written acknowledgement, prior to or at the time of admission and during stay, of these rights and of all rules and regulations governing patient conduct and responsibilities;

2) Is fully informed, prior to or at the time of admission and during stay, of services available in the facility, and of related charges including any charges for services not covered under titles 18 or 19 of the Social Security Act, or not covered by the facility's basic perdiem rate;

3) Is fully informed, by a physician, of his medical condition unless medically contraindicated (as documented, by a physician, in his medical record), and is afforded the opportunity to participate in the planning of his medical treatment and to refuse to participate in experimental research;

4) Is transferred or discharged only for medical reason, or for his welfare or that of other patients, or for non-payment for his stay (except as prohibited by titles 18 or 19 of the SSA), and is given reasonable advance notice to ensure orderly transfer or discharge, and such actions are documented in his medical record;

5) Is encouraged and assisted, throughout his stay, to exercise his rights as a patient and as a citizen, and to this end may voice grievances and recommend changes in policies and services to facility staff and/or to outside representatives of his choice, free from restraints, interference, coersion, discrimination, or reprisal;

6) May manage his personal financial affairs, or is given at least a quarterly accounting of financial transactions made on his behalf should the facility accept his written delegation of this responsibility to the facility for any period of time in conformance with State law;

7) Is free from mental and physical abuse, and free from chemical and (except in emergencies), physical restraints except as authorized in writing by a physician for a specified and limited period of time, or when necessary to protect the patient from injury to himself or to others;

8) Is assured confidential treatment of his personal and medical records, and may approve or refuse their release to any individual outside the facility, except, in case of his transfer to another health care institution, or as required by law or third-party payment contract;

9) Is treated with consideration, respect, and full recognition of his dignity and individuality, including privacy in treatment and care for his personal needs;

10) Is not required to perform services for the facility that are not included for therapeutic purposes in his plan of care;

11) May associate and communicate privately with persons of his choice, and send and receive his personal mail unopened, unless medically contraindicated (as documented by his physician in his record);

12) May meet with, and participate in activities of social, religious, and community groups at his discretion, unless medically contraindicated (as documented by his physician in his medical record);

13) May retain and use his personal clothing and possessions as space permits, unless to do so would infringe upon the rights of other patients, and unless medically contraindicated (as documented by his physician in his medical record);

14) If married, is assured privacy for visits by his/her spouse; if both are inpatients in the facility, they are permitted to share a room, unless medically contraindicated (as documented by his attending physician in the medical record).

Fig. 3.3 The rights of patients in nursing homes. Phrases or sections in parentheses apply only to Skilled Nursing Facilities.

DO NURSING HOMES IN YOUR AREA
COMPLY WITH THE FEDERAL REGULATIONS?

Survey 1—Public Access to the Patients' Bill of Rights and Contents of Facilities' Bills of Rights

The federal regulation states that each Skilled Nursing Facility participating in the Medicare or Medicaid program must establish and implement written policies regarding rights and responsibilities of patients, and that these policies and procedures are public information. The purpose of this survey is to find out whether nursing homes are complying with the federal regulation: will they make their Bill of Rights available to the public and do these documents meet the federal requirements?

Contact the Social Security and Welfare office for a list of area Skilled Nursing Facilities that participate in the Medicare or Medicaid program.

Whenever possible, the patients' rights documents should be requested in person by a pair of surveyors visiting each home and speaking with the administrator. When that is not possible, a written request can be made asking for the documents, citing the federal regulation, and agreeing to pay the cost of duplication. However, many homes interpret the regulation narrowly and, rather than make a copy of the documents available by mail, or even to volunteers in person, will allow a review of the original documents only at the facility. If that is the case, lodge a written complaint with the nearest Regional Office of the Department of Health, Education, and Welfare and send a copy of the complaint to the State Inspection Agency, and the Office of the General Counsel, Social Security Administration, Woodlawn, Maryland.

Review the policy statement of the facility to determine whether all patient's rights included in the federal regulation are written into the facility's document. Any sections not included should be noted and brought to the attention of the nursing home administrator. Whenever possible, speak with nursing home staff about the written procedures and their implementation.

Information on access to nursing homes' written policies, conversations with nursing home staff, and the analysis of the policy statements should be compiled into a written report and turned in to the Project Coordinator. After similar reports have been completed on the other homes in the area, the information can be included in a "Consumers' Guide," made public and sent to the offices mentioned above.

Survey 2—Patients' Rights Questionnaire

The patients' rights questionnaire presented in Fig. 3.4 is designed to test facility compliance with federal regulations. The questionnaire is directed to nursing home residents' next of kin and, in certain circumstances, to residents themselves. Surveying next of kin can be done on a random sample basis, which is considered the most statistically credible method. Limit the survey to next of kin that visit the home frequently because their credibility cannot easily be questioned by those reviewing your survey data.

Survey of Rights of Patients in Nursing Homes

(Questions 1-13 are designed to indicate the relationship between the patient and the next of kin, and how
familiar the next of kin is with conditions at the
nursing home.)

1. How frequent have your visits been with the patient?

   Daily___ Weekly___ Every two weeks___ Monthly___

   If the person answering indicated that visits have

   been less frequent than biweekly do not continue with

   the questionnaire unless: (1) Those who make monthly

   visits indicate that those visits are of long duration

   and feel quite familiar with the patient's circum-

   stances in the home, in which case you may choose to

   continue on with the entire questionnaire; (2) This

   person assisted the patient in becoming admitted to a

   nursing home, in which case you should ask her or him

   questions 2-10.

2. When was the last time you visited the patient?

   _____

3. How are you (or were you) related to the patient you

   have visited most frequently?

   Parent   _____   Son/daughter   _____

   Husband/wife   _____   Friend/associate _____

   Brother/sister   _____   Other (explain)   _____

4. Are you the legal guardian of the patient?

   Yes____ No____

5. What is/was the name of the nursing home that the

   patient is/was most recently staying and where is it

   located?_____

Fig. 3.4 Survey of rights of patients in nursing homes.

6. Did you assist the person in becoming a patient in <u>any</u> nursing home? Yes_____ No_____

   (If yes, ask questions 7-14. If no, go directly to question 15.)

7. Is the nursing home where you assisted this person in becoming a patient the same home as mentioned above? Yes_____ No_____

   If no, what was the name of the home and where is it located:_____

   _____

8. When did you assist this person in becoming a patient?

   _____

9. Before this person became a patient in the nursing home (or subsequent to December 2, 1974, if patient was admitted before that date) was he or she informed by the home about the home's policies and procedures regarding patients' rights and of all rules and regulations concerning patient conduct and respon- sibilities? Yes_____ No_____ Do not know_____

10. Did this person acknowledge in writing his or her having been so informed? Yes_____ No_____

    Do not know_____

11. Are the patients' rights as explained by the home at time of admittance actually complied with by the home? Yes_____ No_____ Do not know_____

    Explain:_____

    _____

Fig. 3.4 *Continued*

73

12. Are there rules and regulations regarding patient conduct and responsibility that were not explained by the home at the time of admittance?

     Yes_____ No_____ Do not know_____

How do you know the information given above?

a) Personal observation_____

b) Conversation with patient_____

c) Conversation(s) with other patients_____

d) Conversation(s) with nursing home staff_____

e) Other (please specify)

13. a) Before, or at the time of admission to the nursing home (or subsequent to December 2, 1974, if patient was admitted before that date) was the patient informed about services available at the home?

     Yes_____ No_____ Do not know_____

b) Before, or at the time of admission (or subsequent to December 2, 1974, if patient was admitted before that date) was the patient also told about all charges for services, including charges not covered by Medicare, Medicaid, or by the home's basic daily rate?

     Yes_____ No_____ Do not know_____

c) Have charges been made which were not explained before, or at the time of admittance?

     Yes_____ No_____ Do not know_____

14. a) Is the patient kept fully informed by a <u>physician</u> about his or her medical condition?

     Yes_____ No_____ Do not know_____

Fig. 3.4 *Continued*

b) If no, do you know if the patient has asked, and if so, why the patient was not told about his or her medical condition?

Yes_____ No_____ Do not know_____

Explain:_____

_____

c) Is the patient made aware of the possible treatments and given the opportunity to participate in the planning of his or her medical treatment?

Yes_____ No_____ Do not know_____

d) Was the patient ever asked to participate in experimental research?

Yes_____ No_____ Do not know_____

e) If the patient was asked, but refused to participate in experimental research, was his or her denial contested?

Yes_____ No_____ Do not know_____

15. a) Was this person ever transferred from any nursing home?

Yes_____ No_____ Do not know_____

b) Was this person ever discharged from a nursing home?

Yes_____ No_____ Do not know_____

c) If yes, what is the name and location of the nursing home and the date of the action? (If before December, 1974, don't record answers as the regulation was not in effect.)_____

Fig. 3.4 *Continued*

d) Who made the decision that the patient was to be transferred or discharged?

_____

e) Was the person told why he or she was being transferred or discharged?

Yes_____ No_____ Do not know

f) If yes, what was the reason? Please explain below.

1. Medical___

2. For his or her welfare___

3. For the welfare of other patients___

4. Nonpayment___

5. Other (please specify)_____

g) How far in advance of the transfer or discharge was the patient given notice?_____

16. a) Has the administration of the nursing home encouraged the patients to exercise their rights as patients and as citizens? Yes_____ No_____ Do not know_____

How do you know the information given above?

1. Personal observation_____

2. Conversation with patient_____

3. Conversation(s) with other patients_____

4. Conversation(s) with nursing home staff_____

5. Other (please specify)_____

b) If the patient is physically able, may he or she go to town meetings or the like?

Yes_____ No_____ Do not know_____

Explain:_____

Fig. 3.4 *Continued*

c) Is transportation arranged by the home?

Yes_____ No_____ Do not know_____

Explain:_____

d) If the patient is physically able, may he or she
go to the polls to vote?

Yes_____ No_____ Do not know_____

17. a) Has the patient ever wanted to voice a grievance
or recommend changes in policy or services to staff
or someone outside the facility?

Yes_____ No_____ Do not know_____

b) If yes, did the patient feel free to do so without fear of restraint, interference, discrimination,
or reprisal?

Yes_____ No_____ Do not know_____

c) Was this patient or another ever interfered with
or discriminated against or were reprisals taken
against her or him because of complains he or she
had voiced?

Yes_____ No_____ Do not know_____

Patient_____ Other patient_____

Explain:_____

18. a) Is the patient legally responsible for handling
his or her finances?

Yes_____ No_____ Do not know_____

b) If no, who is?

1. Family_____

2. Friend_____

3. Facility_____

Fig. 3.4 *Continued*

77

c) Who decided that the patient wouldn't handle his or her own finances?

    1. Patient_____

    2. Family_____

    3. Facility_____

d) If the nursing home is responsible, does the patient receive an accounting of the transactions?

    Yes_____ No_____ Do not know_____

How often?_____ (Under the new federal regulation, such accounting is to be provided every three months.)

19. a) Was the patient ever mentally or physically abused?

    Yes_____ No _____ Do not know_____

If yes, how was he or she abused?_____

_____

b) Has the patient or another ever been restricted to his or her bed or room?

    Yes____ No_____ Do not know_____

    Patient_____ Other patient_____

c) If yes, how was the person restricted?

    1. Given sedative drugs_____

    2. Restrained in bed or chair_____

    3.Locked in room_____

    4. Told not to leave room_____

    5. Other (please specify_____

d) What was the reason given for restriction?

    1. Protect patient from injury____

Fig. 3.4 *Continued*

2. Protect others from injury____

3. Other (please specify)

e) Who decided to restrict the patient?

Doctor____ Staff____ Do not know____

How do you know the information given above?

1. Personal observation____

2. Conversation with patient____

3. Conversation(s) with other patients____

4. Conversation(s) with nursing home staff____

5. Other (please specify)_____

20. a) Have the personal or medical records of the patient been released to anyone outside of the home?

Yes____ No____ Do not know____

b) If yes, to whom?_____

c) Did the patient approve such a release?

Yes____ No____ Do not know____

d) If not, who authorized the release?_____

_____ Do not know____

21. a) Is the patient treated with consideration, respect and recognition of his or her dignity and individuality? Yes____ No____ Do not know____

Explain:_____

_____

b) Does the patient and other patients have privacy (either a separate room or with curtains drawn around patient's bed) when being examined and tested, and when having personal needs (i.e., bathing) attended to?

Fig. 3.4 *Continued*

Yes____ No____ Do not know____

c) If no, who has been present?_____

Were curtains not used?_____

22. a) Was the patient or another patient ever asked to
    perform services for the facility?

    Yes____ No____ Do not know____

    Patient____ Other patient____

    b) If yes, what kinds? Cleaning____ Cooking ____

    Yard work ____ Other(specify)____

    c) Was the patient paid for his or her work?

    Yes____ No____ Do not know____

    d) How do you know the information given above?

    1. Personal observation____

    2. Conversation with patient____

    3. Conversation(s) with other patients____

    4. Conversation(s) with nursing home staff____

    5. Other (please specify)_____

23. When visiting the patient, have you always been al-
    lowed:

    a) To see the patient at anytime during visiting

    hours?   Yes____ No____

    If no, explain:_____

    _____

    b) Privacy with the patient?

    Yes____ No____ Do not know____

    If no, explain:_____

    _____

Fig. 3.4 *Continued*

24. Have anyone who wished to visit the patient been refused permission to do so during visiting hours?

Yes_____ No_____ Do not know_____

If yes, explain:_____

_____

25. a) Is the patient able to make telephone calls in
private?

Yes_____ No_____ Do not know_____

b) Is there any restriction on when telephones are
available to patients?

Yes_____ No_____ Do not know_____

If yes, what are they?_____

_____

26. a) Has the patient's mail ever been opened by someone
else without permission?

Yes_____ No_____ Do not know_____

If yes, by whom?_____

b) Has the patient had difficulty in getting outgoing
correspondence mailed?

Yes_____ No_____ Do not know_____

c) Has the patient's outgoing mail ever been opened
by someone else?

Yes_____ No_____ Do not know_____

If yes, by whom?_____

27. a) Has this person ever wanted to leave the nursing
home to visit someone, attend a meeting, religious
service, etc., but not been allowed to do so?

Yes_____ No_____ Do not know_____

Fig. 3.4 *Continued*

b) If this person was not allowed to leave the nursing home, why was this not possible?_____

_____

28. a) Was the patient allowed to take a reasonable amount of personal clothing and possessions he or she wanted to bring into the nursing home?

   Yes_____ No_____ Do not know_____

   If no, what was the reason given?_____

   _____

   b) Is the patient allowed to wear his or her personal clothing?

   Yes_____ No_____ Do not know_____

   If no, what reason was given?_____

   _____

   c) Is the patient allowed to use and keep those personal possessions he or she brought?

   Yes_____ No_____ Do not know_____

   If no, what reason was given?_____

   _____

29. If the patient is married, is he or she assured privacy during visits by the spouse?

   Yes_____ No_____ Do not know_____

   If no, why not?_____

30. If the patient is married and the spouse is also a patient at the same home, are the two permitted to share a room?

   Yes_____ No_____ Do not know_____

   If no, why not?_____

Fig. 3.4 *Continued*

31. What other problems concerning the dignity of nursing home patients do you think should be considered that have not been mentioned in this survey?

_____

_____

_____

_____

_____

_____

_____

_____

_____

_____

_____

Fig. 3.4 *Continued*

The Maine PIRG completed a survey similar to that in Fig. 3.4 and, if their experience holds true elsewhere, next of kin will be responsive. In Maine, five out of every six next of kin answered the questionnaire. (See Tables 3.1–3.3 for their response data.)

Surveying nursing home residents entails several difficulties. It is not possible to do the survey on a strictly random sample basis as patients must be chosen on the basis of alertness which makes it easy for administrators to claim that surveyors interviewed patients who were particularly disgruntled with the home. Furthermore, many nursing homes will either not allow access to patients or would pressure patients to respond favorably.

It may be possible for volunteers to interview residents with a shortened version of the questionnaire. Develop such a questionnaire after next of kin are surveyed, and include those rights that next of kin indicate are most frequently violated. This information would be useful as a supplement to, but not a substitute for, next of kin data.

How to Obtain Names and Addresses of Next of Kin

Here are three suggested methods for getting the names and addresses of next of kin. The first was used by Maine PIRG who were given the names and phone numbers of next of kin as they appeared on Medicare and Medicaid records at the Division of Hospital Services of the Maine Department of Health and Welfare. This confidential information was made available under a contractual agreement with the Maine Committee on Aging of the Maine Department of Health and Welfare.

Maine Public Interest Research Group

Next-of-kin Response Data

Table 3.1   Response to surveyor by case

Response type	Number of respondents
a) Completed survey	243
b) Refused to do survey	23
c) Respondent did not know anyone in a nursing home	15
d) Never visited relative	7
e) Could not contact	135
Total	423

The major reason for not being able to contact 135 persons was that the telephone numbers provided on the Medicaid forms were inaccurate. Of the 135, 59 fell in this category. The remaining persons not contacted were either never home, had moved, had speech or hearing difficulties, or were ill or deceased.

Table 3.1 Response to surveyor by case.

Table 3.2   Frequency of visits

Response type	Number of respondents	Percent
a) Daily	57	23.9
b) Weekly	121	50.8
c) Monthly	47	19.8
d) Annually	13	5.5
Totals	238	100.0

Table 3.2 Frequency of visits.

Table 3.3   Period of time since last visit

Response type	Number of respondents	Percent
a) Day	56	24.9
b) Week	82	36.4
c) Month	37	16.4
d) Year	49	21.8
	224	99.5

Note: The decline in responses that is evident in Table 3.1 and the sharp increase of annual visits as opposed to Table 3.2 can be attributed to respondents whose relatives had died.

Table 3.3 Period of time since last visit.

84

That committee had legislative authority to "conduct research on the problems of Maine's elderly, and to advise the Maine Department of Health and Welfare"[7] and could authorize Maine PIRG to conduct a research study. The terms of the agreement held Maine PIRG "fully accountable to the Committee in so far as all information derived from the survey would be the sole property of the Committee."[8] Maine PIRG further agreed to "observe all standards of confidentiality to which the Maine Committee on Aging was subject."[9] The agreement was reviewed by the Director of the Division of Hospital Services and approved by the assistant state Attorney General assigned to the Department of Health and Welfare. Names of next of kin were not identified with completed questionnaires, and their anonymity was further protected by grouping and mixing the survey data.

Any group interested in this approach should first find out which state agency is responsible for certifying and inspecting nursing homes and, thus, has next of kin names and addresses. Then find out if there is a semi-independent committee, like Maine's Committee on Aging. Check with the agency responsible for nursing homes, the Governor's office, or the Clerk of the State Legislature.

A second possible way to get names and addresses of next of kin is to contact either the state regulatory agency or the regional office of HEW, asking for access to the names and addresses.

If they are cooperative, decide how many next of kin responses you want for each Skilled Nursing Facility. That number should be no lower than 20 if the data are to be representative and credible. Choose a set number of responses for all homes or scale the number to patient occupancy in each home. Not all names and addresses in the files will be up to date, and not all next of kin contacted will respond to the questionnaire. Thus, the total response rate will probably be under 50 percent. In view of this fact, obtain two to three times the number of names and addresses you will need.

If you want to end up with 20 next of kin responses for each of 100 nursing homes, you should record data on 40 to 60 next of kin for each home. The information on next of kin and the name of the nursing home in which the patient resides are kept in patient files. Surveyors will pull files randomly and record next of kin data on separate sheets for each home until they have the necessary number on each sheet.

The third way to get next of kin names is to have surveyors work at the nursing homes you are including in the study. Similar to "candy stripers" in hospitals, the volunteers could work in the homes on a part-time basis. Through observations and questioning of patients, surveyors might be able to get the names and addresses of a representative number of next of kin. Determine the number of names needed from each home before volunteers begin their work, using the method discussed above. Aim for a larger number of responses for each home if you use this method, to avoid charges that surveyors took a biased, nonrandom sample by getting names of next of kin from patients who seemed to be particularly unhappy.

How to Conduct the Survey

It is best if the questionnaire is conducted as a telephone survey because response to mail surveys is generally low and the subject matter is sensitive. Next of kin will want to know exactly how the information will be used and will need assurance that the data are to be kept confidential. The surveys can best be conducted by volunteers who are mature, articulate, and familiar with the problems of the aged. If these volunteers meet for a group training session before undertaking the phone surveying, better results will be achieved.

The survey can be conducted in one-half hour. If at all possible, begin the survey during the initial call. If necessary, ask about a more convenient time, but set a specific time for the second call. Some next of kin may prefer to have the questionnaire mailed to them. Agree to do so only if they absolutely will not answer the questions over the phone and mail the questionnaires after all phone surveying has been completed. This precaution is necessary because nursing home owners and administrators may have relatives in a home and be included on your next of kin list. With a copy of the questionnaire in their possession, word of your survey would spread overnight and homes could begin cosmetic attempts at compliance before you have contacted all next of kin. For this reason, too, complete all surveying as quickly as possible.

Action to Take after Completing the Survey

Initially, compile the survey data according to frequency of next of kin visits —daily, weekly, every two weeks, and, if you included it, monthly. Then, keeping those categories separate, record the data by question and by nursing home.

Here is a sample format for compiling the answers to one question, followed by an explanation of the data it provides.

Responses	*Number of responses by visit frequency*				*Percent*
	Daily	Weekly	Every two weeks	Monthly	
a) Yes	5 (31%)	6	3	2	6.9
b) No	68 (35%)	52	48	27	82.6
c) Do not know	4 (16%)	5	7	9	10.6
	77	63	58	38	100.0

Total responses 236

The last column indicates the percentage of total responses answering "Yes," "No," and "Do not know" to the question. Review the responses for each category of frequency of visit. It may be that those who visit the patient more frequently will have a consistently better or worse view of conditions in the nursing home. If that is the case consider breaking down the figures more specifically by calculating the percentage of those answering "Yes," "No," and "Do not know" who visited daily, weekly, etc. This is partially done in the chart above; daily visitors accounted for 31 percent of the "Yes" answers, 35 percent of the "No" answers and 16 percent of the "Do not know" answers.

Make your findings public at a news conference and/or in a news release and send copies of the release to citizen groups and individuals working on nursing home reform. Send the final report to the state Department of Health, any commission, committee, or legislative group that is studying nursing homes, the Governor, the district office of the Social Security Administration, and the Secretary of the United States Department of Health, Education and Welfare (300 Independence Ave. S.W., Washington, D.C. 20201).

Ask them all to respond to your report with information about the corrective action they plan to take. This is an important follow-up stage of your effort to make sure that disclosure of abuses lead to real change. If the response of those to whom you sent the report did not include plans for any action, make that known to the public. When corrective action was promised, keep on top of the situation and see whether actual results are forthcoming.

The report can be the basis for a state Patients' Bill of Rights as well as a step toward correcting abuses of patients and improving nursing home care.

BIBLIOGRAPHY

Burger, Robert E. Commercializing the aged. *Nation,* May 11, 1970, pp. 557–560.

Consumer's handbook on nursing homes, Pennsylvania Nursing Home Ombudsman Demonstration Project, Governor's Office for Human Resources, Commonwealth of Pennsylvania, December, 1973.

Developments in aging: 1973 and January, 1974. A Report of the Special Committee on Aging, United States Senate. Report No. 93–846. United States Government Printing Office, Washington, D.C.

Garven, Richard M., and Robert E. Burger, *Where They Go To Die: The Tragedy of America's Aged.* New York, Delacorte Press, 1968.

Horn, Linda L., R.N., *A report on Davenport's health facilities.* Davenport, Iowa, August 8, 1974.

How to choose a nursing home. *Changing Times,* January, 1974, pp. 35–39.

How to set up a health service information center. National Consumers League, Washington, D.C., 1974.

Jacoby, Susan. Waiting for the end: on nursing homes. *New York Times Magazine,* March 31, 1974, pp. 13, 15, and 76.

The law and nursing homes. Health Law Project, Philadelphia: University of Pennsylvania, 1974.

Medicaid: compilation of federal requirements for skilled nursing home facilities. U.S. Department of Health, Education and Welfare, Social and Rehabilitation Service, Medical Services Administration, Washington, 1971 (SRS 73-24351).

Medicaid, Medicare review in skilled nursing homes and mental hospitals: guidelines. Department of Health, Education and Welfare, Social and Rehabilitation Service, Medical Services Administration, Washington, D.C., November 13, 1972 (MSA PRG-25).

Mendelson, Mary Adelaide, *Tender loving greed.* New York: Knopf, 1974.

Nursing Home Care. Consumer Information, Series #2, No. 73-24902, U.S. Department of Health, Education and Welfare, Washington, D.C., 1973.

Nursing home patients, who protects them? an in-depth study of Oregon nursing homes. Oregon Public Interest Research Group, Portland Oregon, June, 1974.

Nursing home services survey. California State Department of Public Health, Bureau of Hospitals, Sacramento, September, 1964.

Patients' rights: how to get them. Health Law Project, University of Pennsylvania Law School, Philadelphia, Pa., 1973.

Peer review, suggested guidelines. The American Nursing Home Association, Washington, D.C., 1973.

Proposal for action: nursing homes. Retired Professional Action Group, Washington, D.C., 1972.

Report on Iowa's nursing homes and related care facilities. Iowa Public Interest Research Group, Iowa City, Iowa, December, 1974.

Townsend, Claire. *Old age: the last segregation.* New York, Grossman, July, 1971.

Thinking about a nursing home? American Nursing Home Association, Washington, D.C., 1972.

We may be they someday. Report and Recommendations of the Joint Religious Legislation Committee, Nursing Home Task Force, Minneapolis, Minnesota, 1973.

"When a relative requires nursing home care." *Good Housekeeping,* October, 1970, p. 185.

PART 2
energy projects

Waste not, want not, is a maxim I would teach.
Let your watchword be dispatch, and practice what you preach;
Do not let your chances like sunbeams pass you by,
For you never miss the water till the well runs dry.

Rowland Howard

INTRODUCTION

Americans are very familiar with the words "waste not, want not" but would seem to believe this message is obsolete in a country with our technology and natural resources. As we waited in gas lines during the oil embargo of 1973-1974 and paid escalating prices for electricity, gasoline, and fuel oil, we were told by the energy industry that somewhere the well was running dry or, at least, proving more difficult and costly to run.

At the same time, we were told that a rise in prices would allow industry to ensure increased production to whatever levels were needed. On the other hand, public interest advocates pointed out that the energy industry had caused continued shortages in order to justify rises in prices.

Several years later, the causes and the solution of our energy problem are still under debate. And the answers are not as clear-cut as either the energy industry or the government would lead us to believe. However, the one point that should have become obvious—we cannot continue to waste our energy supply—still has not been translated into action.

Industry and government assert that our demands for energy now exceed domestic production in an increasingly disproportionate ratio. Both agree that until domestic production nearly equals those demands we will be at the political mercy of outside producers, chiefly the oil-producing nations.

Each segment of the energy industry has proposed solutions that involve its own production and prices. Oil producers clamor for access to offshore deposits and western oil shale. Coal producers want permission to stripmine in western states and sell high-sulfur coal. Electric utilities look to unsafe and uneconomical nuclear power plants for a supply of "limitless electricity in the future." All are scrambling for a piece of the action, saying that we must make whatever sacrifices necessary—environmental and economic—in order to keep the nation running and to eliminate oil imports.

While industry and government frantically stress production, neither has made serious projections of our real energy needs—what we would use if energy waste were eliminated. Nor are producers or utilities being adequately questioned about their costs and rates. Rising prices often reflect not only industry costs but also mismanagement, particularly by electric utilities, and deliberate price gouging. Decreased production is, for the most part, the result of industry policy, not unavailability.

While it is true that we are consuming energy in accelerating amounts, this increased use is due as much to energy waste as it is to increased affluence or population. Our energy demands have risen most dramatically since 1965—the annual growth rate having jumped from 3.5 to 4.5 percent.[1] We now consume one-third of the world's energy, although we have only six percent of the world's population.[2] If current consumption and pricing trends continue, by the year 2000 our energy use will be more than twice what it is today and energy costs will have pushed the prices of all goods and services sky-high. Inflation and recession, or worse, could be the end result.

But what can individuals and citizen groups do about the situation? Most have steered away from energy issues because they seem so complex and out of the control of anyone except industry and government. Many of those who have attempted to tackle energy issues have met with frustration and achieved no real results. However, there are success stories, and there are projects which citizens can undertake with meaningful results. The projects in this section address some of our most important energy problems and provide step-by-step guides which have already proven workable for the citizen groups that have undertaken them.

Energy waste continues to be one of the major contributing factors to growing demands and rising prices. A study prepared for the Federal Energy Administration by the Worldwatch Institute estimates that Americans waste at least 50 percent of the energy they use. The most obvious evidence to support this estimate is that West Germany consumes only one-half as much energy per capita as the United States, while providing an equivalent standard of living. Along with the waste, we squander the billions of dollars spent each year to purchase the lost energy and clean up the resulting pollution. "Project Wastehunt" is a guide to understanding the potentials of energy conservation and outlines how to survey buildings to determine whether or not conservation measures have been adopted. It suggests how the survey data can be used to prod businesses and government to make conservation a priority, to argue against the way utility rates are set, and to point out the lack of need for nuclear power plants.

Sharply rising electricity rates eat away at budgets across the country, and residential users are the hardest hit. The costs of utility policy errors are immediately passed on to consumers, as are the utilities' rising fuel costs, with the approval of state public utility commissions. Consumers see no options—if they want electricity, they can't shop around; they just pay or get cut off. Yet there are ways to challenge utilities and the two projects in Chapter 5, "Fighting for Lower Utility Bills" are designed to show you how.

Inadequate funding is one of the major problems faced by groups that want to fight utility policies and rates. Utilities can afford to hire as many attorneys, accountants, and engineers as necessary and to stay in the fight as long as need be, since they can charge the bills to consumers. Citizen groups often find themselves out of money long before they have achieved their aims. The establishment of a Residential Utility Consumer Action Group—RUCAG—can solve that problem because the RUCAG, as outlined in Chapter 5, will be funded by voluntary consumer contributions made through a checkoff system on utility bills.

"Lifeline" addresses the way utility rates are set and shows groups how to propose lowering or stabilizing the rates charged to residential users for a basic minimum amount of electricity. Citizen groups in California have already been successful in getting "Lifeline" adopted statewide.

None of these projects offers an easy solution to national energy problems, but each provides citizens with the information and action guides necessary to take some significant steps toward a sane, realistic, and economical national energy policy.

CHAPTER 4

wastehunt-
how to find
and eliminate
energy waste

The most immediate way for us to bring energy demand and energy supply into any sort of balance is through a strong decisive energy conservation program.

John Sawhill, former Administrator,
Federal Energy Administration
New York Times, Oct. 7, 1974

A nation that runs on energy cannot afford to throw it away.

Lee Schipper, Energy and Resource Group
University of California at Berkeley
"Understanding Energy Conservation"

The skylines of America shine in the night for miles with a neon glow. Buildings are under construction across the country and their builders give no thought to energy efficiency. Waste heat pours out of utility plants and factory smokestacks and big, gas-guzzling cars with single occupants clog our highways. In 1977, more than three years after the first panic about America's "energy crisis," our habits still reflect the old belief that energy can be wasted with impunity.

Designed to provide citizens with information about the uses and misuses of energy, "Project Wastehunt" outlines methods to develop citizen and business interest in energy conservation by surveying energy waste in the commercial sector. On the following pages you will find statistics on energy use, data on how conservation can affect fuel bills, and a step-by-step guide to monitoring energy waste.

WHY CONSERVE ENERGY?

The enormous potentials of energy conservation take on a new importance as energy prices soar and Americans come to realize the adverse economic, tax, health, and environmental consequences of pell-mell expansion of traditional energy sources. Even the government's conservative estimates project that with simple modifications we could decrease our energy use by 30 percent in residences and industrial processes, 30 percent in existing buildings, 60 percent in new buildings if they are designed to be energy efficient, and 20 to 40 percent in transportation! We can do so using currently available conservation methods that will not result in discomfort, decreased economic activity, or exorbitant costs; in fact, just the opposite would be the case.

Conserving energy simply means cutting down on the amount of energy we now throw out doors and windows, up exhaust stacks, or use to overlight, overcool, overheat, and overventilate buildings. More refined engineering advances in conservation will bring even greater savings in the next 25 years. The American Institute of Architects (AIA) states that, in fact, recent studies show the government estimates of potential energy savings in buildings to be conservative. Even based on the conservative 30 percent–60 percent figures for buildings, the AIA estimates that:

> *If we adopted a high-priority national program emphasizing energy efficient buildings, we could by 1990 be saving the equivalent of more than 12.5 million barrels of petroleum per day. This is about as much energy as the projected 1990 production capacity of any one of the prime energy systems: domestic oil, nuclear energy, domestic and imported natural gas, or coal.*[1]

The numerous and far-reaching benefits of energy conservation would affect our economy, our environment and our hastily drawn energy production plans—and affect them in a major and positive way.

Economic Benefits

Rising fuel prices pervade the cost of everything we buy. Since many energy-saving investments can save a unit of energy at a cost far below the cost of producing the same unit of energy, energy conservation in effect means more efficient and cheaper energy reproduction which leads to lower, and hence anti-inflationary, selling prices. Money saved by conservation and rechanneled into the purchase of other goods and services would stimulate the economy and decrease unemployment, thereby combating recession.

U.S. ENERGY CONSUMPTION BY TYPE OF APPLICATION

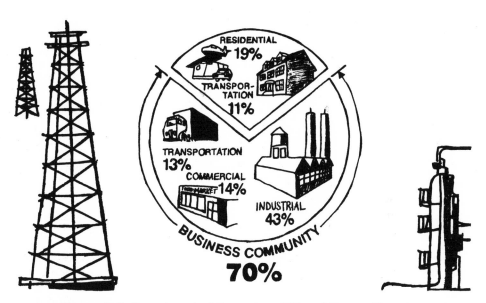

Source: U.S. Department of Commerce, Office of Energy Programs

The estimated total cost of energy in the United States is about 10 percent of the Gross National Product (GNP). This means that energy conservation, if widely adopted, could result in a rechannelling of billions of dollars into other segments of the economy.

Environmental Benefits

Energy conservation is an environmentally sound program. The production and use of energy in present forms significantly contributes to the pollution of our air, land, and water. Decreased energy consumption results in fewer power plants and oil refineries spewing contaminants into the air, less stripmined land, and fewer offshore oil rigs spilling oil into the oceans and onto the shores.

According to one energy expert, saving a third of the energy used today to heat homes and buildings—a very reasonable, short-term goal—would replace an equivalent energy output of oil refineries totaling two million barrels per day.[2]

An Alternative to Production

A barrel of oil saved (or its equivalent) is as good as a barrel produced because the conserved energy is available for the same uses as the newly produced energy. Indeed, saving a barrel of oil is better than producing the same because the environmental impacts of energy production and consumption are avoided. Further benefits of energy conservation occur in those cases when the cost of saving energy is less than the cost of producing the same amount. In addition, the amount of energy used to produce more energy is often greater than the amount needed for conservation modifications.

Given our massive energy waste, a genuine national commitment to energy conservation during the remainder of this century should enable us to cut our energy use per unit of GNP drastically. Our annual growth in energy demand could be reduced sharply from present projections, and zero growth in energy demand could be achieved by the year 2000, while the economy continues to grow.[3] (See *Nuclear plants: the more they build, the more you pay*, by Ron Lanoue, available through Critical Mass, Box 1538, Washington, D.C. 20013.)

This stabilizing of energy demands would eliminate the need to rush into greatly increased production of inefficient, polluting, and unsafe energy sources. Instead, we could, over the next quarter century, push massive development of more efficient, clean, and safe sources such as solar energy in all its forms.

WHY HASN'T ENERGY CONSERVATION BEEN A NATIONAL PRIORITY?

Why, several years after the oil embargo and the onset of increased fuel costs, do we continue to waste precious and finite energy resources? The answer to this question lies in the misconceptions and ignorance about energy conservation shared by individuals and businesses, and in ineffective government efforts to promote and require energy conservation.

The energy industry claims that escalating energy use is a necessary component of a growing GNP. Coming from those who make their money selling energy, this is not a surprising point of view. But too many individuals and government officials unquestioningly accept the industry line, despite overwhelming evidence to the contrary. Other highly industrialized nations with a per capita GNP as high as or higher than ours, such as Sweden, West Germany, and Switzerland, average about 50 percent less energy use per capita annually than we do in the United States.[4] Most thermodynamic engineers, energy experts, and architects agree that, to a great extent, our energy use exceeds that of these other industrialized nations because of the energy we waste.

Federal spending focuses primarily on supporting energy industry monopolies in their production of finite, polluting, increasingly expensive, and, in the case of nuclear power, unsafe energy sources. The Energy Research and Development Administration (ERDA) budget request for research and development for fiscal year 1978 totals $2.8 billion. Of that amount $1.666 billion or 60.6 percent is allocated for nuclear power R & D. Only $244 million (8.9 percent) is allocated for energy conservation and $250 million or 9.1 percent for solar energy R & D. Furthermore, if government continues to rely on commercial and industrial energy users to cut back voluntarily as prices rise, energy conservation will not be effective. Energy costs represent only a small part of overall business costs; before businesses feel the financial crunch, residential users will have been priced out of the energy budget.

This situation cannot be allowed to continue. Energy users must be encouraged or told to conserve. The resulting success stories can provide painless and economical examples of energy conservation and move the community toward a conservation ethic.

WHY SURVEY COMMERCIAL BUILDINGS?

For several reasons the commercial sector provides the most logical place for citizen groups to monitor and encourage energy conservation.

First, although this sector of the economy currently uses less energy than other sectors, prior to the oil embargo and recession, its use of energy was growing at a faster rate than total United States use—5.4 percent per year as compared with the 4.5 percent annual growth of energy consumption in general.[5] Increased use of electricity accounts for this rising energy demand by commercial buildings and electricity is the most inefficient energy source to produce.[6] Conversion losses are the main reason for the inefficiency of electrical generation. That is, 64 percent of the energy consumed in producing electricity is lost as waste heat when the primary fuel is converted to electricity. Furthermore, 10 percent of the electricity that is produced is lost in transmission and distribution.

Second, reductions in commercial energy use are relatively easy and painless to achieve. For example, when the city of Los Angeles required cuts in electricity use during the oil embargo of 1973–1974, commercial users achieved a 28 percent energy cutback, although they had been required to cut only by 20 percent, and did so without evident discomfort or disruption of business. Another outstanding example of energy saving in commercial type buildings has been accomplished by the Ohio State University. The university reduced electricity use by 36 percent and natural gas use by 61 percent in six campus buildings at a cost of $210,000, which was repaid from energy savings in less than eight months.

Third, it is more expeditious for citizens to investigate energy waste in the commercial sector than in the residential or industrial sectors. Energy conservation measures adopted in one large commercial building will equal or surpass the energy savings the same measures would bring about in dozens of homes. Compared with industrial energy waste, commercial energy misuse is relatively easy for citizens to survey.

Finally, conservation awareness in the commercial sector can have a ripple effect; virtually the same conservation measures can be adapted to residences and industrial buildings but not to industrial processes.

WHAT WILL WASTEHUNT ACCOMPLISH?

Using Wastehunt survey results, citizens can prod building occupants and managers to conserve energy and retrofit buildings for greater energy efficiency. As a second step, citizens can demand that local and state governments initiate effective energy conservation programs and update building codes with energy efficiency standards.

Survey data can serve as the bases for recommending changes in electric utility rate structures. Electricity costs are set by declining block rates; the more electricity purchased, the cheaper the price per kilowatt hour (kWh). Commercial users of electricity pay far less per kWh than do residential users, a situation which encourages energy waste. Wastehunt data can provide lawmakers with convincing arguments for encouraging energy conservation by reforming electric rates.

SPECIFIC EXAMPLES OF CUTS IN USE OF ELECTRICITY
DUE TO CONSERVATION MEASURES

Regional Shopping Center

Kilowatt hours billed: October 1973— 652,800
October 1972—1,435,200
55% cut in electric usage due to actions taken

(Does not include tenant usage)

Action taken: Removed 180 40-watt fluorescent lamps in halls and loading areas
that were on 24 hours
Disconnected 200 150-watt lamps 16 hours per day
Replaced 864 300-watt lamps with 150-watt lamps in new wing
Turned off advertising signs
Turned off mall floodlights
Increased chill water temperature from 43° to 48°F
Locked off one 750-HP chiller so two can't operate at once
Issued emergency brownout procedures to tenants

Office Buildings - 9 Floors

Kilowatt hours billed: September 1973—330,240
September 1972—536,160
38% cut in electrical usage

Action taken: Building lights turned off nights and weekends
Operating hours 97 hours per week
Chillers turned off from 8:00 P.M. until 6:00 A.M. instead of running
24 hours
Chill water temperature raised 5°F
Drapes closed to reduce solar gain
Maintenance personnel check to make sure all lights are out at night

Fig. 4.1 Specific examples of how conservation methods save electricity. Source: Report by Southern California Edison Company to the Public Utility Commission of the State of California, November, 1973. **Note:** These examples show extensive cuts in electricity use even though the conservation measures adopted are just a few of those which might be adopted in all commercial buildings. Think what the cuts will be in buildings which adopt all the measures which are recommended in this project!

Evidence of energy waste can also be used to fight the development of unsafe or uneconomical energy sources, because energy saved through effective conservation can remove the immediate necessity for those sources.

ENERGY: HOW IS IT USED? HOW CAN IT BE SAVED?

In the United States, 14 percent of all energy is used in commercial buildings. Even more significantly, 24 percent of our electricity is consumed in commercial buildings.

Heating, cooling, lighting and mechanical drives—running office equipment, elevators and escalators—cause the greatest drain on energy in commercial buildings. Electricity is used as follows: 42 percent for lighting, 30 percent for heating, ventilating and air conditioning (HVAC) systems, and 28 percent for miscellaneous uses such as running office equipment and elevators.

Insulation, Caulking, and Storm Windows

Architects and engineers generally agree that 40 percent of the energy used to heat and air condition buildings, and the money spent on that energy, could be saved by controlling the loss of heated/cooled air from the buildings and the infiltration of unheated/uncooled air into the buildings. This can be accomplished by adding adequate insulation to ceilings, walls, and floors; weatherstripping and caulking around doors and windows; thermopane glass or storm windows; and double doors or automatic close devices. Studies done by the Federal Energy Administration (FEA) show that these conservation measures pay for themselves over a short period of time through lowered fuel bills.

The addition of adequate insulation alone can cut energy loss and fuel bills by 25 percent or more. FEA and the National Bureau of Standards recommend six or more inches of insulation for ceilings, three or more inches in walls and three or more inches in floors. The addition of wall insulation in existing buildings is difficult and costly. Surveyors should concentrate on ceilings and basement floors except when discussing building codes. Of course, much thicker insulation is needed in climates with more extreme temperatures, hot and cold.

A quarter-inch crack at the bottom of a three-footwide door allows the same amount of air leakage as a three-square inch hole in the middle of the door! The addition of caulking and weatherstripping around doors and windows can cut energy loss and fuel bills by 5 percent to 30 percent.

The addition of storm windows to a building that does not have insulating glass will cut heat losses through the windows by 50 percent and bring about a 5 percent to 15 percent savings in energy and fuel costs.

Temperature Levels

For each degree a heating system is lowered or a cooling system raised, there is about a three percent energy saving.[7] FEA has recommended heating and cooling temperature levels which ensure occupant comfort but offer substantial savings in energy and fuel bills. Note that changes in temperature levels are cost free, therefore, all energy savings translate to dollar savings. Since electric heating is the highest priced energy source, dollar savings are greatest when electric heating is the source of building heat.

The FEA recommended levels are: 65-68° for heat during working hours; 55° or lower for heat during nonwork hours; and 78-80° for air conditioning during work hours. During working hours, temperatures in warehouses and other space not generally occupied by employees should be set lower than 65° for heating and higher than 80° for cooling, with exact temperature settings dependent on the use of the space.[8] President Carter urged Americans to adjust heating temperatures even lower, to 60° during the day.

Most commercial buildings can completely shut off air conditioning systems during nonwork hours, turn them on again approximately one hour before the workday begins, and still achieve comfortable temperature levels for the start of the workday.

Heating and Cooling Equipment

Engineers with the National Bureau of Standards and the FEA report that the efficiency of heating and cooling equipment in buildings may be diminished by 30 percent or more because of three factors: poor maintenance, frequent starting and shutting off of equipment to control temperatures, and running heating equipment at less than full capacity.

If heating and air-conditioning equipment is serviced at least once and preferably twice a year, its fuel consumption can be improved 10–20 percent, which will more than repay the cost of servicing the equipment.

Uninsulated steam or hot water pipes lose appreciable heat and energy. Insulation can cut that heat lost by about 80 percent and quickly pays for itself in lower fuel bills. Holes in steam pipes result in significant steam and energy losses and are easily repaired by maintenance personnel or a heating contractor.

Thermostats should be located at places remote from sources of outside air so that the heating/cooling system is not constantly responding to signals produced by outside temperatures. Separate areas of buildings should have separate thermostats to allow shutting off or dialing down temperatures in each area according to need. An electrical engineering company can easily remove and add thermostats. The lowered fuel bills will pay for the removal and installation expenses.

Because heating equipment is 10 to 35 percent less efficient when run at less than full capacity, it is advantageous in large buildings to install standby equipment of smaller capacity for use when the heating load is light.

In larger buildings a great amount of energy can be saved by adding heat exchange equipment to recover and reuse heated or cooled air from exhaust air. Again, the cost of such equipment, in time, will be reimbursed by lower fuel costs.

Ventilating and Humidifying Equipment

Ventilation systems circulate air through a building and exchange conditioned (heated or cooled and humidified) air from inside the building with outside air. This exchange is very energy consuming in schools, hospitals, office buildings, and the like where total inside–outside air changes take place as often as every hour or half hour. If more air is drawn into a building than is actually needed, the energy used to heat or cool and humidify that air is wasted.

Power ventilation systems and humidity control should be used only when needed during working hours and turned off completely when the building is not in use. Check with the building permit department to find out how often building codes require that air be circulated and a complete air exchange made. A HVAC (Heating, Ventilating, Air Conditioning) expert or the company that installed humidity control equipment can advise building managers exactly how often this system should be used.

Lighting

For the last 50 years the Illuminating Engineers' Society (IES) has set lighting standards for commercial and industrial buildings—standards which have increased 2000 percent over those 50 years. The membership of IES is composed largely of industry representatives who manufacture and profit from the sale of lighting equipment, a fact which probably accounts for the increased lighting standards.

After extensive testing, the Institute for Applied Technology of the United States Department of Commerce reported that "there is no concrete evidence that the increased illumination recommended by the IES is of any benefit to the building occupants."[9] On the basis of this data and research of its own, the FEA, in 1974, recommended lighting standards that are considerably lower than the levels recommended by IES and currently used in most buildings. (See Table 4.1.)

Table 4.1 GOVERNMENT RECOMMENDED LIGHTING LEVELS

Type of area	*Definition*	*Footcandle levels*
Nonwork areas	Hallways or corridors	10 plus or minus 5 (5 to 15 footcandles)
Work areas	General areas where people are working	30 plus or minus 5 (25 to 35 footcandles)
Occupied work stations	Normal office work, such as reading and writing (on task only), store shelves and general display areas	50 plus or minus 10 (40 to 60 footcandles)
	Prolonged office work which is somewhat difficult visually (on task only)	75 plus or minus 15 (60 to 90 footcandles)
	Prolonged office work which is visually difficult and critical in nature (on task only)	100 plus or minus 20 (80 to 120 footcandles)

Despite the publicity devoted to the energy conservation merits of decreased lighting, most buildings still have much higher lighting levels than those recommended by the FEA, with benefits to no one except electrical utility companies and lighting equipment manufacturers. Reducing lighting to recommended levels can cut energy use and energy costs significantly. Assuming nine hours of lighting, fluorescent lights in an average five-story office building consume about 1700 kWh of electricity per day. Shutting off two-thirds of the lights during the lunch hour would save 124 kWh per day—the daily electricity needed for five average homes. Disconnecting 20 percent of the bulbs (in areas that are overlighted, in nonwork areas, etc.) would save about 337 kWh per day—the daily electricity needed for 13 average homes.

Permanent disconnection is preferable where feasible because it saves more energy and it avoids the capital cost of early replacement of fluorescent bulbs due to repeated switching on and off.

When possible, the most energy efficient light bulbs (giving the most light per unit of electricity) should be installed. In descending order, the efficiency of various lights is as follows: high pressure sodium vapor, metal halide, fluorescent, mercury, and incandescent. Fluorescent lighting is approximately 70 percent more energy efficient than incandescent lighting. Fewer bulbs of higher wattage are more energy efficient than more bulbs with lower wattage. For example, switching from two 60-watt bulbs to one 100-watt bulb will save 12 percent energy usage and provide about the same amount of light.

If individual light switches are installed in separate areas of a building, it will allow the cutoff of lighting to areas that are not occupied. Installation costs will pay for themselves in greatly decreased electric bills. Obviously, lights should be turned off when sunlight provides adequate illumination, but it is surprising how seldom this is done in commercial buildings.

All inside and outside lighting, except that needed for security, should be turned off at night. If janitorial work is done during the day or on a floor-by-floor basis at night, it is not necessary to illuminate the entire building during the cleaning period.

Water

Heating water constitutes the fifth highest use of energy in commercial buildings. In most of them, the hot water in washrooms can be cut off completely without any great discomfort to users. If that meets with the disapproval of the building occupants, the FEA recommends that water temperatures be cut back to 110°. FEA also states that hot water in cafeterias need not exceed 120° unless dishwashers are used, in which case 140° is sufficiently hot.

If high-pressure nozzles and other valve devices are eliminated from faucets in washrooms, the flow of water (and energy used to heat it) will decrease considerably with no inconvenience to users.

Supermarket Freezers

Sliding glass doors on refrigeration units in supermarket frozen food departments will cut energy use considerably. If merchants argue that the doors would discourage shopper browsing, suggest that they ask their customers how much browsing they do along those freezing cold aisles.

HOW TO CONDUCT AN ENERGY WASTEHUNT

This project has been done by PIRGs across the country. Without exception, their re-sults show that commercial buildings have not adopted even the most basic energy conservation measures.

Buildings surveyed in four states and the District of Columbia in 1974 and 1975 had lighting levels from two to seven times FEA recommended levels! Heating levels ranged from 68° to 78° and averaged 74°, which is 6° higher than the FEA-recom-mended maximum level, with a corresponding 18 percent higher fuel use. In 84.5 per-cent of the buildings surveyed, there were no storm windows or thermopane glass, 40 percent of the buildings did not have individual light switches for separate areas, and in 30 percent outside lights were burning brightly at night. Energy conservation pro-grams had been established in only 14 percent of the buildings surveyed.

It is important to note that energy use in buildings is a total system involving how the building is situated on the land, how it was constructed, the types of equipment used, the kinds of energy used, and occupant habits. Optimum energy conservation in buildings will occur only when energy efficiency becomes a major consideration at each of these stages.

The checklists of conservation measures that make up the Wastehunt survey can-not provide a complete picture of how the building operates as a total energy system, and in some cases energy conservation measures will not be apparent to surveyors. But the experts who have reviewed Wastehunt believe that if this limitation is kept in mind, the survey will provide valid and useful data.

How Big a Wastehunt Should You Attempt?

The survey included in this chapter covers most of the energy conservation measures that could be adopted in commercial buildings. It is broken into two sections. The first is a "walk-thru" survey to be completed by walking through a building, observing, and answering the survey questions. The second is an interview survey which includes questions about conservation measures that cannot be observed, and fuel-use figures. The survey forms are shown in Fig. 4.2.

Wastehunt can be done in its entirety or scaled down to a size that is manageable for you to handle effectively. If surveyors have not read some of the materials listed in the bibliography and are not completely familiar with the conservation measures men-tioned in the interview section, it is wise to limit the survey to the walk-thru section. Some groups have simply checked the lighting and temperature levels of buildings, be-cause if these basic conservation measures are not in effect, it is unlikely that energy conservation measures have been properly considered.

The Massachusetts PIRG used this approach and found that 75 percent of the buildings surveyed had heating temperatures higher than 68°F and that over 50 per-cent had lighting levels in excess of those recommended by FEA. When they released the survey results, Mass PIRG criticized "token energy conservation efforts at both the state and federal levels" and stated that "Massachusetts consumers deserve immediate governmental action, designed to ensure that business and industry do not waste energy while consumers sit in cold, dark homes, awaiting energy bills they can-not pay." Shortly after Mass PIRG's findings were made public, in March 1975, the governor announced a statewide program to cut energy use in government buildings by 20 percent.

ENERGY CONSERVATION SURVEY FOR COMMERCIAL BUILDINGS

Building surveyed_____

Address_____

Building occupant(s)_____

_____

_____

Owner_____

Manager/managing company_____

Age of building_____

Size of building - number of stories and approximate
                   square footage per floor___ _____

Date and time survey conducted_____

Outside temperature when survey conducted_____

Surveyor's name_____

Surveyor's address and telephone number _____

_____

Note: The questions/conservation measures marked with one
or two asterisks relate to building design and their
adoption is most likely, depending on the rental agreement, the responsibility of the building owner not of
occupants.

*Those marked with one asterisk are those which can be
adopted in buildings but involve an initial expense. However, that expense would be recouped over a period of
time because of reduced fuel bills.

**Those marked with two asterisks are those which cannot
be adopted in existing buildings (with the possible exception of storm windows). If your purpose in doing the
survey is strictly to "rate" buildings on adaptable conservation measures, these points do not have to be included. They are important if you plan to make recommendations about revisions in building codes, as are all
questions marked with one asterisk. The information about
the age and size of the building, too, is needed only if
you plan to work on building codes.

Fig. 4.2 Energy conservation survey for commercial buildings.

Part I - Walk-through Survey Questionnaire

Space Conditioning   Heating, Cooling and Ventilation
                      Systems

1. Are there revolving doors, double doors, or automatic
   doors to prevent heat/cool air loss?

   _____ Yes   _____ No

**2. Does the building have windows that can be closed and
   opened?

   _____ Yes   _____ No

3. Are windows and doors closed if the heating/cooling/
   ventilating system is in use?

   _____ Yes   _____ No

**4. Does the building have either storm windows or ther-
   mopane glass?

   _____ Yes   _____ No

*5. Are there venetian blinds, shades, or heavy draperies
   on windows?

   _____ Yes   _____ No

In summer these can be used to cut amount of sunlight
coming into building and thereby reduce air conditioning
load considerably. In winter on cloudy days they can be
used to cut down on amount of heated air that escapes
through windows. In winter on sunny days opening blinds
allows sunlight in and thereby cuts down on heating load.

6. Were blinds,etc., used as mentioned above?

   _____ Yes   _____ No

*7. Is there weather stripping or caulking around windows
   and doors?

   _____ Yes   _____ No

Before checking thermostat settings and recording temperature levels, it is important to determine which system is
in use - heating or air conditioning. To do this, take a
reading of the air temperature directly at the duct
opening to determine whether it is hot or cold. If the
system that is in use is not what would be needed under
normal circumstances, given the outside temperature, make
a note to that effect. Look for conditions within the
building that cause the reverse need. For example, excessive lighting may add so much heat to a building that
air conditioning is needed even on cool days. During the
interview, ask representatives of the company or owner to
explain the need for the reverse conditioning system's
use.

Fig. 4.2 *Continued*

8. Is the heating/cooling system normally needed at the time the one is in use?
                                  _____ Yes _____ No

If no, did you observe a probable cause of the reverse need?

_____

_____

9. Are openings to air ducts (or are radiators) unblocked to permit maximum air (heat) flow?
                                  _____ Yes _____ No

*10. Are thermostats located away from sources of outside air?
                                  _____ Yes _____ No

11. Are thermostats in work areas set at 68°F or lower (heating) or at 78°F or higher (cooling)?
                                  _____ Yes _____ No

*12. Are there separate thermostat controls in nonwork areas (e.g., lobbies, hallways, etc.)?
                                  _____ Yes _____ No

13. Are thermostats in nonwork areas--lobbies, hallways, storage areas--set at 62°F or lower (heating) or at 84°F or higher (cooling)?
                                  _____ Yes _____ No

*14. Are there separate thermostat controls in areas used only during certain hours (e.g., cafeterias, conference rooms)?
                                  _____ Yes _____ No

15. During periods when the area is not in use, are these set at 62°F or lower (heating) or 84°F or higher (cooling)?
                                  _____ Yes _____ No

16. Are thermostats rolled back to 50°F at night? (You will have to ask in interview if you cannot get access to building at night.)
                                  _____ Yes _____ No

Temperature levels should <u>not</u> be recorded on days when the outside temperature is unusual for the time of year that the surveys are being conducted. On an unusually warm day in winter, even if the heating system in the building has been turned down, the temperature levels may record high. The reverse is true for an unusually cool day in summer.

Fig. 4.2 *Continued*

Using a dry bulb thermometer, record temperatures in as many work areas (e.g., reception areas, offices) as you can get access to.

_____   _____

_____   _____

_____   _____

17. Average temperature in work areas_____

Using a dry bulb thermometer, record temperatures in non-work areas (hallways, storage rooms, etc.)

_____   _____

_____   _____

_____   _____

18. Average temperature in nonwork areas_____

Using a dry bulb thermometer, record temperatures in areas used only during certain hours; record them during off-hours.

_____   _____

_____   _____

_____   _____

19. Average temperature in areas used only during certain hours (cafeterias, conference rooms)_____

Lighting

*20. Can lighting in the building be separately controlled (i.e., are there separate light switches for separate areas?)?

_____ Yes   _____ No

21. Is lighting in areas used only during part of the day turned off when areas are not in use?

_____ Yes   _____ No

22. Is lighting turned off where sunlight provides sufficient illumination?

_____ Yes   _____ No

*23. Is fluorescent versus incandescent overhead lighting used?

_____ Yes   _____ No

Fig. 4.2 *Continued*

24. Are desk lamps used to supplement, and thereby allow cutback of, overhead lighting?

_____ Yes _____ No

Using a light meter, record lighting levels in three types of areas. Later compare them with government recommended levels. If unable to use light meter, see light chart in Resource 4.1 to translate camera light meter readings to footcandles (lumens).

A) Nonwork areas: Government recommended level - 10 footcandles.

_____   _____

_____   _____

_____   _____

25. Average lighting level in nonwork areas_____

B) Work areas: Govermnent recommended level--30 footcandles (Work areas are those areas occupied by workers, but not their exact work location, e.g., offices.)

_____   _____

_____   _____

_____   _____

26. Average lighting level in work areas_____

Work stations: Government recommended level--50 footcandles (Work stations are those places where workers are primarily located when doing tasks, e.g., at desks.)

_____   _____

_____   _____

_____   _____

27. Average lighting level at work stations_____

Visit building at night after 8:00

28. Ask the guard if office cleaning is done during the day. This will be verified during interview as it may be done both day and night.

_____ Yes _____ No

Fig. 4.2 *Continued*

If cleaning is done at night, ask to speak with supervisor or one of the cleaners to find out the following:

29. Ask if cleaning is consolidated floor by floor and whether the building manager/occupant requested that lights be turned on only when cleaners are on each floor? [Need two yes answers here, or mark no].

_____ Yes   _____ No

30. Ask if all lights are turned off by employees when leaving the building?

_____ Yes   _____ No

If you could not get an answer to question 29 from cleaning personnel, observe at night from the outside how many floors of the building are lit up and ask the guard how many employees are working in building at that time. Are there no more lights on than could be accounted for by the number of employees still working and one floor of cleaning personnel.

_____ Yes   _____ No

31. Has outside lighting been cut back to a level that seems the minimum necessary for security?

_____ Yes   _____ No

Miscellaneous

*32. Has hot water been cut off or lowered for washrooms?

_____ Yes   _____ No

Part II - Interview Survey Questionnaire

NOTE: Those questions/conservation measures marked with one asterisk are those which, depending on the rental agreement, are most likely to be the responsibility of the building owner. Adoption of the measures, in most cases, involves some expense but not an unreasonable one considering the savings in electricity or fuel bills that would result. Ask in interview who is responsible for each measure.

1. Since October, 1973, have you received any information on energy conservation from the government?

Federal ___ Yes ___ No   State ___ Yes ___ No

Local ___ Yes ___ No

Fig. 4.2 *Continued*

If yes, from what source and in what form (film, brochure, visit, etc.)?_____

_____

Did that information include recommendations about specific energy conservation measures applicable to commercial buildings?

_____ Yes   _____ No

2. Has a coordinator of energy conservation efforts been appointed by the company(ies) that occupy(ies) a substantial portion of the building or by the building owner (if there are many occupants)?

_____ Yes   _____ No

3. Has an energy audit been done for the building and recommendations been made regarding conservation measures that are to be adopted by occupants and/or by the owner?

_____ Yes   _____ No

4. What energy conservation measures have the occupants/ owner put into effect within the last two years? (Compare information here with that from Walk-through Survey, and point out any discrepancies after you have completed all questions, or later by letter.)

_____

_____

_____

5. What, if any, additional energy conservation measures will be put into effect within the next six months?

_____

_____

_____

If the official did not include the following measures when answering questions 4 and 5, mention each measure and ask why it has not been adopted. In some cases the official may have forgotten to mention the measure previously adopted. In other cases he or she may claim to have adopted measures which in fact have not been adopted. In order to verify the statements made, ask questions about where adopted, the expense involved, and whether you may speak with maintenance personnel about the effectiveness of the measures.

Fig. 4.2 *Continued*

*6. Does the building have automatic clock devices for night setback of thermostats?

_____ Yes _____ No

7. Having checked local building codes for require frequency of air changes, ask if the ventilating system (if a power system) is used no more frequently than codes specify during work hours and is turned off at the end of the workday.

_____ Yes _____ No

8. Is humidity control turned off at the end of the workday?

_____ Yes _____ No

*9. If the building is quite large, is there a small standby boiler or furnace to carry building load during mild weather? (It is much more energy efficient than running a larger boiler at low-level.)

_____ Yes _____ No

*10. If building is quite large, is heat exchange equipment used?

_____ Yes _____ No

*11. Does a heating contractor or the utility company check and adjust furnace/boiler with instruments prior to each heating/cooling season and clean or change filters and registers?

_____ Yes _____ No _____ Don't know

12. Is office cleaning done during the day so that lights are not kept on in the evening?

_____ Yes _____ No _____ Don't know

13. If office cleaning is done at night, are janitorial services consolidated by floor or section to eliminate lighting in entire building?

_____ Yes _____ No _____ Don't know

*14. Do walls have 6" of insulation?

_____ Yes _____ No _____ Don't know

Do ceilings have 4" of insulation?

_____ Yes _____ No _____ Don't know

Do floors have 3" of insulation?

_____ Yes _____ No _____ Don't know

*15. Are heating/cooling ducts insulated?

_____ Yes _____ No

Fig. 4.2 *Continued*

*16. Are hot water or steam pipes insulated?

_____ Yes _____ No

17. Are all pipes and ducts checked for leaks at least annually?

_____ Yes _____ No

18. If the heating/cooling system in use is the reverse of what would normally be needed, ask the reason.

_____

19. How much (what percent) has energy consumption been cut back between the periods January 1, 1974 - January 1, 1975 and January 1, 1976 - January 1, 1977?

_____

20. What were the energy cost savings?

_____

Fuel-use Figures

Fuel	Period Jan.1,1975- Jan.1,1976	Period Jan.1,1976- Jan.1,1977	Difference
Electricity kilowatt hours	_____	_____	_____
Btu's	_____	_____	_____
#____ Fuel oil (only need figures in one of these amounts)	_____ Barrels	_____ Barrels	_____ Barrels
	_____ Gallons	_____ Gallons	_____ Gallons
Natural gas (only need figures in one of these amounts)	_____ Lbs	_____ Lbs	_____ Lbs
	_____ Cubic feet	_____ Cubic feet	_____ Cubic feet
	_____ Therms	_____ Therms	_____ Therms
	_____ Btu's	_____ Btu's	_____ Btu's

Were there any changes in equipment or operating conditions that may have caused a difference in the answers to questions above?

_____

Fig. 4.2 *Continued*

112

What Buildings Will You Survey?

Simply defined, the category of commercial buildings includes all structures not used for mining, manufacturing, or as residences. It includes all public buildings, schools, hospitals, office buildings, wholesale and retail stores, hotels, restaurants, theaters, and museums.

The most appropriate buildings to include in a survey vary with the community, but there are some guidelines to consider. Survey public buildings—federal, state, county and local—because they should be leading the way on energy conservation and the owners and occupants are particularly susceptible to public pressure. Schools are also important to include; many have initiated conservation programs and may be able to provide useful data about lowered fuel bills. Don't include hospitals, theaters, or museums in your Wastehunt. They have special lighting and temperature needs and, with the exception of hospitals, are not among the largest energy users.

After selecting building categories, choose specific buildings according to size; the bigger a building, the greater the potential for energy savings. Large buildings with a single enterprise make a better choice than those with many different users because the responsibility for adopting conservation measures is not so diffuse. Although concentrating on large buildings will provide quantitatively better results, be sure to include a representative sample of small buildings. Any occupant can point to a bigger energy user, but that kind of buck-passing must stop.

Walk-Thru Surveys

It would be practical for surveyors to meet before beginning the surveys to discuss the questions, learn how to record temperature and light levels accurately, and make survey assignments. Whenever possible, survey in pairs for purposes of verification.

Walk-thru surveys are more easily done in shopping centers than in office buildings because the public has access to most areas in stores but only to limited areas in office buildings. Therefore, the more confident and resourceful surveyors might go to office buildings, and be prepared to move through them quickly, surveying the lobby, hallways, and other public areas first, and then asking for permission to visit individual offices to record light and temperature levels.

Recording temperature levels The method for determining temperature levels is simple. Use a dry bulb thermometer attached to a metal or wood base. They are available from most hardware stores or electrical supply stores. Place the thermometer in the area to be surveyed for about two minutes and record the temperature.

In *one-floor stores*, take temperature readings in at least two areas in the main section of the store.

In stores with *more than one floor*, take two readings on each floor.

In *shopping centers*, take readings in general areas of the center, and in as many stores as possible.

In *office buildings*, don't record temperatures in the lobby as they will not reflect building temperature accurately. Start in areas with easy access such as hallways, cafeterias, and unused rooms. Record the temperatures and whether or not the areas are unoccupied. Record two readings for these areas if they are particularly large, and record temperatures on each floor when building size permits. Then attempt to get access to occupied areas.

In *very large office buildings (many floors) with one enterprise,* record temperatures for every second, third, or fourth floor.

In *office buildings where separate businesses have several floors each,* record temperature levels for each business.

Recording light levels The most accurate way to record light levels is with a light meter designed for that purpose. Available from electrical equipment stores or lighting supply companies, these meters usually cost about $20. See Resource 4.1 for guidelines on using light meters.

Before recording lighting levels, surveyors must be familiar with the definitions of each of the three types of building space to which the FEA guidelines apply—work stations, general work areas, and nonwork areas. Review the information in Table 4.1.

In *one-floor stores and office buildings,* aim for at least nine readings and be sure that the same number of readings are taken in each building. Four readings should be taken at work stations, three at general work areas, and two in nonwork areas.

In *stores or office buildings with more than one floor,* take seven readings, three at work stations, three at general work areas, and one in a nonwork area.

In *very large office buildings,* record light levels for every second, third, or fourth floor.

On each floor, take the work station readings as follows: two or three at stations which are in between light fixtures and away from windows, and one near a window. General work area and nonwork area readings ought to be taken between light fixtures. All readings should be taken 30 inches from the floor (the height of the average desk).

Interview Surveys

Ideally, building engineers or building managers should be interviewed. Send letter requesting an interview, but be aware that in most cases they will be hesitant to speak with surveyors without the permission of either the building owner or personnel of the occupying company. Figure 4.3 shows a sample letter requesting an interview.

Many groups that have done this project were referred to a public relations department or energy conservation office whose personnel tended to speak generally, glowingly, and not always accurately about energy conservation efforts. For this reason the interview survey is designed so that surveyors first ask officials to outline their energy conservation programs and then discuss specific conservation measures. Fuel-use figures are requested because they indicate the extent to which conservation measures affected fuel use and costs.

It is important to begin the interview by stressing how useful energy conservation can be in cutting fuel costs. If you can afford it, write and distribute flyers with specific information about energy conservation and its financial benefits. Otherwise, consider distributing *33 Money Saving Ways to Conserve Energy in Your Business* available from the United States Department of Commerce.

(Name of Group)

(Address)

(Name of Interviewee)

(Address)

Dear Mr./Ms._____:

  The (name of group), a statewide organization with a
base of _____ thousand citizens, is conducting a survey
of energy conservation measures being employed in the commercial buildings of (name of city, county, or state).
We are attempting to determine what energy conservation
measures have been adopted by business and to what degree
they have been effective. Our experience suggests that
we may be able to spot ways to help you reduce your energy
costs.

  We would like to interview you or your designated representative at the earliest possible time. The interview
will be brief and to the point and will not take more than
a half hour of your time.

  One of our researchers will be contacting your office
within the next few days to arrange an appointment. Thank
you for your cooperation.

Sincerely,

Fig. 4.3 Sample letter requesting an interview.

Compiling the Survey Data

Develop a Data Compilation Form which lists across the top each question (conservation measure) included in your survey. List the buildings surveyed down the side of the
form. For each question, indicate the answer with a yes or no. A sample Data Compilation Form I is included in Fig. 4.4. Include all questions except those relating to
information received by the government. That data can be compiled separately, and a
sample form, Data Compilation Form II, is included in Fig. 4.5.
  When publicizing survey results, summarize the information from those forms in
terms that are easily understood and provide comparisons between buildings. The

Fig. 4.4 (Data computation form I)

	Walk-Thru Questionnaire		Interview Questionnaire	Total Correct Answers
Name and address of building	Space Conditioning	Lighting		
Name of occupant and of owner	1 2 3 4 5 6 7 8 9 10 11 12 13 14 15 16 17 18	19 20 21 22 23 24 25 26 27 28 29 30	1 2 3 4 5 6 7 8 9 10 11 12 13 14 15 16 17 18 19 20	

Fig. 4.4 Data computation form I.

Government Information Received Concerning Commercial Building Data

Name & Address of Company	FEDERAL			STATE			LOCAL		
	None	General Info	Specific Info	None	General Info	Specific Info	None	General Info	Specific Info

Fig. 4.5 Data computation form II.

TOTAL NUMBER of Buildings	Number and percentage in first range (1-12 measures adopted)	Number and percentage in second range (13-24 measures adopted)	Number and percentage in third range (25-36 measures adopted)	Number and percentage in fourth range (37-48 measures adopted)

Fig. 4.6 Data computation form III.

Name of Building and Address	Number of Conservation Measures Adopted	Range in Which Building Is Placed

Fig. 4.7 Data computation form IV.

most equitable and effective way to do this is through a scoring system. Take the total number of questions and divide them into three or four groups or ranges. For example, if you include the entire questionnaire as presented here, there are 48 questions. The first group would include buildings in which zero to 25 percent of the conservation measures, or 1 to 12, were adopted; the second, buildings with 26 to 50 percent or 13 to 24 measures; the third, buildings with 51 to 75 percent or 25 to 36 measures; and the fourth, buildings with 76 to 100 percent or 37 to 48 measures. Then list each building in the appropriate group and compute the percentage of buildings falling into each category on forms like the ones in Figs. 4.6 and 4.7.

If you prefer, the data on lighting and temperature levels can be compiled separately. Summarize information on the number of buildings with lighting and temperature levels above those recommended by the FEA, the average excess levels, and the amount of resulting energy waste.

Action to Take after Completing the Surveys

Prepare a final report including the full survey results, your survey methods, and your group's recommendations for action needed by government and the business community. Send the report to the Governor's office, state and local offices, or commissions working on energy and energy conservation, major businesses in the area, and the Federal Energy Administration, Office of Conservation and the Environment, Washington, D.C.   22101.

Publicize the survey results in a new conference announced in a succinct news release and have available copies of the full report. Large charts illustrating the potentials of energy conservation and the energy waste you uncovered would dramatically emphasize the point of your efforts. Refer to Chapter 12 for more specific information about preparing the news release and running a news conference.

Stick with the issue. Monitor government agencies that are responsible for setting energy policy and make their efforts, or lack thereof, public. Ask businesses to outline their energy conservation programs and provide fuel- and electricity-use figures to show the results. Publicize success stories as well as information on those who continue to do nothing.

One outstanding example of the superiority of investment in energy efficiency over investments in energy production has been provided by Admiral's Walks, a condominium development in Boca Raton, Fla., program of retrofitting existing buildings to use energy more efficiently. Boca Admiral's Walk has cut its use of electricity by more than half by rerouting waste heat from the air conditioning systems to heat the building's water temperature; using computerized controls to regulate temperature, lighting, and various pumps; reducing wattage in corridor light bulbs; and, replacing mercury-vapor lights in the parking lot with energy-saving sodium-vapor lights. The addition of a water softener to the air conditioning system avoids calcium buildup which could otherwise cause a 20 percent reduction in efficiency. The $70,000 investment in modifying the building converted into an annual savings of $30,000 and the condominium is now getting a 43 percent a year return on its investment.

Encourage residential users to adopt energy conservation measures and to demand that the businesses they deal with do the same. Make energy conservation a reality in your community and state.

BIBLIOGRAPHY

Citizen's advisory committee on environmental quality, *Citizen Action Guide to Energy Conservation.* Washington, D.C., Sept., 1973.

Con Edison Utility Company, *Energy management guide for building management.* Sept., 1973.

Ford Foundation, Draft of *Energy and architectural design.* Energy Policy Project and the American Institute of Architecture, Washington, D.C., 1974.

————, Draft of *Exploring energy choices, a preliminary report.* Energy Policy Project, Washington, D.C., 1974.

————, Draft of *Fuel conservation possibilities in the industrial sector.* Energy Policy Project and Thermo-Electron Corp., Washington, D.C., 1974.

————, Draft of *Improving energy efficiency in industry.* Energy Policy Project and the Conference Board, Washington, D.C., 1973.

————, *Recycling opportunities in industry.* Energy Policy Project and the Midwest Research Institute, Washington, D.C., 1973.

————, *A time to choose.* A Report to the Energy Policy Project, Ballinger Publishing Company, Cambridge, Mass., 1974, pp. 45–111.

Freed, Fred, *The energy crisis.* NBC Reports—An American White Paper, Air Date: Tuesday, September 4, 1973.

Goetz, G.J., and Hirst, E.A., *Energy use patterns in United States manufacturing for the period 1950-1970.* Oak Ridge National Laboratory, Oak Ridge, Tennessee.

Herendeen, Robert A., *The energy costs of goods and services.* Oak Ridge National Laboratory, Oak Ridge, Tennessee, Oct., 1973.

New Jersey Public Interest Research Group, Abuse of power: a study of industrial and commercial energy waste in New Jersey. Trenton, N.J., Sept., 1974.

Schipper, Lee. Holidays, gifts, and the energy crisis. Lawrence-Berkeley Lab., University of California, UCID-3707, Nov., 1975, (revised). See also Sierra Club *Bulletin* (Nov.-Dec.) 1975.

U.S. Department of Commerce, National Bureau of Standards. *Technical options for energy conservation in buildings.* Nov., 1973.

————, Office of Energy Programs. *Thirty-three money-saving ways to conserve energy in your business.* Nov., 1973.

U.S. Executive Office of the President, Office of Emergency Preparedness. *The potential for energy conservation—a staff study.* Oct., 1972.

————, Office of Science and Technology. *Patterns of energy consumption in the United States,* Washington, D.C., January, 1972.

U.S. Federal Power Commission, Office of the Chief Engineer. *Guidelines for energy conservation for immediate implementation; small businesses and light industries.* Washington, D.C., Jan., 1974.

————, *A technical basis for energy conservation.* (Staff report), Washington, D.C., April, 1974.

U.S. House of Representatives, Committee on Science and Astronautics. *Individual action for energy conservation.* Washington, D.C., 1974.

U.S. Senate, Committee on Commerce. *Report on S2176: National Fuels and Energy Conservation Act of 1973.* Nov. 16, 1973.

_____, Committee on Government Operations, Permanent Subcommittee on Investigations, *Staff study of the oversight and efficiency of executive agencies with respect to the petroleum industry, especially as it relates to recent fuel shortages.* Nov. 8, 1973.

_____, Committee on Interior and Insular Affairs. *Conservation of energy—a national fuels and energy policy study.* 1972.

CHAPTER 5
fighting for lower utility bills

INTRODUCTION

The cost of electricity has skyrocketed in recent years. Within the past several years, the cost of primary fuels and new generating capacity, as well as other utility costs, have risen sharply, forcing the average prices paid by consumers to rise 70 percent in the 1970–1976 period. The increases in 1974 and 1975 together amounted to $22.2 billion, more than twice as much as all rate increases in the previous quarter of a century.

Nuclear power, promoted as the answer to rising costs and higher electric bills, has proven to be neither safe nor cheap, and the costs are escalating rapidly. Nuclear power plants that came into operation in the mid-1960s cost, on the average, $150 per kilowatt (kW). Plants currently coming into operation have an average cost of $405 per kW, and utility companies project that the plants planned for mid-1980s operation will cost $1000 per kW. Utility bills will continue to rise with the price of nuclear energy.

Other utilities and energy industries are not to be outdistanced by the electric companies in the race for the consumer dollar. The Carter Administration proposed an excessively high price for new natural gas; a move than would yield the industry windfall profits. AT&T has asked for the largest rate increase ever for long-distance calls and for a return to investors that is the highest in the nation for any utility. Local subsidiaries are not far behind with requests for an increase to 20 cents for a pay phone call and a new levy for directory assistance. Consumers are frustrated and angry because they can't see any recourse except to pay and keep paying.

WHY AREN'T CONSUMER INTERESTS PROTECTED?

In theory, public service commissions are supposed to protect consumers; the commissions are supposed to act in the public interest and ensure that utilities—legal monopolies—earn only those profits necessary to maintain their services. In practice, a very different course is followed. Like most regulatory agencies, public service commissions operate at a low level of funding and expertise. As a result, they have been unable, if not unwilling, to vigorously challenge utilities or, indeed, to investigate their rate structures for hidden costs and waste.

It has become clear that utility commissions do not adequately protect the interests of consumers. Public service commissions have proven themselves incapable of answering consumer complaints and often altogether avoid the embarrassing confrontation with the very citizens who pay their salaries.

The regulatory process works only if all sides of an issue are adequately presented before policymakers. Utility companies employ professionals to advocate the industry's viewpoint before public service commissions. But residential utility consumers often go unrepresented, and the regulators are left to act both as judge and, hopefully, consumer advocate. With part-time commissioners wearing two hats—advocate and judge—and hearing only the utility's one-sided arguments, it is not surprising that the consumer gets shortchanged.

What can concerned consumers do about the ever-increasing costs of electricity, natural gas, and telephone service? How can they combat the utilities and those government regulators who have become the partners of the utilities in the raid on consumers' pocketbooks?

The first step is to become as well informed as possible about the operation of the utility you are investigating. One invaluable guide to understanding electric utilities is a booklet prepared by the Environmental Action Foundtion, called *How to challenge your local electric utility: a citizen's guide to the power industry.* This 112-page booklet explains most of what a citizen needs to know to become involved and is available for $1.50 from EAF, 1346 Connecticut Avenue, NW, Room 720, Washington, D.C. 20036.

After consumers become knowledgeable, then what? How are they going to challenge the utilities in a rate proceeding? How are they going to pay the expenses of lawyers, expert witnesses, appeals, and the organizing of citizen opposition? Numerous citizens have intervened in utility proceedings. They have even won small victories. However, the following year the utility returns with another application and you and your friends have even less money with which to challenge them. They can afford to return year after year, they have your money (as a rate payer) to pay their staff, their lawyers, and their expert witnesses.

Some have offered as a solution a "Peoples" or "Consumers' Counsel." A Consumers' Counsel is a lawyer appointed by the Governor or Public Utilities Commission to represent consumer interests in hearings. That may be a small part of the solution but it does not provide enough political balance because it has at least three major drawbacks. Persons holding the position do not owe their appointment to the people and, therefore, will not be as accountable to the people as they should be. The Consumers' Counsel will find it difficult, if not impossible, to get the funds necessary to fight utility requests. And, equally important, it is unlikely that the Consumers'

Counsel will have the desire or capability to involve consumers in the process—organizing busloads of citizens to testify at legislative proceedings, to picket the headquarters of the utility, or to lead proxy fights. A better solution is needed.

Citizens can help themselves by setting up a group—a RUCAG—to monitor utility regulatory bodies and ensure that the consumer is fairly represented.

Consumers can also propose a "Lifeline" electricity rate structure that would guarantee residential users a basic, fixed amount of electricity at a flat rate. These kinds of action will result in lower and more equitable utility rates for residential consumers.

Form a RUCAG

A RUCAG—a Residential Utility Consumer's Action Group—is an organization that has independence, money, and accountability to consumers rather than to the utility commission or utility executives. A RUCAG will have a full-time staff of professionals—lawyers, economists, engineers, accountants, and organizers—funded and directed by residential utility users. That staff can advocate the public's interest in energy decision making before state legislatures, regulatory agencies, and the courts.

Utility consumers can fund the RUCAG through a checkoff system on their monthly utility bill. The checkoff works this way: within each residential utility bill there will be either an envelope addressed to the RUCAG or room for listing a voluntary contribution to support a group of full-time consumer advocates. Utility consumers can then pay their utility bill and fund their own action group at the same time!

The checkoff system to fund the RUCAG can be established by state law, utility commission regulation, or the initiative process. The utility is then obligated, under strict audit, to pass monthly contributions on to the RUCAG. The telephone, electric, or gas utility acts solely as a collection agent, turning over all contributions to RUCAG. Furthermore, to avoid any possible retaliatory action, the utility is forbidden from maintaining a copy of contributor lists.

The translation of consumer support into citizen action occurs only when an organization is structured to meet the needs of its membership. The RUCAG membership—all those residential consumers contributing a set minimum amount to the fund—will annually elect their own Board of Directors. The Board is responsible for hiring the staff, intervening in rate proceedings, monitoring legislative proceedings, handling consumer complaints, and ensuring that consumers and the rest of the public are kept constantly informed of their activities. This includes publishing the minutes of all meetings and distributing them to public libraries as well as requiring that meetings of the Board be open to the public.

Membership is limited to residential customers—those least able to fund organized opposition to rate increases on an ongoing basis. However, residential customers or members of their immediate family who are either employed by or hold shares in a local utility should be barred from becoming members of the Board of Directors, as they have an inherent conflict of interest.

The RUCAG will represent the interests of residential utility consumers: lower prices, better service, and efficient environmentally sound production.

As a participant in all proceedings, the RUCAG will challenge unnecessary expenses claimed by the utility, such as those for advertising and promotion. It will analyze the requests for unfair inclusions in the rate base—that amount of capital equipment upon which a rate of return is to be paid. The RUCAG's accountants can question the data on any claimed expenses in a rate hearing while its engineers determine whether equipment cited in the rate base is "used and useful" to consumers.

The RUCAG can analyze the utility's growth predictions and present counterproposals to the public service commission about the real needs, or lack thereof, for new construction. Because many citizens have expressed concern over the fuel adjustment clause and the effect it has had on their fuel bills, RUCAG can investigate these charges and determine which costs are fairly passed along to consumers.

The law says that a utility's rate of return must be fair to investors and to consumers. The company argues in behalf of investors but there is now no one saying what is fair to consumers. With economists on its staff, a RUCAG would have the expertise to persuasively represent consumers when rates of return are at question.

As an action arm of RUCAG, professional organizers would catalyze citizen involvement and teach consumers how to most effectively fight utilities.

The decisons to build nuclear power plants are made without citizen input. At present, citizens are woefully short of money and expertise to decisively intervene in the proceedings of the Nuclear Regulatory Commission, one of the federal agencies that succeeded the Atomic Energy Commission. RUCAG will give citizen's the funding and expertise needed to become involved in this vital decision-making process.

RUCAG will intervene in requests by telephone companies for rate increases and challenge their unique rate structure. Any phone company that wants to double the price of a pay phone call, add a new charge for directory assistance, or raise residential rates while reducing business rates will have to face consumers on equal terms through RUCAG.

And, equally important, the RUCAG will act as a clearinghouse for consumer complaints—the same complaints that gather dust on the desk of an engineer in the Public Utilities Commission. Employees of the RUCAG can take these complaints to the Public Utlities Commission as a group and demand action.

RUCAG staff time should also be devoted to larger issues: the structure of utilities, their political activity, the need for legislative reform, and the investigation of new technology and alternative forms of energy production.

Finally, RUCAG can reform one major cause of energy waste and inflationary prices, utility rate structures—the way utility companies set their prices for different types of consumers. At present, they are outrageously unjust. Utility rate structures reward the profligate user and punish the frugal or conscientious consumer. Those who use more gas or electricity are rewarded with lower per unit rates; residential telephone users in some states have been hit with rate increases while some business counterparts have received reduced rates on equipment. The RUCAG's engineers and economists can analyze the proposed rate structures of the utilities and help design nondiscriminatory schedules that are related to cost.

How to Form a RUCAG

The first step in every successful political battle is to develop your organization. Contact all groups concerned with the rising costs of utility services, particularly those with a constituency. These may include consumer and environmental groups; groups representing the interests of low-income people and the elderly; and civic associations. Be certain to have within your coalition respected people who have access to elected and appointed officials. Arrange an organizational meeting and plan your action strategy.

Then inform the public, explaining what you hope to accomplish and how. For this you need a provocative media program. If you do not effectively communicate what you are doing to the public, do not expect its support. See Chapter 11 for a guide to dealing with the media.

In some states the battles will be waged before the Public Service Commission. In others it will be decided in the committee rooms and on the floors of the state legislatures, or through a direct statewide election. Refer to Chapter 12 for guides to lobbying and the initiative and referendum process—one of these methods of making laws may be the key to establishing a RUCAG.

Review the legislation (Resource 5.1) designed to establish a RUCAG. If you have questions concerning any aspect of this project, contact Marty Rogol, Box 19312, Washington, D.C.   20036.

Initially, it may seem an impossible task to challenge as powerful and imposing an institution as a public utility. But a journey of a thousand miles, as President Kennedy was fond of saying, begins with a single step.

PROPOSE A "LIFELINE" RATE

A potential reform of utility rate structures is "Lifeline," a proposal to provide electricity to citizens for their basic needs, lighting, cooking, and refrigeration, at an affordable rate.

Traditionally, the utilities have had what are termed *promotional rate schedules* under which large users pay substantially less per unit than do small users. There was a certain logic to this approach during the 1940s and 1950s when new technology and the economies of scale led to cheaper power rates. It was considered reasonable to promote the use of power so that growth would result in even lower rates for all. There seemed to be a direct connection between the cost of serving different users and the actual rates charged.

This situation had changed dramatically by 1970. New and bigger power plants began to exhibit unexpected deficiencies so that economics of scale were less evident. The new technology—nuclear power—began to run into snags of staggering complexity and seriousness. As a result, a kilowatt hour (kWh) of electrical energy from a new plant became much more expensive than energy produced by existing facilities. Residential customers using small amounts of electricity per month are now forced to pay for the larger and, in many instances, more wasteful uses by other consumers.

Because of the changing cost patterns and the inability of many citizens to afford the basic minimum quantity of electricity to sustain life, public interest advocates in Vermont, led by the Vermont PIRG, developed the Lifeline scheme. Lifeline would guarantee residential users a fixed amount of electricity for their basic needs at an affordable fixed rate. Since the Lifeline rate structure was first conceived in 1973, only California has made it law, although it has been proposed in many other states including Vermont, Massachusetts, and Michigan. Such reform may require constant advocacy by an organization like a RUCAG if it is to be realized in other states.

Lifeline is actually more consistent with the cost-of-service doctrine than the present promotional rate structures. The basic reasons for spiraling electric rates are the expensive new plants and the costs of fuel required to meet ever-increasing demand. Increase in demand is attributable to dramatic rises in industrial, commercial, and residential per capita consumption. Therefore, the rising costs of power should be reflected in costs to those whose rising consumption is contributing so heavily to those high costs, not in the rates for the basic amount of electricity used by virtually every family.

It is important to emphasize that the Lifeline rate would apply to everyone, regardless of income, although the small user would be the prime beneficiary. Low-income families are not necessarily low energy users, but the proposal would ensure that a family could at least provide itself with rockbottom necessities at a fair price. The concern of low-income people is that even these rockbottom necessities may be priced right out of sight under present rate policies. But because a certain amount of electricity is a necessity, it cannot be eliminated, and the bill is now being paid from the food budget of too many families.

Such a program is financially feasible. The costs of Lifeline service could and should be absorbed by large industrial, commercial, and residential users. The costs of serving customers by varying utilities are not the same and therefore the standard Lifeline rate does not precisely reflect cost of service. That is the reason why in many states legislative action is required to establish it.

Another reason that Lifeline makes economic sense and is more equitable than the traditional methods of setting rates is found in the elasticity of demand for electricity. Average usage certainly exceeds the amount of kWh per month that would be alloted under the Lifeline concept. What the fixed amount of kWh/month represents is the amount of electricity that must be used for basic necessities that can best be provided by electricity, such as refrigeration and adequate lighting. A family's demand for this basic amount of energy is inelastic, i.e., its consumption to this degree will not be affected by the price of the product.

Beyond this basic amount, however, demand is more elastic; energy is used unwisely and outright waste occurs both in residences and, more spectacularly, in commercial buildings and industry. This demand is elastic. Lifeline would mean that a greater share of costs would be paid by those whose demand is elastic than has been the case in the past.

Lifeline would encourage energy conservation. There is currently little public awareness of the fact that the way electrical rate schedules are set encourages use of electricity by setting lower prices for greater use. There is certainly no real financial *incentive* to use electricity wisely. Lifeline would provide that incentive for the first time.

If electric rates did encourage energy conservation, the end result would be less need for costly new power plants and expensive fossil fuels, with resultant savings to all consumers of electricity. This is another reason why Lifeline is consistent with cost of service thinking.

Of course, wasteful and unnecessary consumption of energy will still continue, but Lifeline is a step toward ensuring that the true costs of this energy will be shouldered by the actual user, not by the user who is merely providing reasonable and moderate necessities for a family.

How to Get Lifeline Accepted in Your State

There are numerous types of Lifeline proposals, all of which require legislative passage or public utility commission approval. Largely through the efforts of the Michigan Public Interest Research Group, the Michigan Public Service Commission adopted Lifeline electric rates for the residential consumers of the area's two largest utilities. You can propose a specific fixed amount of kWh as the amount to be included in the Lifelife rate or allow the local regulatory body to set the amount based on different needs in different portions of a state. In California, the groups that successfully lobbied for Lifeline chose the latter approach because legislators were confused and intimidated by the procedures for deciding upon an appropriate figure.

In Massachusetts and Vermont, where Lifeline was proposed by the PIRGs, specific Lifeline amounts and costs were included in the legislation. The figures were based on the amount of electricity needed to provide basic residential necessities that are usually electrically powered as estimated by the Edison Electric Institute, an industry trade association. Table 5.1 shows their figures for the basic appliances a family of four might own, and the amount of electricity they use.

Table 5.1 ELECTRICITY CONSUMPTION

Appliance	kWh/month
Furnace blower*	103
Oil burner*	19
Refrigerator-freezer	
(14 cu ft manual defrost)	95
Water pump	19
Lights	70
Radio	7
Sewing machine	1
Total	314

*Based on average for whole year

Naturally, there may be some disagreement concerning which appliances are necessities. Also, these figures are averages for people who now own these appliances. Some families use considerably more electricity than these figures indicate, just as some use less. But this list indicates that 300–400 kWh is a good estimate of the minimum electricity required by most families.

The PIRGs then set the cost of this amount under Lifeline by determining the average cost of the amount statewide, and then setting a lower figure for the lifeline amount and slightly raising costs for larger amounts, in order to offset losses to the utility. Such calculations are time consuming to prepare, may not reflect the difference in prices charged by different utilities around the state and, as mentioned previously, legislators may not feel comfortable proposing such specific and complicated figures.

Take these problems into consideration before determining whether you wish to include specific figures in your proposal.

Three different forms of Lifeline legislation are found on the pages following. The first version is the legislation passed in California in the fall of 1975. The California law varies from the Lifeline concept as discussed above in that it does not provide for a fixed amount of residential usage at a lower rate. Instead, the law guarantees that utilities will not be able to raise prices of the Lifeline amount of electricity for residential users. This type of compromise may be necessary in other states.

The second version is part of proposed federal legislation (H.R. 2615 and S. 122) aimed at utility reform and regulation. It provides that a fixed basic amount of electricity (the amount to be determined by the regulatory authority) will be provided to residential users by any electric utility at a cost no higher than "the lowest charge per kilowatt-hour to any other electric consumer" within each jurisdiction of a regulatory agency with rate-making authority.

The third version is a bill that has been proposed in several states, including Maryland. It is similar to the federal bill but includes a provision that a fixed basic amount of natural gas usage also be provided to residential users at the lowest rate at which mcfs (or therms) are sold by a utility. Many now take the position that some relief is necessary for all-electric homes, and this third version of Lifeline requires the establishment of a Lifeline amount for them during the winter months. The rate would only be available for those all-electric homes constructed before the passage of the Act, assuming the house was the principal place of residence of the occupant.

Consider the options these bills present before determining which would be most appropriate and likely to meet with acceptance in your state.

In most states it will be necessary to present a Lifeline proposal to the legislature rather than to the Public Utility Commission. It is a departure from the more traditional cost of service methods of determining rates and, due to bureaucratic inertia, PUCs may refuse to act. You should be prepared for a long, hard fight. Business and industry do not want to see changes that will adversely affect their low rates. Legislators may be wary if they perceive it as a system of welfare, aimed at helping only low-income people. It will be more important to point out that Lifeline helps residential users of low amounts of electricity whether or not they are low income and that Lifeline will encourage energy conservation.

It will be important to oppose efforts by utilities or legislators to promote the use of energy stamps as an alternative to Lifeline or other types of utility reform. Such a plan will inevitably become another demeaning welfare program and remove the pressure for overall rate reform. Utilities know that if one part of the citizen coalition is bought off, there will be fewer problems fighting the rest.

Contact the Citizen Action League for specific information about their successful Lifeline campaign.

LIFELINE LEGISLATION: STATE OF CALIFORNIA

An act to add Section 739 to the Public Utilities Code, relating to public utilities.

LEGISLATIVE COUNSEL'S DIGEST

AB 167, as amended, Miller (Fin., Ins., & Com.). Public utilities: gas and electric rates.

Present law does not require electrical or gas corporations to provide residential customers minimum service at reduced rates.

This bill would direct the Public Utilities Commission to designate a lifeline quantity of gas and electricity necessary to supply the minimum energy needs of the average residential user for end uses of space and water heating, lighting, cooking and food refrigeration.

The bill would direct the Public Utilities Commission to require electrical and gas corporations to file a revised schedule of rates and charges providing a lifeline rate. *It would specify that the lifeline rate shall be not greater than the relative rates in effect on January 1, 1976. It would prohibit any increase in the lifeline rate until the rates for all customers of electrical or gas service, whichever is applicable, exceed the lifeline rate by 25 percent or more, and would require the commission thereafter to maintain a lifeline rate differential of at least 25 percent.* It also would state legislative findings and declarations and define the term "residential."

This bill would require the Public Utilities Commission to report to the Legislature on the effect of this bill upon rates, and the cost to users and utilities.

Vote: majority. Appropriation: no. Fiscal committee: yes. State-mandated local program: no.

The people of the State of California do enact as follows.

SECTION 1.   The Legislature hereby finds and declares as follows:

(a) Light and heat are basic human rights, and must be made available to all the people at low cost for basic minimum quantities.

(b) Present rate structures for gas and electricity serve to penalize the individual user of relatively small quantities, and at the same time encourage wastefulness by large users.

(c) In order to encourage conservation of scarce energy resources and to provide a basic necessary amount of gas and electricity for residential heating and lighting at a cost which is fair to small users, the Legislature has enacted this act.

SEC. 2.   This act may be cited as the Miller-Warren Energy Lifeline Act.

SEC. 3.   Section 739 is added to the Public Utilities Code, to read:

739. (a) The commission shall designate a lifeline volume of gas and a lifeline quantity of electricity which is necessary to supply the minimum energy needs of the average residential user for the following end uses: space and water heating, lighting, cooking and food refrigerating, provided that in estimating such volumes and quantities the commission shall take into account differentials in energy needs between utility customers whose residential energy needs are supplied by electricity and gas. The commission shall also take into account differentials in energy needs caused by geographic differences by differences in severity of climate, and by season.

(b) The commision shall require that every *electrical* and gas corporation file a schedule of rates and charges providing a lifeline rate. *The lifeline rate shall be not*

greater than the relative rates in effect on January 1, 1976. The commission shall autho-
rize no increase in the lifeline rate until such time as the rates for all customers of elec-
trical or gas service, whichever is applicable, exceed the lifeline rate by 25 percent or
more. Thereafter, in establishing electrical and gas rates, the commission shall main-
tain a lifeline rate differential of at least 25 percent.

(c) Nothing shall preclude the commission from reducing any rate established pursuant to subdivision (a) either specifically or pursuant to any general restructuring of all electrical or gas rates, charges, and classifications.

(d) As used in this section, the term "residential" means domestic human needs end use and excludes industrial, commercial, and every other category of end use.

SEC. 4. The Public Utilities Commission shall report to the Legislature, in January, 1977, on the effect of this act upon rates, and the cost to users and utilities.

SECTION OF H.R. 2615, INTRODUCED TO THE UNITED STATES HOUSE OF REPRESENTATIVES JANUARY 27, 1977

National Minimum Standards for Electric Utility Rate Regulation
Sec. 203 (a) Each State regulatory authority which has assumed enforcement responsibilities (within the meaning of section 209 (a)) shall (in order to carry out section 209 (a)) require that each electric utility, with respect to which it has ratemaking authority, comply with the following minimum standards:

(1) Except as otherwise provided in paragraph (3), rates for providing electric service to each electric consumer (or class thereof) shall be designed, to the maximum extent practicable, to reflect the costs of providing electric service to such consumer (or class). Such costs shall be determined by the State regulatory authority in accordance with section 205.

(2) The rate per kilowatt, or per kilowatt-hour, for providing electric service during any period to any electric consumer (or class thereof) shall not decrease as kilowatt, or kilowatt-hour, consumption by such consumer increases, except to the extent that such utility shows in an evidentiary hearing that such decrease reflects costs of providing electric service to such consumer (or class) which decrease as such consumption increases. Such costs shall be determined by the State regulatory authority in accordance with section 205.

(3) (A) Except as otherwise provided in subparagraph (D), each electric utility shall provide for a rate under which the charge for kilowatt-hour at any time of use (including any customer charges) to a residential electric consumer for a subsistence quantity of electric energy in any month (or other applicable billing period) for such consumer's principal place of residence does not exceed the lowest charge for kilowatt-hour at such time of use (excluding demand, capacity, and customer charges) to any other electric consumer (within the jurisdiction of the State regulatory authority) to whom electric energy is sold by such utility.

(B) For purposes of this paragraph, the term "subsistence quantity" means the number of kilowatt-hours which the State regulatory authority determines is necessary to supply the minimum subsistence electric energy needs of residential consumers at their principal place of residence for domestic lighting and food refrigeration.

(C) No provision of this title shall prevent an electric utility, a State regulatory authority, or other State agency from increasing the kilowatt-hours of the subsistence quantity prescribed in this paragraph to include additional domestic end uses.

BILL INTRODUCED TO THE GENERAL ASSEMBLY OF THE MARYLAND LEGISLATURE ON LIFELINE

Section 1. The Legislature hereby finds and declares that:

(a) Light and heat are basic human rights, and must be made available to all residential users at low cost for basic human necessities.

(b) Present rate structures for electricity and gas serve to penalize the individual user of relatively small quantities, and at the same time encourage wastefulness by large users.

(c) In order to encourage conservation of scarce energy resources, it is necessary to provide a basic amount of electricity and gas for space and water heating, lighting, cooking and food refrigeration at a cost which is fair to small users.

Section 2. The Public Service Commission shall not allow as part of any rate schedule for an electric or gas utility any rate which provides that the cost per kilowatt-hour to a residential electric customer for the first kilowatt-hours or to a residential gas customer for the first mcf (or therms) in any month for such consumer's principal place of residence exceeds the lowest cost per kilowatt-hour or mcf to any other electric or gas customer within the jurisdiction of the Public Service Commission to whom electricity or gas is sold by such utility (or any electric or gas utility which is controlled by, or under control with, such utility).

Section 3.

(a) The Public Service Commission shall require that every electric utility file a schedule of rates and charges which provides to those residential consumers who heat their single family residence with electricity the same proportional percentage reduction in their average monthly bill as residential customers who use less than kWh received as a result of the implementation of Section 2 of this Act.

(b) The rate specified in Section 3(a) of this Act shall apply only:

1. To those single family residences with electric heat in which installation of the electric heating system was completed prior to January 1, 1976; and

2. from October 15th of each year to March 31st of the following year; and

3. at the principal place of residence of such residential customer

BIBLIOGRAPHY

Leflar, Robert B., and Martin H. Rogol. Consumer participation in the regulation of public utilities: a model act. *Harvard Journal on Legislation*, 13, 2, February, 1976: 236–296.

PART 3
grocery projects

INTRODUCTION

During the last ten years, the cost of living in the United States has increased 65 percent while food prices rose an even more frightening 79.6 percent.[1] The most substantial increases occurred between 1972 and 1975 when food prices jumped 45 percent. Americans spent an estimated $76.05 billion on food in 1965, but by 1974 that figure had jumped to $143.15 billion.[2] The impact of increasing food prices was intensified by the rising unemployment and deepening recession felt across the country.

Consumers respond to escalating food costs by shopping carefully for quality products at the lowest possible prices. But this is impossible without accurate information on comparative grocery store prices, the freshness and quality of food products, and honest advertising. Without this kind of information, consumers will continue to spend more money than necessary and end up with inferior products.

Ideally government regulation would ensure that advertising, packaging, and labeling provide consumers with this information, but it does not. Instead, the more than $4 billion a year spent on food advertising by manufacturers, the costs of which are included in food prices, offer such helpful "facts" as:

"Imperial Margarine. . . fit for a king"
"Maxwell House . . . good to the last drop"

Food dating and labeling often serve more to confuse than inform the consumer. Many retail food stores compound the problem by not only failing to provide useful information but also by deliberately deceiving harried shoppers and manipulating their purchasing choices, using signs and displays that indicate that items are priced at a discount when in fact they are not.

Escalating food costs affect all Americans and are especially devastating to low-income groups, the unemployed, elderly persons living on fixed incomes, and large families. In 1975 a family of four with an income of $9198 spent 26 percent of that income on food. Families with incomes of $5000 or less spent 32 percent of their income on food.[3]

The prices of raw food products, which has increased only four percent from 1952 to 1971, increased about 60 percent by 1973.[4] In 1974, raw food prices continued to climb at even higher rates due to growing inflation, monopolistic practices, increasing costs of oil and oil-based fertilizers, world shortages of feed grain and other commodities, and heavy demand from foreign markets.

Although increasingly expensive raw food products, packaging, and energy shortages have forced up the expenses of grocery stores, the stores have absorbed none of these costs themselves, and the consumer pays the price.[5] This policy along with the increased cost of food at the retail level, have resulted in "the highest and most prolonged period of inflation since World War II."[6] The refusal of retail food stores to absorb some of the rising costs is particularly irresponsible given the fact that according to government and industry figures,[7] the retail food industry is one of the most profitable in the United States.

Rising food prices have created new awareness and increased concern on the part of consumers, and have made investigations of the pricing, advertising, and consumer information services of grocery stores important and timely issues for individuals and consumer groups. The projects in the following chapters will enable you to address some of the concerns of shoppers and provide them with much needed data about area grocery stores. They can also lead to new laws and changes within the stores themselves—changes which will give shoppers the information they must have to make grocery shopping easier and less expensive.

Alaska PIRG surveyed prices of staple food items and published a shopper's guide to grocery stores. Publication of price data resulted in the highest priced store lowering its prices to meet those of the lowest priced store.

North Carolina PIRG investigated the availability of advertised specials in grocery stores and found that, on the average, specials in grocery stores were unavailable or overpriced 17 percent of the time, with individual stores' percentages ranging from 5 to 40 percent. They made that information public and asked the Federal Trade Commission to investigate the stores with the worst practices.

Oregon PIRG conducted a unit pricing survey, and found that "without unit pricing, comparative pricing of 95 percent of the food items surveyed required difficult mental calculations by the shopper," and that most voluntary unit pricing programs were inadequate because labels were either difficult to understand or missing. Oregon PIRG has used its survey data to support legislation which would make unit pricing mandatory in the state.

SOME PRELIMINARY INFORMATION
ABOUT GROCERY PROJECTS

In doing any of the projects discussed in this chapter, it is important to consider where consumers in your area usually shop. When choosing stores to survey, the most important type to be included are chain stores. Of the approximately 282,300 retail food stores in the United States, only about 46,000 or 16 percent are chain stores. However, in 1968, this 16 percent had an estimated sales of $51.6 billion or 67 percent of the total food sales for that year.[8]

Furthermore, in metropolitan areas the four largest retail food store chains in the United States account for more than 50 percent of the market.[9] Any two stores owned by the same company are considered part of a chain. For survey purposes, larger chains are the more important. Figure P3.1 supplies a list of those chains.

If only one large grocery chain operates in your area, try to include about 50 percent of its stores in any survey and more if it is possible. This is a necessary safeguard against charges that your data is not representative of the chain as a whole. If several large grocery chains operate in your area, survey 50 percent of the stores from each, except in large metropolitan areas where 25 percent may be a more feasible goal. It is important to survey the same percentage of stores from each chain rather than the same number of stores from each. This may sound unreasonably rigid but it will eliminate the opportunity for a chain to charge you with prejudicing your investigation.

If you are surveying a wide area, try to choose stores from each chain which are located in both the inner city and in suburbs, and stores which serve shoppers from different economic levels.

FIFTY-SIX PUBLICLY HELD GROCERY CHAINS LISTED IN ORDER

OF THEIR SALES

SAFEWAY	BIG BEAR
A & P	THRIFTMART
KROGER	FOODARAMA
AMERICAN STORES	MARSH
LUCKY	NIAGARA FRONTIER SERVICES
WINN-DIXIE	ALTERMAN FOODS
JEWEL	SHOP RITE FOODS
FOOD FAIR	SHOPWELL
GRAND UNION	SEAWAY FOODTOWN
SUPER MARKETS GENERAL	KING KULLEN
NATIONAL TEA	BRUNO'S
STOP & SHOP	PENN TRAFFIC
ALBERTSON'S	STAR SUPERMARKETS
FISHER FOODS	BAYLESS
DILLION	BIG V
FIRST NATIONAL	PURITY SUPREME
COLONIAL	THOROFARE
GIANT FOOD	VICTORY
ALLIED SUPERMARKETS	FOODTOWN (N.C.)
FRED MEYER	SCHULTZ SAV-O
WALDBAUM	MOTT'S
BORMAN'S	VILLAGE
PUEBLO INTERNATIONAL	APPLEBAUMS'
CULLUM	MAYFAIR
J. WEINGARTEN	RED FOOD
ARDEN-MAYFAIR	BAZA'R
WEIS	E & B SUPERMARKETS
BI-LO	JURGENSEN'S

Fig. P3.1   Fifty-six largest grocery chains in the United States as of 1976 sales figures. Source: *Progressive Grocer,* April, 1977.

Small chain stores and independents should not be excluded entirely from your survey. In large cities the small chain stores and independents which are most important to include are those which have no competitor in the area. If there are few chain stores in your area, you will want to include more of these small stores.

The Yellow Pages list all stores and their addresses and you may want to mark out the locations of a tentative list of stores to be surveyed on a map to be sure you have a good mix of locations.

GET THE NEWS MEDIA INTERESTED IN THE PROJECT

Over the past few years the news media have devoted increasing amounts of space and time to covering food related issues. The issues of food prices and quality are certainly on everyone's mind. What this means to anyone about to do a grocery survey of any type is that you may, with little effort, be able to attract the interest of local newspapers, radio stations, and especially television stations before beginning your surveys.

The advantages to this approach, rather than waiting until the survey has been completed and you are ready to release the results, is that they may be interested in filming or covering the survey as it takes place and then again when you hold a news conference or issue a news release. We've all seen television spots where reporters discuss how much costs of food have gone up over a week or a month. The survey projects in Chapters 6-9 can offer equally, or more, interesting viewing.

BIBLIOGRAPHY

Consumer price index. Bureau of Labor Statistics, U.S. Department of Labor, Washington, D.C., 1976.

Food from market to consumer. Final Report, National Commission on Food Marketing, Washington, D.C., 1966.

Fortune, 500 Edition. New York: 1965-1974.

On food chain profits. Staff Report, Federal Trade Commission, Washington, D.C., July, 1975.

Ross, Donald K., *A Public Citizen's Action Manual.* New York: Grossman, 1973.

CHAPTER 6

market basket survey - comparative grocery pricing

INTRODUCTION

Shoppers compare retail prices consciously and unconsciously for every type of commodity, but because of the large number of grocery stores, it is often impossible for individuals to compare food prices without considerable trouble and expense. Comparative grocery pricing surveys with properly publicized results are both an aid to the consumer and a catalyst for competitive—and lower—prices. A state-sponsored grocery pricing survey undertaken in Hawaii in 1973 resulted in a four percent overall drop in food prices.

Using the survey described in this chapter, consumers can compare the retail prices of common grocery items which the average family frequently buys. The results will indicate which stores provide the lowest prices for general grocery shopping and for each category of foods most frequently purchased. Using the survey results as a shopping guide, area consumers may save as much as 10 percent of their grocery bills. Surveys done by the Michigan PIRG and the Northern California PIRG showed that prices in the least expensive area stores were, respectively, 9.2 percent and 10.5 percent lower than in the highest priced store.

With food prices climbing and the value of a dollar shrinking, any savings at the supermarket will be welcomed by some shoppers. Area consumers, if informed about store prices, may take their business to lower priced stores. A grocery store manager reported to Indiana PIRG that his business increased by 30 percent after the PIRG survey showed that his store had the lowest prices in the area. On the other hand many shoppers will choose to pay more at stores that offer the conveniences, products, and locations they prefer.

SOME BASICS

To do this project you will need a hand calculator and an adding machine (or a computer if you have access to one), and several volunteers willing to go to grocery stores and record on survey forms the prices of common food items.

Check to see if this sort of survey has ever been done in your area. Call local consumer groups and student groups involved with consumer issues. If studies have been done in the past, analyze their effect before beginning your survey. Has any store raised or lowered its prices in a way which seems to be the direct result of the positive or negative publicity it received from these surveys?

Remember that no one drives to Idaho for cheaper potatoes. Since helping local shoppers is the purpose of this survey, make price comparisons within a radius that an average consumer might travel for a bargain without using much more gas than usual. To simplify the collection and compilation of data, limit the survey to common items, like those in Fig. 6.1, in the project.

Choose a coordinator for the project who will set the schedule for the survey, supervise the surveyors, compile the data, and answer questions or complaints from the public and merchants.

HOW TO DO THE SURVEYING

Generally, it is not necessary to ask permission of store personnel to do this survey. If you go about the pricing in a quiet and unobtrusive manner, you should not have any problems. Some store personnel will be very cooperative and offer to help, while others will be apprehensive and try to make surveyors uncomfortable. Most grocery store personnel are accustomed to government inspectors and other groups doing comparative pricing and will probably not interfere with your survey.

If you are told to leave the store at any time during your survey, ask politely to see the store manager or owner. Explain the nature of the project and express your willingness to abide by any reasonable requests (e.g., not blocking the aisles, not interfering with customers' purchases). In the case of extreme hostility, simply say that you will have to publish the fact that certain store owners or managers refused to allow their prices to be compared with those of other stores. You must, nevertheless, leave if and when you are told to do so; you are on private property, and the store owner can

Grocery Pricing Survey Form

Name of store_____

Location_____

Name of surveyor_____

Phone number_____ Date_____

Date to be returned_____

Amount	Product	Prices	Comments	Brand X
MEATS, POULTRY, and FISH				
1 lb	Hamburger, ground beef, lean			
1 lb	T-bone steak, U.S. choice			
1 lb	Chicken, frying, whole			
1 lb	Frozen turbot fillets, not cooked, not breaded			
1 lb	Hot dogs, cheapest			
1 lb	Pork loin, rib chops			
1 lb	Oscar Mayer bologna			
PRODUCE				
1 lb	Carrots			
1 lb	Iceberg lettuce			
1 lb	Onions (yellow)			
1 lb	Bananas			
5 lb	Potatoes (white)			

Fig. 6.1 Grocery pricing survey form.

Amount	Product	Prices	Comments	Brand X

DAIRY

Amount	Product	Prices	Comments	Brand X
half gal.	Milk, Vitamin D, grade A homogenized			
one doz	Eggs, large, grade A			
1 lb	Butter, salted, cut in quarter lb. sticks			
1 lb.	Blue Bonnet stick margarine			
12 oz	Kraft American sliced cheese, not individually wrapped			
half gal	Ice cream, vanilla, cheapest			

PROCESSED FOODS

Amount	Product	Prices	Comments	Brand X
12 oz	Minute Maid frozen orange juice			
17 oz	Green Giant niblet Corn			
one can	Campbell's chicken noodle soup			
18 oz	Skippy Superchunk peanut butter			
29 oz	Del Monte pear halves			
1 lb	Maxwell House regular ground coffee			
six-pack	Coke, 12 oz cans			
15 oz	Hunt's tomato sauce			
10 oz	Green peas, frozen			

Fig. 6.1 *Continued*

Amount	Product	Prices	Comments	Brand X
6 1/2 oz	Star-Kist, tuna, chunk light			

BAKERY, CEREAL and STAPLES

Amount	Product	Prices	Comments	Brand X
16 oz	Arnold bread, white enriched			
18 oz	Kellogg's corn flakes			
18 oz	Oreo cookies			
1 lb	Mueller's thin spaghetti			
5 lbs	Pillsbury all-purpose flour			
5 lb	sugar (cheapest)			
12 oz	Ritz crackers			

NONFOODS

Amount	Product	Prices	Comments	Brand X
20 oz	Tide laundry detergent			
5 oz	Dial bath soap			
75 sq ft.	Reynold's Wrap aluminum foil			
1 roll 100 sq ft.	Scott Paper Towels			
22 oz	Joy dishwashing liquid			

Any additional comments: (such as "cheaper house brand available.")

Fig. 6.1 *Continued*

143

legally ask you to leave. If you can't negotiate, don't fight! If the store personnel have any questions or complaints, refer them to the project coordinator.

The items recommended for price comparison should be stocked by all grocery stores. The only unavailability problem you are apt to encounter will be items which are temporarily out of stock.

Survey the stores in teams of two, using a Survey Form like that shown in Fig. 6.1. Price items carefully and compare figures with those of your partner *before* leaving the store. Be sure that all the numbers are accurate and legible or the results will be hopelessly distorted. Work slowly until you get the hang of it. Check the weight, brand, volume, etc. of each item to be sure that you have found *exactly* what the survey calls for. Record the price in the column next to the name of the item.

Do not make substitutions! If you can't find the exact item, if the item is not available, or if there is any irregularity whatsoever, follow the specific instructions below. Do not guess at or interpolate prices, or switch brands or sizes. *The comparisons must be exact to be valid.*

If you can't find an item, ask a clerk for its location. Once you have found it, record the price as indicated below:

Amount	Product	Price	Comments	Brand X
one doz	Eggs, Large, Grade A	$.83		

If the store has several items that meet the specifications of the survey, always record the one with the cheapest price.

If the price marked is for more than one package or more than the quantity called for by the survey, (e.g., one box 34¢, but 3/$1.00), record the price that is charged for the amount specified on the survey form but note the price conditions in the "Comments" column.

Amount	Product	Price	Comments	Brand X
10 oz	Frozen Green peas	$.34	3/$1.00	

If identical items are marked with different prices, ask a clerk if there has been a mistake and record the correct price.

If the store does not stock the item, mark the price column with an X and write N/S (does not stock) and your source of information under "Comments."

Amount	Product	Price	Comments	Brand X
1 lb	Muellers thin spaghetti	X	N/S Manager said they don't carry item	

If you fill in the survey form this way, be absolutely certain that the item is not sold in the store, because such items will have to be cut from all the surveys (or the store itself will have to be omitted from the survey) so that the totals balance. (This will rarely be the case if the items surveyed are those on the sample survey form.)

If the survey asks for specific name brands but the store also has a cheaper name brand or house brand available, record the requested brand under product and price and the lower brand and price in the "Brand X" column. Put an asterisk next to the price of the name brand product. On your pricing chart note something like "cheaper house brand available" under comments or next to asterisk at bottom of page. Quality judgments must be left to the individual consumer.

Large chains may charge more for name brands in order to promote their own house brands but, by the same token, they may be offering identical merchandise at a *lower* price than average.

Amount	Product	Price	Comments	Brand X
17-oz can	Green Giant niblet corn	$.45*		*Townhouse* 3/$1.00

* cheaper house brand available

If the item is in the process of a price change, record the more recent price because it is the one shoppers will have to pay by the time the survey is published. Note the former price in the "Comments" column and mark it "changing price."

Amount	Product	Price	Comments	Brand X
22 oz	Joy dishwashing liquid	$.91	*formerly $.85 changing price*	

Do not automatically record prices of items in special displays, often located at the end of aisles or in the front of stores. These may or may not be sale items or specials and, thus, the cheapest item of the product in the store. Sometimes such displays are the result of accidental overstocking, and there will be cheaper brands on the shelves. Other times they are a quick way to get rid of damaged or no longer fresh merchandise (e.g., day-old bread). In any case, always check the prices of all other brands before recording prices. If the special is the least expensive item which meets survey specifications, record the price and note the regular price and duration of the sale under "Comments."

Amount	Product	Price	Comments	Brand X
1 head	lettuce	$.57	*one-week special $.56 a head*	

If an item seems to be out of stock, look for its usual price on shelf labels and signs. If you can't find a price, ask the clerk or cashier how much the item normally costs. Record the price; write O/S (out of stock) and your source of information for the price under "Comments."

Amount	Product	Price	Comments	Brand X
1 lb	Frozen turbot fillets (not cooked or breaded)	$ .79	*O/S cashier gave normal price*	

Before leaving the store, check to see that all the columns are filled in and that all figures and comments are legible.

HOW TO COMPLETE THE MARKET BASKET SURVEY

Scan all survey forms for obvious errors and check with surveyors if any numbers are unclear. Don Ross notes in *A Public Citizen's Action Manual* that "one Washington, D.C., survey revealed mispricing on about two percent of supermarket items surveyed." So if any prices vary greatly from those charged by other stores, go back to the store to see if the figures are correct. Also, check all forms for items marked N/S. If an item is not stocked in one of the stores, the product or the store will have to be omitted from the survey so that the final totals balance.

Compile a chart like the one in Fig. 6.2 which is a complete index of items and prices for all stores surveyed. The fastest, most accurate way to determine store prices is to subtotal the prices from each category (produce, dairy, etc.) on an adding machine and then add up the subtotals. Check your addition by totaling the prices of the same items, but without the subtotals. Repeat this procedure for every store.

Make adjustments in the totals for prices which are lower if items are bought in quantity. For example, if a can of soup costs $.35, but is also sold 3 cans for $1.00, the consumer saves almost $.02 per can by purchasing 3 cans ($.35 $\times$ 3 = $1.05 $-$ $1.00 = $.05; $.05 $\div$ 3 = $.016 = $.02). Compute the savings for each item which is sold with a discount for a larger quantity and subtract the amount of the discount (in the case of our example, $.02) from the original total for each store.

Finally, take the adjusted totals and calculate the percentage by which each store's total varies from that of the least expensive store. Subtract the cheapest store's adjusted total from those of each other store. Then divide that figure by the cheapest store's adjusted total to get "Percentage Difference." For example, if the adjusted total of the cheapest store—the A&P on Elm St.—is $33.24, and the adjusted total of the A&P on Route 353 is $34.19, the latter store is 2.9 percent more expensive than the Elm St. A&P ($34.19 $-$ $33.24 = $.95; $.95 $\div$ $33.24 = .029 = 2.9%). Mark these percentages on the chart.

SAMPLE CHART

Name of Item	A&P Elm Street	Giant	A&P Rt. 353	Acme Walnut Street	Joe's Deli
Hamburger	.99	.97	.99	1.01	1.17
Steak	2.09	2.01	2.09	2.12	2.31
Chicken	.55	.53	.59	.59	.64
Fish	.79	.79	.79	.89	.89
Hot dogs	1.05	1.04	1.09	1.13	1.27
Pork chops	1.69	1.63	1.75	1.81	1.88
Bologna (Oscar Mayer)	.77*	.74*	.79*	.79	.84
Subtotal for meats, poultry, and fish	$7.93	$7.71	$8.07	$8.34	$9.00
Carrots	.31	.32	.33	.35	.38
Lettuce	.51**	.56	.59**	.61	.64
Onions	.15	.15	.15	.15	.15
Bananas	.19	.19	.19	.21	.21
Potatoes	.55	.59	.59	.61	.64
Subtotal for Produce	$1.71	$1.81	$1.85	$1.93	$1.99
Milk	.74	.74	.74	.74	.79
Eggs	.83	.83	.83	.83	.89
Butter	.89	.88	.85	.81	.85
Margarine	.79	.79	.81*	.79*	.83
Cheese	.67	.67	.75	.65	.75
Ice cream	1.27	1.27	1.35	1.27	1.69
Subtotal for Dairy	$5.19	$5.18	$5.33	$5.09	$5.80
Frozen orange juice (Minute Maid)	.67	.67	.67	.72	.71
Corn (Green Giant)	.38	.42	.45*	.45*	.42
Noodle soup (Campbell)	.25	.28	.28	.29	.29
Peanut Butter (Skippy)	.99*	.99*	1.05*	1.04*	1.04*
Pears (Delmonte)	.75	.79	.79	.79	.79
Coffee (Maxwell House)	1.31	1.33*	1.39*	1.44*	1.53*
Coke	1.60	1.59	1.59	1.67	1.71
Tomato sauce (Hunt's)	.37	.37	.37	.37	.37
Peas, frozen	.30	.33	.35	.34	.41
Tuna (Star-Kist)	.63	.63*	.63	.66*	.63*
Subtotal for Processed foods	$7.25	$7.40	$7.57	$7.77	$7.90

Fig. 6.2 Sample chart of grocery items and prices.

Name of Item	A&P Elm Street	Giant	A&P Rt. 353	Acme Walnut Street	Joe's Deli
Bread, Arnold	.59	.60	.59	.61	.64
Corn flakes, Kellogg's	.67	.69*	.69	.69	.67
Cookies, Oreos	1.09	1.09	1.09	1.09	1.09
Spaghetti,Muellers	.53	.53	.53	.53	.53
Flour, Pillsbury	1.88	1.91	1.89	1.91	1.89
Sugar	2.75	2.80	2.79	2.79	2.88
Crackers, Ritz	.69	.69	.69	.69	.69
Subtotal for bakery,cereals, and staples	$8.20	$8.31	$8.27	$8.31	$8.39
Detergent, Tide	.59*	.59	.59*	.63	.65
Soap, Dial	.40	.40	.40	.40	.40
Alum.Foil, Reynolds	.81*	.84	.79*	.81	.81
Paper towels, Scott	.55	.56	.55	.59	.59
Dishwashing liquid, Joy	.86	.86	.85	.89	.91
Subtotal for Nonfoods	$3.21	$3.25	$3.18	$3.32	$3.36
Total	$33.49	$33.66	$34.27	$34.83	$36.44
Adjusted total***	$33.24	$33.50	$34.19	$34.80	$36.44
Percentage higher		0.8%	2.9%	4.7%	9.6%

☐   Cheapest subtotals
*   Cheaper brands also available
**   "Specials"
***   Totals are adjusted to account for lower prices
      available if you buy the item in a larger quantity
      than our survey called for (34¢ a piece, but 3/$1.00)

The following items listed in the chart were on sale when
the pricing survey was done:

Name of store	Item	Duration of sale	Regular price

Fig. 6.2 *Continued*

Mark with an asterisk each item that is available in a cheaper name or house brand. Mark with two asterisks items on special.

```
                                    FOR IMMEDIATE RELEASE
                                    FOR FURTHER INFORMATION
                                    CONTACT: John Doe
                                             382-5663
```

```
     MidPIRG DISCOVERS 9.6% DIFFERENCE IN LOCAL FOOD PRICES
```

MidPIRG announced today that food prices vary by up to 9.6%

in the Mid City area. A recent survey conducted by MidPIRG reveals

that the A&P on Elm Street is the lowest priced market of the

stores surveyed in the area.

The average person in the U.S. spends 17% of his or her overall

budget on food. "By shopping wisely, Mid City residents could

reduce their food bills by up to 10%," said John Doe of MidPIRG,

"and we plan to make sure they know which stores have the lowest

prices by repeating our survey every three weeks."

In the 1/2 mile between the Elm Street A&P and Joe's Deli,

consumers could lose $3.20. The Elm Street A&P charges $33.24

for the 40 staple items chosen for comparison, while at Joe's, the

same 40 items cost $36.14.

The A&P on Elm Street charges the least for fresh produce,

processed foods, and bakery, cereals and staples as well as being

the least expensive store overall. Meats, poultry, and fish

are cheapest at the Giant on Rt. #1, while non-food household items

cost least at the A&P on Rt. #353. The Walnut Street Acme charges the

least for dairy products.

Fig. 6.3   Sample press release.

Release the results of your market basket survey to the press using as a model the Sample Press Release in Fig. 6.3. Attach to the release: a sample list of stores surveyed, their total market basket price and the percentage by which their price was higher than that of the lowest priced store, and your complete pricing chart.

Follow-up surveys should be conducted approximately every three weeks thereafter to provide regular and consistent analysis of food prices in the area. If you don't have the resources for follow-up surveys, try to interest a newspaper or television station in doing them on a regular basis.

CHAPTER 7

fresh food ? it's up to you

INTRODUCTION

It has happened to every consumer on more than one occasion: in the middle of preparing a meal with recently purchased food, a second whiff or look tells you that the product has spoiled and cannot be used. Even if the store refunds the price of the product, it cannot compensate for lost time, irritation, and the inconvenience of being unable to use the product as planned. The seriousness of this problem becomes even more apparent when one considers that for every spoiled or stale product bought, dozens more are purchased that, although not yet spoiled, are too old to offer much nutritional value.

In most stores, consumers find it impossible to determine the freshness of foods before purchasing them because they are systematically denied information about product shelf-life that manufacturers and retailers know. All of the thousands of packaged food products sold in grocery stores are marked with a code date that indicates where the product was manufactured or packed and when it should be removed from the shelves. But each manufacturer marks this information differently and in such a way that it cannot be interpreted by shoppers. The following code data illustrates the problem: D271 (Armour canned meat products), 1175K (Beechnut Baby Foods) and 4B27 (Ann Page products) all mean April 27, 1971. However, one indicates the expiration date and the others, the date of manufacture.

National Consumers United (NCU), a Chicago-based consumer organization, published a booklet in 1971 explaining how to translate many of the hundreds of code dates used by manufacturers. Along with other consumer groups and newspaper reporters across the country, NCU investigated grocery stores and found products still on the shelves that should have been removed days, months, and even *years* before!

As a result of studies like those of NCU, consumers have begun to demand easily understandable information about food freshness. The name given to this marking system is "open dating." Open dating is merely a translation of code dates into dates that can be understood by shoppers—dates that indicate the final day on which a product ought to be sold or used.

Many supermarket chains have responded to consumer demands by voluntarily including open dates on a few products. (See Fig. 7.1.) Some state laws make open dating of certain products mandatory (see Resource 7.1). These are encouraging steps, but they do not solve the problem.

Using this project guide, you can inform other consumers about the usefulness of open dating and support legislation requiring clear, intelligent, and uniform open dates on all perishable and semiperishable food products.

UNDERSTANDING OPEN DATING

The open dates required by law or used voluntarily by stores provide one or more of the following types of information:

a) Manufacturer date—the date the product was manufactured or processed.

b) Packing date—the date the product was finally packaged for retail sale.

c) Shelf display date—the date marked by a retailer to indicate when an item was put on display. The purpose of this date is to aid in proper stock rotation.

d) Freshness date—the last date which the processor estimates the product will retain original freshness or peak quality. It may be entirely usable for a longer period.

e) Pull date or sell by date—the recommended last date for retail sale. This period is usually determined by the processor and allows a reasonable time for home storage after the pull date. Products are to be removed from shelves after this date.

f) Expiration date or durability date—the last date the product can be expected to perform as in a manner equal to consumer expectations. Will be accompanied by a phrase such as "For best results use by. . . ."

Not only does this plethora of definitions make open dating confusing to consumers, but some open dates are not helpful in determining how long a product can be used. Of the six types of dates, three—the date of manufacture, packing date, and shelf display date—are virtually useless to consumers unless they memorize the shelf life of products, an almost impossible job. The other dates—pull, sell by, freshness and expiration dates—are helpful shopper guides *if* stores clarify what the dates mean.

State legislation should mandate the adoption of a uniform open dating system in all stores and initiate a program of consumer education about the meaning of the dates. (See open-dating regulation for the City of New York, Resource 7.1.)

NATIONAL ASSOCIATION OF FOOD CHAINS
OPEN DATING SURVEY—JULY 1972

Acme Markets, Inc.
Albertson's, Inc. (Idaho)
Alpha Beta Acme Markets
Benner Tea Company
The Bohack Corporation
Brockton Public Markets, Inc.
Buttrey Foods (Mont.)
Capitol Super Markets
Colonial Stores, Inc.
Consumers Supermarket (D.C.)
Daitch Crystal Dairies, Inc.
Delchamps, Inc. (Ala.)
Dillon Stores
Dominick's Finer Foods, Inc.
Eagle Food Centers (Ill.)
Eisner Food Stores
S.M. Flickinger Co., Inc.
First National Stores, Inc.
Food Fair Stores, Inc.
Friedman's Super
Furr's, Inc.
Giant Food, Inc. (Md.)
Giant Food Stores, Inc. (Pa.)
Godfrey Company
Golup Coop.
Good Deal Supermarkets
The Grand Union Company
The Great A & P Tea Co., Inc.
Hillman's, Inc.
Hinky Dinky Super Markets
Highes Markets (Calif.)

Iandoli Markets
Jewel Food Stores
Kings Supermarkets, Inc.
The Kroger Company
Louis Stores, Inc.
Lucky Stores, Inc.
Marsh Supermarkets, Inc.
Meijer, Inc.
National Food Dist. Co.
National Tea Company
The Oshawa Group, Ltd., (Canada)
P & C Food Markets
Penn Fruit Company
Piedmont Grocery
Quality Markets, Inc.
Ralphs Grocery Company
Red Owl Stores, Inc. (Minn.)
Safeway Stores, Inc.
Schnuck Markets, Inc.
Sloans
Smiths Management Corp.
Star Markets (Mass.)
Star Supermarkets, Inc., (N.Y.)
The Stop & Shop Companies, Inc.
Sunflower Food Stores
Supermarkets General Corporation
Thorofare Markets, Inc.
Tradewell Stores, Inc.
Wakefern Food Corporation
J. Weingarten, Inc.
Winn-Dixie Stores, Inc.

Fig. 7.1 Listed are 62 food chains and co-ops which have adopted or are in the process of adopting major open-dating programs. Locations of home offices are in parentheses.

SUPPORT FOR OPEN DATING

Studies have shown the extent to which shoppers buy foods that spoil or become stale prematurely and that open dating can ameliorate the problem. An extensive survey conducted in several cities during 1971 by the United States Department of Agriculture and the Consumer Research Institute revealed that 28 percent of the shoppers had, within the two weeks prior to the surveys, purchased one or more items that had spoiled or gone stale before use. In almost half of those cases, spoilage was noticed on the day of purchase.[1]

These surveys were followed by in-store controlled experiments held in 1972 in Ohio supermarkets. Shoppers were polled before and after the stores marked certain perishable and semiperishable foods with a pull date. The reported purchase of spoiled or stale food decreased from 19.4 percent to 9.9 percent.[2] With mandatory and uniform open dating in all stores, the percentage would drop even further.

Both consumers and representatives of the retail food industry support open dating. A nationwide survey of 250,000 shoppers conducted in 1971 reported that 89 percent favored an easy to understand dating system.[3] The trade journal *Chain Store Age* conducted a survey of industry employees in which close to half of those replying called open dating "the single most important [consumer] service," and 95 percent listed open dating as the consumer service "most useful" to stores.[4] The Vice-President of Accounting and Date Processing of Safeway Stores has this answer for critics who claim open dating costs are so high as to push up food prices: "Basically, there are no significantly greater costs inherent in open dating as compared to any other kind of dating system. All producers of perishable foods must date their products in one way or another anyway. It is in the conversion from coded dates to open dates that some costs may arise. Open dating is an aid to store personnel that clearly pays for itself."[5]

Currently, neither laws nor agency regulations mandate open dating at the federal level. However, the United States Department of Agriculture, which regulates the inspection and packaging of meat and poultry products, requires those producers and manufacturers who voluntarily implement open dating to include an explanatory statement on the container about the type of date used. But the regulation applies only to USDA inspected meats and poultry; that is, meat and poultry sold in the same packaging in which it was inspected. Since most meat is recut and repackaged by retailers, the impact of the regulations is severely limited. Any package with a USDA seal falls under this voluntary regulation, such as frozen poultry, prepackaged luncheon meats, and canned meat products. The USDA regulation appears in Resource 7.2.

In March, 1977, a bill introduced in the United States House of Representative HR 4642 which amends the Food, Drug, and Cosmetic Act and the Fair Packaging and Labeling act to require a "sell date" or a "use by" date as well as a statement about the necessary storage conditions on all packaged foods that the Secretary of the Department of Health, Education, and Welfare determines shall fall under this authority. That bill has not yet been passed, but if such a law is passed by both houses without being weakened, there will be no need for legislation at the state level. Should this be the case, it will be important for consumers to survey area stores to see if all manufacturers are in compliance with the federal law.

SURVEY TO USE IN AREAS WITH MANDATORY OPEN DATING

Contact the State Attorney General's office, or Mayor's office, and request a copy of the open dating state legislation or city ordinance, and find out what agency is responsible for enforcing the law. Analyze the law carefully and write all the requirements into a checklist for surveyors, including such points as: products to be dated;

OPEN DATING SAFETY CHECKLIST

STATE, COUNTY OR CITY REQUIREMENTS

Product (specified by state regs.)	Type of date required (top, bottom, etc.)	Stamp Location required (top, bottom, etc.)	Explanatory phrases required

Fig. 7.2 Open-dating safety checklist: state, county, or city requirements.

the type of open date to be used; the manner in which, and where, it is to be stamped on each product; and any explanatory phrases that are to be used. See Fig. 7.2 for a sample checklist.

Then draw up a form like the one in Fig. 7.3 to be used in recording violations. Surveyors should review each product covered by the law for points on the checklist and at the same time look for products that are still on the shelves after a "pull" date or "sell by" date. When compiling the data from these forms, pay special attention to the number of products that remained on the shelves past the "pull" or "sell by" dates. Make this information public, bring it to the attention of the government agency responsible for enforcing the law, and request that action be taken.

Compare the law regulation or ordinance for your state, city, or county with others, using the chart in Resource 7.2 and with the open-dating law in Resource 7.1. If

OPEN DATING VIOLATION FORM

Name and address of store _____

_____

Name of store manager _____

Surveyor's name, address and phone _____

_____

Date and time of survey _____   _____

_____

Products					
Sell by/ pull by dates on packages (list only dates of products that should have been pulled from shelves)					
Date checked					
Number of days over- due to be removed from shelves					
Date in correct place on pack- age and legible?	yes				
	no				
Explanatory phrases (If no, explain on back of form.)	yes				
	no				

Fig. 7.3 Open-dating violation form.

your law does not cover all perishable and semiperishable foods or has insufficient enforcement procedures, then strengthening of the law is called for. Consider surveying shoppers for their views about the usefulness and efficiency of the existing statute and using that data, support a revised statute that will include more food products, possibly a clearer type of open date, and stringent fines for violations. Shoppers can be asked if they understand the open dates, whether the dates are prominently displayed on products, and whether the store adequately explains the method used.

If your survey results indicate strong shopper support for changes in the open dating law or ordinance, write up the survey results along with your analysis of the existing law. Contact the original sponsors of that law, discuss the problems encountered in passing the legislation, and ask for any suggestions and help they can offer with regard to revising the law. Review original testimony and hearing reports. Send for copies of open dating statutes from states with the type of law you wish to promote before drafting your legislation. Try to interest a legislator in proposing more stringent amendments to the law and refer to Chapter 12 for guidelines about lobbying for a new bill.

SURVEY TO USE IN AREAS
WITHOUT OPEN DATING ORDINANCES

It will be important to determine whether shoppers in your area support mandatory open dating, and the Shopper Questionnaire (Fig. 7.4) is designed to provide that information. Survey shoppers outside the store, being careful not to inconvenience those shoppers who do not wish to respond. Each interview will only take above five minutes to complete. Try to interview no fewer than 50 shoppers at each store. Survey results can be compiled on a Questionnaire Compilation Form (Fig. 7.5).

If some stores or products have voluntary open dating systems, they can be surveyed to determine whether food is left on the shelves after the "sell by," "pull by," or "expiration" dates. The Violation Form (Fig. 7.3) can be adapted easily for use by surveyors. Your results will probably show many cases of expired products for sale. For example, as a result of consumer complaints about spoiled dairy products, the South Carolina PIRG surveyed stores to see if dairy products were on the shelves past the manufacturers expiration dates. They reported that items from a few days overdue to six months overdue were found in 29 out of the 33 stores surveyed. In fact, one store had removed the expiration date stickers from expired merchandise but kept stickers intact on unexpired merchandise.

If surveyors have the time, they should consider checking manufacturers' code dates to determine whether the products should still be on store shelves. They can get the booklet which translates many code dates from National Consumers United, 1043A Chicago Avenue, Evanston, Illinois 60202.

This type of survey will most likely provide some very persuasive results. The data from these surveys, along with information in this chapter, can be used to support the passage of strong open dating legislation. Send the data to the United States House of Representatives Committee on Interstate and Foreign Commerce, Washington, D.C. 20515. That committee is currently considering the federal open-dating legislation discussed previously.

SHOPPER SURVEY QUESTIONNAIRE

Name and address of store_____

_____Open dating_____yes_____no

Name of Surveyor_____Date and time_____

1. Please think back over the past two weeks. Other than leftovers, has food you bought from this store spoiled or gone bad before you used it? yes_____ no_____

2. Please think back over the past two weeks. Other than leftovers, have you thrown away any food that might have still been good, but you thought you might have had for too long? yes_____ no_____

3. When you find that food you bought is spoiled in some way, what do you do about it?

     Ask for money back_____

     Ask for replacement_____

     Other_____

4. Does the store comply satisfactorily?* yes_____ no_____

5. A. Some grocery stores and food manufacturers have been putting a date on certain food products to tell the shopper how fresh they are. Have you noticed any such dates? yes____no____

   B. If "yes," on which types of products have you noticed a date and what do you think it means?

Product	What date means to shoppers	What date really means**
_____	_____	_____
_____	_____	_____
_____	_____	_____
_____	_____	_____

    * Data from questions 3 and 4 may show that shoppers find it inconvenient to return spoiled products, or that stores do not always replace or refund money for spoiled items.

    ** To be filled in by surveyor after observing and asking store manager.

6. When items are marked with a date, do you sometimes sort through packages looking for the freshest item? yes_____ no_____

7. There are various dates that a store could put on packages. From the list below, choose which you think would be <u>most</u> helpful. (Check one only)

    a. The date the product was made or picked_____

    b. The date the product was packaged or processed_____

    c. The date the product was placed on the shelf_____

    d. The last date on which the product should be sold_____

    e. The last date on which the product should be used_____

8. Has this store made any genuine effort to promote consumer understanding of open dating systems?
    yes_____ no_____ don't know_____

9. If "no," would you like such a program undertaken? yes___no____

10. Would you and your family benefit from passage of a law requiring that a uniform date, indicating the last date the product should be sold or used be put on all foods with a short product life? yes_____ no_____

             *   *   *   *

    If you are planning to conduct your survey over the telephone, this questionnaire can be modified easily. Remember to first identify yourself and your group, and to explain the purpose of your survey. Then ask to speak with the family member who does the majority of the shopping.

Fig. 7.4 Shopper survey questionnaire.

SHOPPER QUESTIONNAIRE COMPILATION FORM

Name of store_____

Address_____

Total number of shoppers interviewed_____

    1) Percentage of shoppers responding "yes" to question #1_____

    2) Percentage of shoppers responding "yes" to question #2_____

	Number	Percentage
3) Shoppers who asked for refund	_____	_____
Shoppers who asked for a replacement	_____	_____
4) Shoppers who received satisfactory response	_____	_____
5) Shoppers who noticed open dates	_____	_____

Product	Number & Percentage of shoppers who identified meaning of date correctly	
_____	_____	_____
_____	_____	_____
_____	_____	_____
_____	_____	_____

    6) Percentage of shoppers responding "yes" to question 6_____

    7) Shoppers response to what kind of date would be most helpful

Answers:			
	a)	_____	_____
	b)	_____	_____
	c)	_____	_____
	d)	_____	_____
	e)	_____	_____

	Number	Percentage
8) Shoppers responding "yes" to question 8	_____	_____
Shoppers responding "no" to question 8	_____	_____
Shoppers responding "don't know" to question 8	_____	_____
9) Shoppers responding "yes" to question 9	_____	_____

10) Percentage of shoppers responding "yes" to question 10 _____

Fig. 7.5 Shopper questionnaire compilation form.

Informing the public of your results is probably the single most beneficial follow-up action. Write a succinct news release which identifies your group, when and where the survey was conducted, the survey results, and any proposed action or legislation, using as a model the release in Fig. 7.6.

FOR IMMEDIATE RELEASE   CONTACT: SHIRLI AXELROD
                                                 (203)527-7191

STUDY SHOWS CONSUMERS LACK FOOD FRESHNESS INFO

Claiming that food stores in Connecticut are not providing consumers adequate information to avoid unnecessary food spoilage, the
Connecticut Citizen Action Group (CCAG) today called for legislation
to require "pull dates"to be stamped on perishable foods sold in
Connecticut supermarkets. The "pull date" would tell shoppers and
store employees when foods should no longer be sold as fresh produce.

CCAG spokeswoman Shirli Axelrod cited the results of a statewide
survey by the Connecticut Citizen Research Group (CCRG), an offshoot
of CCAG, that showed most of Connecticut's major food stores put dates
on less than half the perishable foods that they sell. "It's frustrating in these times of exorbitant food prices for shoppers to discover that food they bought only two days ago has spoiled by the time
they're ready to use it," Axelrod said. "Also, some foods which have
been on the shelf too long lose their nutritional value, so that consumers are buying worthless food for high prices," she added.

CCRG's survey showed that three of the five chains, A&P, Shop-
Rite, and Food Mart, had dates marked on half or less of the products
surveyed. Stop and Shop dated 64% of its products and Finast dated
85% of the foods surveyed.

CCRG's survey checked at least 15% of the retail outlets for
each of the five major food chains in Connecticut. CCRG staffers
and volunteers checked about 30 food items in each supermarket to
determine whether foods were stamped with dates and whether the
date was understandable. Meats, dairy products, baked goods, frozen foods, and fruits and vegetables were checked.

162

Axelrod said that even when stores date perishable foods, shoppers can be thrown into confusion. "The meaning of the dates isn't clear. Does the date represent when the food was packaged, or when it should be used by? Many stores do not provide this information with the date stamped on the package," Axelrod said. "It becomes a frustrating and expensive guessing game." She added that the CCRG survey showed that substantial numbers of dated food products had unclear labels.

According to Axelrod, "The average family of four will spend nearly $2500 on groceries this year. They can't afford to gamble that their food is fresh. They need to know for sure." She argued, "The food industry itself initiated food dating to cut its own costs. But they often put the dates in codes unknown to customers or, as CCRG's survey showed, don't explain what the date means." Axelrod noted that Connecticut already requires open dating of some milk products to warn consumers.

Axelrod said that government agencies and food industry representatives agree that the cost of an open dating system is negligible and that minor costs are more than offset by reduced losses from returns of stale and spoiled goods by disgruntled customers. She noted that New York City, Washington, and Florida already require dating of some perishable food products. Axelrod added that foods could be sold after the "pull date", so long as they were clearly marked and separated from fresher products. "We've spoken with people in the food industry who agree that good marketing techniques and regular turnover can minimize wasting food."

The proposed open dating legislation, along with other nutrition and food shopping issues, will be considered by the state legislation's General Law Committee in a public hearing at the State Capitol on Thursday, March 27, at 9 a.m.

CONNECTICUT CITIZEN
ACTION GROUP

Fig. 7.6 Model news release.

BOX G, HARTFORD, CONNECTICUT 06106
OFFICES: 130 WASHINGTON ST., HARTFORD, CONN.
PHONE 203/527-7191

BIBLIOGRAPHY

A study of consumer reaction to unit pricing and open dating in metropolitan Washington, D.C. Consumer Research Institute, Inc., Washington, D.C., July, 1971.

Cost aspects of open dating and unit pricing. N.V. Lawson, Vice President of Accounting and Data Processing, Safeway Stores, Inc., Speech to the 21st National Association of Food Chains Controllers' Conference, San Francisco, California, May 23–26, 1971.

Food dating: shoppers' reactions and the impact on retail foodstores. United States Department of Agriculture, Economic Research Service, Market Research Report #984, Washington, D.C., January, 1973.

Food labeling goals, shortcomings and proposed changes. General Accounting Office, Report to Congress, January 29, 1975.

Issue brief: open dating. Grocery Manufacturers of America, Washington, D.C., 1973.

CHAPTER 8.

unit pricing – finding the "best buys" easily

INTRODUCTION

Every day thousands of unaware American consumers are deceived and misled by the variety of package sizes filling supermarket shelves. What ought to be a simple choice of detergent, for example, becomes a mathematical quiz with brands available in different sized boxes—16, 20, or 30 ounces—at different prices—.89 cents, $1.39, $1.29 or $1.76. Even the most diligent shopper cannot make a comparative choice on the basis of price when faced with this baffling selection.

In a New York City Department of Consumer Affairs survey, conducted in 1969, shoppers failed to pick the cheapest product 40 to 50 percent of the time, thereby losing ten cents out of every dollar spent!

Unit pricing cuts through the confusion, by indicating the cost per unit of weight or measure—per ounce, pound, pint, or quart. Syndicated columnist Sylvia Porter calls unit pricing "the food shopper's biggest money-saving weapon" and "virtually the sole means of comparing supermarket costs." According to the New York City Department of Consumer Affairs study, unit pricing encourages retailers to stock even-sized packages and encourages manufacturers to eliminate confusing packaging.

Opponents of unit pricing charge that it emphasizes cost over quality and that it is difficult and expensive to implement, thereby making price increases necessary. But rebuttals to such claims can be found within the food industry itself. The following remarks were made by Mrs. Esther Peterson, when she served as Consumer Advisor to the President of Giant Food:

> Unit pricing has been a marvelous aid to Giant. It has given the store much better inventory control, and since unit pricing was adopted, pricing errors have dropped dramatically. . . . One of the complaints about unit pricing is that the consumer will overlook quality in pursuit of the cheapest product. This is not true. We find that customers are trying less expensive brands and then switching to them only if quality is comparable . . . and contrary to some industry nay-sayers and doom prophets, it has not raised either our costs or our prices.[1]

If grocery stores in your area are not required to provide unit pricing labels, you may want to survey shoppers to determine whether they find comparative price shopping more difficult in stores without unit pricing than in those with voluntary unit pricing systems. The data obtained from such a survey will be valuable in rallying consumer support for either state legislation or a city ordinance making unit pricing mandatory. Surveys of this type done throughout the country present conclusive evidence that without unit pricing, consumers cannot identify "best buys." The data used to demand mandatory unit pricing in your area should demonstrate consumer views in that same area.

In cities or states where unit pricing is mandatory, you can survey stores to determine whether they are complying with the law, and compare the law with those of other states to determine whether or not it needs revision.

SURVEY FOR AREAS WITHOUT MANDATORY UNIT PRICING

In this survey shoppers will be asked to try to determine which particular size and brand of certain products are the most economical regardless of quality, taste, size, and personal preference. Conduct the survey in stores with and without unit pricing systems so the data will show whether shoppers find it easier to shop comparatively with the aid of unit pricing. A list of grocery chains and co-ops with voluntary unit pricing is in Resource 8.1. In those stores surveyors can also check the unit pricing system for effectiveness. Refer to the checklist under Survey for Areas with Mandatory Unit Pricing for ideas about common deficiencies in unit pricing systems.

Survey data will be more persuasive if, at each store, at least ten products are surveyed and no fewer than ten shoppers are questioned about each product. The same products must be surveyed at each store, so choose products which are unit priced in those stores with such systems. It is also important that the products surveyed come in many package sizes and, in order to facilitate data compilation, are measured in ounces or pounds. The following list is recommended as a guide in choosing products:

Canned peas	Long grain white rice	Canned coffee	Detergents
Cold cereals	Peanut butter	Catsup	Dry milk
Fruit cocktail	Grape jelly	Canned ham	
Instant mashed potatoes	Cooking oil	White all-purpose flour	

Date

Manager's name and address
_____
_____

Dear _____ :

    Our group is concerned with consumer issues. We are
conducting a study of unit pricing in the area, and
would like to use your store as the basis for one of our
surveys. We would like to place __(two or four)__ interviewers within __(name of store)__ on __(date)__ . Our
surveyors will approach shoppers and ask them to choose
the cheapest brand of a certain product, regardless of
quality, taste, amount, and personal preference. The
shoppers' responses will be tabulated on Shoppers'
Answer Cards. The survey should take no more than (three
to six) hours.

    The results of this survey will help our group formu-
late a recommendation on the subject of unit pricing,
and whether such a system should be implemented on a
mandatory basis in the (name of city or state.). The
survey results will be made public, along with our
recommendations.

    We hope to gain your help and support in the project.
If you have any questions concerning our plans, please
call (surveyor's phone number). I will be in touch with
you within the next week.

                        Sincerely,

                        Project Director

enclosed: Sample Shoppers' Answer Card

Fig. 8.1 Suggested letter to store manager.

    It may not be possible to complete this survey without attracting the attention of
store managers. Since their reactions will vary, it is important to remember that the
store is private property, and that the manager has the right to tell nonshoppers to
leave. For this reason, some groups may choose to contact managers in advance and
inquire whether they will permit surveyors in their stores. A sample letter to be sent to
managers can be found in Fig. 8.1. If store managers refuse to cooperate, inform them

that many area stores are being surveyed, and their refusal will be made public when the survey results are released. If the store is part of a chain, inform the chain's public relations department about the manager's refusal to cooperate.

Interviewers should review project instructions together before beginning the shopper survey. Most shoppers are rushed, so the suggested survey has been designed to take very little of their time. If interviewers work in pairs, with one asking the questions and the other recording the data, four interviewers should be able to survey a store in about three hours.

Before questioning shoppers about a particular product, record, on the Product Pricing Form (Fig. 8.2), the size and price of each type of that product on the shelf. One interviewer can approach shoppers, explain the purpose of the survey, identify the group conducting the survey, and ask each shopper to identify the "best buy" (i.e., the cheapest product) on the shelf, regardless of brand, quality, personal preference, or amount. The second surveyor records shoppers' responses on the Shopper's Answer Card (Fig. 8.3). Question any shopper that passes by and, when ten or more have responded, move on to the next product to be surveyed.

Be careful not to block the aisle at any time or to interfere with the flow of traffic. Uncooperative shoppers should be thanked quickly and politely.

In order to successfully determine the effect of unit pricing, one person must compile the data using information from the Shopper's Answer Cards and the Product Pricing Form sections completed by surveyors. To determine the money lost by consumers surveyed in stores without unit pricing, refer to the simple procedure below and then compile a Data Compilation Form (Fig. 8.4).

Determining Money Lost

The *Unit Price* is the cost divided by measure (lb, qt, oz). The *Best Buy* is the item with the lowest unit price. The *Shopper's Choice* is the item that the shopper selected.

Step 1 Write the Unit Prices, using the same measures, for the Best Buy and the Shopper's Choice.

Example The *Best Buy* was 30 cents for a measure of 5 oz. The *Unit Price* of the *Best Buy* is 30 cents divided by 5 oz which = 6 cents per oz. The *Shopper's Choice* was $3.20 for a measure of one lb. Therefore the *Unit Price* of the *Shopper's Choice* is 320 cents divided by 16 oz which = 20 cents per oz.

Step 2 Take the difference between the *Unit Price of the Best Buy* and the *Unit Price of the Shopper's Choice.*

Example (20 cents per oz) − (6 cents per oz) = 14 cents per oz.

Step 3 Multiply this number, in our example 14 cents per oz, times the measure of the *Shopper's Choice*, in this case 16 oz.

Example (14 cents per oz) × (16 oz) = $2.24. This is the money the shopper lost by choosing the more expensive product.

Money Lost should be determined for each item included in the survey and recorded on the Product Pricing Form for each store. The next step is to review each

Product Pricing Form

Name of store __*Joe and Doug's*__

Address __*133 C Street., S. E.*__

Date and Time of Interview __*4/12/77*__   __*3:45 P. M.*__

Names of Surveyors __*John Boyd and Sam Geller*__

Name of Store Manager __*Roger McNeal*__

Product	Size	Price	Unit Price	Money Lost
Cut green beans *Del Monte*	*8 oz.*	*$ .24*	*3.0¢ per.oz.*	*$ .06*
whole green beans *Mudds*	*16 oz.*	*$ .42*	*2.6¢*	*best buy*
Cut green beans *Andersons*	*16 oz.*	*$ .46*	*2.9¢*	*$ .04*
whole green beans *Andersons*	*16 oz.*	*$ .49*	*3.0¢*	*$ .07*
French green beans *Kovens*	*16 oz.*	*$ .48*	*3.0¢*	*$ .06*

Note: Surveyors should bring one copy of the Product
Pricing Form to the store for each product to be priced.
Before asking shoppers to pick "best buy" of the product,
fill this form in with the brand name, each size available
and price of each. Unit Price and Money Lost will be
filled in later by the person responsible for data compilation. The Unit Price is the cost of the item divided
by the number of ounces. The best buy is the item with
the lowest unit price. Information on how to compute
Money Lost is in the text. Remember to use the same products while surveying in each store.

Fig. 8.2 Completed product pricing form.

SAMPLE SHOPPER'S ANSWER CARD

Money lost_____

Product_____

Brand name chosen_____

Amount (ounces, pounds, etc.)_____

Cost_____

Date and time of survey_____

Names of surveyors_____

_____

_____

Name and address of store_____

_____

Does store have unit pricing system? yes_____ no_____

Fig. 8.3 Sample Shoppers' Answer Card.

Shopper's Answer Card and, noting the Shopper's Choice, fill in the Money Lost by the shopper. Tally the number of shoppers who choose the best buy in all stores with unit pricing and then for all stores without unit pricing. The last figure to calculate is the total Money Lost by shoppers in all stores with and without unit pricing.

Figure 8.5 shows a sample format for writing up the survey conclusion. Make your results public in a news release like the one issued by Oregon Student PIRG and included in Fig. 8.6.

SAMPLE COMPLETED DATA COMPILATION FORM

Name of Store___Jo and Doug's Mart_____

a. First Product -- Green Beans

1st shopper's choice   "best buy"

2nd shopper's choice   lost $.06

3rd shopper's choice   lost $.04

4th shopper's choice   lost $.06

5th shopper's choice   lost $.06

6th shopper's choice   "best buy"

7th shopper's choice   lost $.07

8th shopper's choice   lost $.04

9th shopper's choice   lost $.06

10th shopper's choice   lost $.07

b.20%___   of shoppers chose "best buy"

c.80%___   of the shoppers did not choose "best buy"

d. On the average, the error cost___$.06 an oz____

(Your form will include the above information for each product surveyed.)

Store figures, ____% of shoppers chose "best buy"

           ____% of shoppers did not choose "best
buy"

On the average, the error for all products priced cost

This figure is arrived at by adding the average error for each product (point d) and dividing by the number of products surveyed.

Fig. 8.4 Sample completed data compilation form.

SAMPLE STATEMENT OF CONCLUSIONS

Our group,_____, a nonprofit organization, has just completed a unit pricing survey in the area. We interviewed ____ shoppers at ____ grocery stores, (list them) from _____, _____, '77 to _____, _____, '77. Shoppers were asked to choose the cheapest brand of a certain product regardless of individual preferences.

From the data collected, we have concluded that the consumer is unable to pick the cheapest buy ____% of the time in those stores with unit pricing and ____% of the time at those stores without unit pricing. Furthermore, for all stores surveyed without unit pricing, the shoppers questioned lost a total _____ because they could not determine which items were the Best Buy.

We recognize that some shoppers choose more expensive products intentionally. However, we feel this data provides conclusive evidence of the need for unit pricing legislation and reform in this city/state_____.

Fig. 8.5   Sample statement of conclusions.

OSPIRG

FOR RELEASE: Monday, February 24, 1975, 9:00a.m.

For further information contact:

    Neil Robblee
        or
    Faith Ruffing
    OSPIRG, 408 S.W. Second Avenue
    Portland, Oregon 97204
    Telephone: (503) 222-9641

The Oregon Student Public Interest Research Group (OSPIRG) today released a report calling for mandatory unit pricing in Oregon supermarkets.

Detailing the results of a survey of 16 supermarkets in Portland and Eugene, the report claims "the pricing practices of many major supermarkets make price comparison a formidable task" for consumers.

The survey found that easy comparison of prices among brands and sizes was possible only five percent of the time. All the rest of the time the consumer must make "difficult mental calculations" to compare prices, the report stated.

The report also criticized voluntary unit

Fig. 8.6 Sample news release by Oregon Student PIRG.

173

pricing systems used by some supermarkets for having
"inaccurate or missing unit price stickers." As a result,
the report said, in more than half the instances checked
the shoppers were unable to use the unit price stickers.

"The average shopper can expect to save up to 10 percent by shopping with the aid of a unit pricing system,"
the report claims, because the consumer often unwittingly
buys more expensive products if unit pricing is not
available.

In addition, the report says that unit pricing would
help consumers find gross price disparities. The report
cited instances where small packages cost "more than
twice as much per unit" than larger packages of the same
commodity.

The surveyors also found that five percent of the
time larger items cost more per unit than smaller sizes
of the same product.

Without unit pricing, the report stated "it is difficult or impossible for the average shopper to find out
exactly which smaller sizes cost grossly more per unit
than larger sizes and vice versa."

A bill requiring unit pricing in large chain stores,
H.B. 2086, has been introduced in the Oregon Legislature.

The report was authored by Tom McIntyre, a former PSU
student and by Faith Ruffing.

Fig. 8.6 *Continued*

SURVEY FOR AREAS WITH MANDATORY UNIT PRICING

If unit pricing is required by law the following survey indicates whether it is efficiently written and properly enforced. Resource 8.2 lists states and cities with unit pricing laws or ordinances.

Read the law or ordinance in order to determine the exact requirements. Survey stores to check compliance with the law or ordinance and compare violations to the following checklist of frequent consumer complaints about unit pricing systems:

1. There is no label for the item.
2. The label is inaccurate.
3. The labels include extraneous and confusing information.
4. The unit price is printed in type too small to be easily read. (A legible size should be specified by law. In New York City, for example, the unit price must at least be the size of pica type.)
5. The label is torn or otherwise illegible.
6. The label is blocked from view.
7. The label is not near the item.

Surveyors can determine all points, except point 2, by observation. To determine point 2, divide the current price of the item by the unit of weight. Record all the data on a survey form like the one in Fig. 8.7.

If the survey results show stores have not complied with the unit pricing law or ordinance, demand that the government agency responsible for enforcement implement an aggressive compliance campaign. At the state level, the Department of Weights and Measures may be the agency with this authority. On a county or city level, check with the Consumer Protection Office.

Managers of stores and presidents of chains where unit pricing was not satisfactorily implemented should be notified, by registered or certified letters, of the survey results and requested to respond with their plans to rectify the situation. Inform them that the survey data was sent to the appropriate government agency. Make the survey results public in a news release.

Compare the law or ordinance for your area with the Model State Unit Pricing Law developed by the National Conference on Weights and Measures (Resource 8.3), and with the Unit Pricing Ordinance for New York City (Resource 8.4.) If the law is inadequate, consider conducting the Shoppers' Survey to provide data encouraging change. Then begin a campaign to have the law strengthened, referring to Chapter 12 for a guide to lobby efforts.

SURVEY FORM FOR STORES WITH UNIT PRICING

Store name_____

Address_____

Street_____

Area_____

What information is on the unit label?

| | Whole Green Beans | | | Cut Green Beans | | |
| | Smiths | | Andersons | | Smiths | | Andersons |
	16 oz	Other	16 oz	Other	8. oz	Other	16 oz	Other
Selling price on package								
Unit price								
Selling price								
Pack- aging size								

Is the label...

Not posted?							
Out of date?							
Not near item?							
Torn?							
Blocked?							
Confusing?							

Fig. 8.7 Survey form for stores with unit pricing.

BIBLIOGRAPHY

A study of consumer reaction to unit pricing and open dating in metropolitan Washington, D.C. Consumer Research Institute, Washington, D.C., July, 1971.

Cagle, Joseph S. 1970. What cost dual pricing? *Progressive Grocer,* November.

Cost of unit pricing in grocery stores. Consumer Research Institute, Inc., Washington, D.C. July, 1971.

Food labeling: goals, shortcomings, and proposed changes. General Accounting Office, Report to Congress, January 27, 1973.

Ross, Donald K. 1973. *A public citizen's action manual.* New York: Grossman.

Unit prices. *New Republic,* New York, New York, July 5, 1969.

CHAPTER 9

advertised specials: promotional gimmick or a real break for the consumer?

INTRODUCTION

In order to attract customers, food stores often advertise "specials," items offered at lower prices for a given period of time. More and more shoppers rely on, and plan their shopping around, these special sales. The promotion of advertised specials is a legitimate practice and one that benefits consumers if the specials are in fact available at the prices advertised. But that is not always the case.

In 1967, the Federal Trade Commission (FTC) responded to consumer complaints about advertised specials and directed its staff to investigate the pricing practices of retail food chain stores. During 1967-1969, survey teams in Washington, D.C., Baltimore, and San Francisco conducted 500 pricing surveys at 147 stores. Those investigations and subsequent hearings revealed widespread unavailability and overpricing of advertised specials. In Washington, D.C., for example, "most of the largest chains had average unavailability plus overpricing (charge more than advertised price) rates ranging between 21 percent and 26 percent."[1]

In July, 1971, the FTC promulgated the Retail Food Store Advertising and Marketing Practices Regulation which sets requirements regarding the availability of advertised specials. Stores that do not comply with the regulation are guilty of unfair methods of competition and unfair or deceptive acts or practices. However, stores across the country continue to mislead consumers by failing to have advertised specials in stock or overcharging for them. The New York PIRG surveyed Syracuse supermarkets in 1974 and reported that in two major chain stores, 13 percent and 43 percent of advertised specials were unavailable or overpriced! A 1975 survey of Durham supermarkets by the North Carolina PIRG showed equally disturbing records; in the twelve stores surveyed, an average 17 percent of advertised specials, or one out of every six advertised items, were unavailable or mispriced. Individual stores' unavailability and mispricing records ranged from 5.1 percent to 40.6 percent. Both groups notified the FTC about the violations, requesting that action be taken against violators and made their survey results public.

This project provides a guide for consumers to use in monitoring grocery store compliance with the FTC regulation, and suggests measures to ensure that corrective action is taken against violators.

Federal Trade Commission Regulation

The FTC regulation (reprinted in Resource 9.1) states that retail food stores are guilty of unfair methods of competition and unfair or deceptive acts or practices if they do not meet the following requirements regarding the availability of advertised specials:

1. Stores that have advertised certain products for sale at a stated price and for a stated period of time, *must* have those products *in stock, conspicuously and readily available to customers at, or below, the advertised price during the effective period of the advertisement.*

2. If the products are not *readily available, clear and adequate notice* must be provided stating that the items are in stock at the sale price and may be *obtained upon request.*

3. The product must have been *ordered in adequate time for delivery and in quantities sufficient to meet reasonably anticipated demands.*

4. There must be *clear and conspicuous disclosure in all such advertisements as to all exceptions and/or limitations or restrictions* with respect to stores, product availability, or prices.

   General disclaimers in advertising relating to product availability are not acceptable, such as: "Not all items at all stores," or "Available at most stores." *Specific, clear, and conspicuous disclaimers* in ads relating to product availabilty only in stores possessing particular facilities are allowed. An example is, "Available only at stores featuring delicatessen departments."

5. Many stores have what they call a *"raincheck"* policy. When advertised items are not available, the customers are given coupons entitling them to buy the product at a later date at the advertised price. The FTC has ruled that the existence of *such a policy,* in and of itself, is not *considered adequate compliance* with the regulation. That is, if rainchecks are offered as a *substitute* for compliance, when there is no indication that the product was ordered in sufficient number to meet reasonably anticipated demands, the store is still in violation of the regulation. The reasoning behind this is that customers come into the store to buy the special at the time it was advertised and probably will do other shopping at that time in that store.

   The FTC considers the *existence of a "raincheck"* policy to be *relevant in determining the retailer's "good faith"* and an attempt at compliance in the following situations:

   a) If products *were ordered* in adequate time and in sufficient quantity but were *not delivered due to circumstances beyond the advertiser's control;*

   b) If products were advertised but not made available at the sale price for *reasons beyond the advertiser's control,* e.g., a mistake in the ad made by the newspaper, or unexpectedly high demand depleting inventory quickly.

6. Under the regulation, retailers are not required to keep adequate records to support claims that advertised products:

   a) were ordered in sufficient time and numbers and delivered in sufficient numbers, but were depleted quickly due to unexpectedly high demand;

   b) were not delivered due to circumstances beyond the store's control or;

   c) were misadvertised by the newspaper. However, if such records are kept and support the claims of the retailers, they will be considered a defense against charges of violations, so it is in retailers' interests to keep such records.

   It is not necessary for surveyors to view store records before charging a store with unavailability and reporting them to the FTC. In investigating complaints, the FTC will review the records to see if they support a manager's claims.

HOW CAN CONSUMERS MONITOR STORES?

Getting Started

Check the local newspapers for one week to determine what day each store to be surveyed runs most of their advertisements for specials, and what days the specials first become available. Such ads are very specific and it is important to know exactly what is being advertised. The Exercise for Surveyors and Correct Answers to the Exercise (Resources 9.2a and 9.2b, respectively) are designed to help you analyze the ads. Surveyors should meet to review the following instructions and Resources 9.2a and 9.2b.

At that time choose a project coordinator and decide what day surveyors will clip the ads for the stores they will investigate, the day the surveying will be done, and the number of specials you will survey. Survey all stores on the same day—the first or the last day that the specials are to be available. Many stores delay making specials available or claim to have run out of them before the last day, but these practices are violations of the FTC regulation except in the special circumstances mentioned in the discussion about the regulation. If possible, plan to survey all the items that are advertised as specials. If that is not feasible, the same percentage of advertised items should be surveyed in every store.

Beware! Some items may be included in the ads that are not really "specials." After investigating the advertising practices of Portland supermarkets, the Oregon PIRG charged six chains with "inaccurate, ambiguous, or misleading" advertising of specials. Many prices called, or implied to be, specials in the ads had regular prices or were actually more expensive than usual! The group sent their report to the FTC and the Consumer Protection Division of the Attorney General's Office, recommending that stores be required to include regular prices in all sale advertisements and in-store signs.

After clipping all the ads for stores to be surveyed, read them carefully and note those that may not be specials. If you find during the survey that they are not sale items, include that information in your survey report. Review the FTC regulation and determine whether the ads meet the requirements. If they do not, make a note to that effect on the back of the Store Survey Form in Fig. 9.1. Then fill in rows 1, 2, and 3 on the Survey Form and attach all the ads to it.

At the Store

Surveyors should bring the Survey Form, the ads, and the Exercise for Surveyors to the store with them to avoid any confusion and to ensure that the data are recorded correctly. It is a good idea to have all surveyors purchase one of the sale items before beginning the survey so they will be treated like any other customer.

Sometimes advertised items are not on display for sale and no notice to request the item is posted. In this situation surveyors should ask a store employee to point out where the item(s) are displayed for sale. If the store representative is unable to do so, surveyors will mark rows 4 and 6 of the Survey Form. If substitution is offered, rows 4 and 6 are still checked, but note the offer on the back of the Survey Form.

Some ads or in-store signs indicate that the item is "available on request," and in these cases surveyors will mark row 5 of the Survey Form. To determine whether this is

Store Survey Form

Name of store_____

Address of store_____

Name of surveyor_____

Date of survey_____ Time arrived_____

Time departed_____ Store manager_____

Were copies of newspaper ads conspicuously posted in the store? ___ yes ___ no
Were copies of newspaper ads posted at or near the check-out counter? ___ yes ___ no
Does the store have a raincheck policy? (ask manager) ___ yes ___ no
Does the store have a substitution policy? ___ yes ___ no

Description and brand name of item				
size and/or amount				
advertised price (note conditional offers)				
Not on display for sale and no notice to request provided				
Not on display; but notice to request provided				
Not available on request				
Price(s) marked on unit(s)				
Posted price				
(if price of items higher than advertised price) number of items checked number overpriced				

Fig. 9.1 Store survey form.

true, ask a store representative to furnish at least one unit of the item. If the representative fails to do so, mark row 6 on the Survey Form. An item can be considered "furnished on request" if it is presented before the surveyor completes the survey. As in the example above, if a substitution is offered, simply note it on the back of the Survey Form.

Inspect several items at the front of the display to determine the price and mark it on the Survey Form. When a unit is marked with two or more prices, record the lower price. If units of the same item are marked with different prices, record all prices in row 7, and in row 9 record the number of items checked and the number overpriced. Also look for signs posted for the special and record the sign price in row 8. If more than one sign appears for an item or if the sign is not near the displayed product, note these facts on the back of the Survey Form.

Purchase all or a certain percentage of the items that were overpriced, since some stores will claim, and the FTC accepts as a defense, that checkout clerks know the advertised prices and charge only those prices even when the items are incorrectly marked. If the costs of purchasing all overpriced items are prohibitive for surveyors, split the purchase costs evenly between surveyors, pool the items, and distribute them among surveyors. Otherwise, before surveying begins decide what percentage of overpriced items surveyors will purchase and purchase the same percentage of items at each store. Receipts should be attached to the back of the Purchase Form (Fig. 9.2).

If the store has anything but a perfect record ask to speak to the manager. Tell the manager: (1) that you could not find certain items or a notice as to where they could be obtained and (2) that certain items were marked with or posted at a price higher than that advertised. If the manager thinks you are incorrect, ask to be shown items or prices.

Return to the store a half an hour after speaking to the manager and check to see if the incorrectly priced items have been re-marked. If so, the store has still violated that section of the FTC regulation, but make a note on the back of the Survey Form.

ACTION TO TAKE AFTER COMPLETING THE SURVEY

Ask the surveyor to complete a Data Compilation Form (Fig. 9.3) as soon as possible by transferring information to it from the Survey Form. The project coordinator then reviews all Survey Forms and Data Compilation Forms before writing up the survey results.

Make the survey information public in a news release similar to the one in Fig. 9.4 issued by the North Carolina PIRG. The release can include the data on all stores and chains, stores where more than five percent of advertised items were unavailable and/or overpriced, or on stores with the highest percentages of unavailable and overpriced items. If the release does not include the survey results from all stores, attach a chart with that information.

Send survey results to store managers and chain presidents via registered or certified letter at the same time they are released to the press. Include a cover letter outlining the data collected, the purpose of the survey, and how the survey was conducted. Request a response describing what action will be taken to correct the abuses indicated in the survey.

PURCHASE FORM

Name of chain store_____ Store No.____

Address of store_____

Date_____ Time form III completed_____

Name of surveyor_____

No. of Items	1 Description and brand name of item	2 Size and/ or amount	3 Advertised price (note conditional offer)	4 Price(s) marked on unit(s)

Attach below register tape, initialed, dated, and noted with identity of item(s) purchased by item number.

Fig. 9.2 Purchase form.

DATA COMPILATION FORM

Name of store/ chain--store number & address	Number of items surveyed	Number of items Unavailable/ Overpriced	Percentage of items Unavailable/ Overpriced
		u/o	u/o

Fig. 9.3 Data compilation form.

NC PUBLIC INTEREST RESEARCH GROUP

STATE OFFICE

704 A Ninth Street   (919) 286-2275
P. O. Box 2901
Durham, N.C. 27705

April 30, 1975
For further information, contact: Rick Kennedy, 379-5750
FOR IMMEDIATE RELEASE

NC PIRG STUDY REVEALS FOOD ADVERTISING DECEPTION

The UNC-G Chapter of the North Carolina Public Interest Research Group (NC PIRG) today releases the results of a six-week investigation into the availability of advertised food specials in the Greensboro area. The study found massive and widespread deception of the public in the advertising and marketing practices of retail chain food stores, and PIRG urged a full-scale investigation of the problem by the U.S. Federal Trade Commission.

Twelve retail chain food stores were surveyed in the period from February 22 through April 5, 1975. The principal findings were as follows:

1. Of the twelve stores surveyed, an average of 17% of the advertised specials were found to be unavailable or mispriced. In other words, one out of every six items listed as specials was not readily available as advertised at the supermarkets surveyed. A thirteenth store, the Food Town store at Golden Gate Center, refused to allow our surveyors to enter the store, and we have no reason to believe that the specials would have been any more available at the Food Town store.

2. Although one store was able to keep 98% of the specials available, the overall average for all stores was four times worse, with 8% unavailable specials.

3. Over 10% of the advertised specials were mispriced on an average, although some stores maintained a rate of 2-3%. The major source of mispricing errors was the overpricing of food specials, which accounted for 70% of all pricing mistakes. The clear impact of mispricing, then, was that consumers were overcharged in most cases.

"In addition to the continuing deception of the public through advertised specials," said Rick Kennedy, project coordinator,"our study indicates that the FTC regulation issued in 1971 has been ineffective in stopping this problem. In light of these conclusions, NC PIRG urges the following actions be taken: comprehensive efforts by Greensboro supermarkets to comply with the FTC rule begin immediately; a full-scale investigation by the FTC of Greensboro food store advertising practices; prompt action by the A&P Food Stores to correct the intolerable situation at their Walker Street store; and renewed hearings and investigation by the FTC for the purpose of revising and strengthening the current rule. We also call upon the N.C. Attorney General to take action to end the deceptive and unfair trade practices which we found under the power given him by N.C. General Statute 75.1."

Fig. 9.4 Sample news release from North Carolina PIRG.

Send survey data on all stores with an unavailability and/or overpricing rate of 2.5 percent or more to an FTC Regional Office (see Resource 9.3 for addresses) with a request that corrective action be taken. Also send copies to the Director, Bureau of Consumer Protection, FTC, Washington, D.C. 20580, the local or state equivalent of the FTC, and the Consumer Protection Division of the State Attorney General's Office.

Rerun the survey in a few months in all stores with unavailable or overpricing rates of 2.5 percent or more. You might also consider proposing or supporting state legislation similar to the FTC regulation. Call the clerk of the legislature for information about any such proposed legislation. The Connecticut Citizen Action Group (CCAG) supported a bill guaranteeing availability of advertised specials in the Connecticut General Assembly. Their testimony follows.

TESTIMONY OF CCAG ON HB 7162, AN ACT CONCERNING WARRANTIES OF ADVERTISED SPECIALS

CCAG also supports HB 7162, requiring retail grocers to have sufficient stock of advertised foods to meet public response. We agree that the conspicuous posting of such advertisements at cash registers, as provided in this bill, will further this endeavor. We also recommend that the Commissioner of Consumer Protection adopt regulations to give the current Retail Food Store Advertising and Marketing Practices requirements more teeth.

According to Public Act 73-615, the "Baby FTC" Act, concerning unfair trade practices, "all the rules, regulations, and decisions interpreting the Federal Trade Commission Act automatically are made the law of this state." In the interest of time, we will not enumerate the requirements regarding the availability of advertised specials. Nevertheless, we urge the DCP to be more aggressive in enforcing the regulation; and we ask the DCP to educate consumers about their rights in this important area.

At present, consumers are led to believe that stores are doing them a favor by issuing "rainchecks," coupons entitling them to buy the advertised product at a later date at the advertised price. According to Ralph Nader's Citizen Action Group in Washington, the FTC has ruled that the mere existence of a raincheck policy is not considered adequate compliance with the regulation, which requires that advertised specials must be in stock during the sale, having been ordered in adequate time for delivery and in quantities sufficient to meet reasonably anticipated demands. As the Nader report points out, customers come into a store for a special at the time it is advertised and probably make additional purchases while there. "Advertising should be more than a false lure."

We recommend that the DCP require retailers to keep adequate records to support claims that (1) advertised products were ordered in sufficient time and quantity but depleted quickly due to unexpectedly high response, (2) products were not delivered due to circumstances beyond the store's control, or (3) products specials were misadvertised by the newspaper.

We ask that you report favorably HB 7162, with adequate provisions to help insure that retailers will live up to their advertising claims.

BIBLIOGRAPHY

Bores, Daniel, and Paul R. Verkuil. Regulation of supermarket advertising practices. *Georgetown Law Journal.* Georgetown University, Washington, D.C., **60**, 5, May, 1972.

Federal Trade Commission, Washington, D.C., 1971. *Retail food store advertising and marketing practices, trade regulation rule, including statement of its basis and purpose.*

North Carolina Public Interest Research Group. *Advertised specials: a continuing deception.* Durham, North Carolina, April 30, 1975.

Verkuil, Paul, R. *Developments in the regulation of supermarket advertising practices: an empirical analysis. New York University Law Review* **48**, 3, June, 1973. New York University, New York.

CHAPTER 10

are you getting what you pay for when you buy meat ?

INTRODUCTION

Consumers today pay as much as 70 percent more for meat than they did ten years ago. As food budgets feel the pinch, it becomes extremely important that shoppers receive the quality and amount of meat paid for, but often they do not. Two of the most common and costly ways that consumers are deceived when buying meat are: "short-weighting," the practice of labeling a package at more than the actual weight and charging for the inflated weight figure; and the selling of ground beef that either contains more than the maximum amount of fat allowed by law or is mislabeled in such a way as to indicate a lower fat content than it actually contains.

The two projects in this chapter explain how citizen groups can investigate stores to determine whether they are defrauding consumers by such practices, and outline action that will ensure that corrective measures are taken against violators.

ARE YOU PAYING FOR GROUND BEEF OR FAT?

The increased cost of ground beef has not been accompanied by improved quality. In fact, many wholesale and retail meat distributors are responding to their own rising costs by selling lower grade meat with a higher fat content.

A federal regulation exists to protect the consumer from these practices. The United States Department of Agriculture's Meat and Poultry Inspection Regulations, 319.15 (a) and (b), state that "chopped beef, ground beef, and hamburger shall consist of chopped fresh and/or frozen beef with or without seasoning and without the addition of beef fat as such, and shall not contain more than 30 percent fat." (See Resource 10.1 for a copy of this regulation.) Many states have similar regulations limiting fat content in ground beef, regulations that are enforced by the state Department of Agriculture. Often those regulations require stores which sell ground beef according to grade, to post a statement describing the fat content of each grade.

Despite these regulations, consumers are often sold substandard or mislabeled ground beef and may be paying increased prices for meat with a high fat content. The Oregon PIRG, in a 1973 survey, found that 11 of the 54 stores surveyed (15 percent) did not comply with the 30 percent fat content limit for ground beef. Furthermore, among the 34 stores that sold several grades of ground beef, eight stores (23 percent) had higher fat content in the higher priced grades! The fat content in the same grade of beef varied from store to store by as much as 18 percent.

Unfortunately there is no way for individual consumers to easily determine the fat content of the meat they purchase. Shoppers will continue to be misled and overcharged unless they are given specific information about variances of fat content in the same grade of beef from store to store, and about stores that violate federal and state regulations. This project outlines how a consumer group can make that information available to the public and to state and federal regulatory agencies.

Some Basics

To complete this survey you may choose to determine all of the following points or points 1 or 2 only:

1. The percentage of retailers in compliance with the USDA 30 percent fat content standard;
2. The percentage of retailers in compliance with state regulations;
3. The difference between fat content of "regular" ground beef and the higher grades sold by stores. (The higher grades might not be worth the extra money.);
4. The range of fat content within the same grades of ground beef from store to store;
5. The clarity of labels describing different grades.

After completing the initial project planning stages—choosing a project coordinator, checking with other groups for similar projects, determining the geographic area to be covered by the survey, and choosing stores to be surveyed, decide how you will test meat samples for fat content.

It is best to have a laboratory run two tests on two sections of each meat sample provided. Unfortunately many laboratories may charge as much as $10 per sample, but some have run these tests at a lower cost because they are interested in assisting consumer groups with such a survey. The Micronomics Environmental Consultants Laboratory, in El Cajon, California, tested meat samples for consumer groups at $4 per sample. For more information, contact the laboratory staff, at P.O. Box 1485, El Cajon, California 92022, or by phone at 714/453-0060, extension 321.

The most exact testing method, for which many laboratories are equipped, is the "ether-extract method" which has been recognized as accurate by the Association of Official Analytical Chemists and the United States Department of Agriculture (USDA). The USDA advises that this method be used in any analysis which may result in litigation or similar action against a store. If you have questions about the method, speak with a local laboratory which tests foods or contact the Supervisory Chemist, USDA, Washington, D.C.

Another option is to purchase a Univex Fat Analyzer (model FA-B) and run the tests yourselves. This device cooks the meat sample and leaves the fat for measuring. Measurements are accurate to the nearest 0.5 percentile, which is not as accurate as measurements determined by the "ether-extract method." Although these test results might have to be verified by USDA or a state agency before stores can be charged with violating regulations, they will be accurate enough to be publicly disclosed.

If your group cannot afford testing by a private laboratory or the Univex machine, check with nearby university or college laboratories to see if one of them can set up a system for testing by the "ether-extract method."

Determine what day samples are to be sent to the testers, the amount of each sample required for testing, and how the samples are to be packed and transported. Shipping will probably involve purchasing styrofoam containers and dry ice for packing.

Compile a list of stores to be surveyed, give each store a code number and each surveyor an assignment. Whenever possible surveyors should work in pairs and verify the purchasing procedures.

This information is then filled in on a Master List of Stores to be surveyed, like that in Fig. 10.1. Assign a code letter for each grade of meat to ensure that samples are not identifiable at the lab by store or grade type so the testing is nonprejudicial.

How to Purchase and Prepare Meat Samples for Testing

If you have decided to test only for compliance with the USDA 30 percent fat content regulation, purchase samples of the lowest grade of ground beef or hamburger. If you are going to compare fat content in different grades of meat, purchase samples from each grade the stores regularly sell. Meat packages should be chosen on a random sample basis, and more than one package of each grade of meat must be purchased at each store. A store cannot be charged with noncompliance with regulations on the basis of one sample, so purchase 5–10 percent of the total number of packages of each grade of meat displayed. Purchase the same percentage of packages from each store surveyed. In order to have a representative sample of each grade, all the packages of

Masterlist of Stores
to Survey

Store
code

Number   Store and address   Surveyors
_____ _____ _____
         _____ _____
_____ _____ _____
         _____ _____
_____ _____ _____
         _____ _____
_____ _____ _____
         _____ _____
_____ _____ _____
         _____ _____
_____ _____ _____
         _____ _____
_____ _____ _____
         _____ _____
_____ _____ _____
         _____ _____
_____ _____ _____

(Each separate store of a chain should be given a
different number)

Compiled by_____

Fig. 10.1 Masterlist of stores to be surveyed.

each grade should be mixed together, either by the butcher or at home by surveyors. The grade sample will be a part of this mix.

If there is a state regulation requiring retailers to post a statement which explains their grading terms, note whether there is such a sign and write down exactly what it says. The Store Record Form in Fig. 10.2 and the Meat Sample Forms in Fig. 10.3 are to be filled in at the store. Use separate Meat Sample Forms for each grade of meat, but not for each package within that grade.

Select a test sample of the same amount (specified by the lab or testing machine instructions) for each grade of meat. If the meat is being shipped to a lab or is not going to be tested by the group within a day or two, the samples must be frozen. Wrap each sample tightly in plastic wrap or aluminum foil and seal it in two plastic bags to prevent moisture loss which results in a higher fat content count. Do not use freezer paper

Store Record Form

Name of store:_____Code No.:_____

Address of store:_____

Date of purchase(s):_____

Name(s) and Address(es) of Surveyor(s):

_____

_____

Grade	Grade code letter	No. of packages of grade	No. of packages purchased	Weights	Price per pound	Total cost	If sale price, what is regular price?
Hamburger meat	D						
Regular	A	33	3	1.3	1.29	1.67	
				1.2	1.29	1.58	
				1.0	1.29	1.29	
Lean	B						
Extra lean	C						

Explanation of ground beef grades as appeared on store signs (Applicable only if state law requires such signs or if you wish to lobby for such legislation.)

1. Regular_____

2. Lean_____

3. Extra lean_____

4. Super lean (or other superlative label_____

5. Other _____

Attach receipt to form immediately. Attach meat package labels after packages of each grade have been mixed and sample taken.

Fig. 10.2 Store record form.

193

Meat Sample Form

Store code_____ Meat Grade Code Letter_____

Date purchased_____ Date on label(s)_____

_____

_____

Fig. 10.3 Meat sample form.

Handling Form

Location of freezer_____

Put in freezer by_____ Time_____

Removed from freezer by_____ Time_____

Was the ground beef frozen?_____ Signed_____

Where samples were packed for shipment?_____

_____

Packed by_____ Time_____

Container number_____

Fig. 10.4 Handling form.

because it draws moisture from the meat. Mark each sample with a Meat Sample Form attached to the inner package with freezer tape.

Samples must be frozen for a minimum of three hours before being transferred to containers for shipment. A Handling Form (Fig. 10.4) should be filled in at that time. When the samples are packed according to the lab instructions complete the Handling Form. If possible, all samples ought to be prepared, frozen, and packed for shipment at the same location to further ensure that each step will be uniform since stores may question the methodology and uniformity of your survey. Fill in a Container Form like the one in Fig. 10.5.

The Packing Form in Fig. 10.6 is to be filled in at the lab to verify that the samples arrived frozen.

Final Report and Follow-Up Action

After the meat samples have been tested, write a report that includes information about how the survey was conducted, its results, and your group's recommendations.

Container Form

Container number_____

Packed by_____ Date_____ Time_____

Mode of transportation_____ Operator_____

Time (bus/train/car) left_____

Put on(bus/train/car) by_____ Time_____

Taken off (bus/train/car) by_____ Time_____

Received at Laboratories (address)_____

_____ Time_____

The container was sealed and packed in the proper fashion

Signed:_____ (by laboratory personnel)_____

Fig. 10.5 Container form.

Packing Form

Container number_____

Packed by_____ Time_____

The following samples were packed frozen and were still
frozen when the package was opened at __(name of lab)____

_____ (address of lab)_____

Fill in store code and grade code for each sample packed

_____ _____ _____

_____ _____ _____

_____ _____ _____

_____ _____ _____

The above samples were received in good condition for
testing for fat content.

Signed: __(by laboratory personnel)_____

Laboratory:_____ (name and address)_____

Fig. 10.6 Packing form.

195

Release the results to the media in a news conference with the lab spokesperson present to answer any technical questions. (Refer to the press release in Fig. 10.7 that was issued by OSPIRG.) A large chart outlining the survey findings would be useful.

If the USDA fat content standard was violated by a store, give written notice to the Regional Office of USDA, your State Department of Agriculture and the State Attorney General's Office, requesting remedial action. Ask for a reply to your complaint, and send a copy of the letter to the Compliance Division, USDA, Washington, D.C. 20027.

Based on survey and tests results presented by the California PIRG, the State Attorney General's Office filed suit against a grocery chain. The chain was charged with selling ground beef which had fat content higher than the 30 percent allowed by law and mislabeling packages. The labels did not denote real or significant differences in the fat content among the different grades.

Consider lobbying for legislation which would make the grade names for ground beef uniform at all stores statewide, with each grade representing a maximum fat content.

Write letters to the managers of the stores in which violations of federal or state regulations were found, where grading levels were not indicative of fat content, or where content within grades was not standard throughout branch stores. Send the letters by registered or certified mail with return receipt requested. Send copies to headquarters offices of all chain stores. A sample letter is included in Fig. 10.8. If stores do not reply with information on action they plan to take to remedy the situation, make that information public.

In several months, rerun the survey in those stores that had violations. If the violations are still occurring, consult legal counsel.

ARE YOU BEING SHORTWEIGHTED WHEN YOU BUY MEAT?

When you buy a four-pound roast or a seven-pound ham, you pay as much as 70 percent more than you would have ten years ago. At the same time, you may not be getting the amount of meat you paid for. Public Interest Research Groups in several states discovered that some shoppers were being shortweighted when they purchased meat and poultry. "Shortweighting" is selling a product that weighs less than the amount stated on the label and charging consumers for the inflated weight figure; it can be the result of a deliberate attempt to overcharge, an inaccurate store scale, or the carelessness of store personnel.

Shortweighting is a violation of state weights and measures law. *Media and Consumer* reported that in 1973 Criminal Court Judge Justin C. Ravitz of Detroit sentenced the meat manager of Wrigley Supermarket to a day in jail for cheating consumers. The Wrigley manager had pleaded guilty to shortweighting 33 cuts of meat. Judge Ravitz also notified Detroit's six major food chains that if they were violating Michigan's food laws, they would be comparably penalized.

Company personnel are seldom treated as they were in Detroit for cheating consumers, and may retain virtually unlimited freedom to defraud consumers. Citizens can change this situation. Find out if consumers in your area are cheated when they

For release 8:30 A.M., Wednesday, Dec. 5, 1973

OSPIRG Ground Beef Study

Ground beef sold in some Oregon supermarkets needs to go on a diet, according to the Oregon Student Public Interest Research Group. A recent OSPIRG study concluded some makers of ground beef are exceeding state and federal fat content limits.

Results of the ground beef fat content study indicates that in some cases consumers may actually be paying more money for more fat in supposedly leaner grades of meat.

On the whole, however, the OSPIRG study determined that most Oregon supermarkets who prepared their own ground beef are complying with state and federal standards. Federal standards limit fat content of ground beef to 30 percent. Stricter state laws regulate the allowable fat content level between various grades of ground beef-- regular, lean, extra lean, and super lean.

"On the average, it appears that the consumer gets what he pays for," the report said. "However, upon analysis, the consumer may often be paying 20 to 30 cents (per pound) more for meat only slightly lower in fat content--or at times even higher."

"In addition, he (the consumer) can be unwittingly deceived if he thinks what is lean in one store is lean in another," the report said. "For example--a regular grade, a lean grade, and an extra lean grade from three different stores all had a fat content of 22.5 percent.

"Obviously the consumer is unable to determine which grade is best to buy or which store has the lowest fat content in its ground beef. His basis for comparison-- the fat content spelled out on the label or other qualifying statements--is often meaningless," the report said.

OSPIRG volunteers purchased ground beef samples from randomly selected supermarkets in western Oregon. The beef samples were turned over to an independent food testing lab for a fat content analysis. Twenty volunteers purchased the ground beef samples in 54 stores on Nov. 13, 1973.

Fig. 10.7 Sample news release.

Results of the chemical analysis conducted by Food Quality Testing Inc. of Portland show:

--43 of 54 stores (85 percent) surveyed complied with the 30 percent fat limit.
--25 of 35 of the surveyed stores (71 percent) that sell more than one grade of beef complied with their posted statements quoting fat content (either by labels or meat case placards).
--Samples from 8 of 35 stores (23 percent) had actual increases of fat content from one grade to the next leaner grade.
--Fat content in the various grades of ground beef ranged from 18 to 34.5 percent for regular, 11.5 to 30 percent for lean, and 3 to 22.5 percent for the extra lean grade.

Although the study indicated the Oregon Department of Agriculture is doing an adequate job in its general meat inspection program, OSPIRG noted discrepancies go undetected under the present state inspection system. OSPIRG made several recommendations to the Department of Agriculture:

--The department must set specific uniform definitions for the comparative/superlative labeling of the various grades of beef.
--The department should specify that respective grades of ground beef have at least a five percent difference in fat content as implied by maximum fat content limits.
--The department should sample all grades of beef simultaneously rather than only one grade to determine if mislabeling is occurring.

The report noted that three generations of Americans have grown up on ground beef. But because of beef's popularity, the meat industry is susceptible to a variety of frauds. "Excessive fat levels are probably the most common of these abuses," the report concluded.

Director for the study was John Savage, an Oregon State University student and member of the OSPIRG student executive committee.

Students surveyed supermarkets in five regions in the Willamette Valley and Southern Oregon. The areas were Ashland-Medford, Salem-Minnville-Independence-Monmouth, Corvallis, Eugene, and Portland.

Fig. 10.7 *Continued*

Mr. John X. Doe
More Money Market
0 Bleeker Street
Brownsville, Wh.   20000

Dear Mr. Doe:

Last month (Name of Group) conducted ground beef fat content surveys
on the 9 major retail food chains in _____ . Five stores
from each chain were selected at random, and our surveyors purchased
10% of packages of each grade of ground beef on the shelf. These
samples were then repackaged and delivered to _____ Laboratories for testing, using the ether-extract method.

Results of our tests in the More Money Market's samples were as
follows:

Date	Store Address		Percent Fat	
		Regular	Lean	Extra Lean
5/7		34.7	20.0	20.8
5/10		17.8	12.6	14.8
5/15		22.5	26.1	15.2

As is evident, the fat content of one sample was in violation of
USDA regulations allowing a maximum 30% fat content in ground beef.
In addition, there were discrepancies between grade labels and the
actual fat content of the ground beef, and there were wide variations in fat content between the same grade of ground beef at different More Money Market stores. These discrepancies appear to
violate Section 403(a) of the Federal Food, Drug, and Cosmetic Act,
as amended, and Section _____ of the State Civil Code.

We believe that continued mislabeling defrauds consumers and must
be rectified. Accordingly, (Name of Group) requests that you provide
us with the following information, in writing, no later than (Date):

(1)   The method by which fat content in ground beef is deter-
      mined, and the approximate frequency of such determinations
      at More Money Market stores or processing facilities;

(2)   Any changes from previous methods you intend to introduce,
      or have introduced, to upgrade ground beef fat testing;

(3)   Any other comments you would like to make.

Thank you for your cooperation.

Sincerely,

Fig. 10.8   Sample letter.

199

purchase meat and, if they are, force state officials to take action to correct this abuse. Using one of the survey methods outlined below you can compare the weight of meat purchased with that stated on the label.

The types of meat recommended for the survey are relatively inexpensive and commonly purchased—chuck roasts, whole frying chickens, and store-packaged (not canned) hams. In order to ensure that data are representative, survey a minimum of four items of each type of meat chosen randomly from the counter at each store. Compile a list of stores to be surveyed using the form in Fig. 10.9.

Decide which of the survey methods below best serves your purposes, and then establish the true weight of the meat samples. Whichever method you choose, the instructions for determining true weight remain the same and appear after the survey method outlines.

First Survey Method

Contact the county or state Department of Weights and Measures (Resource 10.2) and explain that you plan to conduct a shortweighting survey and ask if the office is interested in participating by authorizing an inspector to accompany your surveyors. The advantage of this arrangement is that although inspector authority varies from state to state, most inspectors have the right to open and weigh packages without purchasing them, using their own or store scales. If this survey is done in cooperation with a government office, make it clear at the outset that you intend to release results to the public and do not want stores forewarned of the survey. Formulate a written agreement outlining survey methods. If the survey is done in conjunction with a state inspector using store scales, be sure that the inspector "calibrates" the scales, that is, that he verifies that the scales weigh properly.

Second Survey Method

Although this method involves more coordination than the others, it is likely to work the best. Volunteers arrange to purchase meat on a specified day. Pool your resources before buying the meat so surveyors do not bear the entire cost of their purchases, as costs will vary from store to store. Weigh the meats in one place on an accurate scale, either at the Weights and Measures Office, a retail store that has agreed to cooperate, or at a school lab. In the latter cases, calibrate the scale. If samples are found to have been shortweighted, keep a few for use during the press conference held to announce the survey results.

Third Survey Method

Prepare flyers explaining some facts about your group, the purpose of the survey, and the meats to be weighed. Then set up a weighing station in the stores' parking lots, perhaps in a van. Pass out flyers to shoppers before they enter the store and ask for permission to weigh their puchases after they are through shopping. Bring plastic wrap so that meats can be rewrapped after they are weighed with and without the packaging. Be sure that the weighing station is clean and well organized.

Masterlist of Stores to Be Surveyed

Store	Location	Surveyor
_____	_____	_____
_____	_____	_____
_____	_____	_____
_____	_____	_____
_____	_____	_____

Compiled by _____

Fig. 10.9   Masterlist of stores to be surveyed.

If the store manager asks you to leave the lot, explain who you are, the purpose of the survey, and the fact that noncooperativeness will be made public. If she or he persists, complete the survey on public land or, if this isn't practical, by using one of the other survey methods.

Weighing the Meat

The true weight of meat is its weight without store wrappings. First, the package is weighed in its wrapping so that no juices are lost. (The juices are included in the store weight.) Then the "tear weight" or the weight of the wrappings alone is determined. The first figure minus the tear weight is the true weight of the meat.

Compiling Survey Data

Using Data Compilation Form I in Fig. 10.10 for each store, determine if there is a difference between the weight of the meat stated on the label and the meat's true weight. For each discrepancy, fill in Data Compilation Form II in Fig. 10.11 with the name of the store, the type of meat, and the amount it was shortweighted.

Action to Take after Completing the Survey

If the survey uncovered substantial incidents of shortweighting, call a news conference or issue a news release to announce the results. Public knowledge of your information may ensure that the Department of Weights and Measures will be more vigilant in protecting consumers.

Shortweighting of Meat - Data Compilation Form I

Name of store_____

Address of store_____

Store manager_____

Date and time of survey_____

Name(s) and address(es) of surveyor(s)

_____   _____

_____   _____

Type of meat	Weight on store label	Weight of meat & wrapper	Wrapper weight	Actual weight of meat	Price per pound	Price charged
1.						
2.						
3.						
4.						

Fig. 10.10 Data compilation form I.

SHORTWEIGHTING OF MEAT
Products Shortweighted

Name of store_____

Address of store_____

Store manager_____

Type of meat	Amount shortweighted	Price per pound	Amount Overcharged
1.			
2.			
3.			
4.			

Fig. 10.11 Data compilation form II.

202

Informed consumers can save money by continuing to monitor shortweighting. Your news release might recommend that shoppers buy small, inexpensive scales to check their purchases, notify the Department of Weights and Measures about instances of shortweighting, and return overpriced products to the store.

At the same time, or before making your results public, notify store managers, state or county Departments of Weights and Measures, and the office of the city attorney or state attorney general of any shortweighting discovered. Send the letters by registered or certified mail and ask for a response outlining what measures will be taken to remedy the situation.

Before issuing the release, you might call or visit the county or state Department of Weights and Measures or ask to be referred to a local office. Ask for information about the number of times they have cited stores for shortweighting, the action taken against the stores, and the authority of the office, and its staff size.

It might become apparent that law enforcement by the Department of Weights and Measures has not solved shortweighting problems. If so, new state laws or city ordinances may be in order. Contact the Office of Weights and Measures, National Bureau of Standards, Washington, D.C.   20234, for a copy of the Model Weight and Measures Ordinance, 1974, for help in recommending the rewriting of legislation.

Repeat the survey in two or three months in the stores that had shortweighted products.

BIBLIOGRAPHY

Association of Analytical Chemists. *Official Methods of Analysis.* Washington, D.C., Section 24.005, (11th ed.), 1970.

California Public Interest Research Group. *Ground beef fat content survey.* San Diego, California, 1975.

Meat and poultry inspection regulations, 319.15 (a) and (b). United States Department of Agriculture, Washington, D.C.

Mleczka, Lou. Warning to shortweighters: you may be thrown in jail. *Media and Consumer* **9**, 1974.

Oregon Public Interest Research Group. *Fat content in ground beef: a study of western Oregon supermarkets.* Portland, Oregon, 1974.

PART 4

the media and effecting legislation

CHAPTER 11

working effectively with the media

INTRODUCTION

Given the deceptive nature of many activities historically practiced by public relations people and advertising agencies, an organized public relations effort is sometimes looked upon as being somehow improper for citizen and consumer groups. This attitude is unfortunate and without merit. Consumer groups have vital information and a message for citizens. For these groups to ignore the normal channels of communication with the general public is unrealistic and impractical.

Begin your communications campaign by preparing a list of all newspapers, magazines, radio, and television stations in the area. Start with the Yellow Pages of the telephone directory and, if that does not provide a sufficiently inclusive list, check the *Broadcasters' Yearbook* for TV and radio stations and the *Editors' and Publishers' Yearbook* for newspapers and magazines. Both yearbooks are probably available in your local library. The list you develop should include names, addresses, phone numbers, audiences, and names of such key contact people as editors, publishers, program directors, and news directors.

Next, visit the offices on your communications list. Be prepared to give the people you meet some literature about your group and what it is doing. At newspapers, try to meet with editors, publishers, reporters, and stringers. (Stringers are nonsalaried reporters, paid for each column inch of material published, and therefore have quite an incentive to cover a story and get it published.) At radio and television stations, you will want to meet the news and assignment editors, political reporters, the director of public affairs, and the people with interview shows, particularly consumer-oriented shows. The key to coverage is to learn with whom you are dealing; who is friendly, who is not, and the form and amount of information they like to receive.

NEWS RELEASES—DOS AND DON'TS

The major vehicle for dissemination of information is the news (or press) release. If you are aiming for TV or radio coverage as well as newspapers, remember, it is a *news* release, not a press release. Do not expect the media to automatically cover what you think is important. Use news releases to announce events that you consider news-worthy but which otherwise probably would not receive coverage. A release is best written in the third person so that it may be printed or read without revision. If you are advocating a point of view, do so by quoting sources, whether they be members of your group or some other spokesperson.

A news release is typically double-spaced on 8½" by 11" paper (so that one sheet will probably suffice). At the top left, type "For Further Information" followed by the name and phone number of your project coordinator. On the next line indicate the release time, "For Immediate Release" or "For Release September 20, 1975, Morning," etc. Next, type the title of the release across the page, for example: "The D.C. Public Interest Research Group Announces Suit against Corporate Power and Electric Company." Prepare and send the release at least 48 hours before it is to be released to allow time for its review.

Write the release using the "inverted pyramid" structure used by journalists. The first paragraph contains the basic idea expressed in the release, and following paragraphs contain details in descending order to importance so that if the news director or editor cuts your story short, only the least important parts will be deleted. The first paragraph should answer the questions *Who?*, *What?*, *Where?*, *When?*, and *How?*, (and sometimes *Why?*), and at the same time remain short.

Use names, quotes, and other specifics to support your story. *Be absolutely certain of your facts;* be able to attribute your information to sources, and make sure you haven't misrepresented them. Avoid sensationalism, exaggeration, and clichés (especially radical ones which might turn off some of the people you are trying to reach). Yet don't resort to the other extreme and let your point disappear in mush. Acquiring a newsworthy sense will help you to strike a balance between the extremes of bland and sensationalized press releases. For example, which of the following stories makes its point best?

Citing instances of "gross criminality," the South Borneo PIRG today charged the American Pharmaceutical Testing Laboratory, an industry puppet, with embezzling federal research funds, pandering to special interests, and making blatantly illegal campaign contributions to candidates of both national political parties.

South Borneo PIRG said today that the Pharmaceutical Testing Laboratory may have unwisely used federal research funds, became involved in a "questionable relationship" with a number of major drug firms, and made cash contributions to political candidates.

At a news conference held today at the Headhunter Hilton, South Borneo PIRG charged the Pharmaceutical Testing Laboratory, an industry group, with instances of "administration neglect" involving a federally funded research program, conflict of interest with major drug firms, and making secret cash campaign contributions to candidates of both parties.

If, in spite of your group's attempts at accuracy, it develops later that you were inaccurate, be quick to admit it. If you decide to take the approach in the first story, be sure you have enough evidence for an indictment.

NEWS CONFERENCES

Reserve news conferences for major news stories; stories that are important and demand strong play. Don't call conferences too frequently or for minor news items. If news conferences are used wisely, the press will likely attend.

In preparation for a news conference at which you will release a major study, you may want to distribute your report in advance with a release time stated, to give the media a chance to look it over, prepare a story, and prepare for the conference. If the nature of the conference is such that a prerelease is either unnecessary or inappropriate, use what is known as an "editors' advisory," a short announcement of the press conference stating when and where it will be held and, in general terms, what it is about. The advisory should be delivered 48 hours in advance of the conference. Always follow up the advisory with phone calls to ensure maximum attendance. Everyone, including the wire services, to whom you will send a news release should receive an advisory.

At the news conference, make sure there is adequate space and that there are enough electrical outlets for TV cameras. Provide chairs for the reporters, sample copies of the report and the accompanying news release, and a table in front of the person(s) speaking or leading the conference, with room for microphones, recorders, and other equipment. Have someone with a notebook at the door and see to it that members of the media sign their names, and give addresses and affiliations. Always try to have *Visuals* (charts, diagrams, etc.) available for background interest for photographers and TV camera operators.

The group's spokesperson customarily opens the conference with a brief statement and then takes questions from the media. Once the questions become redundant, or when interest seems to be waning, end the conference and thank the attendees.

After the conference, the spokesperson normally is available for personal interviews with radio and TV commentators and reporters. Alert all those connected with the project beforehand that if they are not adequately familiar with the subject matter they should refer questions to the appointed spokesperson.

TIPS ON SCHEDULING

Good scheduling is an important aspect of a successful news release or news confer-ence. Keep in mind the time of the week and the time of the day. Weekend news conferences (any time after 3:30 P.M. on Friday) are likely to be poorly attended, while weekend news releases often get good coverage, particularly if they are developed by Thursday and timed and geared for the Sunday papers. News conferences should be held in the morning for good coverage—9:30 A.M. or 11:00 A.M. until noon—unless it is likely to be a heavy news day. In that case TV crews and reporters may be tied up in the morning and you should aim for 2:30 P.M. Avoid lunch hour scheduling.

Never hold a news conference after 3:30 P.M. There is no surer way to miss out on coverage than to present an editor with the problem of getting a TV crew through evening rush hour traffic and rushing the film back in time to incorporate it into the evening news.

Newspaper Coverage

If you have more than one paper per town, then there will be a trade-off in determining whether you should release your material for the morning or afternoon paper. Rotate release times so that no one becomes upset. For example, if you release your report at 2:00 P.M.; it becomes a morning story and will get much less attention the following afternoon.

For news releases, coverage on the weekends and holidays is important to investi-gate; with government offices closed, news is slower. After determining the weekend policies of the media, and of the newspapers in particular, you may find it most effec-tive to use the weekends for important news releases. You will have to decide whether losing TV and radio coverage is worth the gain in newspaper coverage.

Saturday afternoon papers have little impact, while Saturday morning and Sunday papers are usually well read. Make sure you know the papers' deadlines for stories.

Radio Coverage

When you are dealing with radio stations, you may find that audio feeds (also known as "beepers" or "actualities") are just as important or possibly more important to the station than the news release is. When you make your initial round of call and introductions, find out it they take feeds and whether they like to get one along with a news release. To do audio feeds you will need to make 30- to 45-second voice clips of the spokesperson on a tape recorder. Find out whether the stations take cassette or reel-to-reel recordings. Ask for suggestions for a good quality, inexpensive tape recorder. You will also need a "patch cord" with two "alligator clips" on one end and with a minijack on the other. An electronics store can explain how to use the equipment.

After you've recorded your statement, call the station. The process of transmit-ting the audio feed is easiest if there are two phones close to one another. Call on one phone and ask the station if it wants the audio on your story. If it does, have the recorder attached to the second phone. To do this, unscrew the mouthpiece and take out the disk voice piece. Attach an alligator clip to each of the two prongs you see. The other end of the patch cord is plugged into the monitor or earplug hole. When the station is ready to take your feed, depress the *play* button. (If you have only one phone, remember, after sending the message you can no longer speak into the phone. You must disconnect the clips and replace the disk to the mouthpiece before you can be heard.)

The most important time for radio stations, and the time that costs the most for advertisers, is "drive time," i.e., commuting time to and from work. Since the audience is biggest then, you should try to schedule your audio feeds to reach drive time. Give the station time to edit. If you want morning drive-time coverage, then you will have to give it to the station late the night before or *early* that morning.

Television Coverage

Television news provides the largest audience and the greatest coverage, but is usually the hardest to get, especially if the local news segment is only one-half hour long. TV news is headline coverage for the most part, and the stations want material that is crisp and newsworthy.

Be sure to send news releases and news conference invitations to all TV stations. Sometimes, by dropping by the stations and delivering the release, you can set up a short interview to supplement the release. If you have a good story and if the news is slow that day (by making a few calls ahead of time you can find out), the news people may welcome you. You'll find that you are more likely to get coverage over a weekend when news tends to be slow. Call the news room on Thursday to let them know you have something planned for the weekend.

The over-the-air broadcasters have a competitor, albeit a minor one. In many communities homes are wired to a master antenna which provides improved reception, coverage, and programming. Sometimes this cable system provides original programming produced by citizens or their local production personnel. Determine whether or not there is a significant number of people in your area wired to the local cable system and, if so, whether the system carries any local news. Some systems broadcast only the wire service tickers, but you may find that cable television is a major force in your community.

Public Service Announcements

Radio and television stations are required by federal law as part of the licensing process to air a prescribed number of public service announcements (PSAs) each license term. In their application for license renewal, the stations state that they will air a certain number of PSAs per week.

Take advantage of this opportunity whenever possible. Stations usually are receptive to the least controversial groups in the community. However, some stations may be more courageous. Determine the policy of the local radio and television stations. Usually they will at least allow PSAs that seek support and volunteers for a project, and on occasion for fund-raising spots.

The PSA must be catchy. In 10 to 60 seconds you want to attract the attention of the viewers or listeners and communicate your point of view. If your message is put together well, audience response is apt to be good.

Stations must air PSAs, but they do not have to air yours. Therefore, determine their policies, work with them, and use good copy. Sometimes they may even help to develop the copy.

MEDIA REGULATION

It is important to have a basic understanding of the regulatory process of the broadcast media. This section briefly outlines that process. If you are interested in more details, contact the Citizens' Communications Center, 1914 Sunderland Place, NW, Washington, D.C.   20036, and ask for its *Primer on Citizens' Access to the Federal Communications Commission.*

Currently, federal law states that a station's license is due for renewal every three years. At renewal time, the FCC reviews the application, compares it with previous applications and the promises of the last application, and determines whether it would be in the public interest to renew the license. Unless there is opposition, such as the filing of a Petition to Deny by a citizens' group or the filing of a competing application, the license will be renewed.

The political climate created by citizens filing hundreds of Petitions to Deny over the last four or five years has caused much greater broadcaster sensitivity to the needs and aspirations of local communities and citizen groups.

Broadcasters, however, are now trying to get the Federal Communications Act amended to allow for longer license terms and a lighter burden of proof that they have acted in the public interest. They now want the FCC to find that their licenses should be renewed before dealing with competing licenses, basically eliminating all elements of competition in an already monopolistic enterprise. It behooves public interest groups to express complaints about this proposed change to the broadcasters and to the FCC.

Another important issue is the application of the "fairness doctrine." Under its present application, the fairness doctrine requires a station to provide a balance in its news coverage. This includes responses to advertisements if they are "controversial in nature." The doctrine requires the station "to afford reasonable opportunity for the discussion of conflicting views on issues of public importance." This does not mean equal time. It does mean that the station must develop balance and it has the opportunity to do that in any form it desires.

If you believe a station has not provided a balanced view on a story, file a complaint with the station, asking for time to provide the balance you thought lacking. If your request is denied, file a complaint with the FCC and also seek legal counsel. The *Primer* from the Citizens' Communications Center will be helpful if you intend to pursue the issue.

CHAPTER 12
changing the laws

INTRODUCTION

Those who work on consumer or public interest projects find that effecting permanent change almost inevitably leads to changing laws—drafting legislation, and lobbying or using the initiative. Laws must be promulgated or amended to guarantee consumer rights and protection.

Our legislative system works as it should only when all interest groups make their opinions known to their representatives, and lobbying, when conducted in a proper way, is a legitimate part of the legislative process. Public interest lobbying is a response to a serious imbalance created in the system when special interests exert powerful influences on legislative decision making by speaking with dispropor-tionately loud voices. You can respond either by wringing your hands or by working to restore balance to the system, speaking for interests that are too easily and too often ignored. While all lobbyists want to influence legislation, as a public interest lobbyist you seek to represent the concerns of a traditionally unorganized, often inarticulate, and generally diverse constituency.

The initiative process is self-government in one of its truest forms. It enables citizens to circumvent the traditional legislative process and propose laws themselves. Through the initiative, citizens may submit a law directly to the voters for enactment or defeat, provided they have secured, through petition public support to place the law on the ballot. This process has been used successfully by public interest groups and may prove to be the most fruitful method of getting the laws you support passed.

Both legislative processes are discussed in this chapter.

USING REPRESENTATIVE DEMOCRACY: LOBBYING

Rule 1: *The effectiveness of public interest lobbyists is directly proportionate to the number of citizens* (or votes) *they represent.*

Legislators may be influenced by any of the following: a genuine interest in your issue, favorable publicity, the stand taken by committee chairpeople and other legislative or political party leaders, views of staff people, and loyalty to friends, lobbyists, and campaign contributors. But for most legislators, the desire for the support of the voting public proves the most important motivating factor. Reelection or election to a higher office is never far from their minds, and only public support can elect. Votes talk and legislators listen.

If you represent substantial numbers of strongly committed and politically active voters who make it clear to legislators that their vote on the bill will be remembered at election time, your influence can outweigh that of any other group or individual—campaign contributors notwithstanding. That is not to say that a large constituency can guarantee you success; the way in which you organize the group and their diligence in responding are essential.

In the broadest sense, any citizen can lobby (attempt to get legislatures to vote for a measure) simply by expressing views on a particular bill to legislators. However, lobbying has come to mean a much more intense and ongoing effort to influence our elected representatives. Legally, anyone who plans to represent the views of a group to legislators must register as a lobbyist with the Office of the Secretary of State.

Even if your aim is to propose or support one piece of legislation rather than to develop an ongoing consumer or public interest lobby, it is imperative that you develop a strong citizen support group and that your group leaders register as lobbyists.

Your support group or citizen lobby should be active in as many member districts as possible, particularly in the districts of legislative leaders and of legislators who hold positions on committees that will be key to your success. Those constituents will contact their member by letter or in person as soon as your issue has been raised, at the time of committee votes and immediately before the floor vote. At this last step mailgrams or telegrams are effective. They lend an air of urgency and real concern. (Public opinion telegrams may be sent at reduced rates in most areas.) A strong petition drive may be appropriate at some point, but should never be considered a substitute for individual visits and letters. Voters often shy away from writing to legislators, fearful that the letter will not be well written enough to influence the member. If you have done your job well—informed your supporters on the issue and stressed that the letters do not have to be literary masterpieces—this should not be a problem. Never supply form letters to be mailed by your supporters; contrived efforts to indicate support will backfire on you.

A second important function of the citizen support group is attending public hearings on the bill you support and, when appropriate, testifying at those hearings. They will also attend important committee hearings, particularly constituents of the committee members, informing the member of their intention to attend before the meetings convene.

How to Develop a Citizen Lobby

Begin by giving the group a name that is brief and as self-explanatory as possible. Develop a position paper that describes the issue you are concerned with, the major problems that need corrective action, and the kind of legislation or ordinance you think is necessary to correct the situation. Draft your proposal with public support in mind. While your position paper and proposed bill should be as specific as possible, it's best to frame your issue so that it will generate the broadest possible base of public support (and the narrowest possible base of opposition) without becoming watered down and useless. Include an outline of the types of support activities you need from the citizen lobby. Elect co-chairpeople from your core group.

As soon as you begin to organize, the decision must be made whether or not to incorporate. A nonprofit group that meets certain federal and state requirements can qualify as a nonprofit, nonpartisan corporation eligible for "tax-exempt"status. The factors to consider before making the decision to incorporate include: (1) The amount of funding you will need to operate and where you plan to get that funding; (2) the size of the group and the length of time you expect to be in operation; and (3) the fact that a corporation cannot be held legally accountable for the actions of individuals in the corporation. Be sure to consult a local attorney for aid in making your decisions and filing the necessary legal papers.

If your group plans to do substantial fund raising, pay a staff, have an office, or work on the issue for a lengthly time period and in many areas, it may be wise to incorporate as a nonprofit, nonpartisan corporation. If you will be relying on a small core group of volunteers, working out of homes and keeping to a modest budget with little fund raising, the benefits of tax-exempt status may not outweigh the time and effort entailed in filing incorporation papers and meeting the requirements to retain the status. Incorporation costs money, approximately $40. A tax-exempt, nonprofit corporation must keep complete and detailed financial records, conduct periodic fiscal audits, and organize all their materials into a comprehensive filing system (again, for auditing purposes). These requirements are time consuming, but the order they impose will prove advantageous, particularly to a large group; a well-run operation and easy access to materials is essential to your credibility and effectiveness.

A nonprofit citizen group can seek tax-exempt status under 26 United States Code 501 (c) 3 or under 26 United States Code 501 (c) 4:

> 501 (c) 3 status is granted to corporations organized and operated exclusively for "religious, charitable, scientific, testing for public safety, literacy or educational purposes...."
> 501 (c) 4 status is granted to corporations "not organized for profit but operated exclusively for the promotion of social welfare."

Under 501 (c) 3 status, contributor donations are tax deductible and therefore easier to solicit. However, such status is more difficult to obtain, involving a longer time period, and corporations with such status *may not devote any substantial part of its activities to lobbying or to organizing activities which result in lobbying.*

A group that plans to engage in lobby activities must apply for 501 (c) 4 status. It is easier to obtain, but contributor donations to (c) 4 corporations are not tax deductible. Nor, with few exceptions, can a (c) 4 corporation receive funding from foundations.

Now you're ready to start building a coalition of groups and individuals to join with you.

Step 1. Contact all potentially interested groups and organizations. These might include: consumer and public interest groups working on such issues as energy, challenging utilities, tax reform, ecology, health, food and nutrition, problems of the elderly or of minorities, and tenants' rights; womens' rights groups; civic groups such as the American Association of University Women and the League of Women Voters; and labor unions.

Most groups have full-time commitments involving their own issues and work. However, if they philosophically agree with the stand you are taking on your issue and can be convinced of its importance, they may be willing to join your coalition and publicly support you. When asking groups to join with you, do not ask that they automatically agree to devote a great deal of time to your issue; instead try to persuade them simply to take a public stand and to commit their members to joining your phone lobby described below. Of course, those with the time and interest should be encouraged to work more closely with you.

Step 2. Contact individuals, particularly those with expertise in areas such as law, economics, engineering, accounting, architecture, health and nutrition which are directly related to your issue(s) and ask that they either work with you in a consultant capacity or that they simply join your coalition and add their names to the phone lobby.

Budget permitting, send personal letters to as many persons as possible, buying mailing lists from other public interest groups, political parties, and appropriate magazines. Outline the information in your position paper, ask for support, and include the name and phone number of the contact person in their area.

Step 3. Hold a news conference announcing the formation of the coalition group. Refer to Chapter 11 for specific information about issuing news releases and holding a news conference.

Step 4. Use a "telephone tree" like that developed by the Connecticut Citizen Action Group (CCAG) to develop the citizen lobby. Begin by creating regions around the state based on phone company exchanges; in that way no one within a region need make long-distance calls. Select a coordinator for each region who will recruit five people to work with them. The coordinators will have copies of the position paper to distribute to all who join or express an interest in joining the lobby. They should stress to everyone called that a full-time commitment on the issue is not demanded from all lobby members. Concern about the issue, an agreement to express their views to their legislator, and an attempt to contact five other interested voters is sufficient. Again, those with more time can be asked to help with coordinating and public information functions.

The regional coordinators should keep informed about the persons in their region who are working with the lobby, the amount of time each has to contribute, and any special skills they have. Your co-chairpersons will keep each regional coordinator informed as to the status of the legislation, when letters and visits are needed, and when hearings and meetings are to be held.

Now you can begin working and lobbying on your issue, keeping in mind that the coalition group and phone lobby must be continuously kept active parts of that process. You may often find yourselves in opposition to relatively wealthy, well-organized, major industry lobbyists with significant economic interests at stake. Out of necessity as well as choice, your tactics will not be those associated with special interest lobbyists on expense accounts—no cocktail parties or dinners at expensive restaurants. The role of the public interest lobbyist is not only to get legislation passed but also to open the decision-making process to legitimate and much needed public input.

Rule 2: *A public interest lobbyist's conduct should be above reproach.*

Doubters and opponents will watch your actions closely if you claim to advocate the concerns and interests of the public, and you should behave accordingly.

The CCAG was once invited by a political reform group to co-sponsor a cocktail party for legislators on a campaign reform issue. They respectfully declined, feeling that sponsoring legislative cocktail parties was appropriate neither for business and industry associations nor for good-government groups. The reputation of one very active public interest group in another state was badly damaged when allegations were made that one of its lobbyists was arranging social engagements for legislators.

Rule 3: *Lobbying is a time-consuming job.*

If you become a public interest lobbyist, don't expect the lobbying life to be one of constant glamour and excitement. Many hours will be spent waiting for repeatedly (and perhaps purposely) delayed hearings to start, sitting through boring meetings once they have started, and so forth. Although this may seem to be wasted time, it is extremely important that you establish a full-time presence at the capitol, able to endure the drudgery so that you are sure to be there when the decisions are made.

The importance of a strong commitment cannot be overemphasized if you hope to achieve real results. You may find that just as you are about to abandon a meeting in which an interminable discussion of bills in which you have no interest is taking place, the bill on which you have worked for three months comes up for consideration. Adding a conjunction here and deleting a plural there can ruin the bill, so you've got to be there—awake. Providing last-minute reminders, answering a crucial question for the hundredth time, or just making eye contact with a key supporter at a critical moment may be the thread on which your success or failure hangs. One of CCAG's lobbyists saved an important utilities bill by being present when its sponsor had stepped out of the room and the committee was about to vote to dump the bill. As a general rule, attend everything that you possibly can.

And don't leave early. You may think the committee has finished with your piece of legislation, but while the meeting is still in session, decisions can be changed. CCAG learned this lesson the hard way several years ago. They had worked very hard to get favorable committee action on a campaign-spending reform bill, and were delighted when the bill cleared the committee by a vote of 8 to 6. Their lobbyist left the meeting to celebrate the "victory" only to find out several hours later that the vote has been reversed when two of their supporters left the meeting and another opponent arrived. Had CCAG's lobbyist been there, they might have found those two supporters in the building and saved the bill.

Preparing for Lobbying

Your ability to influence legislation depends on your knowledge of both the legislative process and the legislators. A lobbyist functions most effectively when the legislators respect his or her competence and understanding of how the legislature works.

Step 1. Prepare your legislation and research ahead of time.

Let's assume that you have an issue you are concerned about and at least a general idea of legislation you would like to see passed. It is helpful to have a model law to work with, whether an actual law from another state, a bill from a previous year's attempt in your state, or a proposal from a research group, a national legal institute, or a sympathetic local attorney. If it is possible to prepare a bill that looks professional, do so. Also provide a memo summarizing the bill's intent and key provisions in plain English. Most legislators are no more eager than you are to read formal, technical language. Because your memo conveying the sense of your bill may be all they'll ever read, it should be clear, concise, and convincing.

You'll always be ahead of your opposition if you do the writing of any bill. If you write the bill, you control its contents. Whenever possible volunteer to draft a bill, or to write revisions or amendments. Since most legislatures are part-time and poorly staffed, legislators will appreciate your work. If you cannot prepare a draft of the bill, most states allow "skeleton" proposed bills, written in ordinary English, to be introduced and have staff do the technical drafting. Work closely with the drafter to ensure that your ideas are properly expressed in statutory language and are not changed by the drafter.

Step 2. Anticipate any problems that your proposal may cause.

Be sure to think out the implications of your proposed bill in advance. The economic consequences of any bill are likely to be the keys to its success or failure. Will appropriations be necessary to carry it out? Will it require new taxes or changes in existing taxes? Is it necessary or advisable to include specific directions or deadlines for actions or should the enforcing agency be given latitude in formulating a program? Will it require the establishment of a new state agency to enforce it? If not, which of the existing agencies should be charged with enforcement?

Which agency is designated to enforce your legislation can be critical in determining whether the law is gutted by bureaucratic scheming or given real meaning through vigorous enforcement by concerned and sympathetic state officials. CCAG struggled for more than a year over a simple set of regulations to enforce a law permitting pharmacists to post prescription drug prices. The legislature had designated the Pharmacy Commission, over their opposition, to draft the regulations. Like most professional boards, the commission is composed entirely of the more traditional members of the pharmacy profession. Had the more distant Department of Consumer Protection, or a special commission of sympathetic individuals, been responsible for drafting the regulations, a lot of the problems CCAG encountered could have been avoided.

Make your proposal as specific as possible. (Don't ask for a bill prohibiting business personnel from being nasty to consumers.). Be sure that the action you are seeking is appropriate for state government, rather than for federal or local governments. Make your proposal sound moderate, one that no reasonable person could object to: a proposal that appears to be radical, even if only in the rhetoric used to describe it, simply has less chance of passing.

Step 3: Develop thorough background material.

It is also advisable to compile general information on your issue, particularly newspaper clippings and any materials you can get from other states, other groups, and state agencies. The legislature itself may not be equipped to do this kind of research, and it is not difficult to become more knowledgeable than most legislators on a given subject. Many legislators work only part-time at the capitol. Because of this, they are not likely to be experts and are not inclined to become experts. At best they may be genuinely interested but lack the time to follow through on all the legislation that sounds good to them. State legislatures also have a relatively high rate of turnover, which further reduces the number of old pros and technical experts.

Your research must fill a serious information gap. You can be sure that the legislators will receive a steady barrage of information from the special interest groups presenting their side of any issue of importance. Pharmaceutical lobbyists, for instance, bring movies and leave flashy notebooks full of glossy photos and articles that sound authoritative. If you don't provide the counterarguments and the facts to support your position, no one else will. On credit-billing questions, an uninformed committee invited a friendly credit department manager of a large retail department store to explain an issue: you can be sure he did not present it from the consumer's point of view. The institutions of state government do not ensure that the many sides of an issue are presented fairly and in a balanced manner. Furthermore, by providing information, you establish yourself as a resource person on your subject, which is an extremely valuable position to occupy.

Step 4. Know the legislature: the who, the what, the how.

It is essential that you become familiar with the calendar, the procedures, and the people in your legislature. Know when the deadlines are; where to find the journals, bulletins, or other records of actions; how to get copies of bills and other publications. Find out what stages bills go through and when. If your state publishes a picture book of the legislators, study it. Be certain to get a complete list of the names and addresses of legislators and their committee assignments. Learn the geography of the capitol. Attending an orientation session held for first-term legislators is one good way of picking up this sort of information. The point is that you must know how things get done at the capitol.

The who: the players For the novice, sizing up the legislators can be a long and arduous undertaking. Generally, very little information is available in handy form.

Connecticut is a notable exception. In 1972 and 1974, CCAG undertook 1500-page projects compiling and evaluating the records of all Connecticut legislators. (The New York Public Interest Research Group did a similar project in 1974 for that state.) CCAG staff members interviewed all incumbents who were running for reelection (about 150 each year) and analyzed all debates on the floor of the House and the Senate. For each legislator a 10- to 15-page profile was prepared. The projects had such an impact at the capitol that legislators were heard to remark: "If we vote on this issue, it will be sure to end up in CCAG's book." A similar effort may be beyond your resources, but any information you can compile, including that based on your own experiences, will be invaluable both to you and to other public interest lobbyists. Other sources of information are offices in the capitol, legislative records, voter education groups, and other lobbying groups.

As mentioned previously, legislators are moved to act by a variety of motivations. Try to identify what motivates whom under what conditions.

The what: the stage A legislature permanently employs a great variety of people, from elevator operators to state police, from "go-fers" to counsel. While the House and Senate chambers are the most visible, the nitty-gritty work of the legislature is carried on by staffers working in less august chambers in the wings. Find out your state's equivalent for the following staff offices:

☐ The bill writers, who not only write bills but also check bills written by others for language and compatibility with existing statutes.

☐ The researchers, who do research for individual legislators and committees.

☐ The money specialists, who do general budgetary research and determine the fiscal impact of all tax and appropriations bills and, at the request of a legislator, of any other proposal.

☐ The housekeepers, who administer the legislature.

☐ The information givers, who provide information on the status of a bill, its current stage in the legislative process.

And, to help you keep track of what's going on, find out what daily bulletins, calendars, or other publications your state puts out, listing meetings, hearings, and other events, as well as what happened yesterday and what will happen today on particular bills.

The how: the script Though the details may differ from state to state, the general procedure by which a bill becomes law is the same everywhere. Make sure you know the specific rules that apply in your state. Here are some fundamental questions all lobbyists must be able to answer about their legislature:

☐ How are bills introduced? By legislator? by committee? by initiative?

☐ How are bills referred to committee?

☐ How are committees structured (joint or separate)?

☐ Are committee meetings open to the public and are the votes recorded?

☐ What is the procedure for public hearings?

☐ What actions can a committee take on a bill?

☐ If a bill fails to get out of committee, what alternative procedures are there to get it to the floor?

☐ What are the parliamentary rules?

☐ What information is public and how may it be obtained?

☐ Are party caucuses open to the public?

You should also keep a good handle on the timetable for the major steps in the legislative process, which usually follow a schedule established by statute or rule. For example, make sure you know when the session convenes and adjourns, what the deadlines are for introduction, drafting, and reporting of bills, and what the schedule is for floor debates on bills of interest.

While you will want to thoroughly understand how the legislature works in formal terms, remember that there are many points in the legislative process at which personalities and politics determine the course of events. Don't expect the rules to keep the process tidy. It will take some time to figure out the ins and outs of your legislature, so keep your eyes open for the ways that issues are diluted, sidetracked, or hidden by smokescreens.

Your resources again will determine how you go about reaching the public. Mass mailings, letter-writing, the telephone network, speech-making, and the communications media are the standard channels. Keep in mind that some issues or events lend themselves well to TV coverage while others are better handled in newspaper stories. Try to tailor your activities to maximize coverage. Don't forget letters to editors, replies to editorials, feature stories, and press conferences. The media are undoubtedly the best way to inform the largest number of people, so cultivate your relations with them. Get to know reporters, particularly regular staff reporters at the capitol (they are also a good source of information on what's happening there, as they are generally relatively uninvolved observers with a useful perspective on events and people). You need coverage and reporters need stories. Refer to Chapter 11 for more specific information about working effectively with the media.

AT THE LEGISLATURE

Step 6: Find a sponsor for your proposal with interest and political clout.

Probably the most important trait to look for in a sponsor for your proposed bill is a strong interest. If you're completely new at lobbying, you'll have to do some research to learn which legislators might be willing to sponsor your bill. Start reading current and back issues of your state and local newspapers with this in mind. See what reference tools your state library has available. Some libraries and newspapers have clipping files that you can use. Look for voting records as well as campaign statements on issues. Voter education groups such as the League of Women Voters may have this information. Ask groups with related interests who have worked at the capitol in the past. If the issue has come up before the legislature in previous sessions, examine the transcripts of the debates and public hearings, which should be available at your state library. If this precise matter is new to the legislature, look for persons who have introduced bills on related subjects.

Think about pairing a relatively unknown legislator who has a strong interest in the bill with a powerful member of the leadership or a committee chairperson as a co-sponsor. Try to secure a broad sponsorship for your legislation—different wings of the same party, members of different parties. And of course, try to get sponsors from both houses of the legislature.

Given an interest in your bill, your ideal sponsor would be a member of the leadership in the legislature. Next in order of desirability as a sponsor would be the chairperson of the committee that will consider the bill, a member of that committee, and finally any sympathetic legislator (you might start with your own local legislator).

Once you have a potential sponsor, sit down with the legislator and discuss your bill. Personal contact is important: don't depend on the mails or a telephone call. A general rule to be followed in all contacts with legislators: *always follow up*. Try to give them some kind of memo after every conversation. If you telephone them, send a follow-up letter; if you write them, make a follow-up phone call. Your goal is to establish yourself as a resource person on all questions pertaining to your issue.

Step 7: Make sure the committee process is open.

Committees should be open to public participation and public scrutiny. If they're not, then getting them open should probably be one of your first priorities. Because what happens in committee determines whether or not legislation will ever reach the floor, plan to monitor the appropriate committees and take part in their activities as fully as possible.

Step 8: Get to know the committee: its legislators, staff, other lobbyists, and process.

Try to attend *all* meetings. In addition to participating informally in their proceedings, you'll have a chance to observe how the various legislators work. It's at committee meetings that you'll first have an opportunity to see the results of the behind-the-scenes activities. You may learn that the debate and decision on a matter have already occurred in the washroom.

At breaks in the committee meetings, take the opportunity to get to know the legislators. As a public interest lobbyist, you may feel uncomfortable about adopting the old-buddy behavior of other lobbyists, and be tempted to adopt a holier-than-thou attitude, but this will only alienate legislators and will not encourage them to accept your proposals. You don't have to be a back-slapper if that goes against the grain, but being sociable and approachable is really more effective than appearing aloof and superior to the whole scene. You may find that legislators are most receptive to your arguments in the least structured settings, that is, in the cafeteria rather than in the committee room. Without going overboard on the friendliness bit and compromising your own integrity, use informal opportunities.

Friendliness toward the staff people as well as the legislators is similarly helpful. Members of the staff of a committee keep track of all the bills, often determine which messages get through to the legislators, and what background information is filed or distributed to the committee members. Legislators may rely on staff people for opinions and answers to questions simply because the staffers are there every day. Friends on a committee staff can help to keep your bill in a harried chairperson's mind. Members of the staff of other offices in the capitol are assigned such important tasks as researching issues, officially drafting bills, and reporting fiscal impact. They can pass along useful information and timely observations. They'll appreciate the same from you.

The committee meetings will probably also provide your first chance to size up your opposition—the other lobbyists. Since many of the issues of concern to public interest lobbyists are likely to draw heavy opposition from vested interests, you can generally count on the presence of opposing lobbyists. Your adversaries will be using all the tactics you'll be using to persuade the legislators, and probably some you wouldn't use (the expense account again). Get to know them as well as possible. You may be surprised to find them acting extremely nice to you. If you can remain on civil terms with them, you may get some useful information.

You may also find it disconcerting that the special interest lobbyists seem to be really at home in the capitol, perhaps even more so than many of the legislators. It's no wonder they act at home—they're probably there full-time, and the capitol has been their almost exclusive preserve for many years. (They may be former legislators themselves.) That's why you're there now.

Keep in mind here your role as a watchdog of the legislative process. If you see the process becoming secretive, complain and call attention to that secrecy. This is at least as important as any substantive issue.

Finally, legislative committees have three crucial functions: (1) they hold public hearings and sometimes special (educational) hearings, (2) they decide the actual provisions of bills, and (3) they decide whether or not bills actually reach the floor.

Step 9: Use public hearings as a platform to tell legislators and the general public about your bill.

Public hearings provide the formal setting for the committee to obtain information. Use them fully as a forum for your position. Bring in experts to testify when possible and appropriate, and bring in the public when possible (it's always appropriate). Get there early and try to speak first. Have your testimony written and give a copy of it to every legislator there. But don't read from your text, *speak*! You'll get more attention. Use your imagination to do something unusual with your testimony, such as providing audiovisual materials to go with it. Nevertheless, don't expect to see a line of fully attentive legislators: they may be chatting, doodling, or dozing while you talk. Try to take it in stride.

The hearings are for the benefit of lobbyists as much as legislators: you'll have a chance to hear your opponents' case. Hearings are also the time when your issue gets media coverage if it ever will. If you can, work for a media story focusing on your group and your issue. Try to get the reporters to cover *you* testifying at the hearing, not the fact that a hearing was held. Before a hearing on a bill to require new buildings to be made accessible to the handicapped, a wheelchair brigade circling in front of the room drew sufficient attention to ensure that the bill passed unanimously, without debate.

Step 10: Use public hearings as a means to demonstrate your clout on an issue.

Hearings are the place for you to show the public support for your position by locating interested members of the public and making sure they attend. The more people, the better: a room packed with new faces makes a great impression on legislators. It also makes a good media event. Remember that hearings are important only if you can make use of them for your own purposes: to get the public's attention or demonstrate your political clout. Even your most rational arguments on the merits of your legislation may fail if you cannot demonstrate public support for your position.

As the committee deadline draws near, things are bound to become hectic and probably confused. Be sure that you're there to answer questions, remind the legislators about your bill, and just keep an eye on things. Bills can often be turned around and gutted in order to complete work before a deadline.

Step 11: Check for methods to bring your bill to the House or Senate floor even after it has died in committee.

The moment of truth comes when the committee votes on whether your bill goes to the whole assembly for consideration. If the committee blocks your bill, check your state's rules and speak with strong supporters to see if there is some way it can be resurrected.

There are often ways to use other rules in such circumstances.

Step 12: In lobbying the floor, try to personally contact as many legislators as possible.

You have been working in the committee with a relatively small group of legislators, but once the bill reaches the floor you are going to face perhaps ten times as many people who will vote on your bill. How can you get to them all? You'll have to make some difficult decisions based on your assessment of the climate in which you are working. Among the things to consider are whether or not your issue is well known, the existing support or opposition, the position of the leadership, and what other bills are before the legislature (remember that your number one issue will not be the top priority for everyone else).

You'll have to decide whether to try to reach every legislator or whether to work on or with a key group of legislators who will lobby their colleagues as a matter of course. Your staff limitations will probably be the determining factor. You can stuff mailboxes or talk personally to the legislators but, if you have sufficient personnel to do so, talking and providing memos on your bills is the best way to gain support.

Some bills show up on the calendar a few days after the committee votes; others disappear for months. Sometimes there is a deliberate effort to lose a bill, so don't assume that the legislative process will ensure that your bill comes to the floor. There are controversial issues on which legislators prefer not to have to make a decision. One of your most important functions may be to force lawmakers to take public stands on such issues and be accountable in the political process.

Be aware that amendments may be introduced before and during the debate. Some amendments substitute an entirely new bill for your proposal. Other changes may be so drastic that you'd prefer to see your own bill defeated: you must be there to decide and to let your allies know. In other cases, it may simply be extremely important for you to be present to answer questions at the last minute. If the issue or the sponsoring legislator is new, it may be possible for you to influence what is said in the opening statement and what answers are prepared for expected questions.

A CCAG-backed bill, requiring landlords to pay double damages if they failed to return the tenants' security deposits, appeared to be in trouble on the floor and was withdrawn from debate. Their lobbyist scurried down to the chambers and discussed the bill right on the spot, working out a slightly weaker but still very good bill. If the lobbyist hadn't been there, ready to respond to unexpected events, the bill probably would have been gutted by amendments or left to die.

Legislators often have decided how they will vote long before the debate. The debate itself may be largely a matter of form. Legislators are supposed to engage in debate, and to constituents it looks like something important is going on. However, on some controversial and emotional issues, the debate may really be the decisive time for making up sluggish minds.

Nebraska has a unicameral, or one-house, legislature. All other states have a bicameral, or two-house, legislature. When your bill passes one house, it still has a second house to get through. Remember that each house may have very different characteristics. In addition, bills that carry appropriations or change or establish taxes may be required to go to additional committees, where economic considerations can sidetrack the issue. For example, one bill introduced in the Connecticut legislature to set up a nuclear power study group almost died in the appropriations committee because it was thought that the bill would cost the state $10,000. In fact, however, the money was to come from the utility companies, not the state and, by pointing this out, CCAG managed to save the bill.

AFTER THE LEGISLATURE

Step 13: After your bill passes, work to get the governor to sign it.

Don't sit back and breathe your sigh of relief yet. You still have the possibility of the governor's veto to contend with. Even if you think the governor will sign the bill, it helps to have the supporters of the bill write to him or her on the issue. If the governor is hostile to the bill, a big public campaign is in order—press releases, letters, telephone calls.

Step 14: After your bill becomes law, you must monitor what happens to the legislation.

The governor signs. Sigh-of-relief time? Sorry, not yet. There are regulations to be drafted to implement the bill. Poor regulations or foot-dragging by a state agency can totally undermine all that you've worked for. Draw up your own draft of regulations and submit them to the appropriate agency. Attend hearings on the regulations. If the regulations that the agency finally issues are still horrible, appeal them to the state's legislative regulations review committee, if there is one, or consider going to court.

OK. Now you can take your sigh of relief. But make it quick, because you've now got to prepare to monitor the state agencies. Let them know you're watching them—it should help to keep them on their toes.

Here are some problems to guard against when regulations are written. Bad regulations can make your legislation useless or even harmful.

☐   Watch for unfriendly agencies being made responsible for regulation writing and enforcement.

☐   Watch for endless postponement and delays in adopting regulations.

☐   Watch for regulations being ignored by the enforcing agency.

☐   Watch for bad appointments to a newly created agency to carry out your legislation.

The entire lobbying process described here, in order to be done well, takes full-time commitment. Special interest lobbyists know this and act on it. While your resources are likely to be more limited than those of other lobbyists, come as close as possible to this goal.

Accountability

Ultimately, the legislators must be held accountable for their votes. They must answer to their constituents: if they vote for the public interest, you should make this known; if they vote against the public interest, you *must* make this known.

For our system to work, legislators must believe that their actions will be scrutinized by an informed citizenry. There are several ways, ranging from the simple to the comprehensive, to help make legislators accountable. You can blow the whistle on conflicts of interest and tip off reporters to any shenanigans you discover. You can compile indexes of how the legislators have voted on those issues you are concerned with and publicize your results. For example, if your state has a "Dirty Dozen" who always vote against environmental bills, their constituents ought to be so informed. If you have the resources, you may be able to produce detailed evaluations on a variety of issues for every legislator, based on his or her voting record, campaign promises, public statements, and personal interviews, as CCAG did in 1972 and 1974, just in time for the elections.

Why you shouldn't give up: *the other side won't.*

LAWMAKING BY THE PEOPLE: THE INITIATIVE

The initiative is the process by which people, through petition, may write laws to be submitted directly to the voters of their state for passage or defeat. The initiative process is self-government in its truest form, giving any citizen or group of citizens the power to enact laws.

Before a proposed law (called a proposition in most states) can be submitted to the electorate, a certain percentage of voters must have indicated, by signing petitions, their wish to see the proposition on the ballot. The exact percentage varies from state to state and ranges from about 5 percent to 10 percent.

This type of lawmaking by direct election is not new. For nearly 20 years after the founding of Plymouth colony, lawmaking was done in a primary assembly of freemen. When the colony grew so large that it was difficult for people to meet in this manner several times a year, every town elected two delegates to join in enacting ordinances, and the whole population met once each year to have general overview, to repeal all acts deemed ill-advised, and to pass any new legislation desired. This government lasted from 1638 to 1658, and in a modified form until 1686.

After 1686, lawmaking by direct election was set aside and representative democracy was developed. It wasn't until 90 years ago that South Dakota brought back direct legislation by adopting the initiative process. Currently, 22 states have the initiative process. A list of these states and their initiative laws can be found in Resource 12.1.

Examples of initiative propositions in recent years range from general political and environmental reforms to prohibiting public boxing matches on Sunday. In 1971, 350,000 Californians signed initiative petitions for an act to ban DDT, phase out leaded gasoline at filling stations, and impose a five-year moratorium on nuclear power plant construction. A Colorado initiative featured provisions to regulate state lobbyists, boost corporate taxes, and reform the state utility commission. The state of Washington saw initiative bills aimed at protection of shorelines from offshore oil drilling and limitation of the amount of solid waste through requirement of refunds on all beverage containers.

The initiative is a powerful tool but one that is often difficult and time consuming to implement. Although citizens live much closer together than they did in the days of Plymouth Colony, they have difficulty in communicating with one another because they do not control their communications systems. For this reason, use of the initiative—specifically signature gathering—has become an art which requires tight organization and training to be successful.

Know the Initiative Law

The first step in any initiative campaign is to become completely familiar with state laws governing the process. The guidelines for drafting the legislation, filing the initiative with state officials, and collecting signatures on a petition will be quite specific and even a slight error may invalidate your efforts. After you have reviewed the law, consult with the office of the Secretary of State about drafting and filing requirements.

The most important consideration with regard to drafting the law is its constitutionality. An otherwise successful initiative effort will become a futile exercise in self-government if, after passage, your law is declared unconstitutional by the courts. Consult with law professors and attorneys who know this area of the law. Find out if a similar statute has been adopted in another state and whether it was tested for constitutionality.

Pay careful attention to the phrasing of the law, keeping it as simple and precise as possible. Your proposition may be defeated because voters either do not understand the issue or cannot understand whether a yes or a no vote is needed to support it!

When analyzing the sections of the initiative law relating to signature gathering, be particularly attentive to restrictions governing who can circulate and who can sign petitions, whether or not signatures must *exactly* duplicate the name under which the voter is registered, time restraints for signature gathering, and any other technicalities.

After you have become familiar with state law, fulfilled any technicalities, and have drafted your law, file the initiative with state officials.

The next step is to set out your organizing strategy. Media coverage of your issue and a well run drive are the two essential elements of such a strategy.

The media coverage must begin before petitioning, as people will be hesitant to sign if they are not somewhat familiar with the proposed law already. Your group cannot educate people during the time they are gathering signatures. Well in advance of the petition drive, decide exactly what information voters must have about the issue, how you are going to get that information to them, and what other groups should be asked to work with you.

Begin your media campaign with a press conference in the state capital and other large cities. Refer to Chapter 11 for specific information about effective press conferences, news releases, and other aspects of dealing with the media. Keep the momentum high and interest growing by arranging for coverage on radio and television talk shows, making speeches before community groups, sending letters to newspapers, and distributing flyers and pamphlets at places where large numbers of people congregate. The drive for press coverage should be intensified as the signatures are being collected.

Signature-gathering

Successful signature-gathering is an art that can become the basis of a successful initiative drive. Good signature-gathering involves hard work, perseverence, and tight organization.

Determine ahead of time which are the best places for signature-gathering in each community—places where you can find the largest numbers of people. Appoint a chairperson of the effort who will make personal visits and telephone calls before charting out the target places.

If your media program has been successful and you do a good job of organizing, the ranks of your core group should swell considerably during the period of the petition drive. Many people who did not have the desire or ability to help with other aspects of your effort may be willing to devote time to getting people to sign the petition. However, you can make no worse mistake than to allow people to solicit signatures for the petition who have not been "trained" in the issue and in the signature-gathering techniques discussed below. Untrained workers will be ineffective, turn off the people they approach, and become discouraged quickly.

Set up several training sessions during the course of the petition drive so new volunteers can be put to work quickly. Invite experts who have successfully run initiative campaigns to train your workers.

Have factsheets on hand explaining the issue and the law you have drafted as well as *numbered* petition forms. The petition forms should be headed with the law you are proposing, translated into easily comprehended, nonlegal language. Include the name and address of a person from whom additional petition forms may be obtained. Be sure to record to whom each petition form is given at the time they are first distributed or your record keeping will become hopelessly confused. In addition, you may wish to expand the factsheet into a "petitioner's handbook" with questions and answers about the issue and the law you are proposing, instructions on how to petition, a map of the petition stations you have decided to use, and a time grid for volunteers to use to record the times and locations they have agreed to canvass. Wrap up the meeting by having your workers sign up for specific locations and time slots on volunteer sheets prepared for the training session by the organizers.

Your workers cannot be expected to educate the public about the details of the petition. If your media campaign has been successful, most persons asked to sign the petition should be somewhat familiar with your proposed law and should need little explanation from your helpers. Remind those persons who seem undecided that by signing the petition they are not voting yes to the law but merely requesting the opportunity to vote for or against it at election time.

The most effective method for collecting signatures is to set up tables in well-traveled traffic areas and organize your efforts around them. Petitions should be attached to the tables with masking tape. This permits several persons to sign simultaneously and requires fewer volunteers at each station. Two or three people should work at each table, one or two in front to bring the people to the table and one in back of the table to make sure that people sign properly. Never provide chairs! Action is the key word and you must keep people moving. If you get tired, take a break, but never sit behind the table.

Discourage people from taking petitions away from the table. If they insist, hand them a blank petition and move them away from the front of the table so the area will not become too crowded for others to move in and sign.

Don't leave pens near each taped petition. The person behind the table should hand the pen to each person being asked to sign. This approach is more personal and will cut down on the number of pens accidentally removed.

Do not overload your table with literature. Keep a small amount available for those people who simply will neither sign nor leave until they get something to take along to study. Give these people a blank but numbered petition along with the literature.

The basic method of approaching people follows: The helper in front of the table should approach people one by one, make eye contact and ask, "Are you registered to vote?" or (depending on the requirements of your state initiative law), "Did you vote in the last election and are you registered to vote this year?" If the person replies "Yes," the helper should turn towards the table with a gesture and say, "Please sign for safe nuclear power," (or whatever the appropriate request, given your proposed law). Usually the person will move to the table at that point and it will not be necessary for you to say anything else. The person behind the table stands with the pens in hand and says, "Are you registered in_____county?" If the person replies yes, hand him or her a pen, point out a petition that is not being signed by someone else, and ask the person to sign with exactly the signature used when he or she registers to vote. Most people will or will not sign at this point—and usually they sign.

If someone asks a question, they should be answered specifically but with the shortest possible answer. Remember, you are trying to get a rhythm and flow of signers at the table. Any interruption of this process will stop the signatures. If someone starts an argument—don't debate the issue. Instead arrange to discuss it with that person at another time.

Always be polite and cheerful. Rude remarks can give your effort a bad name. If you are getting a lot of "Nos," take a break. A good appearance, pleasant smile, positive attitude, and enthusiasm in your voice and movement are all-important to the petition drive.

Place the table so that it doesn't interrupt the natural flow of traffic. Often this means that your table will be placed at the left of a doorway because people frequently turn to their left (a psychological anomaly) after they have left a doorway.

Dress neatly and wear comfortable shoes. Keep your station neat and do not eat at the table. If you are hungry, go elsewhere to eat. Beverages are OK, but never put a cup on the table, or the contents will invariably end up all over your petitions.

The first few thousand signatures will probably be rather easily obtained. The last ones are almost always the most difficult to get, so it is important that the press coverage be intensified during the time. Keep daily tallies of how many signatures are collected at each station. As an area begins to slack off, consideration should be given to moving on to another spot. Keep petitioners informed about the progress of the signature drive to keep up their enthusiasm.

Don't stop the drive when you have obtained the requisite number of signatures. A certain percentage of those signatures will not be valid and you must have several thousand over the limit as insurance. Some groups have stopped what they thought was a successful petition drive only to discover a week or two later that they fell short of the required number of validated signatures by only a few hundred or thousand. Resparking the drive at that point would be very difficult.

Once the initiative proposition has been qualified, you must campaign for approval of the proposition by the electorate. Use of the referendum has been demonstrated repeatedly by political candidates and the fight for approval of your ballot proposition must take on all the trappings of a good political campaign. You need the support of a majority of those who vote and will have to campaign to get it. This is best done with professional assistance. Consult those who have been successful in initiative campaigns and be prepared to raise campaign funds to get your message to the voters.

resources

State Statistics on Disclosure of Prescription Drug Prices*

SYMBOLS

M – Disclosure mandatory
R – Prohibited by Board of Pharmacy Regulations
S – Prohibited by statute
C – Prohibited by rule or statute as to some or all controlled substances but not all prescription drugs
I – Extensive medical or other information required or considered necessary
? – Unclear or undetermined

DISCLOSURE TECHNIQUE

1. In-store verbal disclosure to person with prescription
2. In-store verbal disclosure to person without prescription
3. Telephone disclosure to caller with prescription
4. Telephone disclosure to caller without prescription
5. Within store posting of prices (1 sign) not visible from outside
6. Within store posting of prices (1 sign) visible from outside
7. Within store posting of prices (more than one sign)
8. Newspaper ad – "price posters/lists available in store"
9. Radio/TV ad – "price posters/lists available in store"
10. In-store list of prices removable from store
11. Mailing or distributing (other than removable lists) a list of prices
12. Discount ads (e.g. "10% off", "cut rate")
13. Comparative newspaper ad – "Rx prices lower than competitors"
14. Comparative radio/TV ad – "Rx prices lower than competitors"
15. Newspaper ad – discloses actual Rx prices
16. Radio/TV ad – discloses actual Rx prices

STATE	1	2	3	4	5	6	7	8	9	10	11	12	13	14	15	16
Alabama	R	R	R	R	R	R	R	R	*S/R	S	R	S/R	S	S/R	R	R
Alaska	S	S	S	S	S	S	S	S	*S/R	S	S	S/R	S	S	S/R	S/R
Arizona		?	?		?	?	?	?								
Arkansas	C	C		C	?	?	?	?		?		?	?	?	?	?
California	M	M	M	M	C/M	?	?	?		?		?	?	?	?	?
Colorado																
Connecticut			M					S	S	S						
Delaware																
D.C.																
Florida					C	C	C	C	C	C		C	C	C	C	C
Georgia					S/R	C/R	S/R	S/R	C/R	S/R		S/R	S/R	S/R	S/R	C/R
Hawaii		M		M	C	C	S/R	C	C	S/R		C	S/R	S/R	C	C
Idaho																
Illinois								C/R		C/R		C/R		C/R	C/R	C/R
Indiana								C/R		C/R		C/R		C/R	C/R	C/R
Iowa					R	R	R	R/I	R	R/R		R	R	R/I	R/R	R/I
Kansas								R/I		R/I		I	I	I	R/I	R/I
Kentucky					C	C	C	C/I		C/S		C	C	C	C	C
Louisiana					C/S	S		C/S	S	S		S	S	S	C/S	C/S
Maine					M/M	C/S		C/S		C/S					C	C/S
Maryland					S	S/C		S		S/C					S	S
Massachusetts								C/R		C/R		R	R	R	C/R	C/R
Michigan					M/M	?		?		C		C	C	C	C	C
Minnesota	M		M		M/M			C		C		R	R	R	C	C
Mississippi																
Missouri					C	C		C		C		C	C	C	C	C
Montana																
Nebraska																
Nevada	M	M	M	M	M/M											
New Hampshire					M/M											
New Jersey					S			S		S		S	S	S	S/C	S/C
New Mexico								I/C		S/I		R/R	R/R	R/R	I/C	I/C
New York	M			M				R		R		R	R	R	R	R
North Carolina																
North Dakota					?	S	?	S	S	S	S	S	S	S	S	S
Ohio					S/I	S/I	S/I	S		S/I	S/I				S/I	S/I
Oklahoma					S	S	S	S	S	S					S	S
Oregon																
Pennsylvania										I					C	C
Rhode Island					C/R	C/R	C/R	C/R	C/R	R		C/R	C/R	C/R	C/R	C/R
South Carolina																
South Dakota	M	M	M	M	S	S	R	R	S/R	S/R	S	S/R	S/R	S	R	R
Tennessee																
Texas			M	M	S/R	S/R		S/R	S/R	S		S	S	S	S/R	S/R
Utah																
Vermont				M												
Virginia																
Washington	M	M	M	M				R		R		R	R	R	R	R
West Virginia								R		R		R	R	R	R	R
Wisconsin																
Wyoming																

*Prepared by the Federal Trade Commission, 1976

Notes for 1.1

ALABAMA Present prohibitions on price disclosures are found in Rule 8, Code of Professional Conduct, effective October 1, 1967. The Board of Pharmacy was permanently enjoined in 1974 from enforcing Rule 9, Code of Professional Conduct, which prohibited the use of discount terms or comparative advertising. This rule was also effective on October 1, 1967, and remained in effect until *Revco Southern Drug Centers, Inc. v. Alabama State Board of Pharmacy,* No. 38860 (Cir. Ct., Montgomery County, Ala., Feb. 12, 1974).

ALASKA Section 08.80.420 (b) which prohibits most forms of price disclosure was added to the Alaska Pharmacy Act in 1972.

ARIZONA Arizona Pharmacy Act Section 32-1932 B.3 was effective August 11, 1970. Arizona Board of Pharmacy Rules and Regulations, Rule 6.6120, was effective October 26, 1970.

ARKANSAS Regulation 18 of the Arkansas Board of Pharmacy was repealed in February, 1975; it had been in effect at least since the early 1960s. This regulation prohibited most forms of price disclosure.

Act 1436, Arkansas Acts of 1975, Section 5, specifically authorizes but does not mandate the display of prescription drug prices; however, it prohibits the display of prices of controlled substances. The statute prohibits controlled substances prices on posters but does not specifically prohibit them on price lists. Since the act does not regulate media advertising it appears that the controlled substances prohibition does not apply to media advertising. Thus, it appears that the only current restriction on price advertising in Arkansas is the prohibition on posting prices of controlled substances.

CALIFORNIA Price disclosures are restricted by Section 651 and 651.3 of the California Business and Professions Code. Section 651.3 which prohibits price advertising was added to the Business and Professions Code in 1961. Stats. 1961, c. 199, p. 1205, Section 1. Section 651, which prohibits discounts, was added in 1955. Stats. 1955, c. 1050, p. 2001, Section 1. The Board of Pharmacy was enjoined from enforcing Sections 651, 651.3 and 652.5 in *Terry v. State Board of Pharmacy,* 395F Supp. 94, May 12, 1975). This has been appealed to the United States Supreme Court, No. 75-336.

California has a mandatory posting law, Business and Professions Code, Section 4333 (b) which became effective January 1, 1974. Business and Professions Code Section 4333 (a), also effective January 1, 1974, mandates disclosure of price information by telephone.

COLORADO H. B. 1154, effective July 1, 1975, permits all price disclosures. Prior to this, Section 48-1-2 (d) 1, effective April 1, 1972, required extensive medical information about each drug advertised, including warnings and contraindications. This was enjoined in *Dillon Companies, Inc. v. Moore,* Civil Action No. C-38188, (Dist. Ct., Denver, Colo., May 30, 1974). Prior to the promulgation of this regulation in 1972, a much stricter regulation was in effect which completely prohibited the posting or advertising of prescription drug prices and the use of discount or cut-rate phrases. This latter regulation had been in effect at least since 1964.

CONNECTICUT The advertising of cut-rate or discount prices is prohibited by Connecticut General Statutes, Chap. 382, Section 20-175, Article 18, which became effective in 1961. Article 18 was not changed by new pharmacy laws which eliminated Article 17 which had further prohibited disclosure of price information since 1961. PA 75-543, effective October 1, 1975, removes the prohibition on posting of controlled substances. PA 75-95, Connecticut General Statutes, effective May 12, 1975, removes the prohibition on advertising prescription prices in the media.

PA 75-543 made posting mandatory, effective October 1, 1975. The Commissioner of Consumer Protection has authority to draft regulations under this statute. Prior to this, Connecticut had a statute which permitted posting although it did not require it; PA 73-480, effective July 1, 1974. This latter statute permitted posting and advertising of the fact that prices were posted.

FLORIDA Court cases overturned rule and portion of earlier statute prohibiting promotion of some prescription drugs. *Florida Board of Pharmacy v. Webb's City, Inc.*, 219 S.2d 681 (Fla. 1969); *Stadnick v. Shell's City, Inc.*, 140 So. 2d 871 (Fla. 1962). Prohibitions still in effect for all narcotics, central nervous system stimulants, tranquilizers, barbiturates, and other hypnotic and somnifacient drugs. Florida Rules and Laws, Section 465.23 (a) - (e) was effective in 1965; 465.23 (f) which prohibited the promotion or advertising of any prescription drug was added in 1967. 465.23 (f) was declared unconstitutional in *Webb City* in 1969, and was removed from the statute by the legislature in 1974.

GEORGIA Section 79A-408 (8), Georgia Pharmacy Laws, which restricts disclosure of price information, was effective on July 1, 1967. Georgia Pharmacy Rules 480-16.01 (5) were filed on June 30, 1965, effective October 26, 1970.

HAWAII Rule permits posting (except for controlled substances); must include 100 drugs in three quantities plus services and be located within prescription department area.

Telephonic disclosures required (other than controlled substances).

Media price ads permitted if they include, at a minimum: those drugs (in three quantities) most frequently prescribed; availability of services; and notice of price availability by telephone. Media ads not specifically authorized are prohibited.

ILLINOIS A court case permanently enjoined enforcement of Board of Pharmacy rules and regulations V1 and V21 which prohibited prescription advertising. *Osco Drug, Inc. v. Dept. of Registration and Education*, No. 71-Ch5276 (Cir. Ct., Cook County, Ill., Oct. 23, 1973). This case is presently on appeal. The regulations were promulgated in 1962; prior to this there may have been other prohibitions on price advertising in Illinois. The board revised its regulations, August 22, 1975, to eliminate all references to advertising.

"Advertising" of controlled substances by name is still prohibited; definition of "advertising" is unclear. Illinois Controlled Substances Act. Section 315, effective August 16, 1971.

INDIANA Advertising of prescription prices is prohibited by Regulation 20, Section 1 (b), which was adopted May 14, 1962, filed June 18, 1962. This was challenged in

PIRG v. Cohan, which was dismissed on technical grounds with leave to amend the complaint.

IOWA Regulation 9.4 (205) which restricts prescription advertising was first promulgated in 1962 and was enforced until 1966. Board indicates that although rule has remained in the regulations since then, it has not been enforced. Pharmacy Board suggests that rule prohibiting advertising not enforced for media ads if extensive medical information about each drug is included.

Rule requires reminder sign in store that prices are available upon request and presentation of prescription.

KANSAS Kansas has currently no laws or regulations relating to prescription price advertising. However, the Board has the power under K.S.A. 1974 Supp. 65-1650 to "regulate the advertising" of prescription drugs. The Board is currently drafting regulations under this statute. 65-1650, which became effective July 1, 1975, specifically states that the Board may not require, regulate, or prohibit posting of prices nor may it restrict the offering of discounts on prescription drugs.

Prior to July 1, 1975, advertising of prescription drug prices was regulated under Sec. 68-2-17, a regulation promulgated by the Board of Pharmacy in January 1, 1966. Subsection (a) of this regulation prohibited the advertising of prescription prices. This regulation was declared an invalid exercise of the Board's authority in Opinion 74-45 by the Attorney General, issued February 11, 1974. Board states that it did not enforce this section of the regulation after the Attorney General's opinion was issued.

The Attorney General's opinion did not affect Subsections (b) and (c) of KAR 68-2-17, and these remained in effect until the new Pharmacy Law became effective July 1, 1975. These prohibited advertising of professional superiority, and advertising which tends to cause excess purchases of prescription drugs. One case held that the Board could not prohibit the name "Rx for Less" under these sections of regulation, but did not overturn the regulation. *Rx for Less v. State Board of Pharmacy,* No. 125558 (Shawnee Cty. Dist. Ct., Topeka, Kan., October 4, 1974).

KENTUCKY Statute expressly prohibits Pharmacy Board from regulating advertising of prescription drugs. Controlled Substances Act prohibits advertising of controlled substances by brand or generic name, KRS Section 218 (a) .140. This became effective in 1972.

LOUISIANA Louisiana Rev. Stat. 37 Section 1225 (11), which prohibits advertising, has been in effect approximately 20 years. The Board stated that the prohibition was apparently contained in the Code of Ethics promulgated in 1956 and was put into the statute about 1960. In addition, Board Regulation #22, which prohibits use of discount phrases and reference to prescription prices, has been in effect for approximately the same period.

MAINE Board of Pharmacy Regulation #21 which previously prohibited advertising was in effect for at least 20 years, and remained in effect despite Attorney General's indication that it was invalid. It was replaced by a new statute governing prescription price disclosures, 22 MRSA Section 220 (4) (D). This became effective May 12, 1975 and permits advertising except for controlled substances, needles and syringes, and television advertising.

The statute 22 MRSA Section 2204-F, also effective May 12, 1975, makes posting mandatory.

MARYLAND The Controlled Dangerous Substances Act, Article 27 Section 300 (e) (*ii*), which was enacted in 1961, makes it a criminal offense to advertise controlled dangerous substances or prescription drugs by trade name or by generic name. A recent letter from the Attorney General to the Board of Pharmacy expresses reservations about this section in light of *Maryland Board of Pharmacy v. Sav-A-Lot, Inc.,* 311 A.2d 242 (Md., 1973).

Maryland Board of Pharmacy v. Sav-A-Lot, Inc. overturned another statutory provision regulating prescription price advertising, Article 43, Section 266A (c) (4) (*iv*), which prohibited the use of discount or cut-rate terms. This section was also apparently enacted in 1961.

Posting became mandatory in Maryland on January 1, 1976; controlled substances may not be posted: H.B. 1026, Article 43, Section 271A. Another recent letter of the Attorney General's office indicates that the Board does not have the power to stop pharmacies from voluntarily posting prices prior to the distribution by the Board of the posting charts authorized in this statute.

MASSACHUSETTS Rule 49, Code of Professional Conduct of Pharmacy, which has several provisions which relate to prescription price advertising, was adopted on September 29, 1961. Chapter 94 (c), Section 46 of the Massachusetts Pharmacy Laws was enacted in 1971, effective July 1, 1972. Prior to the present regulatory and statutory restrictions on price advertising, there were other similar restrictions in both the regulations and the statutes, although apparently prior restrictions related mostly to narcotic drugs.

MICHIGAN Section 15 (e) which prohibits the "promotion" of prescription drugs was promulgated in 1962. It has been interpreted by the Board of Pharmacy in a declaratory ruling issued in February, 1975, to not include simple price disclosures. Board maintains that it now recognizes distinction between "promotion" of prescription drugs and "price information."

The mandatory price posting bill, Act 155, which was effective June, 1975 has been implemented by Board of Pharmacy regulations effective July 24, 1975.

MINNESOTA Regulation 37 (k) which prohibited the advertising of prescription prices was first enacted in 1960; it was revised or enlarged in 1969, and revised again effective April 29, 1975. Board maintains that present revisions are intended to differentiate between the providing of prescription price information and the promotion of prescription drugs. The new regulation prohibits representations about efficacy or safety of the drugs, prohibits price information for Schedule II-IV drugs and requires that the advertisement include a termination date for the prices given.

Minnesota has a mandatory posting law, Section 151.06 Subdivision 2A which was effective August, 1973. This revision also requires that price information be given upon request by telephone or in person to anyone holding a valid prescription.

MISSISSIPPI Board of Pharmacy adopted new regulations effective January 1, 1976, which eliminated both Article 1, Section 8 and Article 15 from the Pharmacy Law, leaving no restrictions on advertising prescription prices.

Article XV was overturned in a court case, *Mississippi State Board of Pharmacy v. Steele,* 317 So. 2d 33 (Miss., 1975) because the Board exceeded its statutory authority in promulgating the regulation.

Article 1 Section 8, which is the same as Section 8 of APhA's Code of Ethics, was adopted as a board of Pharmacy regulation effective September 27, 1973. Article 15 has been in effect since about 1970. There were apparently no restrictions on prescription price advertising in Mississippi prior to these provisions.

MISSOURI Section 195.060 (4), which prohibits the advertising or promotion of narcotics or hallucinogenic drugs, was enacted in 1971. There apparently was no prior regulation of prescription price advertising. Board indicates that this restriction would probably apply to posting, to distribution of in-store price lists, and to mailing of price lists.

NEBRASKA Section 71-147 and Section 71-148 of the Nebraska Pharmacy Law which prohibited price advertising for the health professions generally were held not to prohibit the advertising of prescription drug prices in an opinion issued November 19, 1974 by the Attorney General. These provisions were added to the Nebraska Statutes in 1935 but were originally only applicable to the dentistry professions. They were extended to all health professions in 1943.

NEVADA Restrictions on price disclosure, NRS 639.261 and 639.262, were in effect in Nevada from 1967 until July 1, 1973. No. 639.261 prohibited the advertising of prescription prices; 639.262 prohibited the giving of discounts to particular groups such as senior citizens groups. Both sections were repealed effective July 1, 1973, at which time 639.2802 came into effect which requires that a pharmacist furnish price information upon request regardless of whether that person is in possession of a valid prescription.

Nevada has a mandatory posting law which was effective July 1, 1975; posters went up September 1, 1975.

NEW HAMPSHIRE New Hampshire has a mandatory posting law, House Bill 222,146:6, approved June 2, 1973, effective August 1, 1973.

NEW JERSEY The New Jersey statute which restricts prescription price advertising, Section 45:14-12 (c), has been in effect since 1965.

NEW MEXICO Board adopted new regulations effective September 20, 1975, which distinquish between "price disclosure" and "advertising." "Price disclosure" is defined as in-store verbal disclosure, price lists, posters, and telephone disclosures and no requirements or prohibitions exist for this category. "Advertising" which includes shelf tags, preticketing, display cards, bills, billboards, and media advertising has certain restrictions. Each advertisement must contain extensive information about the product; the price must include certain services. If such services are not included in the price, then the advertisement must indicate that they are not provided. These services include the professional fee for cost of the product and the markup, family prescription records, delivery, charge privileges, pharmaceutical counsel, emergency after-hours service, and tax or insurance information. In addition, advertising is not permitted for any controlled substance or any prescription drug that FDA requires to carry a warning statement on its box label, or any drug which is rated "possibly effective."

Comparative and discount advertising is restricted under Section 316, Guidelines. No comparative prices may be given unless the reference price is also given and unless the advertising can substantiate this price. Similarly, no phrases such as "10% Off" or "Discounts" can be used unless the advertiser gives the reference.

Regulation 11, which formally dealt with prescription advertising has been repealed, except for the initial sentence prohibiting false and misleading advertising. This regulation was in effect since the mid-1960s.

NEW YORK New York has had statutes and regulations prohibiting price advertisements since July 1, 1945, L. 1945c. 744. Education Law Section 680r (l) (d), prohibiting price advertisements was repealed by L. 1971c.987, effective September 1, 1971. The prohibition was continued, however, by Rules of the Board of Regents, Section 291, effective September 1, 1971. The regulations of the Commission of Pharmacy defining unprofessional conduct have included price advertising prohibitions since February 28, 1947. 8 NYCRR 63.3 was amended effective June 1, 1972, adding (c) which prohibits the advertising of prices or the use of cut-rate or discount terms.

8 NYCRR 63.3 (m) provides that it is not advertising to make prescription prices available to a person with a prescription. New York has had mandatory posting since January 1, 1974, L. 1973 (c) 751.

NORTH CAROLINA Court case overturned earlier Board Code of Professional Conduct prohibition on prescription drug advertising, *Revco v. North Carolina Board of Pharmacy*, 204 S.E. 2d 38 (N. C. 1974). Code of Professional Conduct Section 8 was effective January 1, 1971.

NORTH DAKOTA Section 43-15-10 (1) (b) which prohibits prescription price advertising was enacted no later than 1959.

OHIO—Section 4729.36 requires a brief statement of use and caution when dangerous drugs, which are defined to include prescription drugs, are advertised by name or therapuetic class. This provision was enacted December 31, 1971.

The City of Cleveland requires posting of drugs most frequently prescribed.

OKLAHOMA 59 O.S. Section 736.1 which restricts prescription price advertising was enacted in 1961. Board suggests that telephone disclosure is also discouraged.

OREGON A regulation prohibiting advertising was promulgated in 1963, but invalidated in *Oregon Newspaper Publishers Association v. Peterson*, 415 P.2d 21 (Ore., 1966). The Board did not remove the regulation from Oregon Pharmacy Law, however, until 1972.

PENNSYLVANIA Court case overturned unethical conduct code of Board which prohibited prescription price advertising, *Pennsylvania State Board of Pharmacy v. Pastor*, 441 Pa. 186, 272 A.2d 487 (1971). This section defined grossly unprofessional conduct subject to suspension or revocation of license to include the advertising to the public of prescription prices. Pharmacy Act 699 Section 5 (*ii*), effective January 2, 1962.

Media price advertisements must be for a "commercially reasonable quantity" and must include a price per unit or per smallest saleable quantity.

Promotion of Schedule II controlled substances and barbiturates is prohibited. Rules and Regulations p. 1056 (r) (2) effective June 2, 1973.

RHODE ISLAND Rule No. 11 which restricts prescription price advertising was promulgated May 19, 1958. The statute which prohibits soliciting of controlled substances, 21-28-3.23, has been in effect at least 25 years.

SOUTH DAKOTA South Dakota has had prohibitions against price advertising since 1957 when the Board promulgated a rule prohibiting price advertising. This regulation was codified in 1967, 36-11-47, SL 1967, Ch. 102, Section 20 (c). In 1973 posting of prescription prices was determined not to be advertising within the meaning of this statutory prohibition. Regulation E-13 which was enacted September 12, 1967 also prohibits price disclosures. This regulation was amended September 24, 1975, to permit advertising of the fact that prices are posted.

South Dakota has a statute which requires the pharmacist to make available prescription price information upon request. This law, SDCL 36-11, amended by SD 13, just filed March 14, 1975, became effective July 1, 1975.

TEXAS Two provisions in Texas Pharmacy Law relate to prescription price advertising: Article 4542 (a) Section 17 (d) (3) and Article 4542 (a) Section 20 (A). Section 17 (d) (3) provides that the pharmacy Board may cancel, revoke, or suspend pharmacy permits for pharmacists who have advertised the selling price of a prescription drug. This statute became effective May 12, 1959. Before this, there was no similar provision in Texas law. Section 20 (A) requires mandatory posting, and prohibits all other means of price disclosure. This became effective August 27, 1973.

These provisions have been challenged in *Gibson's Discount Centers v. Texas State Board of Pharmacy*, No. 215, 694 (Travis Cty., 147th Dist., Austin, Tex., Mar. 10, 1975). Advertising prohibitions codified in Art. 4542 (a), Section 20 (A), II (a) and II (d) were found unconstitutional as improper use of state police power. The provision relating to the mandatory posting of prices was upheld. Section 17 (d) (3), which allows the pharmacy Board to take disciplinary action against a price advertiser, is still in effect. This case was argued on appeal November 5, 1975. The Board has been enjoined from enforcing the statute against Gibson's Discount Centers, but has not been enjoined from enforcing it against other pharmacies.

In addition to the statutes there is a regulation which relates to advertising, Regulation 5 (i), which purports to clarify the provisions of Section 17 (d) (3). This makes it a violation of 17 (d) (3) for pharmacists to disseminate the selling price of prescription drugs to members of the general public except upon specific request. This regulation was enacted in February, 1961.

VERMONT Attorney General official opinion invalidated earlier Board rule prohibiting price advertising. Board does not enforce the rule, but has not so notified pharmacists. The rule was promulgated about 1962 and was in effect until it was invalidated by the Attorney General's opinion in 1974.

Posting requires the 100 most frequently prescribed drugs and manufacturer's name. Ch. 29, T. 26, Section 1898 became effective July 1, 1972.

VIRGINIA Court case now on appeal to United States Supreme Court permanently enjoined enforcement of earlier Board rules prohibiting price advertising. *Virginia Citizens Consumer Council, Inc. v. State Board of Pharmacy*, 373 F. Supp. 683 (three-judge panel, E.D. Va., 1974), *appeal granted*, U.S., 43 U.S.L.W. 3493 (Mar. 18, 1975), (oral argument, November 11, 1975). The statute involved, Sec. 54-524.35, became effective in 1968.

In addition, there is a Board regulation, Regulation 14, which is based on the statute. Although it is still on the books, Board states it is not enforced in light of the *Virginia Citizens* case. This regulation was originally promulgated in 1965. It was amended in 1971 pursuant to the *Patterson* case in order to permit advertising of senior citizens discount plans. From 1960 to 1965 there were no provisions in Virginia Pharmacy Law or Regulations which regulated prescription advertising.

WASHINGTON Promotional ads for prescription drugs must include extensive medical information about each drug advertised. Promotion of controlled substances prohibited. Attorney General indicates that these requirements do not apply to price ads.

WAC-360-24-020 and WAC-360-24-035 which prohibited advertising were in effect at least through the 1960s until they were repealed in October, 1974.

Washington has had a mandatory price disclosure law, WAC-360-23-050, since October, 1974. This includes both telephone requests and in-store requests for price information.

WEST VIRGINIA Pharmacy Board Rule prohibits promotion of narcotic or prescription drugs, which promotion tends to cause such drugs to be used excessively. The Board regulations have been in effect since 1968.

WISCONSIN There have been no provisions relating to price disclosures since 1974 when a court case overturned prior Board Rules prohibiting prescription price advertising. *Osco v. Wisconsin Pharmacy Examining Board*, 214 N.W. 2d 47, (Wisc., 1974). Prior to the *Osco* case, Phar. Secs. 1.17, 1.18, promulgated in 1961, found in 6 Wisc. Admin. Code, prohibited advertising of dangerous drugs by name and all prescription drugs by price.

Model Substitution Statute*   1.2

Although outright repeal of an antisubstitution provision should enable pharmacists to substitute, it will be politically more practical to offer a new provision to replace the old one. A simple model provision allowing substitution might read:

a) As used in this section, brand name means the proprietary name the manufacturer places upon a drug product or on its container, label, or wrapping at the time of packaging; an established name shall have the same meaning as assigned that term by the Federal Food, Drug and Cosmetic Act as amended, Title 21, U.S.C. 301 *et seq.*

*Developed with Public Citizens' Health Group.

b) Unless the physician or other authorized prescriber explicitly states otherwise, when transmitting an oral prescription or in the instance of a written prescription indicated in his or her own writing, a different brand name product of the same genus may be dispensed by a pharmacist.

c) In any instance in which a pharmacist pursuant to this section dispenses a different drug product from that prescribed, the pharmacist shall pass on the savings in cost, being the difference between the wholesale prices of the two drug products, to the consumer.

State legislatures will probably want to build some protections into the law when they allow substitution. The reform substitution bills which have been passed in Kentucky and Maryland have included provisions establishing state formularies. The basic concept of a formulary is this: experts in the drug field evaluate available data to determine which drugs are chemically and therapeutically equivalent. A positive formulary is one which lists drugs which are determined to be equivalent and only allows the pharmacist to substitute from drugs listed. A negative formulary is one which lists only those drugs determined not to be equivalent and allows a pharmacist to substitute any drug not listed.

Reliance on a formulary, particularly on a positive formulary, makes it more difficult for pharmacists to substitute and causes lengthy delays while the list of approved/disapproved drugs is drawn up. Furthermore, when a formulary is established, the large drug companies and their lobbying associations are likely to exert heavy pressure on the members of the committee in attempts to keep the number of drugs approved for substitution small.

Because the vast majority of drug products are equivalent, the best substitution bill will not include a formulary provision. If there is to be a formulary at all, it should be negative, placing the burden of proof on those opposed to substitution, who then must establish unequivalency in order to prohibit substitution.

A second provision that has been included in recent substitution bills requires the pharmacist to pass on cost savings of supplying a generic drug to the purchaser. This is included in the model law, and is desirable to prevent pharmacists from using lower cost products but charging the same high prices.

The Kentucky substitution bill also contains a provision which requires physicians to inform patients of the availability of equivalent generic drugs whenever the physician believes the brand and generic to be equivalent. Such a provision, although of little legal effect, encourages a physician to consider the costs of the prescription and increases the consumer's awareness of lower cost products.

The Michigan bill allows substitution *if* requested by the purchaser, unless the physician has specifically indicated on the prescription that a substitution is not to be made. That bill also requires that, when a substitution is made, the prescription label identify as such both the name of the drug prescribed and the drug dispensed.

Set forth below are the two trade regulation rules, modified from those initially recommended by Staff, which the Commission has published for comment. (The numbering system is that which Staff expects to be used in the Federal Register.)

Part DISCLOSURE REGULATIONS CONCERNING RETAIL PRICES
      FOR PRESCRIPTION DRUGS

Section
.1 Coverage
.2 Rule I
.3 Rule II
.4 Definitions
.5 Declaration of Commision Intent

Authority: 38 Stat. 717, as amended (15 U.S.C. 44 *et seq.*)

§.1 Coverage

These Trade Regulation Rules apply to acts or practices in or affecting commerce and to all persons, partnerships and corporations, as hereafter defined, over which the Federal Trade Commission has jurisdiction under the Federal Trade Commission Act.

§.2 Rule I

It is an unfair act or practice for any person, partnership, or corporation directly or indirectly to prohibit, hinder, or restrict, or attempt to prohibit, hinder, or restrict, the disclosure by any retail seller of accurate price information regarding prescription drugs, whether such disclosure is made by means of advertisements in print media, broadcast media, or in any other way.

§.3 Rule II

a) It is an unfair act or practice for any retail seller to fail to disclose adequate price information regarding prescription drugs to potential purchasers.

b) Adequate price information is not disclosed and the requirements of this Rule are violated if the retail seller:

1) Changes, restricts, burdens, makes or fails to make any disclosure of accurate price information by print media, broadcast media, telephone, leaflets, mailings, or in any other way, because of or in connection with any law, rule, regulation or code of conduct of any nonfederal legislative, executive, regulatory, or licensing entity or any other entity or person whatsoever, including but not limited to professional associations; *provided* however, that it is not a violation of this Rule for a retail seller to make disclosures because of an exempt price disclosure requirement.

2) Advertises the price of a prescription drug without also disclosing in such advertisement each item listed in the definition of "price information."

§.4 Definitions

As used in this part:

a) "Person, partnership, or corporation" means any party, other than a state, over which the Federal Trade Commission has jurisdiction, and may include in appropriate circumstances, but is not limited to, individuals, groups, organizations, and professional societies.

b) "Price information" means (1) the regular price at which a retail seller intends to sell an identified prescription drug to anyone with a valid prescription, unless otherwise specified; together with, in an easily understandable manner, whatever information is required to be disclosed by the Food and Drug Administration pursuant to its regulations pertaining to reminder advertisements or labeling and whatever information is required to be disclosed pursuant to these Rules; or (2) general comparative, discount, or other price claims whether or not identifying any particular prescription drug; *provided* that any requirements of the previous paragraph are satisfied.

No additional information need be disclosed in conjunction with or in reference to any price claims. Any representation concerning the safety, effectiveness, or use of a prescription drug is outside the purview of these Rules.

[Alternative definition of "price information":

[b) "Price information" means:

[(1) The regular price at which a retail seller intends to sell an identified prescription drug to anyone with a valid prescription, unless otherwise specified; together with, in an easily understandable manner, whatever information is required to be disclosed by these Rules and

any [*i*) the proprietary (brand) name, if

any [*ii*) the established (generic) name, if

[*iii*) the established name and quantity of each active ingredient, unless the drug has more than three active ingredients other than aspirin, phenacetin, and caffeine;

[*iv*) the quantity and dosage associated with the disclosed price;

[*v*) the name of the packer, manufacturer or distributor if no propriety name exists;

[*vi*) optionally, package or dosage form trade names; or [(2) general comparative, discount, or other price claims whether or not identifying any particular prescription drug; *provided* that any requirements of the previous paragraph are satisfied.

[No additional information need be disclosed in conjunction with or in reference to any price claims. Any representation concerning the safety, effectiveness, or use of a prescription drug is outside the purview of these Rules.]

c) "Prescription drug" means a drug which may be dispensed only upon a written or oral prescription of a practitioner licensed by law to administer such drugs, except that drugs classified as Schedule I under the Controlled Substances Act, 21 U.S.C. 812

(1970) (*i.e.*, those drugs therein declared to have no currently accepted medical use in treatment in the United States) shall not be considered prescription drugs.

d) "Retail seller" means any person, partnership, or corporation which transfers and sells to consumers any prescription drug without assuming control over and responsibility for its administration. Mere advice or instructions regarding administration shall not constitute control or establish responsibility for purposes of this definition.

e) "Exempt price disclosure requirement" means a nonfederal legal requirement upon a retail seller to disclose prices of identified prescription drugs by means of a poster or placard designed to remain on or within the premises of the retail seller, by means of a leaflet designed to be removed from the premises and available to all potential purchasers with or without prescriptions and/or by means of a telephone; *provided* that the poster or leaflet explicitly indicates by such language as "Our Prices" that disclosed prices are uniquely those of the retail seller; and *provided further* that the legal requirement is wholly independent of and is not conditioned upon disclosures made pursuant to these Rules.

§.5 Declaration of Commission Intent

a) It is the purpose of these Rules, subject only to the requirements of federal statutes and regulations, to allow disclosure of accurate prescription drug price information by retail sellers to prospective purchasers and to eliminate restraints, burdens or controls imposed by nonfederal law and by private, state, and local governmental action on such disclosures by any means of communication, including but not limited to advertising (other than exempt price disclosure requirements). It is the intent of the Commission that these Rules shall preempt all nonfederal laws, ordinances, or regulations that in any way frustrate the purpose of these Rules, that would in any way prevent or burden any disclosures of accurate prescription drug price information by retail sellers to potential purchasers, or that would impose standards for prescription drug price disclosure by retail sellers to potential purchasers (other than exempt price disclosure requirements), except that if such law is coextensive with and word-for-word identical to any provisions of these Rules, notwithstanding that differences in jurisdictional provisions are not permissible, such law, and the proper enforcement thereof, shall not be affected by these Rules, and shall have concurrent application with these Rules.

b) The Commission intends these Rules to be as self-enforcing as possible. To that end it is the commission's intent that these Rules may be used, among other ways, as a defense to any proceeding of any kind which may be brought or threatened to be brought against any retail seller who truthfully advertises or otherwise discloses, according to these Rules, price information of prescription drugs which he may offer for sale, or as the basis for declaratory, injunctive, or other relief against the threatening or bringing of any such proceeding.

c) These Rules, requirements, and declarations of intent and their application are each separate and severable.

Determining standard deviation Ask a person with a statistics background to explain this method to you if the following instructions do not answer all your questions.

The most important and widely used measure of variability is the standard deviation, which will indicate to what extent most of the prices of a given drug vary from the average (mean) price.

$$s_x = \frac{1}{-n} \sqrt{n \Sigma x^2 - (\Sigma x)^2},$$

where

s_x = the standard deviation;
n = the number in the sample;
Σx^2 = the sum of the squares of the individual prices in the sample;
$(\Sigma x)^2$ = the square of the sum of the individual prices in the sample.

The usefulness of determining the standard deviation is evident from the following calculation examples.

Example 1. Assume that in a sample of 15 stores, the following prices for 30 tablets of Valium 5 mg were recorded during a pricing survey:

Store	Cost for Rx (x)	x^2
1	$ 3.00	$ 9.00
2	2.95	8.70
3	3.15	9.92
4	2.85	8.12
5	4.50	20.25
6	1.95	3.80
7	2.95	8.70
8	2.60	6.76
9	4.25	18.06
10	2.25	5.06
11	2.50	6.25
12	3.25	10.56
13	2.75	7.56
14	3.90	15.21
15	2.15	4.62
$\Sigma x =$	$45.00	$\Sigma x^2 = $142.57

High price = $4.50
Low price = $1.95
Mean (average price) = $3.00

$s_x = \frac{1}{15} \sqrt{(15) \ (142.57 - (45.00)^2}$
$s_x = \frac{1}{15} \sqrt{2138.55 - 2025.00} = \frac{1}{15} \sqrt{113.55} = \frac{1}{15} (10.66)$
$s_x = 0.71 = $ *Standard Deviation*

Example 2. Assume that in a second sample of 15 stores the following prices for 30 tablets of Valium 5 mg were recorded:

Store	Cost for Rx (x)	x^2
1	$ 3.00	9.00
2	4.50	20.25
3	1.95	3.80
4	2.95	8.70
5	2.95	8.70
6	2.95	8.70
7	2.95	8.70
8	2.95	8.70
9	2.95	8.70
10	2.95	8.70
11	2.95	8.70
12	2.95	8.70
13	3.00	9.00
14	3.00	9.00
15	3.00	9.00
$\Sigma x =$	$45.00	$\Sigma x^2 = \$138.35$

High price = $4.50
Low price = $1.95
Mean = $3.00

$$s_x = \tfrac{1}{15} \sqrt{(15)(138.35) - (45.00)^2} = \tfrac{1}{15} \sqrt{2075.25 - 2025.00}$$
$$s_x = \tfrac{1}{15} \sqrt{50.25} = \tfrac{1}{15}(7.09)$$
$$s_x = 0.47 = Standard\ Deviation$$

Note that in both of the samples above the range is $1.95 to $4.50 (or $2.55 difference) and the mean is $3.00. However, the standard deviation in Example 1 is 0.71 while the standard deviation in Example 2 is 0.47. This particular statistic is useful in that the lower standard deviation of Example 2 is representative of the fact that most prices are clustered around the mean with few extremes while the higher standard deviation in Example 1 depicts greater variability in prices with less clustering.

I. Price Posting Requirements

II. Telephone Disclosure Provision

III. Media Advertising

I. PRICE POSTING REQUIREMENTS SHOULD INCLUDE:

☐ Posting signs should provide the minimum amount of information needed to inform consumers about drug prices and store services—otherwise the signs will be confusing and meaningless.

☐ The drugs to be listed on posters must be: the same for all stores so that inter-store comparisons can be easily made; the most frequently prescribed 50 or 100 drugs; and the list of drugs and dosages should be drawn up by the State Board of Pharmacy or by the State Health Department and should be updated annually or semiannually.

☐ Price Posters should include the following information:

1) the trade name of the drugs, if any;

2) the generic name or composition (by name only, not by amount);

3) the dosage for which the posted price applies;

4) the amount for which the posted price applies;

5) the price.

☐ Additionally, a checklist of the professional and convenience services offered by the pharmacy should be included on posters.

☐ Provision should be made to educated consumers about the meaning and interpretation of information on the price posters.

☐ Drugs available under a brand name only should be listed by that brand name. Drugs available under a generic name as well as by brand name should be listed *first* by the *generic* name and under that by those brand names available which are among the top 50-100 drugs followed by the unbranded product(s) available. For example:

Drug	Dosage	Price	Amount
Chlorpheniramine Maleate	4 mg.		20 tablets
Chlor-Trimeton			
Chlorpheniramine Maleate			
Chlorpheniramine Maleate			

☐ Specific guidelines should be established regarding the location of the posters within a store. This should include, but not necessarily be limited to, placement

---

*Source: *HMO Sourcebook* (1973 Edition), The Health Law Center, Aspen Systems Corporation, Rockville, Md.

in a conspicuous position in the proximity of the pharmacy counter and in store windows.

☐ Specific guidelines should be established regarding poster size and color and print size and type.

☐ Prices that have changed since first posted should be marked with an asterisk (*) and, an explanatory note should be printed on the poster.

☐ It should be required that pharmacies make available, upon request, the prices of all drugs which are not included on the price posters.

☐ It must be assured that price posting will not be based on "loss-leader" tactics, as they tend to distort a pharmacy's pricing structure, and that the prices for posted drugs actually reflect the overall pricing policies of the pharmacy, and that the appropriate state agencies must increase surveillance of store prices to check for compliance with this loss-leader provision of the law.

☐ Enforcement provision should include:

a) routine spot monitoring by appropriate state agency to determine if stores are in compliance with the posting law and whether they offer the customer services they claim to offer and do so effectively.

b) *education of consumers about their rights* under the law, type of violations that may occur, and the importance of reporting violators.

c) appropriate state agency should routinely make public the names of violators and should take disciplinary action against repeated violators.

II. TELEPHONE DISCLOSURE PROVISION

☐ Telephone disclosure of prescription drug prices should be mandatory.

Telephone disclosure is a necessary component to price disclosure. The obvious deficiency of in-store price posting is that a customer must be at the store in order to have price information available. Thus, comparative shopping is difficult for all and impossible for some, such as the elderly, the lame, and the bedridden.

An argument used against telephone disclosure is that patients may misinterpret the name or dosage of a prescription when calling and, thus, not be given pricing information for the actual prescription. Although this may occur at times, the misinterpretation will be corrected when the prescription is filled and patients cannot be expected to argue that the original price should still apply. Moreover, if the patient called several pharmacies, he or she will have made the same error in all calls and will still have received information about comparative pricing patterns between stores.

It must be assured that pharmacies do not price those drugs for which it receives telephone requests on a "loss-leader" basis.

III. MEDIA ADVERTISING

Media advertising of prescription drug prices cannot be made mandatory, but should be allowed. Stores cannot be required to shoulder the expenses of media advertising. However, media advertising may voluntarily follow the lifting of anti-advertising statutes. Therefore, strict guidelines for such advertisements should be included in any legislation eliminating the prohibition on advertising, in order to eliminate any fraudulent or misleading advertising practices. This should include requirements about ad size, print size, and information that must be included in the ads. It should be required that ads are not to be used to promote "special sales" or "loss-leader"* tactics, and that prices advertised in the mass media must be maintained for at least six months, unless legitimate increases in costs occur.

Media advertising of prescription drug prices should be considered to be allowed only in the *printed media.* The concept of advertising the prices of any type of drug in the broadcast media should be severely questioned. It would be wise to limit the media advertising of prescription drug prices to the printed media only. If broadcast media advertising of prices is not to be allowed, a provision to that effect should be included in the legislation. Note that policy advertising (i.e., 10 percent discount for senior citizens) is quite different from drug price advertising, (i.e., Valium 5 mg. only $7.98 per 100), and should not fall under the same restriction.

Promotional advertising of any type of drug in the mass media should be prohibited; that is, advertising referring to the "advantages" or uses of the drug.

ADDITIONAL SUGGESTIONS REGARDING PRICE POSTING LAWS

The Massachusetts Public Interest Research Group, which has done extensive work aimed at a price posting law in that state, suggests that you may wish to add an enforcement clause calling for a fine for the first violation and suspension of license for any subsequent offense.

State Physician Antiadvertising Statutes: A State-by-State Survey 2.1

Flat prohibition on all advertising:

> *Alaska* Stat. § 08.64.380 (Supp. 1971); *Ariz.* Rev. Stat. Ann. § 32-1401 (Supp. 1971); *Ark.* Stat. Ann. § 72-613 (Supp. 1971); *Colo.* Rev. Stat., 1963s 12–36-128; *Fla.* Stat. Ann. §§ 458.12 *et seq.*; 91 *Ill.* Ann. Stat. §§ 16a, 16a-1; *Kans.* Stat. Ann. § 65-2836, 2837; *Ky.* Rev. Stat. Ann. §§ 311.595, .600, 438.065; *Me.* Rev. Stat. § 3203-A; 43 *Md.* Ann. Code § 129; *Minn.* Stat. Ann. § 147.02; *Mont.; Neb.* Rev. Stat. §§ 21-2201 *et seq.; N. J.* Stat. Ann. § 45:9-16 as annon. N.J. Ch. 453 (Laws 1971); *N.C.* Gen. Stat. § 90-14; 59; *Okla.* Stat. Ann. § 509.736.1 (1971); *Tenn.* Code Ann. § 63-123 § 63-619; *Utah* § 58-12-36

---

*"Loss-leader" is the practice of marking advertised products, or in this case, posted products, low to attract customers and at the same time marking all other products higher to make up the financial loss.

Prohibition of advertising in an unethical or unprofessional manner:

> *D.C.* Code Ann. § 2-123 (1966, as amended Supp. 1971); 24 *Del.* Code Ann. § 1741: *Ga.* Code Ann. § 84-916; *Idaho* Code Ann. § 54-1810 (Supp. 1971); *Iowa* Code Ann. §§ 147.55, .56; *Miss.* Code § 8893.1; *Mo.* Rev. Stat. § 334.100; *N.Y.* Ed. L. § 6509 (McKinney Supp. 1971); *N.D.* Cent. Code § 43-17-31; *S.C.* Code §§ 56-1355, 56-1368; *Wisc.* Stat. Ann. § 448.18 (Spec. Pamph. 1972); *Wyo.* Comp. Stat. Ann. § 33-340 (1959)

Prohibition of price advertising:

> *Cal.* Bus. & Prof. Code §§ 651,651.3; §§ 2361 *et seq.* (West. 1962, Supp. 1971)

Prohibition of patient solicitation:

> *La.* Rev. Stat. & 37.1285; *N.M.* Stat. Ann. § 67-5-9; *Ohio* Rev. Code §§ 4731.22; S.D. (see misl.)

Prohibition of misleading or deceptive advertising:

> 46 *Ala.* Code Ann. § 270 (Supp. 1969); *Conn.* Gen. Stat. § 20-45 (1970); *Ga.* Code Ann. § 84-916; *Hawaii* Rev. Stat. § 453-8; *Iowa* Code Ann. §§ 147.55, .56; *Mich.* Comp. Laws Ann. § 750.429; *Mich.* PA 12,368 (1972); *Miss.* Code § 8893.1; *Mo.* Rev. Stat. § 334.100; *Nev.* Rev. Stat. § 630.030 § 631.050; *Ohio* Rev. Code § 4731.22; *Ore.* Rev. Stat. § 677.190; 63 *Pa.* Stat. Ann. § 411; *R.I.* Gen. Laws Ann. § 7-5-1 *et seq.* (1970, as ann. Supp. 1971); *R.I.* Ch. 100 (Laws 1972); *S.D.* Comp. Laws Ann. § 36-4-30, *Tex.* Rev. Civ. Stat. Ann. art. 4505; 26 *Vt.* § 1398,1399; *Va.* Code Ann. § 54-317; *Wash.* Rev. Code §§ 18.72.030, 19.68.010 (1971)

Summary of HEW Regulations for Skilled Nursing Facilities (SNFs) Certified to Participate in the Medicare Program   3.1

OVERVIEW—MAJOR AREAS COVERED

Licensure—Ownership—Administration
Patient Care
    Physicians
    Nursing
    Drugs
    Diet
    Specialized Rehabilitative Services—Lab and Radiological Services—Dental Services
    Medical Records—Transfer Agreements—Infection Control
    Social Services—Patient Activities
Physical Environment
    Disaster Preparedness
Utilization Review

LICENSURE-OWNERSHIP-ADMINISTRATION

The facility and its staff must be licensed according to all federal, state, and local regulations.

Each person who has at least 10 percent ownership interest in the facility, whether direct or indirect, must be identified to the state survey agency.

A single qualified individual must be appointed administrator to take responsibility for the overall management, rule enforcement, and protection of personal and property rights of the patients.

PATIENT CARE

Physicians

The health care of every patient must be under the supervision of a physician, who sees the patient at least once every 30 days during the patient's first 90 days following admission, and at least every 60 days thereafter.

Nursing

The skilled nursing facility must provide licensed nursing care 24 hours a day every day. There must be registered nurses on duty at least during the day tour of duty, seven days a week.

Drugs

Procedures must be established so that drugs are checked against physicians' orders prior to administration, patient must be identified, and all administrations of drugs must be properly recorded in medical record. The facility is responsible for providing drugs to its patients, and for ensuring that pharmaceutical services are provided in accordance with accepted professional principles and appropriate federal, state, and local laws.

Diet

The facility must provide a hygienic dietetic service that meets the daily nutritional needs of patients, ensures that special dietary needs are met, and provides palatable and attractive meals. There must be either a full-time qualified dietician, or frequent, regularly scheduled consultation with one. Menus must be planned in accordance with physicians' orders and the recommended dietary allowances of the Food and Nutrition Board of the National Research Council, National Academy of Sciences. Food must be attractively served at the proper temperatures, and in a form to meet individual needs. If a patient refuses food served, appropriate substitutes of similar nutritive value must be offered.

Specialized Rehabilitative Services—Lab and Radiological Services—Dental Services

Upon the written order of the patient's attending physician, the facility must provide or arrange for specialized rehabilitative services such as physical therapy, speech pathology and audiology, and occupational therapy.

The facility must have provisions for promptly obtaining required laboratory, X-ray, and other diagnostic services.

The facility must have satisfactory arrangements to assist patients to obtain routine and emergency dental care. The facility must assist the patient, if necessary, in arranging for transportation to and from the dentist's office.

Medical Records—Transfer Agreements—Infection Control

The facility must maintain clinical medical records on all patients that are completely and accurately documented, readily accessible, and systematically organized to facilitate retrieving and compiling information.

The facility must have in effect a transfer agreement with one or more approved hospitals to provide patients with inpatient hospital care when needed.

The facility must establish an infection control committee of representative professional staff with responsibility for overall infection control. All necessary housekeeping and maintenance services must be provided to maintain a sanitary and comfortable environment and to help prevent the development and transmission of infection.

Social Services—Patient Activities

The facility must provide the appropriate social services or provide referrals to the appropriate social service agencies to help each patient to adjust to the social and emotional aspects of his or her illness, treatment, and stay in the facility.

The facility must provide an activities program, appropriate to the needs of each patient, to encourage self-care, resumption of normal activities, and maintenance of the physical, social and mental well-being of the patients.

PHYSICAL ENVIRONMENT

The facility must meet such provisions of the Life Safety Code of the National Fire Protection Association as are applicable to nursing homes. A waiver may be granted if strict application would result in unreasonable hardship on the facility, and a waiver would not adversely affect the health and safety of the patients. The facility must have an emergency power source adequate to maintain lighting to all exits, fire detection, alarm and extinguishing systems, and all like support systems. All necessary accommodations must be made to meet the needs of persons with semiambulatory disabilities, sight and hearing disabilities, disabilities of coordination, as well as other disabilities. Patient rooms must be designed and equipped for adequate nursing care and the comfort and privacy of patients. Each room must be equipped with, or conveniently located near, adequate toilet and bathing facilities.

Disaster Preparedness

The facility must have a written plan, periodically rehearsed, with procedures to be followed in the event of an internal or external disaster and for the care of casualities arising from such disasters.

UTILIZATION REVIEW

The facility must carry out utilization review of its services to patients receiving Medicare benefits. There are two elements to utilization review: medical care studies that identify and examine patterns of care provided in the facility, and review of extended duration cases which is concerned with efficiency, appropriateness, and cost effectiveness of care.

Summary of HEW Regulations for Intermediate Care Facilities (ICFs) Certified to Participate in the Medicare and/or Medicaid Programs 3.2

OVERVIEW-MAJOR AREA COVERED

Administration
Hospital Transfer Agreements
Arrangements to Provide Medical and Remedial Care Not Provided within the Facility
Records
Life Safety Code Compliance
Enviornment and Sanitation
Diet
Drugs
Health Care

ADMINISTRATION

There must be on duty all hours of each day sufficient staff to carry out the policies, responsibilities, and programs of the facility. There must be written policies, available to the staff, residents, and public to govern admission, transfer, and discharge of patients; to outline the rights of residents and prohibit their mistreatment or abuse; and provide for registration and disposition of complaints without reprisal against any employee or resident. A written account must be available to residents and their families for all personal possessions and funds received by or deposited with the facility and for all disbursements made to or on behalf of the resident. The facility must have a written and regularly rehearsed plan for emergencies, fires, and explosions.

HOSPITAL TRANSFER AGREEMENTS

The facility must have a transfer agreement with a nearby hospital to ensure the availability of inpatient hospital services when needed. If it is essential to assuring intermediate care facilities services for eligible persons in the community, a facility may be deemed to have an agreement even if it does not in fact, as long as it has made a "good faith" effort to secure one.

ARRANGEMENTS TO PROVIDE CARE
NOT PROVIDED WITHIN THE FACILITY

The facility must maintain effective arrangements to provide medical and remedial care to residents for required services not regularly provided by the facility.

MEDICAL RECORDS

There must be available to professional and other staff directly involved with the resident, and to the appropriate representatives of the state agency, medical records that include at least the following information: identification and past medical and social history; copies of initial and periodic examinations, including all plans of care; an overall plan of care; entries describing all treatments and medication; all symptoms and other indications of illness or injury.

LIFE SAFETY CODE COMPLIANCE

The facility must meet such provisions of the Life Safety Code of the National Fire Protection Association as are applicable to institutional occupancies, except those provisions of the Code which apply to small homes primarily for the care of alcoholism and drug abuse, or where state law imposes an "adequate" fire and safety code.

ENVIRONMENT AND SANITATION

Resident living areas must be designed and equipped for the comfort and privacy of the resident. Each room must be equipped with, or conveniently near, adequate toilet and bathing facilities. Provision must be made for isolating residents with infectious diseases. The facility must provide one or more areas for resident dining, diversional and social activities; and areas used for corridor traffic shall not be considered as areas for these purposes. All necessary accommodations must be made to meet the needs of persons with semiambulatory disabilities, sight and hearing disabilities, disabilities of coordination, as well as other disabilities.

DIET

The facility must provide at least three meals or their equivalents served daily. A designated staff member suited by training or experience in food management or nutrition must be responsible for planning and supervision of menus and meal service. If the facility accepts or retains individuals with special medically required diets, the menus for such patients must be planned by a professionally qualified dietician, or reviewed and approved by the attending physician.

DRUGS

The facility must either employ a licensed pharmacist, or have a formal arrangement with one to provide consultation on methods for ordering, storage, administration and disposal, and record keeping of drugs and biologicals. All medications administered are ordered by a physician, either in writing or orally to a licensed nurse, pharmacist, or physician. Oral orders are immediately recorded and signed by both the prescribing physician and the person who received it. A registered nurse must review monthly each resident's medication, and medications are reviewed quarterly by the attending or staff physician.

HEALTH CARE

The facility must provide health services that assure that each resident receives treatments, medications, diet, and other health services as prescribed and planned, all hours of each day. The facility's health services are supervised every day by either a registered nurse or by a licensed practical nurse who is in regular consultation with a registered nurse. Responsible staff members are on duty and awake at all times to assure prompt, appropriate action in cases of injury, illness, fire, or other emergencies. A written health care plan must be developed and implemented for each resident, and be reviewed by the attending or staff physician at least quarterly. Restorative nursing care must be provided to each resident to achieve and maintain the highest possible degree of function, self-care, and independence. The facility must provide specialized and supportive rehabilitative services either directly or through arrangements with qualified outside resources, to preserve and improve abilities for independent function. Social services and an activities program must be provided to promote preservation of the resident's physical and mental health, to encourage restoration to self-care and maintenance of normal activity. Each resident's health care must be under the continuing supervision of a physician who sees the resident as needed, and at least every 60 days, unless justified otherwise and documented by the attending physician.

§ 422.428 Where requests for information or records may be made.

Requests for information, for copies of records, or to inspect or copy records may be made at any of the Social Security Administration district offices or branch offices. Similar requests relating to information or records available in the Bureau of Hearings and Appeals may be made at any of its field offices. For materials which are available or will be made available at district offices and branch offices, see § 422.430. Although all of the materials listed in § 422.430 are not maintained in all district offices and branch offices, any item listed will be obtained by an office and made available to the requester. For materials in the Bureau of Hearings and Appeals field offices, see § 422.432. The materials available at district offices and branch offices are also available at the Social Security Administration headquarters, 6401 Security Boulevard, Baltimore, MD 21235, and at the Washington Inquiries Section of the Office of Public Affairs, Social Security Administration, Department of Health, Education, and Welfare, North Building, Room 4146, 330 Independence Avenue SW., Washington, DC 20201, except as provided in § 422.430(b). (19). The materials available at the Bureau of Hearings and Appeals field offices are also available at the latter office. In addition, a request for information or a record may be submitted through any office of the Social Security Administration or to any employee of the Social Security Administration in the regular course of his conduct of official business.

[38 FR 7223, Mar. 19, 1973]

§ 422.430 Materials available at district offices and branch offices.

(a) *Materials available for inspection.* The following are available or will be made available for inspection at the district offices and branch offices:

(1) Compilation of the Social Security Laws.

(2) The Public Information Regulation of the Department of Health, Education, and Welfare (45 CFR Part 5).

(3) Regulations of the Social Security Administration under the retirement, survivors, disability, health insurance, and supplemental security income programs, i.e., Regulation No. 1 (Part 401 of this chapter), Regulations No. 5 (Part 405 of this chapter); regulations under Part B of title IV (Black Lung Benefits) of the Federal Coal Mine Health and Safety Act of 1969, Regulations No. 10 (Part 410 of this chapter), Regulations No. 16 (Part 416 of this chapter), and Regulations No. 22 (this Part 422).

(4) Social Security Rulings.

(5) Social Security Handbook.

(b) *Materials available for inspection and copying.* The following materials are available or will be made available for inspection and copying at the district offices and branch offices:

(1) Claims Manual of the Social Security Administration.

(2) Department Staff Manual on Organization, Department of Health, Education, and Welfare, Part 8, Chapter 8000.

(3) Handbook for State Social Security Administrators.

(4) Disability Insurance State Manual.

(5) Parts 2 and 3 of the Part A Intermediary Manual (Provider Services under Medicare).

(6) Parts 2 and 3 of the Part B Intermediary Manual (Physician and Supplier Services).

(7) BHI (Bureau of Health Insurance) Intermediary Letters Related to Parts 2 and 3 of the Part A and Part B Intermediary Manuals.

(8) State Buy-In Handbook (State Enrollment of Eligible Individuals under the Supplementary Medical Insurance Program) and Letters.

(9) Group Practice Prepayment Plan Manual (HIM-8) and Letters.

(10) State Operations Manual (HIM-7).

(11) BHI Letters to State Agencies.

(12) Extended Care Facility Manual (HIM-12).

(13) Hearing Officers Handbook (Supplementary Medical Insurance Program—HIM-21).

(14) Hospital Manual (HIM-10).

(15) Home Health Agency Manual (HIM-11).

(16) Outpatient Physical Therapy Provider Manual (HIM-9).

(17) Provider Reimbursement Manual (HIM-15).

(18) Audit Program Manuals for Hospital (HIM-16), Home Health Agency (HIM-17), and Extended Care Facilities (HIM-18).

(19) Statements of deficiencies based

256

upon survey reports of health care institutions or facilities prepared after January 31, 1973, by a State agency, and such reports (including pertinent written statements furnished by such institution or facility on such statements of deficiencies), as set forth in § 422.433(a). Such statements of deficiencies, reports, and pertinent written statements shall be available or made available only at the district office and the regional office servicing the area in which the institution or facility is located, except that such statements of deficiencies and pertinent written statements shall also be available at the local public assistance offices servicing such area.

(20) Supplemental Security Income Handbook.

(21) Service Area Directory (including the addresses and geographic areas serviced by district offices, branch offices, regional offices, and payment centers).

(22) Indexes to the materials listed in paragraph (a) of this section and in this paragraph (b) and an index to the Bureau of Hearings and Appeals Handbook.

[39 FR 26722, July 23, 1974, as amended at 40 FR 27650, July 1, 1975]

§ 422.432 Materials in field offices of the Bureau of Hearings and Appeals.

(a) *Materials available for inspection.* The following materials are available for inspection in the field offices of the Bureau of Hearings and Appeals:

(1) Title 45 of the Code of Federal Regulations (including the public information regulation of the Department of Health, Education, and Welfare).

(2) Regulations of the Social Security Administration (see § 422.430(a)(3)).

(3) Title 5, United States Code.

(4) Compilation of the Social Security Laws.

(5) Social Security Rulings.

(6) Social Security Handbook.

(b) *Handbook available for inspection and copying.* The Bureau of Hearings and Appeals Handbook is available for inspection and copying in the field offices of the Bureau of Hearings and Appeals.

[36 F.R. 18949, Sept. 24, 1971]

§ 422.433 Availability of official reports on providers of services, State agencies, intermediaries, and carriers under title XVIII of the Social Security Act.

The following shall be made available to the public under the conditions specified:

(a) *Statements of deficiencies and survey reports on providers of services prepared by State agencies.* (1) Statements of deficiencies based upon official survey reports prepared after January 31, 1973, by a State agency pursuant to its agreement entered into under section 1864 of the Social Security Act and furnished to the Social Security Administration, which relate to such State agency's findings on the compliance of a health care institution or facility with the applicable provisions in section 1861 of such Act and with the regulations, promulgated pursuant to such provisions, dealing with health and safety of patients in such institutions and facilities; and (2) such State agency survey reports. Such statement of deficiencies or report and any pertinent written statements furnished by such institution or facility on such statement of deficiencies shall be disclosed within 90 days following the completion of the survey by such State agency, but not to exceed 30 days following the receipt of such report by the Administration. (See § 422.430(b)(19) for places where statements of deficiencies, reports, and pertinent written statements shall be available.)

§ 422.436 Requests for information or records.

A request for information or records may be made orally or in writing. The requester has the sole responsibility to identify each record sought in sufficient detail so that it can be located by personnel familiar with the filing of Administration records. When more than one item is requested, the requester shall clearly itemize each record or other item of information requested so that it may be identified and its availability separately determined. A request for copies should include a check or money order in the amount of the necessary fee (see § 422.440) made payable to the Social Security Administration.

§ 422.440 Fees and charges.

(a) *Applicability.* The provisions of this section do not apply to a request for information pursuant to Part 401 of this chapter (see §§ 401.5 and 401.6 of Part 401 of this chapter) or to a request for a detailed statement of earnings for a purpose not related to title II of the Act (see § 422.125(e)(2)).

(b) *Policy on fees.* It is the policy of the Social Security Administration to provide routine information to the general public without charge. Special information services involving a benefit that does not accrue to the general public are subject to the payment of fees which are fixed in such amounts as to recover the cost to the Government of providing such services. Fees will be charged for the following special services:

(1) Reproduction, duplication, or copying of records;

(2) Searches of or for records;

(3) Certification or authentication of records; and

(4) Preparing materials from punch cards, magnetic tape, or microfilm.

No charge will be made for time spent in making an administrative decision regarding whether to provide the requested copies, or for time spent securing authorization. Similarly, there will be no charge for forwarding the materials to the requester.

(c) *Copying.* A charge of 10 cents per page (one side of a sheet) will be made for the first copy of documents or records; a fee of 5 cents per page (one side of a sheet) will be made for each subsequent copy based on the same request; except that no fee will be charged if total copying cost is less than $1.00. If we furnish copies which were already printed, the actual printing costs per page or cost of printing the report should be charged, in lieu of copying costs.

(d) *Searches.* No fee will be charged for searching for materials described in §§ 422.430 and 422.432. In the event a search is required to locate other materials, a charge of $3 per hour will be made (fractional parts of an hour will be charged on a one-half hour basis) except that no charge will be made for the first one-half hour.

(e) *Certification.* A fee of $3 will be charged for each certification of records or documents if certification is requested.

(f) *Preparing other materials.* The actual cost, determined on a case-by-case basis, will be charged for preparing materials from punch cards, magnetic tape, or microfilm. (Costs are determined according to type of request and the processing necessary to prepare the materials; thus the costs will be determined on a request-by-request basis.)

(g) *Applicability.* These policies and fees are applicable for all components of the Social Security Administration.

[39 FR 26722, July 23, 1974]

(k) *Standard: Patients' rights.* The governing body of the facility establishes written policies regarding the rights and responsibilities of patients and, through the administrator, is responsible for development of, and adherence to, procedures implementing such policies. These policies and procedures are made available to patients, to any guardians, next of kin, sponsoring agency(ies), or representative payees selected pursuant to section 205 (j) of the Social Security Act, and Subpart Q of Part 404 of this chapter, and to the public. The staff of the facility is trained and involved in the implementation of these policies and procedures. These patients' rights policies and procedures ensure that, at least, each patient admitted to the facility:

(1) Is fully informed, as evidenced by the patient's written acknowledgment, prior to or at the time of admission and during stay, of these rights and of all rules and regulations governing patient conduct and responsibilities;

(2) Is fully informed, prior to or at the time of admission and during stay, of services available in the facility, and of related charges including any charges for services not covered under titles XVIII or XIX of the Social Security Act, or not covered by the facility's basic per diem rate;

(3) Is fully informed, by a physician, of his medical condition unless medically contraindicated (as documented, by a physician, in his medical record), and is afforded the opportunity to participate in the planning of his medical treatment and to refuse to participate in experimental research;

(4) Is transferred or discharged only for medical reasons, or for his welfare or that of other patients, or for nonpayment for his stay (except as prohibited by titles XVIII or XIX of the Social Security Act), and is given reasonable advance notice to ensure orderly transfer or discharge, and such actions are documented in his medical record;

(5) Is encouraged and assisted, throughout his period of stay, to exercise his rights as a patient and as a citizen, and to this end may voice grievances and recommend changes in policies and services to facility staff and/or to outside representatives of his choice, free from restraint, interference, coercion, discrimination, or reprisal;

(6) May manage his personal financial affairs, or is given at least a quarterly accounting of financial transactions made on his behalf should the facility accept his written delegation of this responsibility to the facility for any period of time in conformance with State law;

(7) Is free from mental and physical abuse, and free from chemical and (except in emergencies) physical restraints except as authorized in writing by a physician for a specified and limited period of time, or when necessary to protect the patient from injury to himself or to others;

(8) Is assured confidential treatment of his personal and medical records, and may approve or refuse their release to any individual outside the facility, except, in case of his transfer to another health care institution, or as required by law or third-party payment contract;

(9) Is treated with consideration, respect, and full recognition of his dignity and individuality, including privacy in treatment and in care for his personal needs;

(10) Is not required to perform services for the facility that are not included for therapeutic purposes in his plan of care;

(11) May associate and communicate privately with persons of his choice, and send and receive his personal mail unopened, unless medically contraindicated (as documented by his physician in his medical record);

(12) May meet with, and participate in activities of, social, religious, and community groups at his discretion, unless medically contraindicated (as documented by his physician in his medical record);

(13) May retain and use his personal clothing and possessions as space permits, unless to do so would infringe upon rights of other patients, and unless medically contraindicated (as documented by his physician in his medical record); and

(14) If married, is assured privacy for visits by his/her spouse; if both are inpatients in the facility, they are permitted to share a room, unless medically contraindicated (as documented by the attending physician in the medical record).

All rights and responsibilities specified in paragraphs (k) (1) through (4) of this section—as they pertain to (a) a patient adjudicated incompetent in accordance with State law, (b) a patient who is found, by his physician, to be medically incapable of understanding these rights, or (c) a patient who exhibits a communication barrier—devolve to such patient's guardian, next of kin, sponsoring agency(ies), or representative payee (except when the facility itself is representative payee) selected pursuant to section 205(j) of the Social Security Act and Subpart Q of Part 404 of this chapter.

§ 249.12 Standards for intermediate care facilities.

(a) The standards for an intermediate care facility (as defined in § 249.10(b) (15) of this part) which are specified by the Secretary pursuant to section 1905 (c) and (d) of the Social Security Act and are applicable to all intermediate care facilities are as follows. The facility:

(1) Maintains methods of administrative management which assure that:

(i) There are on duty during all hours of each day staff sufficient in numbers and qualifications to carry out the policies, responsibilites, and programs of the facility. The numbers and categories of personnel are determined by the number of residents and their particular needs in accordance with guidelines issued by the Social and Rehabilitation Service;

(ii) There are written policies and procedures available to staff, residents, their families or legal representatives and the public which:

(A) Govern all areas of service provided by the facility:

(1) Admission, transfer, and discharge of residents policies shall assure that:

(i) Only those persons are accepted whose needs can be met by the facility directly or in cooperation with community resources or other providers of care with which it is affiliated or has contracts;

(ii) As changes occur in their physical or mental condition, necessitating service or care which cannot be adequately provided by the facility, residents are transferred promptly to hospitals, skilled nursing facilities, or other appropriate facilities; and

(iii) Except in the case of an emergency, the resident, his next of kin, attending physician, and the responsible agency, if any, are consulted at least 5 days in advance of the transfer or discharge of any resident, and casework services or other means are utilized to assure that adequate arrangements exist for meeting his needs through other resources;

(2) Policies define the uses of chemical and physical restraints, identify the professional personnel under subparagraph (a)(1)(ii)(B)(7) of this section who may authorize the application of restraints in emergencies and describe the mechanism for monitoring and con-

trolling their use;

(3) Policies define procedures for submittal of complaints and recommendations by residents and for assuring response and disposition; and

(4) There shall be written policies governing access to, duplication of, and dissemination of information from the resident's record;

(B) Ensure that each resident admitted to the facility:

(1) Is fully informed of his rights and responsibilities as a resident and of all rules and regulations governing resident conduct and responsibilities. Such information must be provided prior to or at the time of admission or, in the case of residents already in the facility, upon the facility's adoption or amendment of resident right policies, and its receipt must be acknowledged by the resident in writing; and in the case of a mentally retarded individual, witnessed by a third person;

(2) Is fully informed in writing prior to or at the time of admission and during stay, of services available in the facility, and of related charges including any charges for services not covered under the title XIX program or not covered by the facility's basic per diem rate;

(3) Is fully informed by a physician, of his health and medical condition unless medically contraindicated (as documented by a physician in his resident record), and is afforded the opportunity to participate in the planning of his total care and medical treatment and to refuse treatment, and participates in experimental research only upon his informed written consent;

(4) Is transferred or discharged only for medical reasons or for his welfare or that of other patients, or for nonpayment for his stay (except as prohibited by the title XIX program);

(5) Is encouraged and assisted, throughout his period of stay, to exercise his rights as a resident and as a citizen, and to this end may voice grievances and recommend changes in policies and services to facility staff and/or to outside representatives of his choice, free from restraint, interference, coercion, discrimination, or reprisal;

(6) May manage his personal financial affairs, and to the extent, under written authorization by the resident, that the facility assists in such management, that it is carried out in accord-

ance with paragraph (a)(1)(iii) of this section;

(7) Is free from mental and physical abuse, and free from chemical and physical restraints except as follows: when authorized in writing by a physician for a specified period of time; when necessary in an emergency to protect the resident from injury to himself or to others, in which case restraints may be authorized by designated professional personnel who promptly report the action taken to the physician; and in the case of a mentally retarded individual when authorized in writing by a physician or Qualified Mental Retardation Professional for use during behavior modification sessions;

(8) In the case of a mentally retarded individual, participates in a behavior modification program involving use of restraints or aversive stimuli only with the informed consent of his parent or guardian;

(9) Is ensured confidential treatment of all information contained in his records, including information contained in an automatic data bank, and his written consent shall be required for the release of information to persons not otherwise authorized under law to receive it;

(10) Is treated with consideration, respect, and full recognition of his dignity and individuality, including privacy in treatment and in care for his personal needs;

(11) Is not required to perform services for the facility;

(12) May communicate, associate and meet privately with persons of his choice, unless to do so would infringe upon the rights of other residents, and send and receive his personal mail unopened;

(13) May participate in activities of social, religious, and community groups' at his discretion, unless contraindicated for reasons documented by a Qualified Mental Retardation Professional as appropriate in his resident record;

(14) May retain and use his personal clothing and possessions as space permits; and

(15) If married, is ensured privacy for visits by his/her spouse; if both are residents in the facility, they are permitted to share a room.

(C) Provide that all rights and responsibilities of the resident devolve to the resident's guardian, next of kin, or sponsoring agency(ies), where:

(1) a resident is adjudicated incompetent in accordance with State law; or

(2) his physician or, in the case of a mentally retarded individual, a Qualified Mental Retardation Professional has documented in the resident's record the specific impairment that has rendered the resident incapable of understanding these rights.

(iii) A written account, available to residents and their families, is maintained on a current basis for each resident with written receipts for all personal possessions and funds received by or deposited with the facility and for all disbursements made to or on behalf of the resident.....

§ 249.13 Standards for intermediate care facility services in institutions for the mentally retarded or persons with related conditions.

Effective not later than 3 years after the effective date of these regulations, the standards for intermediate care facility services (as defined in § 249.10(b)(15)) in an institution for the mentally retarded or persons with related conditions which are specified by the Secretary pursuant to section 1905(c) and (d) of the Social Security Act and referred to in § 249.12(c)(6), are specified in this section. At such time as an institution is deemed to meet the standards contained in this section, such institution will no longer be required to meet the following provisions of § 249.12: (a)(1)(i), (ii), (iv), (v) and (vi); (a)(4); (a)(6), (i)(B), (iii), (v), (vi), (vii) and (viii); (a)(7); (a)(8); (c)(4); and (c)(5).

(a) *Administrative policies and practices*—(1) *General policies and practices.* (i) The facility shall have a written outline of the philosophy, objectives, and goals it is striving to achieve, that is available for distribution to staff, consumer representatives, and the interested public, and that shall include but need not be limited to:

(A) Its role in the State comprehensive program for the mentally retarded;

(B) Its goals for its residents; and

(C) Its concept of its relationship to the parents of its residents, or to their surrogates.

(ii) The facility shall have a written statement of policies and procedures concerning the rights of residents that assure the civil rights of all residents.

(iii) The facility shall have a written statement of policies and procedures that protect the financial interests of residents and when large sums accrue to the resident, provide for counseling of the resident concerning their use, and for appropriate protection of such funds. These policies shall permit normalized and normalizing possession and use of money by residents for work payment and property administration as, for example, in performing cash and check transactions and in buying clothes and other items.

(iv) Policies and procedures in the major operating units of the facility shall be described in manuals that are current, relevant, available, and followed.

(v) The facility shall have a plan for a continuing management audit to insure compliance with State laws and regulations and the effective implementation of its stated policies and procedures.

(vi) A governing body of the facility shall exercise general direction and shall establish policies concerning the operation of the facility and the welfare of the individuals served.

(vii) The governing body shall establish appropriate qualifications of education, experience, personal factors, and skills for the chief executive officer.

(viii) The chief executive officer shall make arrangements so that some one individual is responsible for the administrative direction of the facility at all times.

(ix) A table of organization shall provide for and show the major operating programs of the facility, with staff divisions, the administrative personnel in charge of the programs and divisions, and their lines of authority, responsibility,

and communication.

(x) The administration of the facility shall provide for effective staff and resident participation and communication.

(A) Standing committees appropriate to the facility, such as human rights, research review, and infection shall be constituted and shall meet regularly. Committees shall include the participation of direct-care staff, whenever appropriate.

(B) Minutes and reports of staff meetings, and of standing and ad hoc committee meetings shall include records of recommendations and their implementation, and shall be kept and filed.

(xi) There shall be an active program of ready, open, and honest communication with the residents and families.

(A) The facility shall maintain active means of keeping residents' families or surrogates informed of activities related to the residents that may be of interest to them or of significant changes in the resident's condition.

(B) Communications to the facility from residents' relatives shall be promptly and appropriately handled and answered.

(C) Close relatives and parent surrogates shall be permitted to visit at any reasonable hour, and without prior notice unless contra-indicated by the residents' needs. Steps shall be taken, however, so that the privacy and rights of the other residents are not infringed by this practice.

(D) Parents shall be permitted to visit all parts of the facility that provide services to residents.

(E) Frequent and informal visits home shall be encouraged, and the regulations of the facility shall facilitate rather than inhibit such visitations.

A handy guide:

Step 1: Set the ASA (film speed) on the light meter to
         200.

Step 2. Take a light reading (using the 200 ASA setting)
         and use the following chart to determine the
         approximate number of footcandles.

ASA	Seconds of Exposure	Lens Opening	Footcandles
200	1/4	5.6	10
200	1/8	5.6	20
200	1/15	5.6	40
200	1/30	5.6	70
200	1/60	5.6	150
200	1/125	5.6	300
200	1/250	5.6	600

(Source, G. Electric Exposure Calculator)

*Note: This table gives only approximate light levels
        and is only useful in determining the gross
        light abusers. Since light levels can vary
        even within one room, the average of three
        readings should be used. The government recom-
        mended lighting standards are:

        10 footcandles for public areas such as lobbys
           and hallways;
        30 footcandles for general work areas such as
           offices or conference rooms;
        50 footcandles for work stations such as a desk.

TABLE OF CONTENTS

Section 1. *Short Title*

This Act may be cited as the [State] Residential Utility Consumer Action Group Act.

COMMENT: Proponents of the Model Act in some states have chosen to give the organization a different title.

*Robert B. Leflar and Martin H. Rogol. Harvard Journal on Legislation, Volume 13, No. 2. February 1976. Copyright © by the Harvard Legislative Research Bureau. Reprinted with permission.

Proponents of the statute may wish to introduce the substantive Comments following the provisions of the statute, as well as relevant parts of the discussion preceding the statute, into the legislative record. As part of the legislative history they will aid in subsequent judicial and administrative interpretation of the Act.

Section 2. *Statement of Legislative Intent*

The purpose of this Act is to ensure effective and democratic representation of residential utility consumers before regulatory agencies, legislatures, and other public bodies by:

(a) creation of a permanent nonprofit organization whose sole duty is the representation of the interests of residential utility consumers before such bodies;

(b) provision for democratic accountability of the Board of Directors of the organization to the will of its consumer constituency through open elections of Directors with thorough financial disclosure requirements and campaign spending limitations;

(c) encouragement of active citizen participation in the regulatory process through involvement in the activities of the organization; and

(d) creation of an efficient funding mechanism for the organization, involving no compulsory burden whatsoever on the taxpayers of this State, whereby residential utility consumers and others may voluntarily contribute to the organization by adding a sum to their utility payments.

Section 3. *Definitions*

(a) "Public utility" means a corporation or other entity engaged in the business of supplying utility services to persons within this State if rates or charges for such utility services have been established or are subject to approval by a local, state, or federal authority.

COMMENT: This definition may be keyed to the definitions in the state statutes providing for public utility regulation. Publicly owned utilities should be included in the definition, however, even if the state statutes do not include them.

(b) "Utility services" means electricity, water, natural gas, and telephone services supplied by a public utility.

COMMENT: Railroads, municipal transport systems, broadcasters, and the like are outside the scope of the Model Act.

(c) "Residential utility consumer" means any resident of this State whose residence is furnished with a utility service by a public utility.

COMMENT: The term "residence" is not confined to resident-owned dwellings, but includes any inhabited premises.

(d) "Regulatory agency" means any local, state, or federal commission or other public body with the legal authority:

(1) to establish or alter rates or charges for the provision or sale of utility services within this State;

(2) to plan or to approve, reject, or modify plans for the construction of facilities for the production or provision of utility services within this State;

(3) to formulate or review energy policies affecting this State; or

(4) otherwise to regulate the activities of public utilities doing business within this State; *provided* that local, state, and federal courts and legislative bodies shall not be deemed to be "regulatory agencies" for the purposes of this Act.

(e) "Proceeding" means any formal meeting of a regulatory agency or subdivision thereof, including a meeting conducted by a hearing examiner or other agent of the regulatory agency, regarding:

(1) the establishment or alteration of rates or charges for the provision or sale of utility services within this State;

(2) the establishment, abrogation, or amendment of rules or regulations concerning residential utility consumers, public utilities, or energy policies affecting this State, or concerning the conduct of regulatory agency proceedings themselves; or

(3) adjudication of the claims or petitions of residential utility consumers, public utilities, or other persons or groups of persons.

(f) "The Corporation" means the Residential Utility Consumer Action Group, Inc.

(g) "Member" means any person who meets the requirements for membership in the Corporation set forth in Section 4(b) of this Act.

(h) "Director" means any person serving on the Board of Directors of the Corporation.

(i) "District" means any political subdivision from which one member is elected to the Upper House of this State.

(j) "Campaign expenditure"

(1) means a purchase, payment, distribution, loan, advance, deposit, or gift of money or anything of value, made for the purpose of electing a candidate to the Board of Directors of the Corporation; and

(2) means a contract, promise, or agreement, express or implied, whether or not legally enforceable, to make any campaign expenditure; but

(3) does not include the use of real or personal property and the cost of invitations, food, and beverages, voluntarily provided by an individual to a candidate in rendering voluntary personal services on the individual's residential premises for candidate-related activities if the cumulative value of such activities by such individual on behalf of any candidate does not exceed [$100.00] for any election.

COMMENT: The language of this definition is taken from the Federal Election Campaign Act[139] with certain modifications to adapt the provision to the local nature of RUCAG campaigns.

The provisions of (j) (3) exclude from the campaign expenditure limitations of Section 10(f)(1) certain types of activities common to grass-roots campaigns, particularly a candidate's use of a supporter's house, on a voluntary basis, as a local headquarters for canvassing, telephoning, etc. Underlying the provision are the policy of encouraging public participation in political campaigns at the grass roots level and the recognition that to require accounting of all such minor in-kind contributions would be an unduly burdensome imposition upon individual candidates. Lest a candidate seek to subvert the Section 10(f)(1) campaign spending limitation through excessive use of the 3(j)(3) exclusion, however, it is suggested that individual supporters be limited to $100.00 worth of such unrecorded in-kind donations.

The use of office space, equipment, and staff services, and the

---

139 2 U.S.C. § 431(f) (Supp. 1975).

provision of transportation, among other in-kind contributions, fall within the scope of "campaign expenditures."

(k) "Campaign contribution"

(1) means a gift, subscription, loan, advance, or deposit of money or anything of value, made for the purpose of electing a candidate to the Board of Directors of the Corporation; and

(2) means a contract, promise, or agreement, express or implied, whether or not legally enforceable, to make any campaign contribution; but

(3) does not include

(A) the value of services provided without compensation by individuals who volunteer a portion or all of their time on behalf of a candidate or political committee; or

(B) the use of real or personal property and the cost of invitations, food, and beverages, voluntarily provided by an individual to a candidate in rendering voluntary personal services on the individual's residential premises for candidate-related activities if the cumulative value of such activities by such individual on behalf of any candidate does not exceed $100.00 for any election.

COMMENT: The language of this provision is also taken from the Federal Election Campaign Act,[140] with certain modifications. The considerations underlying the provision are similar to those underlying subsection (j).

(*l*) "Political committee" means any committee, club, association, or other group of persons which makes campaign expenditures or receives campaign contributions during the year before an election of the Board of Directors.

COMMENT: This provision is adapted from the Federal Election Campaign Act.[141]

(m) "Periodic customer billing" means a demand for payment for utility services by a public utility to a residential utility consumer on a monthly or other regular basis.

(n) The "immediate family" of a person means the person and his or her spouse, and their parents, children, brothers and sisters.

---

140 *Id.*, § 431(e). See also Model Act Section 10(f) and Comment following.
141 2 U.S.C. § 431(d). See Model Act Section 10(f)(1).

Section 4. *Creation of Corporation; Membership*

(a) There is hereby created a [not-for-profit] membership corporation to be known as the Residential Utility Consumer Action Group, Inc., hereinafter referred to as the Corporation.

COMMENT: Some jurisdictions use the term "not-for-profit corporation" to designate corporations not organized for business purposes; others use terms such as "membership corporation," "nonstock corporation," "nonprofit corporation," or "corporation not for pecuniary profit."[142] The legislature should choose the appropriate term.

(b) The membership of the Corporation shall consist of all residential utility consumers of sixteen years of age or older who have contributed to the Corporation at least [two dollars] [an amount to be set by the Board of Directors] in either its preceding or its current fiscal year; *provided*, that any person may resign from membership.

COMMENT: Sixteen years is set as the minimum age for membership in order to encourage young people of high school age to become acquainted with public issues and to give them an opportunity to participate in public affairs. Sixteen-year-olds in many states are given the responsibility of operating motor vehicles, and must pay taxes on their earnings. It is felt that they are likewise mature enough to participate in RUCAG activities, and that they would gain from such participation valuable experience in preparation for exercising the responsibilities of voting citizens.

The provision for membership for both the "preceding and current" fiscal years of RUCAG is (1) for administrative convenience in the keeping of membership rolls and (2) to ensure that persons who have qualified for membership in the past year, but whose contributions in the current fiscal year have not reached the requisite minimum for membership as of the election date (which might conceivably be set for early in the fiscal year), are not barred from voting. If the contribution records are computerized and turned over to RUCAG each month,[143] it would be

---

142 *See* 19 W. FLETCHER, CYCLOPEDIA OF LAWS OF PRIVATE CORPORATIONS § 9001 (1975 rev. vol.).

143 See Section 8(d)(3) *infra*.

feasible to change this provision to read "preceding twelve months" and to purge the membership rolls every month.

A person becomes a member of RUCAG as soon as his or her contributions, as recorded on the RUCAG books, reach the requisite minimum.[144] Proponents of the Act may wish to give the Board of Directors the discretion to set the membership fee at whatever level it determines would best serve the goals of obtaining a broad membership base and of maximizing total contributions. The Board would be democratically accountable to the membership for its decisions on this as on other policy questions.

A contribution to RUCAG is not to be considered refundable if the contributor resigns from membership.

Section 5. *Duties, Rights, and Powers*

(a) It shall be the duty of the Corporation effectively to represent and protect the interests of the residential utility consumers of this State. All actions which it undertakes under the provisions of this Act shall be directed toward that goal.

(b) The Corporation shall have all rights and powers accorded generally to, and shall be subject to all duties imposed generally upon, not-for-profit membership corporations under the laws of this State.

(c) The Corporation may seek tax-exempt status under state and federal law.

(d) The Corporation may conduct, support, and assist research, surveys, investigations, planning activities, conferences, demonstration projects, and public information activities concerning the interests of residential utility consumers. The Corporation may accept grants, contributions, and legislative appropriations for such activities.

COMMENT: This provision would permit RUCAG to investigate the books of utility companies to the extent permissible by law. It would also permit RUCAG to present its case to the public through the mass media, by paid or donated advertising or by other means.

---

144 See text accompanying note 115 *supra* for a discussion of the suggested two-dollar membership fee.

As RUCAG develops expertise in the field of utility issues and builds up a network of contacts with citizens' groups across the state in question, it is conceivable that the state legislature may wish to employ RUCAG to perform research or public information activities. This provision permits RUCAG to accept such work. It is the only exception to the general policy against the use by RUCAG of tax monies, legitimized by the fact that it would be a specific legislative authorization of payment for work done.

This provision in conjunction with subsection (c) also opens up the possibility that RUCAG could establish a tax-exempt subsidiary foundation to solicit foundation grants for its research or educational efforts.

(e) The Corporation may contract for services which cannot reasonably be performed by its employees.

COMMENT: This provision permits RUCAG to employ on a temporary basis accountants, engineers, lawyers, and others whose expert services are necessary in constructing an effective presentation at, for example, a rate proceeding.

Note that Section 9(l), *infra,* which limits compensation of Directors to "expenses necessarily incurred by them in the performance of their duties," would rule out the employment by RUCAG of its Directors to perform such expert services on a paid basis. A directorship in RUCAG is not to be a means of soliciting business for one's private occupation.

(f) The Corporation may represent the interests of residential utility consumers before regulatory agencies, legislative bodies, and other public authorities, except as this Act otherwise provides.

COMMENT: A discussion of consumer representation by RUCAG is set forth in the text.[145]

(g) The Corporation shall not sponsor, endorse, or otherwise support, nor shall it oppose, any political party or the candidacy of any person for public office.

---

145 See text accompanying note 105 *supra.*

(h) The Corporation may support or oppose initiatives or referenda concerning matters which it determines may affect the interests of residential utility consumers.

(i) The Corporation, upon receipt of any written complaint regarding a public utility, shall promptly transmit the complaint to the appropriate regulatory agency or other public authority. The agency or authority shall inform the Corporation of its response to the complaint.

(j) The Corporation shall have, in addition to the rights and powers enumerated in this Act, such other incidental rights and powers as are reasonably necessary for the effective representation and protection of the interests of residential utility consumers.

Section 6. *Representation of Utility Consumers in Regulatory Agency Proceedings*

(a) Notification of Impending Proceedings. Each regulatory agency of this State as defined in Section 3(d) shall notify the Corporation in advance of the time, place, subject, and names of parties of each proceeding of the agency, unless the agency reasonably determines that the proceeding will not affect the interests of the residential utility consumers of this State. The agency shall so notify the Corporation at least thirty days before the scheduled date of the proceeding or within five days after such date is fixed, whichever is later.

COMMENT: The purpose of this provision is to alert RUCAG to hearings in which residential utility consumers may have a stake in time to prepare adequately for participation in the hearings. The agency holding the proceeding is in the best position from an efficiency standpoint to make the determination of its relevance to residential utility consumer interests, and so is given the authority to do so within the bounds of "reasonableness." Thus local zoning commissions, which might be considered "regulatory agencies" for some purposes (e.g., when ruling on proposed power plants), could reasonably determine that the vast majority of their proceedings would not call for notification to RUCAG.

If, however, a regulatory agency fails to notify RUCAG of a proceeding affecting the interests of residential utility consumers, RUCAG may still intervene or otherwise participate in the proceeding under Section 6(b), *infra,* and may seek judicial review of the agency decision under Section 7, *infra.*

(b) Intervention and Participation in Proceedings.

(1) The Corporation may intervene as of right as a party or otherwise participate in any regulatory agency proceeding which the Corporation reasonably determines may affect the interests of residential utility consumers.

(2) The intervention or participation of the Corporation in any such proceeding shall not affect the obligation of the regulatory agency to operate in the public interest.

COMMENT: The statutory grant to RUCAG in Section 6(b)(1) would in practice differ little in content from liberal intervention standards now in effect in most state agency proceedings.[146] The agency would pass judgment on the reasonableness of RUCAG's determination that consumers' interests "may [be] affect[ed]." A decision against intervention would be a final judgment appealable to the courts.

(c) Conduct of the Proceeding. When the Corporation intervenes or participates in a regulatory agency proceeding, it shall be subject to all laws and rules of procedure of general applicability governing the conduct of the proceeding and the rights of interveners and participants. The Corporation shall have the same rights regarding representation by counsel, participation in pre-hearing conferences, discovery, requests for issuance of subpoenas by the agency, stipulation of facts, presentation and cross-examination of witnesses, oral and written argument, participation in settlement negotiations, and other aspects of the proceeding as are accorded to other interveners under the laws of this State, except as otherwise provided in this Act.

COMMENT: The Model Act essentially preserves agency procedures as they presently exist. Though in some jurisdictions reform of administrative procedures, particularly in the area of discovery powers, might well be a topic for citizen groups' reform agendas, it is not the purpose of the Model Act to legislate changes in how the utility commissions are to conduct their business other

---

146 See note 41 *supra.*

than those minimal changes necessary to allow RUCAG effective participation in agency proceedings.

Two other alternatives for reform might have been proposed in the Model Act. The first alternative would be to grant RUCAG all procedural rights deemed necessary to effectuate its statutory role as representative of residential consumers in agency proceedings. RUCAG would be given broad powers in each of the areas listed in Section 6(c). In the discovery area, for example, the agency would be obliged to issue subpoenas for relevant material at RUCAG's request. RUCAG would also be authorized to send interrogatories which the agency could compel a utility to answer, and to take depositions. Moreover, RUCAG would have access to the fruits of the utility commission's investigations and to the utility commission's experts. Such proposals, however, would be vulnerable to attack on fairness grounds, in that they would give RUCAG an undue advantage over other parties and interveners.

The second alternative would be to institute a thorough-going procedural reform granting the rights and powers mentioned above to all parties and interveners. It seems unwise to incorporate such a sweeping reform in the RUCAG proposal if it is to apply to all state regulatory agencies; RUCAG itself could get sidetracked in the ensuing debate. If the reform is to be confined to utility commission procedure, however, a stronger argument exists for inserting it in the RUCAG Act, although the fact that the procedural reform proposal would probably require an additional committee of the state legislature, the Judiciary Committee, to pass on the entire Model Act might raise a significant obstacle to the Act's adoption.

The principal problem in utility commission proceedings is not the rules of the proceedings themselves, however, but rather the inadequacy of effective and accountable residential consumer representation. In most proceedings, for example, once consumer representatives are granted leave to intervene, discovery is not a major difficulty: agencies generally issue subpoenas on request,[147]

---

147 Letter from Elliot Taubman, National Consumer Law Center, Boston, to the HARVARD JOURNAL ON LEGISLATION, Jan. 23, 1976, on file at the HARVARD JOURNAL ON LEGISLATION. There is little judicial precedent available, however, to define the rights of the parties regarding administrative subpoenas. F. COOPER, note 26 *supra,* at 294-95.

and in some states are required by statute to do so.[148] Only in those states in which consumer interveners have had significant problems in obtaining information from utilities or in which other agency procedures have been burdensome on consumer advocates in important respects should proponents of the Act add provisions to it to institute broad procedural reforms.

In any case, RUCAG, once established, may petition the agency or the legislature under the general authority accorded by Section 5(f) of the Act to undertake whatever procedural reforms RUCAG deems desirable.

Section 7. *Judicial Review of Regulatory Agency Decisions; Enforcement Actions*

The Corporation shall be deemed to have an interest sufficient to maintain, intervene as of right in, or otherwise participate in any civil action for the review or enforcement of any regulatory agency decision which the Corporation reasonably determines would adversely affect the interests of residential utility consumers.

COMMENT: The Section 7 grant of standing to RUCAG is within the mainstream of recent judicial decisions[149] on both the federal and state levels regarding standing to seek review of administrative actions. The decisions hold that a party sustaining an "injury in fact" from an agency action, where "the alleged injury was to an interest 'arguably within the zone of interests to be protected or regulated' by the statutes that the agencies were claimed to have violated," possesses standing to obtain judicial review of the agency action.[150] The federal decisions are grounded on Section 10(a) of the federal Administrative Procedure Act, granting judi-

---

148 Among these states are California (CAL. GOV'T CODE § 11510 (West, 1966)), Alaska (ALASKA STAT. § 44.62.430 (1967)), Massachusetts (MASS. GEN. LAWS ANN. ch. 30A § 12(3) (1966)), Missouri (Mo. REV. STAT. § 536.077 (Supp. 1975)), North Dakota (N.D. CENT. CODE § 28-32-09 (1960)). Ohio (OHIO REV. CODE ANN. § 119.09 (Page, 1969)), Oregon (ORE. REV. STAT. § 183.440 (1974)), and Virginia (VA. CODE ANN. § 9-6.10(d) (1973)).

149 *See* cases cited in the Comment and in notes 150 to 153.

150 Sierra Club v. Morton, 405 U.S. 727, 733 (1972); Associated Data Processing Service Organizations v. Camp, 397 U.S. 150 (1970); Barlow v. Collins, 397 U.S. 159 (1970).

cial review to persons *"adversely affected* or aggrieved by agency action within the meaning of a relevant statute" (emphasis added).[151] This language corresponds to that of Section 7 of the Model Act. The degree of injury alleged need not be large; indeed, the Supreme Court has quoted approvingly Professor Davis's conclusion that ". . . an identifiable trifle is enough for standing to fight out a question of principle; the trifle is the basis for standing and the principle supplies the motivation."[152] State courts have moved to adopt the Supreme Court's standards in ruling on standing questions arising from state agency proceedings.[153]

In seeking review of agency decisions "adversely affecting" its members, RUCAG would be in essentially the same position as the public interest groups (whose members were alleged to be "injured in fact" by agency decisions) granted standing by the courts in *SCRAP*[154] and *Wisconsin Environmental Decade*.[155] The reasonableness of RUCAG's determination that its members would be "adversely affected" would presumably be judged by the court on the basis of a standard quite similar to, if not identical with, the "injury-in-fact" standard handed down by the Supreme Court in *SCRAP*.

Section 7 is also consistent with the "zone of interests" test in regard to the type of judicial review RUCAG is likely most often to seek: review of utility commission actions. It is clear that residential utility consumers' interests are within the "zone" regulated by the utility commission. The Model Act may be somewhat more liberal than the "zone of interests" test, however, in that it also grants RUCAG the right to obtain review of other regulatory agencies' actions which adversely affect its constituency, even if the statute the agency is interpreting or from which it derives its authority is not construed to "protect or regulate" the

---

151 5 U.S.C. § 702 (1970).

152 Davis, *Standing: Taxpayers and Others,* 35 U. CHI. L. REV. 601, 613 (1968), cited in United States v. SCRAP, 412 U.S. 669, 689 n.14 (1973).

153 Wagstaff v. Superior Ct., Family Ct. Div., 535 P.2d 1220 (Alas. 1975); De Vargas Savings & Loan Ass'n. of Santa Fe v. Campbell, 535 P.2d 1320 (N.M. 1975); Wisconsin Envir. Decade v. Public Serv. Comm'n of Wis., 230 N.W.2d 243 (Wis. 1975). See also note 41 *supra.*

154 United States v. Students Challenging Regulatory Agency Procedures (SCRAP), 412 U.S. 669 (1973).

155 Wisconsin Envir. Decade v. Public Service Comm'n of Wis., 230 N.W.2d 243 (Wis. 1975).

interests of residential utility consumers. In this respect the Model Act is consonant with the criticisms of judges and scholars that the "zone of interests" test is overly restrictive.[156]

Section 8. *Funding of the Corporation*

(a) The Corporation shall have the authority to prepare and furnish to each public utility in this State, not less than [fourteen] calendar days and not more than one year in advance of the date of each of the public utility's periodic customer billings, the following materials:

(1) a statement, not to exceed the folded size of [x] inches and [   ] ounces avoir., concerning the organization and activities of the Corporation and other matters which the Corporation determines may affect the interests of residential utility consumers; and

(2) a card, leaflet, or similar enclosure, not to exceed [x] inches and [   ] ounces avoir. or a statement to be printed upon the face of the billing in [   ] point or larger type,

(A) indicating that the utility consumer billed and others in his or her household may contribute money to the Corporation by a payment to the public utility in excess of his or her payment for utility services and that such excess payment will be transferred to the Corporation; and

(B-1) containing a box of dimensions [x] and a statement next to it indicating that if the utility consumer billed checks the box and adds [twenty cents or such amount as the Corporation may determine] to his or her payment, such excess payment will be transferred automatically to the Corporation as a contribution from the utility consumer billed; [and]/[or]

(B-2) containing a box of dimensions [x] and a statement next to it indicating that if the utility consumer billed checks the box, [twenty cents or such amount as the Corporation may determine] will be added automatically to his or her next periodic billing, and that such amount when paid will be transferred automatically to the Corporation as a contribution from the utility consumer billed; [and]/[or]

---

156 Barlow v. Collins, 397 U.S. 159, 167 (1970) (Brennan, J., concurring and dissenting); K. DAVIS, 3 ADMINISTRATIVE LAW TREATISE §§ 22.00-3 (1970 Supp.).

(C) containing a space no smaller than [x] inches in which the utility consumer may enter the names of contributors in his or her household sixteen years of age or older and the amount each contributes to the Corporation.

COMMENT: Proponents of the Act should choose which method among the alternatives (B-1), (B-2), and (C), or which combination of methods, would best serve the goals of encouraging contributions and reducing processing costs. Another possibility is to grant the Board of Directors of RUCAG the discretion to make the choice of method.

The Act's proponents must tailor these provisions to the specific billing practices of each utility in their respective states. Billing formats differ widely, as do the type and quantity of additional materials inserted by the utility companies into their billings.[157]

The weight limitation is of particular significance in view of the one-ounce allowance for first class mail. Although postal costs are to be borne by the utility under Section 8(e)(1), efforts should be made to keep the total weight of the bill, the return envelope, the RUCAG statement, and any informational or publicity material inserted by the utility within the one-ounce limit. Fairness dictates that the RUCAG statement and the utility's informational material be of approximately equal size and weight. The weight limitation should be set with these considerations in mind.

(b) Each public utility furnished with such statements or other enclosures in accordance with the provisions of subsection (a) of this Section shall print or otherwise include or enclose such statements or enclosures within, upon, or attached to each periodic customer billing which the public utility mails or delivers to any residential consumer.

COMMENT: How the utilities are to carry out this requirement is discussed in the text.[158]

(c) There is hereby created in each public utility's Uniform System

---

157 See text accompanying notes 84 to 86; see generally the section of the text entitled "Funding," accompanying notes 107 to 122, particularly the paragraph accompanying notes 110 to 112 and note 112.
158 See text accompanying note 113 *supra*.

of Accounts an account to be called the Residential Utility Consumer Action Group Account. All contributions to the Corporation received by the public utility and all other moneys due the Corporation under the control of the public utility shall be deposited in this Account immediately upon receipt of such contributions or when such moneys become due. Interest, calculated at [the current prime rate], shall be added daily to this Account.

COMMENT: When a residential utility customer in paying a monthly billing (1) makes a contribution to RUCAG and (2) has a dispute with the utility over the proper amount of the billing and withholds a part of the amount demanded by the utility, the utility may not apply the RUCAG contribution to the customer's balance due. It must place the contribution in the RUCAG Account to be forwarded to RUCAG under Section 8(d)(1). Disputes over billings must be resolved through normal procedures independent of the RUCAG funding mechanism.

(d) Each public utility which receives contributions to the Corporation shall transfer to the Corporation by the [fifteenth] day of each month

(1) the entire contents of the Residential Utility Consumer Action Group Account as of the date of transfer;

(2) the name and address of each contributor and the amount he or she contributed during the previous month, in the following manner:

(A) a contribution made by checking the box described in Section 8(a)(2)(B) shall be attributed to the consumer billed;

(B) each contribution made by entering the name of the contributor and the amount he or she contributes in the space described in Section 8(a)(2)(C) shall be attributed to such contributor; *provided,* that

(C) if the actual amount the consumer billed adds to his or her payment as a contribution to the Corporation is inconsistent with the amount the consumer states by the methods described in Sections 8(A)(2)(B) and (C) that the members of his or her household are contributing, the actual amount contributed shall be attributed entirely to the consumer billed; and *further provided,* that

(D) if a consumer neither checks the box described in Section

8(a)(2)(B) nor enters the name of any contributor in the space described in Section 8(a)(2)(C), any payment by the consumer in excess of the amount demanded in the periodic customer billing shall not be considered a contribution to the Corporation; *and*

(3) if the public utility operates its billings and customer accounts on a computerized basis, a statement of the cumulative amount contributed by each contributor during the Corporation's current fiscal year.

COMMENT: The operation of this provision is explained in the text.[159] Section 8(d)(2)(C) covers the case in which the consumer billed errs in adding up the contributions of individual household members, or in adding the household's total contributions to the utility payment. So that the utility will not have to determine which part of the miscalculated amount contributed is attributable to each of the contributors in the household, the entire contribution is to be attributed to the consumer whose name appears on the periodic customer billing.

The final phrase of Section 8(d)(3) may be changed to "during the preceding twelve months," depending on the membership requirements.[160] See the Comment following Section 4(b), *supra.*

(e) The Corporation shall promptly reimburse each public utility for all reasonable costs incurred by the public utility, above the utility's normal billing costs, in complying with this Section; *provided,* that

(1) All postage costs of mailings pursuant to Section 8(a) shall be borne by the utility; and

(2) the Corporation may postpone reimbursement of the public utilities for costs incurred through the first election of Directors until [twelve months] after such Directors are installed.

COMMENT: The purpose of this provision is to avoid placing a financial burden on utilities in carrying out the requirements of this Act.[161]

---

159 See text accompanying notes 84, 85, and 110 to 113, and note 112.
160 See Comment following Section 4(b), *supra.*
161 See text accompanying notes 120 and 121, *supra.*

Proviso (e)(1) is made necessary by the possibility that a utility would force RUCAG to bear tremendous additional postal costs by including in the billings the utility's own publicity materials taking up the entire one-ounce first-class allowance, and then arguing that inclusion of the RUCAG material required additional postage. The proviso creates an incentive for the utility to keep the weight of its billing materials to a minimum.[162]

In states in which utility payments are made automatically from the consumer's bank account to the utility through a so-called Electronic Funds Transfer System, the procedures for solicitation and collection of contributions for RUCAG must be modified.

(f) Any disputes arising from the operation of this Section shall be resolved by negotiations between the Corporation and the public utility if possible, or by a civil proceeding in the courts of this State. Neither the public utility nor the Corporation may fail to comply with the provisions of this Act by reason of the existence of such a dispute.

COMMENT: Disputes over the costs of funding mechanism could be a life-or-death matter for RUCAG, especially in its early stages. Given that some state utility commissions are likely to be hostile to RUCAG at first, it seems wise to give jurisdiction of these disputes to the judicial system rather than to the agency.[163]

(g) No public utility or officer, employee, or agent of a public utility may interfere or threaten to interfere with or cause any interference with the utility service of, or penalize or threaten to penalize or cause to be penalized, any person who contributes to the Corporation or participates in any of its activities, in retribution for such contribution or participation.

(h) No public utility or officer, employee, or agent of a public utility may prevent, interfere with, or hinder the activities described in subsections (b), (c), and (d) of this Section.

(i) A person who violates subsections (g) or (h) of this Section shall be subject to a civil penalty of not more than [$5,000]. Each such violation shall constitute a separate and continuing violation of

---

162 See Comment following Section 8(a), *supra.* For an explanation of proviso (e)(2), see text accompanying note 122, *supra.* See also Section 10(a)(1).

163 See text accompanying notes 120-122 *supra.*

the Act. [A person who knowingly and willfully violates subsections (g) or (h) of this Section shall also be liable to imprisonment for a term not to exceed six months.]

(j) No person shall use any list of contributors to the Corporation, nor any part of such list, for purposes other than the conduct of the activities described in subsections (b), (c), and (d) of this Section, or the conduct of other business of the Corporation as prescribed in this Act. No person shall disclose any such list or part thereof to any other who the person has substantial reason to believe does not intend to use it for the lawful purposes described in this subsection. A person who violates this subsection shall be subject to a civil penalty of not more than [$5,000].

COMMENT: This provision is designed to protect the privacy interests of RUCAG members. The only persons outside of RUCAG with access to the membership lists will be the utility companies which compile the lists of contributors for RUCAG.[164] Use of the lists by these firms is strictly limited to the operation of the funding mechanism. Membership lists would be available to RUCAG members considering running for Director, since they would be essential to a petition campaign. Such members, however, would be prohibited from disclosing the lists to those not involved in RUCAG.

Section 9. *Board of Directors*

(a) Function. The affairs of the Corporation shall be managed by a Board of Directors.

(b) Term of Office. The term of office of elected Directors shall be three years, with the exception of Directors drawing shortened terms under the provisions of subsection (c) of this Section. The term of office of Directors appointed pursuant to subsection (e) of this Section shall end when the first elected Directors are installed in office. No Director shall serve more than two consecutive terms.

COMMENT: The prohibition against long, unbroken tenure in office is a safeguard against the establishment of personal fiefdoms within the organization. It will ensure a continual turnover of

---

164 See note 119 and accompanying text.

RUCAG leadership, which should combat tendencies toward bureaucratic stagnation.

(c) **Staggering of Terms.** One-third of the Directors first elected to the Board shall serve for a one year term, one-third of such Directors shall serve for a two year term, and one-third of such Directors shall serve for a full three year term. The Directors shall draw lots upon their installation in office to determine the length of their first terms.

(d) **Qualifications.** Directors shall be residents of this State who are members of the Corporation. No officer, employee, consultant, attorney, accountant, real estate agent, shareholder, bondholder, or member of the immediate family of an officer, employee, consultant, attorney, accountant, real estate agent, shareholder, or bondholder, of any public utility doing business in this State shall be eligible to become a Director.

COMMENT: The purpose of the second sentence of this provision is the elimination of conflicts of interests among Directors. Proponents of the Act may wish to consult their state law regarding conflicts of interest of public utility commissioners.[165]

(e) **Appointed Directors.** Within sixty days after this Act becomes effective, the Attorney General, the Speaker of the House, the President Pro Tempore of the Senate, the majority and minority leaders of the House, and the majority and minority leaders of the Senate of this State shall each appoint one Director of the Corporation to serve until the first elected Directors are installed in office. The appointed Directors shall be installed in office by the Governor.

COMMENT: Many states have set practices regarding appointment of commissions, agencies and the like. State practice may be followed in this respect.

(f) **Special Duties of Appointed Directors.** The appointed Directors shall:
(1) inform the residential utility consumers of this State, by the means provided for in Sections 5(d), 8, and elsewhere in this Act,

---

165 See also Section 14, *infra,* Corrupt Practices and Conflicts of Interest, and Comment following.

of the existence, nature, and purposes of the Corporation, and shall encourage residential utility consumers to participate in the Corporation's activities and contribute to its operating funds;

(2) elect officers as provided in Section 11;

(3) employ such staff as the Directors deem necessary to carry out the purposes of this Act;

(4) make all necessary preparations for the first election of Directors, oversee the election campaign, and tally the votes, as provided in Section 10; and

(5) carry out all other duties and exercise all other powers accorded to the Board of Directors in this Act.

COMMENT: Specification of the duties of the appointed Directors is necessary because (1) these Directors will not have been subjected to the rigorous formal and informal processes designed to assure that elected Directors have a sense of accountability to the consumers — and indeed may conceivably be hostile to the very conception of RUCAG; and (2) it is particularly essential that the appointed Directors carry out the initial publicizing of RUCAG, as required in Section 9(f)(1), in a whole-hearted fashion. Specification of duties should encourage the appointed Directors to perform their statutory obligations in an acceptable manner.

(g) Elected Directors. One Director shall be elected, pursuant to the procedures set down in Section 10, from each District in the State. Each Director shall represent the interests of the residential utility consumers of his or her District and of the State. Each Director shall have one vote in the Board of Directors. Elected Directors shall be installed in office by the President of the outgoing Board of Directors.

COMMENT: Election of Directors from geographical districts is desirable for several reasons. (1) The interests of residential consumers living in different areas of a state may be distinct. For instance, residents of an area where a power plant is to be built may have different views as to its desirability than residents of other areas which are to receive the power it generates. A scheme of statewide at-large representation, for example, would tend to increase the difficulty of geographically based interest groups obtaining adequate representation on the RUCAG Board. (2) Election by geographical district is the most practical form of selecting

Directors. Campaign expenses for gathering petition signatures and the like will be lower than if the elections were statewide. Candidates' mailings will need to go to fewer members. (3) Members will be better acquainted with a small number of candidates from their areas than with a large number from across the state, and will be able to make more intelligent choices among them.

It is suggested that, for administrative convenience, districts for the purpose of electing RUCAG Directors be coextensive with the state senatorial districts.[166]

(h) Recall of Directors. Upon receipt by the President of the Board of Directors of a petition to recall any Director with the valid signatures of at least forty percent of the members from such Director's District, the President shall call an election for the District, to be held not less than four months and not more than six months after his or her receipt of the petition, for the purpose of electing a Director to serve out the term of the recalled Director; *provided,* that no petition to recall a Director may be filed within six months of his or her election. An election following recall shall be conducted in accordance with the provisions of Section 10. A Director may become a candidate in an election following his or her own recall. The Director recalled shall continue to serve until the installment in office of his or her successor.

COMMENT: The four-to-six month delay in calling the election is to allow candidates for the recalled Director's position time to obtain signatures for nomination and to conduct the campaign as provided in Section 10. A newly elected Director is given six months' "immunity" from recall to establish a reviewable performance record.

(i) Vacancies. When a Director dies, resigns, is disqualified, or otherwise vacates his or her office, except as provided in subsection (h) of this Section, the Board of Directors shall select within three months a successor from the same District as such Director for the remainder of the Director's term of office. Any Director may nominate any qualified person as successor. The Board of Directors shall select the successor from among those nominated, by a [two-thirds] majority

---

166 See Section 3(i), *supra.*

of the remaining Directors present and voting. The successor shall be installed in office by the President of the Board of Directors.

(j) Duties of Board of Directors. The Board of Directors shall have the following duties:

(1) to maintain up-to-date membership rolls, and to keep them in confidence to the extent required by the provisions of Section 8(j);

(2) to keep minutes, books, and records which shall reflect all the acts and transactions of the Board of Directors and which shall be open to examination by any member during regular business hours;

(3) to make all reports, studies, and other information compiled by the Corporation pursuant to Section 6(d) of this Act, and all data pertaining to the finances of the Corporation, available for public inspection during regular business hours;

(4) to prepare quarterly statements of the financial and substantive operations of the Corporation, and to make copies of such statements available to the general public;

(5) to cause the Corporation's books to be audited by a certified public accountant at least once each fiscal year, and to make the audit available to the general public;

(6) to prepare and mail, as soon as practicable after the close of the Corporation's fiscal year, an annual report of the Corporation's financial and substantive operations to each member and to each public library in the State;

(7) to report to the membership at the annual membership meeting on the past and projected activities and policies of the Corporation;

(8) to employ an Executive Director and to direct and supervise his or her activities; and

(9) to carry out all other duties and responsibilities imposed upon the Corporation and the Board of Directors by this Act.

(k) Meetings of the Board of Directors.

(1) The Board of Directors shall hold regular meetings at least once every three months on such dates and at such places as it may determine. Special meetings may be called by the President or by any [   ] Directors upon at least five days' notice. [   ] of the Directors shall constitute a quorum.

(2) All meetings of the Board of Directors and of its committees and subdivisions shall be open to the public. Complete minutes of

the meetings shall be kept and distributed to all public libraries in the State.

(l) **Expenses.** The Treasurer shall reimburse Directors for actual expenses necessarily incurred by them in the performance of their duties, and for such expenses only.

COMMENT: Section 9(l) would rule out the employment by RUCAG of its Directors to perform services on a paid basis.[167]

(m) **Bonding.** Directors and employees eligible to disburse funds shall be bonded. The cost of such bonds shall be paid by the Corporation.

Section 10. *Election of Directors*

(a) **Time of elections.**
(1) When the membership of the Corporation has reached [1,000] persons and the Corporation has received [$10,000] in contributions, the appointed Directors shall promptly fix a date for the first election of Directors. The election shall be held not less than four months and not more than six months after the membership and contributions have both reached the prescribed levels.

COMMENT: This provision is designed to allow RUCAG to organize and commence its activities and to build up a fairly broadly based membership before its first election. RUCAG should initially accumulate sufficient funds to pay for the election and begin its consumer representation activities. The appropriate requirement regarding the number of members and amount of contributions received before the first election can be held will vary with the size of the state in question; the figures for New York or California, for example, would be much higher than those suggested in the text of the Act.

The four-to-six-month delay in the election is to give candidates an adequate period to obtain signatures for nomination and to conduct the campaign as provided in this Section.

---

167 See Comment following Section 5(e), *supra.*

(2) Subsequent elections of Directors shall be held at approximately yearly intervals after the first election. The dates of such elections shall be fixed not less than four months in advance by the Board of Directors.

(b) Qualifications of Candidates. To be eligible for election to the Board of Directors, a candidate must:

(1) meet the qualifications for Directors prescribed in Section 9(d) of this Act;

(2) be a resident of the District which he or she seeks to represent;

(3) have his or her nomination certified by the Board of Directors pursuant to subsection (c) of this Section;

(4) submit to the Board of Directors a statement of financial interests in accordance with subsection (d) of this Section and a statement of personal background and positions in accordance with subsection (e) of this Section; and

(5) make the affirmation prescribed in subsection (f)(3) of this Section.

(c) Nomination of Candidates.

(1) A candidate for election to the Board of Directors shall submit to the Board, not later than [sixty] days prior to the election, a petition for nomination signed by at least [five percent] of the members residing in his or her District.

COMMENT: In larger states or where the five percent requirement might impose undue obstacles to candidacy, it may be desirable to reduce the required percentage. There is a trade-off between limiting the field to candidates who are dedicated enough to engage in what could be a difficult petition campaign on the one hand, and discouraging qualified people who lack the time or the resources to undertake such a project on the other. In small states in which the signature requirement could be so easily met that the field of candidates becomes crowded, a candidate might be elected with only a small percentage of the vote. (There is no provision for a runoff election because of the expense and loss of voter interest inevitably associated with it.) In such areas it may be desirable to raise the signature requirement to ten or even fifteen percent of the membership.

(2) The Board of Directors shall verify the validity of the sig-

natures. Upon determination that a sufficient number are valid, the Board shall certify the nomination of the candidate.

(d) Statement of Financial Interests.

(1) A candidate for election to the Board of Directors shall submit to the Board, not later than [sixty] days prior to the election, a statement of financial interests upon a form approved by the Board of Directors.

(2) The statement of financial interests shall include the following information:

(A) the occupation, employer, and position at place of employment of the candidate and of his or her immediate family members;

(B) a description of all significant personal or professional transactions by the candidate and by his or her immediate family members with any public utility during the previous three years;

(C) a list of all corporate and organizational directorships or other offices, and of all fiduciary relationships, held in the past three years by the candidate and by his or her immediate family members; and

(D) an affirmation, subject to penalty of perjury, that the information contained in the statement of financial interests is true and complete.

COMMENT: The rationale underlying the financial disclosure requirements is discussed in the text.[168]

(e) Statement of Personal Background and Positions. A candidate for election to the Board of Directors shall submit to the Board, not later than [sixty] days prior to the election, a [two] page statement concerning his or her personal background and positions on issues relating to public utilities or the operations of the Corporation. The statement shall contain an affirmation, subject to penalty of perjury, that the candidate meets the qualifications prescribed for Directors in Section 9(d) of this Act and is a resident of the District which he or she seeks to represent.

COMMENT: The purpose of the Statement of Personal Background and Positions is described in the text.[169]

---

168 See text accompanying notes 123 and 124, *supra.*
169 See text accompanying note 126, *supra.*

(f) Restrictions on and Reporting of Campaign Contributions and Expenditures.

(1) Each candidate may accept no more than [$50.00] in campaign contributions, as defined in Section 3(k) of this Act, from any person or political committee from one year before the date of an election through the date of the election.

(2) Each candidate shall keep complete records of all contributions to his or her campaign of five dollars or more made from one year before the date of an election through the date of the election.

(3) Each candidate may incur no more than [$____] [____] per member of the Corporation residing in the candidate's District as of sixty days prior to the election] in campaign expenditures, as defined in Section 3(j) of this Act, from the time he or she commences circulation of petitions for nomination or from four months prior to the election, whichever is earlier, through the date of the election.

(4) Each candidate shall keep complete records of his or her campaign expenditures, and shall make such records available for inspection during normal business hours to any member or employee of the Corporation.

(5) Each candidate, within twenty-one days after the election, shall submit an accurate statement of his or her campaign contributions accepted and campaign expenditures incurred to the Board of Directors, and shall affirm to the Board, subject to penalty of perjury, that he or she has fully complied with the requirements of subsections (f)(1) through (f)(4) of this Section.

COMMENT: The Supreme Court's decision in Buckley v. Valeo,[169a] which was handed down just before this article went to press, casts some doubt upon the constitutional validity of Section 10(f)(3) of the Model Act. The decision struck down the Federal Election Campaign Act's restrictions on expenditures in campaigns for federal offices[169b] as an impermissible burden on the freedom of expression protected by the First Amendment.[169c]

The restrictions on campaign contributions and expenditures are designed to preclude candidates with access to substantial fi-

---

169a 44 U.S.L.W. 4127 (U.S. Jan. 30, 1976).

169b Federal Election Campaign Act of 1971 § 608(c), Pub. L. No. 92-225, 86 Stat. 3, *as amended,* Federal Election Campaign Act Amendments of 1974, Pub. L. No. 93-443, 83 Stat. 1263.

169c 44 U.S.L.W. at 4143-44.

nancial resources from overwhelming those without. The amount of permitted campaign expenditures will vary with the size of the state and the number of RUCAG members. Proponents of the Act should consider the kinds of campaign they are willing to permit and estimate the likely cost of such a campaign. One possible measure would be the estimated cost of one mailing to each RUCAG member in the candidate's District, plus an allowance for costs of campaign organization. Addition of an index to compensate for inflation may also be appropriate.[170]

The maximum permissible amount for a campaign contribution may vary somewhat with the campaign expenditure limit and the type of campaign that proponents of the Act would find acceptable.[171]

(g) Election Procedures.

(1) The Board of Directors shall send or have sent by first class mail to each member, not sooner than [twenty-one] and not later than [fourteen] days before the date fixed for the election:

(A) an official ballot listing all candidates for Director from the member's District whose nominations the Board has certified and who have complied with the requirements of subsections (d) and (e) of this Section;

(B) each such candidate's statement of financial interests; and

(C) each such candidate's statement of personal background and positions.

(2) Each member may cast a vote in the election by returning his or her official ballot, properly marked, to the head office of the Corporation by [8 p.m. of] the date fixed for the election.

(3) Voting shall be by secret ballot.

(4) The Board of Directors shall tally votes with all reasonable speed and shall inform the membership promptly of the names of the candidates elected.

(5) In each District, the candidate with the most votes shall be declared elected.

COMMENT: A plurality-vote provision was decided upon because of the expense and loss of popular interest involved in the run-

---

170 See also the Comment following Section 3(j), *supra.*
171 See Section 3(k) and Comment following.

offs which would be required by a provision for election by majority vote.

(h) **Installation of Elected Candidates.** The President of the Board of Directors shall install in office within [thirty] days after the election all elected candidates who meet the qualifications prescribed in subsection (b) of this Section.

(i) **Election Rules.** The Board of Directors may prescribe rules for the conduct of elections and election campaigns not inconsistent with this Act.

Section 11. *Officers*

(a) **Election of Officers.** At the first regular meeting of the Board of Directors, at which a quorum is present, subsequent to the initial appointments of Directors and at the first regular meeting of the Board, at which a quorum is present, subsequent to the installation of new Directors following each annual election, the Board shall elect by majority vote of members present and voting from among the Directors a President, a Vice-President, a Secretary, and a Treasurer. The Board shall also have the power to elect a Comptroller and such other officers as it deems necessary.

(b) Term of Office; Removal from Office.

  (1) Officers shall be installed by the President immediately upon their election. The term of office of officers shall be one year; *provided* that an officer may resign, or may be removed from office by a [two-thirds] vote of all the Directors. After an officer's term of office has expired, the officer shall continue to serve until his or her successor is installed.

  (2) When an officer dies, resigns, is removed, or otherwise vacates his or her office, the Board of Directors shall elect a successor to serve out such officer's term of office.

(c) **Duties and Powers of Officers.** The officers shall exercise such powers and perform such duties as are prescribed by this Act or are delegated to them by the Board of Directors.

Section 12. *Executive Director*

(a) The Board of Directors shall employ an Executive Director.

(b) The Executive Director shall have the following powers and duties, subject at all times to the directions and supervision of the Board of Directors:

(1) to decide upon the course of action of the Corporation regarding appearances before regulatory agencies, legislative bodies, and other public authorities, and regarding other activities which the Corporation has the authority to perform under Sections 5, 6, 7, and 8 of this Act;

(2) to employ and discharge employees of the Corporation;

(3) to supervise the offices, the facilities, and the work of the employees of the Corporation;

(4) to have custody of and to maintain the books, records, and membership rolls of the Corporation, in accordance with the provisions of this Act;

(5) to prepare and submit to the Board of Directors annual and quarterly statements of the financial and substantive operations of the Corporation, and financial estimates for the future operations of the Corporation;

(6) to attend and participate in meetings of the Board of Directors as a non-voting Director; and

(7) to exercise such other powers and perform such other duties as the Board of Directors delegates to him or her.

(c) The Executive Director may be discharged by [two-thirds] vote of all the Directors.

COMMENT: The relationship between the Board of Directors and the Executive Director is discussed in the text.[172]

Section 13. *Annual Membership Meeting*

(a) An annual meeting of the membership shall be held in the month of _____ on a date and at a place within the State to be determined by the Board of Directors.

(b) All members shall be eligible to attend, participate in, and vote in the annual membership meeting.

(c) The form of the annual membership meeting shall be as provided in the law of this State regarding not-for-profit membership corporations.

(d) The annual membership meeting shall be open to the public.

---

172 See text accompanying notes 132 and 133, *supra,* for comment.

COMMENT: The Board of Directors may find it desirable to rotate the annual membership meeting among different areas of the state, in fairness to the entire membership.

Section 14. *Corrupt Practices and Conflicts of Interest*

(a) Neither the Corporation nor its Directors, employees, or agents shall offer anything of monetary value to, or accept anything of monetary value from, any public official or official or employee of any public utility or agent thereof, except as otherwise provided in this Act.

(b) No Director shall personally or through any partner or agent render any professional service or make or perform any business contract with or for any public utility.

(c) No public official or official or employee of any public utility or agent thereof shall offer anything of monetary value to, or accept anything of monetary value from, the Corporation or its Directors, employees, or agents, except as otherwise provided in this Act.

(d) Any person who violates subsection (a), (b), or (c) of this Section shall be subject to a civil penalty of not more than [$5000], or imprisonment for a term not to exceed [five years], or both.

(c) The office of a Director found in violation of subsection (a) or (b) shall be declared vacant.

COMMENT: Proponents of the Act may wish to consult their state law regarding conflicts of interest of public utility commissioners and bring this Section into accord with its language.

A member of a law firm or accounting firm, for example, which numbers among its clients a public utility would be ineligible to become a Director under Section 9(d). Note that under subsection 14(b), such a person would also become subject to civil liability. He or she would be required to cease activity with the firm before becoming Director.

Section 15. *Construction of the Act*

(a) The provisions of this Act shall be construed in such a manner as best to enable the Corporation effectively to represent and protect the interests of the residential utility consumers of this State.

(b) Nothing in this Act shall be construed to limit the right of any person to initiate, intervene in, or otherwise participate in any regulatory agency proceeding or court action, nor to require any petition or notification to the Corporation as a condition precedent to the exercise of such right, nor to relieve any regulatory agency or court of any obligation, or to affect its discretion, to permit intervention or participation by any person in any proceeding or action.

COMMENT: This subsection is designed to protect minorities within RUCAG as well as interests outside it.[173]

Section 16. *Severability*

If any provision of this Act shall be declared unconstitutional or invalid, the other provisions shall remain in effect notwithstanding.

Section 17. *Effective Date*

This Act shall become effective on the date of its enactment.

---

173 See text accompanying note 136, *supra*.

DEPARTMENT OF CONSUMER AFFAIRS

Notice of Opportunity to Comment on Proposed Amendments to Regulation 55 Relating to the Labeling of Perishable Foods.

BY VIRTUE OF THE AUTHORITY VESTED IN ME AS COMMISSIONER of the Department of Consumer Affairs under the provisions of Section 1105 of the New York City Charter and Section 2203(e) of said Charter, the following amendments are hereby proposed to the Rules and Regulations governing the labeling of perishable foods, pursuant to Section 36-120.3 of Title B, Article 12, Chapter 36 of the Administrative Code of The City of New York.

Written comment regarding the proposed amendments must be submitted to the undersigned on or before the 14th day of May, 1973.

Note—New matter in *italics*, matter in brackets [ ] to be omitted.

Regulation 55.

A. Definitions—For the purposes of the application of this Regulation 55 (unless the context indicates otherwise) the following definitions apply:

1. "Sell" or "offer to sell" shall mean the act of selling, displaying, or offering for sale by a retailer or retail entity to the public for off-premises human consumption.

2. *"Foil Packaging" shall mean a metallic wrapping with or without a backing material.*

B. Display of Required Information—

1. On the containers of all foods specified in Section C below of this Regulation 55, there shall be stamped, printed or otherwise plainly and conspicuously marked, a statement indicating recommended conditions and methods of storage.

2. On the containers of all foods specified in Section C below of this Regulation 55, there shall be stamped, printed or otherwise plainly and conspicuously marked either the last day or date of sale or the last day or date of recommended usage.

3. The information required in Paragraphs (1) and (2) of this Section B shall be clearly marked on each and every package or item as follows:

(a) the information shall appear on the top cover or principal panel or of its container, or, on a label affixed thereto; or

(b) a notice shall appear on the top cover or principal panel or on a label affixed thereto indicating the location on the package of such information.

4. *When any of the information required to be plainly and conspicuously marked by Paragraphs (1) and (2) of this section is imprinted on packages of foods specified in Section C of this Regulation 55, that information shall appear as follows:*

(a) The last day or date of sale or last day or date for recommended usage may be expressed by either:

1. the first three letters of the month followed by the numeral or numerals constituting the appropriate calendar date. Example: Jun20.

2. numerals expressing the month, calendar date, and year, with a space or other separating character between the month and the calendar date and the calendar date and the year. Example: 6-20-73.

3. At least the first three letters of the appropriate day, for those products customarily rotated within one week.

(b) When an additional numeral or letter is used for a batch code or other purpose, it may not appear on the same horizontal line as the date.

(c) The last day or date of sale or last day or date for recommended usage shall be clearly expressed by indelible inking, branding, stamping or a similar process. Embossing or debossing without the use of one of the processes listed above is not acceptable, except that deep embossing or debossing will be permitted on foil packaging.

(d) "twist ties", when used to provide date information on food packaging subject to this regulation, must be at least 5/32 inch in width; the day or date must appear in characters at least ⅛ inch in height; the day or date must be printed on both sides of the tie; and at least one full date must remain fully exposed on each untwisted tie end.

5. *Notwithstanding full compliance with the requirements set forth in Paragraph (4) of this section, each failure to mark the last day or date of sale or the last day or date of recommended usage in a plain and conspicuous manner shall constitute a separate violation.*

*Reprinted from The City Record of April 23, 1973

C. Perishable Foods Covered—The following commodities shall be labeled in accordance with the provisions of Section B36-120.2 "Perishable Foods", and Section B of this Regulation 55 governing the labeling of perishable foods:

  1. Eggs—Grade AA, Grade A and Grade B shell eggs.

  2. All pre-packaged, fully or partially prepared baked goods, which have a moisture content exceeding 18 per cent, with or without additives known as:

  (a) Bread, rolls and buns as defined in Title 21, Chapter 1, Part 17 of the Code of Federal Regulations, except those products traditionally known as "fruitcake";

  (b) Cakes, pastries and cookies, except those that are offered for sale in individual, portionpack, snack type packages;

  (c) English muffins, corn muffins, bran muffins and other similar products.

  3. The following pre-packaged dairy and dairy-type products:

  (a) Those products with or without additives or flavorings, known as cheese, as defined in Title 21, Chapter 1, Part 19, Sections 19.499 through 19.685 of the Code of Federal Regulations, that contain 50 per cent or more moisture in the finished product;

  (b) Low-fat, multi-vitamin, multi-mineral type milk products, which are normally stored at temperatures between 32 degrees Fahrenheit and 40 degrees Fahrenheit;

  (c) flavored milk;

  (d) cultured milk, cultured milk products, cultured skim-milk and cultured skim-milk products, with or without fruits, vegetables, meats or cheeses, or other additives;

  (e) milk-shake;

  (f) eggnog;

  (g) yogurt, made from skim-milk or whole milk, with or without fruits, vegetables, meats or other additives;

  (h) whipped cream and instant whipped cream;

  (i) sour cream, cultured cream, salad cream, and non-cultured sour cream, with or without fruits, vegetables, meats or cheese or other additives;

  (j) sour half and half, cultured half and half, non-cultured sour half and half and non-cultured half and half;

  (k) dairy dressing, and dairy dip;

  (l) non-dairy coffee creamers which are normally stored at temperatures between 32 degrees Fahrenheit and 40 degrees Fahrenheit.

  4. All pre-packaged, prepared foods which require refrigeration.

D. Exemptions—

  1. This regulation shall not include any product stored in a retail store at or below a temperature of 32 degrees Fahrenheit, in accordance with the recommendations of the manufacturer or processor.

  2. This regulation shall not include any product hereinabove designated which is sterilized when hermetically sealed and packaged and is so maintained until the time of sale by a retailer to the public.

  3. This regulation shall not include products made from products after the date marked where such secondary products are the result of an additional processing stage.

  4. Upon written application to the Commissioner, and upon a showing of exceptional circumstances, a manufacturer or processor may be granted an extension in writing, not to exceed six months, in which to comply, in whole or in part, with the requirements of Section B above. In the event that a manufacturer or processor has substantially complied with Section B above during the previously granted extension period, but exceptional circumstances exist which render full compliance during the extension period impossible, impracticable, or create undue financial hardship, a manufacturer or processor may apply in writing to the Commissioner for an additional final extension in order to fully comply with Section B. Any request for an additional final extension must be supported by evidence of exceptional circumstances and substantial compliance during the previously granted extension period. The granting of a further extension, if any, shall be in the discretion of the Commissioner.

EXPLANATION

These amended regulations establish uniform standards for providing the dating information required by the City's "open-dating" law. The Department had permitted individual manufacturers wide latitude in their efforts to imprint the dating information required by law. The Department has found that the variations that resulted from this procedure substantially reduced the uniformity of presentation and format which are necessary to make "open-dating" requirements meaningful and intelligible to consumers.

These regulations follow the mandate of Local Law 17 of 1971, which was enacted to help prevent the consumer from purchasing perishable foods which are no longer fresh.

a23,m7   BETTY FURNESS, Commissioner.

PART 317—LABELING, MARKING DEVICES, AND CONTAINERS

1. In § 317.8 of the meat inspection regulations, paragraph (b) is amended by adding a new subparagraph (32) to read as follows:

§ 317.8 **False or misleading labeling or practices generally; specific prohibitions and requirements for labels and containers.**

* * * * *

(b) * * *

(32) A calendar date may be shown on labeling when declared in accordance with the provisions of this subparagraph:

(i) The calendar date shall express the month of the year and the day of the month for all products and also the year in the case of products hermetically sealed in metal or glass containers, dried or frozen products, or any other products that the Administrator finds should be labeled with the year because the distribution and marketing practices with respect to such products may cause a label without a year identification to be misleading.

(ii) Immediately adjacent to the calendar date shall be a phrase explaining the meaning of such date, in terms of "packing" date, "sell by" date, or "use before" date, with or without a further qualifying phrase, e.g., "For Maximum Freshness" or "For Best Quality", and such phrases shall be approved by the Administrator as prescribed in § 317.4.

PART 318—ENTRY INTO OFFICIAL ESTABLISHMENTS; REINSPECTION AND PREPARATION OF PRODUCTS

2. Paragraph (f) of § 318.11 of the meat inspection regulations is revised to read as follows:

§ 318.11 **Canning with heat processing and hermetically sealed containers; cleaning containers; closure; code marking; heat processing; incubation.**

* * * * *

(f) All canned products shall be plainly and permanently marked on the containers by code or otherwise with the identity of the contents and date of canning. The code used and its meaning shall be on record in the office of the inspector in charge. If calendar dating is used, it must be accompanied by an explanatory statement, as provided in § 317.8(b)(32)(ii).

(Secs. 7 and 21, 34 Stat. 1262 and 1264, as amended (21 U.S.C. 607, 621); 37 FR 28464, 28477)

PART 381—POULTRY PRODUCTS INSPECTION REGULATIONS

3. The section heading and paragraphs (a) and (c) of § 381.126 of the poultry products inspection regulations are revised to read as follows:

§ 381.126 **Date of packing and date of processing; contents of cans.**

(a) Either the immediate container or the shipping container of all poultry products shall be plainly and permanently marked by code or otherwise with the date of packing. If calendar dating is used, it must be accompanied by an explanatory statement, as provided in § 381.129(c)(2).

* * * * *

(c) All canned products shall be plainly and permanently marked, by code or otherwise, on the containers, with the identity of the contents and date of canning, except that canned products packed in glass containers are not required to be marked with the date of canning if such information appears on the shipping container. If calendar dating is used, it must be accompanied by an explanatory statement, as provided in § 381.129(c)(2).

* * * * *

4. Section 381.129 of the poultry products inspection regulations is amended by adding a new paragraph (c) to read as follows:

§ 381.129 **False or misleading labeling of containers.**

* * * * *

(c) A calendar date may be shown on labeling when declared in accordance with the provisions of this paragraph:

(1) The calendar date shall express the month of the year and the day of the month for all products and also the year in the case of products hermetically sealed in metal or glass containers, dried or frozen products, or any other products that the Administrator finds should be labeled with the year because the distribution and marketing practices with respect to such products may cause a label without a year identification to be misleading.

(2) Immediately adjacent to the calendar date shall be a phrase explaining the meaning of such date in terms of "packing" date, "sell by" date, or "use before"

date, with or without a further qualifying phrase, e.g., "For Maximum Freshness" or "For Best Quality", and such phrases shall be approved by the Administrator as prescribed in § 381.132.

(Secs. 8 and 14, 71 Stat. 445, 447, as amended (21 U.S.C. 457, 463); 37 FR 28464, 28477)

It does not appear that further public participation in rulemaking proceedings on these amendments would make additional information available to the Department which would significantly alter the decision. Furthermore, the foregoing amendments apply only when a voluntary election is exercised by the labeler. Therefore, under the administrative procedure provisions in 5 U.S.C. 553, it is found upon good cause that further notice and other public procedure concerning these amendments are impracticable and unnecessary.

These amendments shall become effective September 8, 1974.

Done at Washington, D.C., on: July 31, 1974.

G. H. WISE,
Acting Administrator, Animal and Plant Health Inspection Service.

[FR Doc.74–17787 Filed 8–7–74;8:45 am]

Title 9—Animals and Animal Products

CHAPTER III—ANIMAL AND PLANT HEALTH INSPECTION SERVICE (MEAT AND POULTRY PRODUCTS INSPECTION), DEPARTMENT OF AGRICULTURE

PART 317—LABELING, MARKING DEVICES, AND CONTAINERS

PART 381—POULTRY PRODUCTS INSPECTION REGULATIONS

Calendar Date on Labeling of Meat and Poultry Products; Correction

The amendments to the Federal meat inspection regulations and the poultry products inspection regulations published in the FEDERAL REGISTER of August 8, 1974 (39 FR 28515–28516, FR Doc. 74–17787), concerning calendar dates on labeling of meat and poultry products contain an error, in that they do not reflect an amendment to § 381.126(a) published in the FEDERAL REGISTER on February 5, 1974 (39 FR 4569).

The first sentence of § 381.126(a) is changed to read as follows: "Either the immediate container or the shipping container of all poultry food products shall be plainly and permanently marked by code or otherwise with the date of packing."

Done at Washington, D.C., on: September 30, 1974.

F. J. MULHERN,
Administrator, Animal and Plant Health Inspection Service.

[FR Doc.74–23139 Filed 10–3–74;8:45 am]

Mandatory Open Dating Laws (Prepared by the Grocery Manufacturers of America) 7.3

State	Products covered	Date required	Manner of disclosure
Alabama—Jefferson County	Dairy products	"Quality Assurance Date"	To be marked on the container
Arizona (If open dating is provided, it must comply with Arizona regulations)	Any perishable or semiperishable product on which open dating information is provided or products specified by the Assistant Director of Weights and Measures	Pull date	The date shall show the month and the day of the month, followed by the year, if used. The month is to be shown using letters identifying the month or by the digits 1–12; the day shall be shown by the digits 1–31. Bakery products with a shelf life of 7 days or less may show the day or use a color-coding system
California	Dairy products including milk, cream, buttermilk, cottage cheese and sour cream	Pull date	To be displayed on the package
Connecticut	Milk	Pull date	To be determined by the Milk Regulation Board
Florida—Dade County	Perishable foods; meat, poultry, fish and eggs	Terminal shelf life date; for meat this can be no more than 42 hours; for poultry and fish, no more than 18 hours; 90 hours for milk products (pull date)	The date is to be on the top cover or principal panel, or a label affixed to the top cover or principal panel indicating where the information appears on the container
Florida	Dairy products	Shelf life (pull date)	To be conspicuously displayed in boldface type contrasting to the background colors

State	Products covered	Date required	Manner of disclosure
Maine	Dairy products	Pull date	Not specified
Maryland	Milk and milk products	Last date of sale (pull date)—not more than 7 days from the day of production	To be conspicuously marked on the container
Massachusetts Regulations (pending in court)	All food products except alcoholic beverages; fresh meat, poultry and fish, and foods in hermetically sealed glass containers	Pull date for perishables (60-day shelf life); expiration date for other foods; and a coded date of manufacture if such is used	Stamped, imprinted, or otherwise plainly and conspicuously marked as the common abbreviation for the calendar month and numerals for day and year (i.e., Feb. 9, 73)
Michigan	Prepackaged meat, fish, seafood, poultry, eggs, bakery products and other perishable foods (fresh fruits and vegetables, canned food, frozen food, milk and milk products are exempted and covered by the specified section of the Michigan law	Recommended last day of sale; sale after date is permitted if food is wholesome and sound, and if it is clearly identified as past the recommended date	Date shall be identified by month and day as prescribed by the department to protect the public health and safety. Bakery products may be dated with days of the week
Minnesota	Perishables (90-day shelf life) except meat, poultry, fresh fruits and vegetables and frozen foods	"Quality Assurance Date"	To be determined by the Department of Agriculture
New Hampshire	Cream	Pull date	

New Jersey	Milk	Pull date (not to exceed five days from the time of production)	The date is to be preceded by the statement "NOT TO BE SOLD AFTER. . . ." The month must be represented as an abbreviation.
New York—New York City	Perishable foods as designated by the Commissioner of Consumer Affairs	Pull or expiration date	The date is to be stamped, imprinted, or conspicuously marked on the top cover or principal panel or on any label affixed thereto
Ohio—Cleveland	Perishables including eggs, baked goods and dairy products (frozen foods and hermetically sealed foods are exempt)	Pull or expiration date	To be clearly marked on the top cover or principal panel of the container or on a label affixed thereto, or on a notice indicating where the date can be found on the package
Ohio	Packaged perishable food products with a Quality Assurance period of 30 days or less (Exempts fresh fruit, vegetables, meat & poultry)	Sale date	To be determined by the Director of Agriculture
Oregon	Packaged perishable food to include meats, seafood and poultry, dairy products, bakery products and foods which have been refrigerated (canned and frozen exempted)	Pull or pack date (date of slaughter for fresh fowl, including poultry)	To be determined by the Department of Agriculture
Rhode Island	Packaged bakery goods	Pull date	To be conspicuously marked on the package

State	Products covered	Date required	Manner of disclosure
Rhode Island	Milk and milk products	Pull date	
Virginia	Grade A milk and milk products	Pull date	To be expressed in a conspicuous manner as the common abbreviation for calendar month or numerical representation (Jun 1) or (06-01)
Washington	Perishables (30 day shelf life) except alcoholic beverages, frozen foods, fresh meat and poultry, fish and raw agricultural commodities	Pull date	To be determined by the Department of Agriculture
District of Columbia	Fresh milk, meat, poultry, fish, bread products, eggs, butter, cheese, cold meat cuts, mildly processed pasteurized products and other potentially hazardous foods	Pull date	To be prominently displayed on the container

*Prepared by the Grocery Manufacturers of America.

1725 Eye Street
Northwest
Washington, D. C.
20006
Telephone:
(202) 331-7822

May 1, 1973

The nation's food retailers have always tried to fulfill the demands
and needs of their customers.

Over 129 of the nation's major food chains and co-ops, with 1972
gross sales of well over $33 billion, have adopted unit pricing
programs.

The list is as follows:

Acme Markets, Inc. (Pa.)	Dillon Co. (Kansas)
Albertson's, Inc. (Idaho)	D'Agostino Bros. (NY)
Allied Supermarkets, Inc. (Mich.)	Dominick's Finer Foods (Ill.)
Almacs, Inc. (R.I.)	E & B Supermarkets
Alpha Beta Acme Markets (Ca.)	Eisner Food Stores (Ill.)
Associated Food Stores, Inc. (co-op)	Fedco Food Corp.
A.J. Bayless (Ariz.)	Fernandes Super Markets, Inc.(Ma.)
Benner Tea Company (Iowa)	First National Stores, Inc. (Ma.)
Big Bear Stores Co. (Ohio)	S.M. Flickinger Co., Inc. (NY)
Bohack Corporation (N.Y.)	Foodarama Supermarkets, Inc.
Borman's, Inc. (Mich.)	Food Cart, Inc.
Brockton Public Market (Ma.)	Food City Markets (Texas)
Buddie's Super Markets (Texas)	Food Fair Stores, Inc. (Pa.)
Buttrey Foods (Montana)	Foodland Super Markets (Hawaii)
Capitol Super Markets (Ma.)	Food Lane (Pa.)
Carrs Food Centers (Alaska)	Food Pageant, Inc.
Certified Grocers of Illinois	Fox Grocery Co. (Pa.)
Central Groceries Co-op (Chicago)	Fred W. Albrecht Grocery Co.(OH)
Central Markets, Inc. (N.Y.)	Friedman's Foodland Markets, Inc.
Chatham Super Markets (Mich.)	Giant Eagle Markets, Inc. (Pa.)
Colonial Stores, Inc. (Ga.)	Giant Food, Inc. (Md.)
Consumers Cooperative (Berkeley, Ca.)	Giant Food Stores (Pa.)
Co-op Shopping Centers (Minn. & Wisc.)	The Grand Union Company (NJ)
Co-op Supermarkets	The Great A & P Tea Company (NY)
Copps Distributing Co. (Wisc.)	Great Scott, Inc. (Oh.)
Cross Co. (Vt.)	Gristede Bros., Inc. (NY)
Curtis Farms, Inc.	Greenbelt Consumer Services, Inc.
Daitch-Shopwell (NY)	Hannaford Bros. Co. (Me.)
Dan's Supreme Super Markets, Inc.	Harnes Foodway Corp.
Delchamps, Inc. (Ala.)	Harvest Food Stores, Inc.

NAFC UNIT PRICING LIST CONT'D
May 1, 1973

Hillman's, Inc. (Ill.)
Hills Supermarkets, Inc. (N.Y.)
Hinky Dinky Stores (Neb.)
Hyde Park Co-op
IGA (Fla)
Iandoli's Super Markets (Ma.)
International Super Markets, Inc.
Jewel Food Stores (Ill.)
Jumbo Food Stores (Md.)
Key Food Stores Cooperative, Inc.
King Kullen Grocery Co., Inc. (NY)
King "Soopers" Inc. (Colo.)
Kohl's Food Stores (Wisc.)
The Kroger Company (Ohio)
Liberal Markets, Inc. (Ohio)
Louis Stores, Inc. (Ca.)
Lucky Stores, Inc. (Ca.)
Marsh Supermarket, Inc. (In.)
Meats and Treats, Inc.
Meijers Super Markets, Inc. (Mich.)
Met Food Corp.
Milgram Food Stores (Mo.)
Nash Finch Co. (Minn.)
P & C Food Markets, Inc. (NY)
Penn Fruit Company (Pa.)
Peter Reeves Markets
Piedmont Grocery Co. (Ca.)
Pioneer Markets (co-op)
Publix Super Markets (Fla.)

Quality Food Centers, Inc. **(Wash.)**
Ralph's Grocery Co. (Ca.)
El Rancho Markets (Ca.)
Red Owl Stores, Inc. (Minn.)
Royal Farms, Inc.
Rusty's Food Center
Safeway Stores, Inc. (Ca.)
Schnuck Markets, Inc. (Mo.)
Sentry Food (Wisc.)
Shop Rite Markets (N.J.)
Sloans Supermarkets
Smiler's Food Stores, Inc.
The Southland Corp. (Tx.)
Star Markets (Ma.)
Star Supermarkets, Inc. (N.Y.)
Stop & Shop, Inc. (Conn.)
Sunflower Stores (Miss.)
Supermarkets General Corp. (NJ)
Super Valu Stores, Inc. (Minn.)
Tampa Wholesale Co. (Fla.)
Thorofare Markets, Inc. (Pa.)
Times Super Market Ltd. (Hi.)
Tradewell Stores (Wash.)
United Supers
Von's Grocery Co. (Calif.)
Waldbaum, Inc. (NY)
Wegman's Food Markets, Inc. (NY)
J. Weingarten, Inc. (Tx.)
Wetterau Foods (MO
Winn-Dixie Stores (Fla.)

State Laws and Regulations

ARIZONA
Assistant Director of
Weights and Measures
Products covered: Meat, poultry and seafood; dry detergents, soap
powder and cleaning products; wrapping products; rice, beans, candy,
cereals, cookies and crackers, and cheese; paper products; jams,
jellies, preserves, peanut butter, coffee, tea and cocoa; fruits and
vegetables; cooking oils, shortening, condiments, relishes, liquid
soups and syrups; liquid detergents, disinfectants and household
cleaners; fruit and vegetable juices and drinks, salad dressings and
soft drinks; personal deodorants, hair and shaving preparations,
toilet water and cologne

Products exempted: small packages of quantities of less than one
ounce or when the total selling price is ten cents or less;
covered commodities when only one brand in one size is available
in a particular retail establishment; any covered commodity whose
net quantity is the specified whole unit and which has the retail
price plainly marked thereon

Distributors exempted: to be specifically designated by the Assistant
Director

Base units: as specified -- pound, 100 sq. feet, count or whole
unit of dry measure, quart, or fluid ounce. Cost-per-unit information
to be shown by the units listed, the appropriate sub-unit or in
metric measure

Disclosure: Unit price information shall be computed to the nearest
tenth of a cent when less than one dollar and to the nearest cent when
a dollar or more. Price information shall be displayed on a sign
showing the unit price for one or more brands and/or sizes of a given
commodity, by a sticker, stamp, sign, label or tag attached to the
shelf on which the commodity is displayed, or by a sticker, stamp, sign,
label or tag attached directly to the item.
   If a sign provides unit price information for one or more sizes or
brands of a given commodity, the sign shall be in a central location
as close as possible to all items to which it refers. Signs or tags
listing information for more than one brand or size of a given commodity
shall include the following information: 1)identity and brand name of
the commodity, 2)quantity of the packaged commodity if more than one
package per brand, 3)total retail sales price, and 4)price per
appropriate unit in accordance with these regulations.

Compliance date: January 1, 1976

****

*Prepared by the Grocery Manufacturers of America.
  October 1976.

CONNECTICUT
Commissioner
of Consumer
Protection

Products covered: consumer commodities -- any food, drug, device,
cosmetic, or other article, product, or commodity of any other kind
or class customarily produced for sale to retail agencies or instrumen-
talities for individual consumption, personal care, or services
rendered in or around the household

Products exempted: prescription drugs; alcoholic beverages;
commodities sold in even pounds, pints, quarts or gallons which are
price-marked; different brands or products sold in one container in
connection with a one-price sale; products sold in one size only
of 3 ounces or less; snack foods such as cakes, candies or chips in
packages of less than 5 ounces

Distributors exempted: any owner-operated single retail store designated by the Commissioner

Base units: pound or ounce, and the same unit of measure must be
used for the same commodity sold in all sizes: pint, quart or
gallon; 50 feet; 500 square feet; or 100 units

Disclosure: Unit price information shall be computed to the nearest
whole cent or the nearest fraction thereof. Price information
shall be displayed by the attachment of a stamp, tag or label on
the adjacent shelf, at the point of sale, or attached directly to
the product. If the total price is stated, the unit price must also
be stated.

The words "Unit price" must appear to the left of the selling price
with the numerical designation of the unit price. The price per
measure must be carried to three digits. The unit price must be in
a type size which is not smaller than the retail price and not smaller
than pica type.

Advertising: All advertisements for covered commodities must state
the unit price.

Violations: Fine not exceeding $100 for first offense; up to $500
for subsequent violations. The owner, manager or person in charge
of the store and employer of such persons is responsible for compliance.

****

FLORIDA
Department of
Agriculture and
Consumer Services

Products covered: any consumer commodity used by individuals for
personal care and usually consumed in the course of use

Products exempted: durable articles, textiles, apparel, appliances,
paints, writing supplies, special orders and prescription drugs

Distributors exempted: any seller who does not voluntarily establish
a unit pricing program

Base units: ounce, unit, square foot, linear food, pound, or other
units approved by the Department

Disclosure: display unit price in close proximity to the item

Advertising: as determined by the Department

Effective date: July 1, 1972

****

MARYLAND
Division of
Consumer
Protection

Products covered: consumer commodities -- any food, drug, cosmetic
or other article, product or commodity which is produced for sale for
use by individuals for purposes of personal care or in the performance
of services or for household use, and usually consumed in the course
of usage

Products exempted: items which wear or deteriorate from use;
prepackaged food containing separately identifiable items separated
by physical division within the package; prescription items; alcoholic
beverages subject to federal pricing requirements; vending machine items

Distributors exempted: retail sales agency which during the preceding calendar year grossed less than one million dollars, which
derive less than 15% of its total revenues from commodities covered
by this act, or which is owned and operated by one individual and
members of his immediate family; and which is not using a system of
unit pricing

Base unit: any unit of measurement in common use if appropriate
to the item

Disclosure: Total price and unit price shall be displayed by
attachment of a stamp, tag or label directly to the item or its
package; or directly adjacent to the item or on the shelf on which
the item is displayed; or, by means of a sign or list containing the
required price information. The stamp, tag or label shall also dis-

close the name and content amount of the commodity.

Effective date: as amended, July 1, 1976

****

MASSACHUSETTS
Consumer Council

Products covered: 35 categories of packaged commodities

Products exempted: prescription items; alcoholic beverages;
packaged commodities sold in even pounds, pints, quarts, or gallons;
packaged commodities required to be individually marked with the
unit cost (meat, poultry and fish)

Distributors exempted: distributors with only one place of business

Base unit: pound, 100 units, pint, quart, gallon, 50 feet, 50 sq. feet

Disclosure: orange stamp, tag or label on item or shelf with price
per measure carried to three digits; price to be shown in type no
smaller than 7/16" high

Violations: Fine for first offense of $10 to $50; $25 to $100 for
each subsequent offense

Effective date: in three stages from May 24, 1971 to September 1, 1971

****

NEW JERSEY
Division of Consumer Affairs
Products covered: consumer commodities -- any merchandise of any kind
or class produced for retail sale for individual consumption (other
than at the retail establishment), personal care, or services rendered
in the household

Distributors exempted: retailer whose combined annual gross receipts
from the sale of food products, non-prescription drugs, personal care
products and household service products is less than 30% of the
total annual receipts

Base unit: price per measure

Disclosure: to be determined by regulations promulgated through
the Division of Consumer Affairs

Effective date: April 27, 1976

****

NEW YORK
Commissioner
of Agriculture

Products covered: food, pet food, napkins, facial tissues, toilet
tissues, foil and plastic wrapping, paper towels, disposable plates
and cups, detergents, soap and other cleaning agents

Products exempted: prepackaged food with separate and identifiable
food segregated by package divisions; gourmet or specialty foods;
commodities with net quantities and price marked plainly on the
product; food sold for consumption on the premises; commodities sold
as one pound, one ounce, one pint, one quart, 100 count, one foot,
one hundred feet, one square foot or one square yard, and fresh
food produce if the retail price is marked thereon

Distributors exempted: specialty trade stores exempted by the
Commissioner; stores with gross annual sales in the previous year
of less than $2 million unless part of a chain with gross sales of
$2 million or more

Base unit: pound, ounce, pint, quart, 100 units, food and ply count,
square foot or square yard and ply count -- the same unit shall be
used for all sizes

Disclosure: stamp, tag or label indicating unit and total price
directly under the item on the shelf; sign or list near place of
sale for items not visible to consumer

Violations: fine not exceeding $200 for first offense; not more
than $400 for each subsequent offense

Effective date: January 1, 1975

****

RHODE ISLAND
Director of
Business
Regulations

Products covered: detergents, household cleansers, waxes and deodorizers
cereals, instant breakfast foods, butter, oleomargarine, coffee, cocoa,
tea, jelly, jam, sandwich spreads, honey, cooking oils, grains, fruits,
vegetables and juices, pet foods, baby foods, shortenings, flour,
baking mixes and supplies, canned fish and meats, sanitary paper
products (napkins, towels, tissues), aluminum and plastic wraps, waxed
paper, spaghetti and pasta products, ketchup, mustard, sauces, snack
foods (such as potato chips and pretzels, but only in packages of 5
ounces or more), soups, frozen fruits, vegetables and juices, bread
and pastry products, bottled beverages, flavored syrups, powdered

drink mixes, cookies and crackers, salad dressings, toothpaste, deodorants, shampoos, shaving cream, cold cuts, fowl, fish, fish products and meat sold in bulk if weighed or measured at the time of sale, and any other products designated by the Director

Products exempted: prescription drugs, alcoholic beverages, packaged products sold in units of even pounds, pints, quarts or gallons which have the price marked on the container

Distributors exempted: Director may exempt classes of retail establishments if compliance would be impractical; stores with fewer than 5 employees and less than two outlets are exempt

Base unit: price per measure -- pound, pint, quart, gallon, 50 feet, 50 square feet or 100 units

Disclosure: Orange stamp, tag or label on the item or attached to shelf directly above or below the item, showing the words "unit price" with the numerical designation of the price per measure carried to three digits; if price over one dollar, the unit price may be expressed to the nearest cent

Advertising: advertisements showing retail price must also indicate the unit price

Violations: imprisonment not exceeding 6 months or fine not more than $500, or both; manager or person in charge of the store and persons employing the same, are responsible for compliance

Effective date: October 1, 1972

****

VERMONT
Commissioner of
Agriculture

Products covered: aluminum foil, bread, carbonated soft drinks, cereals, cooking oils, dog or cat food, facial tissues, fish, fowl, fruits, vegetables, grains, meats, napkins, plastic food wrapping, waxed paper

Products exempted: prescription drugs, packaged commodities required to be marked individually with cost per unit or weight by weights and measures provisions, products where all brands are sold in one size only and which are price-marked, different brands or products co-mingled in one receptacle for the purpose of a one-price sale, packages containing one ounce or less in weight or less than one fluid ounce, commodities used or consumed on the premises where sold

Distributors exempted: Stores grossing less than $500,000 in the
preceding calendar year; independent family stores unless part of
a chain grossing $1 million during the preceding year; stores
specifically exempted by the Commissioner

Base unit: pound, quart, 100 count, 50 square feet or as otherwise
determined by the Commissioner

Disclosure: Orange label attached to the item or to the shelf
directly above or below the item; total price and unit price shall
be shown; unit price shall be shown in type no smaller than the
retail price and no smaller than pica type

Violations: fine up to $500; owner, manager or person in charge
of the store are responsible for compliance

Effective date: September 1, 1972

Local Regulations

CHICAGO, Ill.

Products covered: meat, poultry, seafood; fruit and vegetables;
fruit and vegetable drinks; detergents, soaps, cleansers; relishes
and condiments; liquid and condensed soups; cereals; candy;
sanitary paper products; film and wrapping paper, foil; cooking
oils; jams, jellies and preserves; coffee, tea and cocoa; syrups;
cheese; rice; pet food; toothpaste; deodorants; colognes; and
hair preparations

Products exempted: sale items, vending machine items

Distributors exempted: retail establishments which do not have their
own computer warehouse operation; retail establishments whose annual
sales of the covered commodities are less than 10% of the total sales

Violations: fine of not less than $50 nor more than $500

****

ANN ARBOR, Mich.

Products covered: most foodstuffs and household goods

Base unit: product's most common unit of measure

Disclosure: orange stamp, tag or label on item itself or directly
under or over the item on the shelf

Effective date: three stages -- June 12, 1973; August 12, 1973 and October 12, 1973

****

NEW YORK, N.Y.

Products covered: 18 categories of consumer commodities

Products exempted: commodities in one, two, five or ten units of the applicable base unit

Distributors exempted: those with volume of less than $2 million annually; those for whom the covered items comprise 20% or less of total sales

Base unit: pound, 50 units, pint or quart

Disclosure: stamp, tag, label or sign at point of display

Effective date: June 1, 1971

****

CLEVELAND, Oh.

Products covered: aluminum and plastic wraps, waxed paper; baby foods; baking mixes and supplies; bottled and canned beverages; bread products; candy; canned poultry, fish and meat; meat, poultry and fish products; cereals; cocoa, coffee; convenience dinners; cookies and crackers; dairy products; deodorants; detergents and soaps; flour; fresh vegetable and produce; frozen foods; juices; hair conditioners; household cleanser instant breakfast foods; jellies, jams, preserves and sandwich spreads; ketchups, mustards and condiments; mouthwash; butter and margarine; pet foods; plastic and paper bags; powdered mixes; cold cuts; salad dressings; salt; sanitary paper products; seasonings and spices; shampoos; shaving cream; shortenings; snack foods; soups; sugar; syrups; tea; toothpaste; grains and beans

Products exempted: prescriptions; alcoholic beverages; food sold for consumption on the premises; commodities for which the net quantity is one base unit, provided the retail price is marked plainly thereon

Distributors exempted: operations which are the sole place of business and have gross annual sales less than $750,000

Base unit: pound, pint, quart or gallon; 50 feet or square feet; 100 units

<u>Disclosure</u>: attachment of stamp, tag or label directly to the
product or the shelf on which the product is displayed; on a sign
near the point of procurement. Such stamp, tag or label shall
show the total selling price and the unit price. The words
"unit price" shall appear as a heading directly over the numerical
designation of the unit price. The unit price shall be expressed
in terms of dollars or cents, as applicable, in three digits.

<u>Effective date</u>: July 5,]975

****

MINNEAPOLIS, Minn.

<u>Products covered</u>: canned, bottled or frozen fruits and vegetables;
canned, bottled, real and imitation vegetable and fruit juices;
frozen vegetable and fruit juice concentrates; canned and bottled
baby food; cooking and salad oils, shortening; canned and bottled
fish and meats; canned and bottled tomatoes, tomato sauce, tomato
paste, tomato puree and other tomato products; ketchups, mustards
and other sauces; jams, jellies and preserves; peanut butter and
sandwich spreads; flour, sugar, coffee, cocoa and tea; dog and
cat foods; breakfast foods; macaroni, spaghetti and dry pasta products;
salad dressings; dishwashing and laundry soaps and detergents;
scouring powders; mouthwashes, deodorants, bath soaps, shampoos;
household cleaning products

<u>Products exempted</u>: covered commodities if only one size of one
brand is offered; commodities sold for immediate consumption on the
premises where sold; vegetables sold by the head or bunch; commodities
in containers standardized by state or federal law

<u>Base unit</u>: commodities in liquid form shall be sold by liquid
measure or by weight; commodities not in liquid form shall be sold
only by weight, by measure of length or by count

<u>Disclosure</u>: Unit price label containing a description of the item,
the selling price, the quantity, and the unit price shall be affixed
by stamp, tag or label directly adjacent to the commodity on the
shelf, or on the commodity itself. If the commodity is not conspicuously visible, a list with the price information shall be placed
near the point of procurement.

<u>Effective date</u>: July 1, 1973

****

SEATTLE, Wash.

<u>Products covered</u>: cereals; grains, meals, rices, lentils, pastas,

flour, cornstarch and all mixes containing such products; frozen,
bottled or canned vegetables; frozen, bottled and canned fruits;
cooking oils, shortening and salad oils; packaged canned and
bottled prepared food mixes; canned and bottled food sauces;
instant food products; canned and bottled jams, jellies, preserves,
syrups, honey and honey products; peanut butter; packaged foods
including raisins, nuts, dried and candied fruit; frozen foods,
excluding prepared meals, ice cream, ice milk, sherbets, ice
cream novelties and imitations thereof; cheeses; bottled and canned
seafoods, seafood products and imitations thereof; bottled and
canned meat, meat products, and imitations thereof; bottled and
canned poultry and poultry products and imitations thereof; baby
food; soups; sugar, salt, pepper, tenderizers, vinegar, baking
powder, and all derivatives and imitations thereof, but excluding
other spices and herbs; pet foods; toilet tissue, paper towels,
paper napkins, facial tissue, paper cups, paper plates, sanitary
napkins, waxed paper and other food wrappings or bags, shelf paper
and contact paper; laundry and cleaning products; air fresheners,
disinfectants, waxes and household polishes; coffee, tea, cocoa;
powdered and instant drink products; other products specified
by the City Sealer through regulation

Distributors exempted: gross receipts are less than $750,000 per
year; more than 30% of gross receipts are from the sale of imported
foods or food related commodities

Base unit: pound, ounce, pint or liquid ounce, one hundred items,
square foot or linear foot, one hundred grams, inches

Disclosure: Unit price shall be computed to the nearest one-hundredth
of one cent and shall be displayed by attachment of a stamp, tag or
label either directly to the item, to the shelf, or at the closest
available location to the commodity if no shelf is available. The
stamp, tag or label shall indicate the brand name, total price, unit
price and quantity or xize of the product by weight, measure or count.

Violations: fine not to exceed $500 or imprisonment for not more
than 6 months, or both

Effective date: August 1, 1972

SECTION 1. <u>APPLICATION</u>.--Except for random weight
packages unit priced in accord with existing regulations
and uniform weight packages of cheese and cheese products
unit priced in the same manner and by the same type
equipment as random weight packages,any retail establishment providing unit price information in addition to the
total price, for any commodity listed herein, shall also
provide the unit price information for all packaged commodities listed herein and in the manner prescribed
herein.

SECTION 2. <u>COMMODITIES</u>.--

Meat, Poultry, and Seafood	Price per pound
Fruits and Vegetables	Price per pound or per individual unit, or whole unit of dry measure
Fruit and Vegetable Juices and Drinks	Price per quart
Dry Detergents, Soap Powders, and Dry Household Cleaners	Price per pound
Liquid Detergents and House- hold Cleaners and Disinfec- tants	Price per quart
Relishes and Condiments	Price per pound or quart
Liquid Soups and Condensed Liquid Soups	Price per pound or quart
Cereals	Price per pound
Candy	Price per pound
Cookies and Crackers	Price per pound
Sanitary Paper Products	Price per 50 sq.ft.,or if by count, per 50 units, including ply
Foil, Film, and Other Rolls of Wrapping (except gift wrap)	Price per 50 sq.ft.
Cooking Oils and Shortening	Price per quart or pound
Salad Dressings	Price per quart
Soft Drinks	Price per quart
Jams, Jellies, Preserves, and Peanut Butter	Price per pound
Coffee, Tea, and Cocoa	Price per pound

---

*As adopted by The National Conference on Weights and Measures 1972

Syrups, Table and Topping	Price per pound or quart
Cheese, Natural and Processed	Price per pound
Rice	Price per pound
Pet Food	Price per pound
Toothpaste	Price per ounce
Deodorants, Personal	Price per ounce
Shaving Preparations	Price per ounce
Toilet Water and Colognes	Price per ounce
Hair Preparations	Price per ounce

The standard of reference for all categories listed above shall be the latest edition of the "Standard Industrial Classification Manual" published by the Executive Office of the President, Bureau of the Budget.

SECTION 3. EXEMPTION: SMALL PACKAGES.--Any of the commodities listed herein shall be exempt from these provisions when packaged in quantities of less than one ounce (avoirdupois) or one fluid ounce or when the total retail price thereof is ten cents or less.

SECTION 4. EXEMPTION: SINGLE ITEM.--Any of the commodities listed herein shall be exempt from these provisions when there is only one brand in only one size appearing in a particular retail establishment.

SECTION 5. PRICING.--The unit price information shall be to the nearest tenth of one cent when less than one dollar and to the nearest cent when a dollar or more.

SECTION 6. PRESENTATION OF PRICE.--

(a) In an retail establishment in which unit price information is provided in accordance with the provisions of the Regulation, that information may be displayed by means of a sign, which offers the unit price for one or more brands and/ or sizes of a given commodity, by means of a sticker, stamp, sign, label, or tag affixed to the shelf upon which the commodity is displayed, or by means of a sticker, stamp, sign, label, or tag affixed to the consumer commodity itself.

(b) Where a sign providing unit price information for one or more sizes or brands of a given commodity is used, that sign shall be provided clearly and in a nondeceptive manner in a

central location as close as practical to all
items to which the sign refers.

(c) If a single sign or tag does provide the unit
price information for more than one brand or
size of a given commodity, then the following
information shall be provided:

  (1) The identity and the brand name of the
  commodity.

  (2) The quantity of the packaged commodity if
  more than one package size per brand is
  displayed.

  (3) The total retail sales price.

  (4) The price per appropriate unit in accordance
  with SECTION 2. COMMODITIES.

SECTION 7. EFFECTIVE DATE.--

(a) Not less than one-third of the commodity categories listed in section 2 of this Regulation
shall be unit priced by any individual retail
establishment within 90 days after this Regulation, by its terms,becomes applicable to
such establishment.

(b) Full compliance with this Regulation by any
individual retail establishment shall be at-
tained within 120 days after this Regulation,
by its terms, becomes applicable to such establishment.

NOTICE IS HEREBY GIVEN THAT PURSUANT TO SECTIONS 1105 AND 2203(e) of the New York City Charter, due and proper publication in The City Record having been made, and an opportunity for comment having been duly afforded, amended regulations regrading unit pricing are adopted pursuant to Section B64-4.0 of Chapter 64 of the Administrative Code of The City of New York, effective July 10, 1972, to read as follows:

1. Definitions

    a. "Self service" shall mean the offering or display of consumer commodities for retail sale in such a manner that the consumer may examine and select commodities for purchase without the assistance of sales personnel.

    b. "Retail establishment" shall mean a single geographical location in which consumer commodities are sold, displayed or offered for sale at retail.

    c. "Retail entity" shall mean any person, partnership, corporation or other organization engaged in the sale, display or offering for sale of consumer commodities at retail from one or more retail establishments. For the purposes of these regulations, retail establishments owned or controlled by different persons, partnerships, corporations or other organizations, but associated together for the purpose of sharing a trade name or advertising expenses or for joint or cooperative purchase of merchandise or services, shall not constitute a single retail entity.

2. Exemptions

    a. B64-3.0, "Display of Price per measure," shall apply only to consumer commodities sold, displayed or offered for sale by self service.

    b. B64-3.0, "Display of Price per Measure," shall not apply to any consumer commodity packaged without a declaration of volume, weight, quantity or other appropriate size declaration.

    c. B64-3.0, "Display of Price per Measure," shall not apply to any consumer commodity sold in one, two, five, or ten units of the applicable standard measure designated in regulation 3(b) below.

    d. B64-3.0, "Display of Price per Measure," shall not apply to any consumer commodity whose method of sale is governed by 191, 193, or 193-d of the New York Agriculture and Markets Law.

    e. B64-3.0, "Display of Price per Measure," shall not apply to any retail establishment in which the total dollar volume sales of consumer commodities constitutes 20 per cent or less of the total dollar volume of sales from such retail establishment.

    (d.) f. B64-3.0, "Display of Price per Measure," shall not apply to any retail entity whose gross receipts from retail sales of merchandise of any sort for the preceding tax year of such retail entity were less than two million dollars.

3. Calculation and Display of Price Per Measure.

    a. Price or measure shall be expressed in terms of dollars or cents, as applicable, carried to three digits. If the price is $1.00 or over, it is to be stated to the nearest full cent, provided that said price is rounded off from one-half cent or over to the next higher cent; and, if less than one-half cent, reduced to the next lower cent. Example: "$1.35 per pound." If the price is less than $1.00, it should be stated to the nearest tenth of a cent. Example "24.8¢ per pound."

    b. Price per measure shall be expressed as follows:

        i. price per pound for commodities whose net quantity is stated in units of pounds or ounces or both;

        ii. price per 100 units for commodities whose net quantity is stated by numerical count;

        iii. price per pint or quart for commodities whose net quantity is stated in fluid ounces, pints, quarts or gallons or a combination thereof; provided that the same unit of measure is used for the same commodity in all sizes sold in the retail establishment;

    iv. price per 50 feet or per 50 square feet, as appropriate, for commodities whose net quantity is stated in units of inches, feet, yards, square inches, square feet or square yards, or whose net quantities are stated in units of length or area and the "ply" count, if any.

    c. All price information required by B64-2.0 and B64-3.0 shall be clear and conspicuous and shall be on a stamp, tag, label or sign directly above, below, adjacent to, or on the consumer commodity to which it relates. Such stamp, tag, label or sign shall:

    i. state the total selling price;

    ii. state the price per measure;

    iii. identify sufficiently the consumer commodity to which the price information relates, if not affixed to the consumer commodity;

    iv. indicate the total selling price on the right side of a horizontal label or on the upper part of a vertical label;

    v. indicate the price per measure on the left side of a horizontal label or on the lower part of a vertical label;

    vi. contain the words "Unit Price" above or below the price per measure;

    vii. indicate the price per measure and unit of measure on an orange background, exeept that packages which are prepriced by the manufacturer shall not be required to use an orange background on a label affixed to the consumer commodity;

    viii. indicate the price per measure in type no smaller than that used for the total selling price, but in no event smaller than pica type

    ix. be submitted to the commissioner for approval prior to its use in any retail establishment.

    d. Every retail establishment required to post price per measure by the regulations governing Truth-in-Pricing, in those cases where shelf labels are used, shall conspicuously post a sign for every two thousand square feet of sales area, but in no event less than two signs nor more than five signs in any retail establishment, which explains the use of price per measure information to the consumer. The price per measure, as used in examples on these signs, shall appear on an orange background in type no smaller than that used for the selling price.

    e. Upon written application to the commissioner, and upon a showing of exceptional circumstances, a retail establishment or retail entity may be granted an extension in writing, not to extend beyond December 31, 1972, in which to comply, in whole or in part, with the requirements of section c above

4. Consumer Commodities Regulated

The following commodities shall be labelled in accordance with the provisions of B64-3.0. "Display of Price per Measure," and of the regulations governing Truth-in-Pricing.

    a. canned and bottled vegetables which do not require refrigerated storage.

    b. canned and bottled fruits which do not require refrigerated storage.

    c. canned and bottled real and imitation vegetable and fruit juices which do not require refrigerated storage.

    d. canned and bottled tomatoes, tomato sauce, tomato paste, tomato puree and other related tomato products which do not require refrigerated storage.

    e. cahned and bottled baby foods which do not require refrigerated storage.

    f. cooking and salad oils

    g. canned and bottled salmon, tuna and sardines which do not require refrigerated storage.

    h. jams, jellies and preserves.

    i. peanut butter

j. carbonated beverages.
k. coffee, instant and regular.
l. dog and cat foods
m. breakfast cereals (does not include corn meal, rice, maize)
n. cake, pie crust and other pastry mixes
o. macaroni, spaghetti and other dry pasta products (does not include prepared or pre-flavored convenience pasta foods).
p. paper towels, napkins, facial tissues, plates,cups and toilet paper
q. dishwashing and laundry soaps and detergents
r. scouring powders

The above regulations shall be known as Truth-in-Pricing Regulations 1,2,3 and 4

EXPLANATION

The proposed amendments to the unit pricing regulations are designed to permit retailers with stores in more than one jurisdiction which requires unit pricing, to comply with each jurisdiction's regulations while using only one style of label. At present, Massachusetts, Connecticut, Maryland and New York City have requirements for unit pricing which may in certain instances conflict with requirements in other jurisdictions. The Department of Consumer Affairs, in cooperation with the retail food industry, has determined that these dissimilar requirements create substantial problems for retailers and that uniform requirements, where possible, would be desirable.

j10   BESS MYERSON, Commissioner

Reprinted from The City Record of June 10, 1972.
Effective July 10, 1972.

RETAIL FOOD STORE ADVERTISING
AND MARKETING PRACTICES

THE RULE AND ITS APPLICATION

VII. *The Rule*

The Commission, on the basis of the findings made by it in this proceeding, as set forth in the accompanying Statement of Basis and Purpose, hereby promulgates as a trade regulation rule its determination that:

In connection with the sale or offering for sale by retail food stores of food and grocery products or other merchandise, subject to the jurisdictional requirements of Sections 5 and 12 of the Federal Trade Commission Act, it is an unfair method of competition and an unfair or deceptive act or practice to:

(1) Offer any such products for sale at a stated price, by means of any advertisement disseminated in an area served by any of its stores which are covered by the advertisement which do not have such products in stock, and readily available to customers during the effective period of the advertisement. (If not readily available, clear and adequate notice shall be provided that the items are in stock and may be obtained upon request.)

Provided, however, that it shall constitute a defense to a charge under Part (1) of the rule, supra, if the retailer maintains records sufficient to show that the advertised products were ordered in adequate time for delivery and delivered to the stores in quantities sufficient to meet reasonably anticipated demands.

(2) Fail to make the advertised items conspicuously and readily available for sale at or below the advertised prices.

Unless, in each of the above cases, there is clear and conspicuous disclosure in all such advertisements as to all exceptions and/or limitations or restrictions with respect to stores, products or prices otherwise included within the advertisements.

Note I: In determining whether the rule will be applied the Commission will consider (a) all circumstances surrounding nondelivery of advertised products which were actually ordered in quantities sufficient to meet reasonably anticipated demands but were not delivered due to circumstances beyond the advertiser's control, and (b) all circumstances surrounding failure to make advertised items conspicuously and readily available for sale at or below the advertised prices, but were not made available at those prices due to circumstances beyond the advertiser's control. In such cases, the availability of "rain checks" will also be considered by the Commission as relevant. However, the existence of a "rain check" policy, in and of itself, will not be considered as compliance with the rule.

Note II: General disclaimers in advertising relating to product availability will not be considered to be in compliance with the disclosure provisions of the rule. Examples of such general disclaimers would be:

(a) "Not all items available at all stores."

(b) A statement that a particular item or group of items is "Available at most stores."

Note III: Specific clear and conspicuous disclaimers in advertising relating to product availability only in those stores possessing particular facilities will be considered to be in compliance with the disclosure provision of Part (1) of the rule. An example of such a disclaimer would be:

"Available only at stores featuring delicatessen departments."

VIII. *The Application of the Rule*

The Commission has noted that the public record contains a number of suggestions that the application of a rule of this nature should be extended so as to cover all retail establishments[7], or to specific types of retailers such as drug stores, furniture stores, clothing stores, appliance stores. The latter suggestions were apparently generated by unhappy consumer experiences[8]. The Commission has concluded that the public record of this proceeding would not support an extension of the applicability of this rule beyond retail food stores.

However, while the applicability of the rule itself is restricted to retail food stores, the Commission wishes to take this opportunity to announce that the legal principles inherent in the rule are in general applicable to the advertising of other commodities. Consequently, in the future the Commission will consider matters involving unavailability and mispricing of other advertised commodities in that spirit.

Promulgated: May 13, 1971.

Effective: July 12, 1971.

By the Commission.

Charles A. Tobin,
Secretary.

---

[7] Mrs. Virginia Knauer, Special Assistant to the President for Consumer Affairs, Tr. 100; Department of Consumer Affairs of New York City, R 141; See also R 160, 170, 264.

[8] See R 17, 20, 107, 152, 170, 189, 206, 214, 265, 266, 295, 366, 368, 387; Tr. 336, 348.

This exercise for surveyors is adapted from a form
developed by the FTC for its investigators.

(Correct answers are given on the answer sheets at the
end of this exercise. Do not read them until you have
completed the exercise.)

1. An ad states: "Redi Whip Topping 9 oz can $.49."
    Manager states Redi Whip doesn't come in a 9-oz can;
    it comes only in an 11-oz can. Manager says that
    reference to a 9-oz can in ad was advertising mis-
    print.

    _____a)   Should surveyor check column 4 in this instance?

    _____b)   If so, is a note on the back of Form I necessary?

    c)   If a note is necessary, write the note:

    _____

    _____

2. Ad states "A&P instant coffee 18-oz jar $.99."
    Manager says, "This item sold out." He offers same
    size jar of instant Maxim coffee, which regularly
    sells for $1.29 a jar, as a substitute.

    _____a)   Should the surveyor check column 4 in this
    instance?

    _____b)   If so, is a note necessary?

    c)   If a note is necessary, write the note:

    _____

3. Ad states, "Tu-Small Frozen dinners 3 for $2.70.
    Normally $1.00 each." Surveyor finds only one dinner
    on display in the freezer. Manager says, "This is
    the last Tu-Small Frozen dinner we have, but it is
    being offered at ninety cents, the sale price."

    _____a)   In this instance, should column 4 be checked for
    Tu-Small frozen dinners?

    _____b)   Should column 6 be checked?

    _____c)   Is a note on the back of the form necessary?

    d)   If a note is necessary, write the note:

    _____

4. Ad states, "Tu-Small Frozen Dinners, 3 for $2.70.
    Varieties: chicken, turkey, and beef." Surveyor
    finds freezer filled with chicken dinners, but
    turkey and beef dinners are not in freezer. Sur-
    veyor asks manager to produce turkey and beef din-
    ners. Manager says, "We don't have a turkey or beef
    dinner in stock. The warehouse goofed and delivered
    only chicken dinners."

    a) Correctly mark the below form for this situation.

	Column 4	Column 5	Column 6
	Not on display for sale	Not on display for sale; notice to request provided	Not available on request
1.Tu-Small Frozen Dinners:Chick			
2.Tu-Small Frozen Dinners:Turk.			
3.Tu-Small Frozen Dinners:Beef			

_____ b) Are any notations required?

c) If notations are required, write the notes:

_____

_____

5. Surveyors, looking for Smith's canned peas, find as
    empty shelf at the place canned peas are normally dis-
    played. However, on the floor immediately below the
    shelf, surveyors find an open carton filled with
    Ptomaine canned peas.
    _____ a) In this instance, should the surveyor check
    column 4?

    _____ b) In this instance, should the surveyor check
    column 6?

6. Surveyor looking for Smith's canned peas cannot find
    any in the canned vegetable section. Store manager
    says Smith's canned peas are on special and thus are
    displayed in front of aisle. Manager points out dis-
    play of Smith's canned peas in front of aisle.

_____a)   Should the surveyor check column 4?

_____b)   Should the surveyor check column 6?

7.   Surveyor views the units on the surface of a display
     of Smith's canned peas. Surveyor cannot see the price
     marking on any unit.

     Circle which of the actions below the surveyor should
     take.

     a) Go on to next item on survey sheet and leave
     column 8 blank for Smith's canned peas.

     b) Ask store representative which price should be
     marked on units, and record what store manager says in
     Column 8.
     c) Pick up one unit of Smith's canned peas and record
     in column 7 the price, if any, marked on that unit.
     d) Pick up units of Smith's canned peas until a unit
     with a price marking is found and record the price
     marked on that unit in column 8.

8.   Surveyor views the units of Smith's canned peas on the
     surface of a display. Surveyor cannot see the price
     marked on any unit. Surveyor picks up one unit and
     finds that it is not marked with any price.

     What,if anything, should the surveyor record in column
     7?

     _____

9.   Surveyor views the units of Smith's canned peas on the
     surface of a display. Surveyor can see the price
     marked on 20 cans. Ten cans are marked $.43. Ten
     cans are marked $.46.

     Record in the partial form below, what the surveyor
     should record in column 8.

	Column 8
	Price(s) marked on Unit(s)
Smith's canned peas	

10. Near a display of Smith's canned peas, surveyor finds a sign, which appears to be temporary, stating, "Special Sale Price, $.38 per can." This sign is taped over another sign which appears to be more permanent. The taped over sign says, "Peas, $.43."

_____What price, if any, should be recorded in column 8?

11. Ad states "Smith's canned peas, $.38 per can." Surveyor sees that there are 20 cans on the surface of the display of Smith's canned peas. Surveyor can see the prices on all 20 cans. Surveyor finds that ten cans are marked $.38, and ten cans are marked $.42.

What, if anything, should the surveyor record in column 9?

_____

12. Same facts as in question 10, except that all 20 cans are marked at $.43, but prominent shelf sign says, "Smith's canned peas, sale price $.38 per can."

What, if anything, should the surveyor record in column 9?

_____

13. Same facts as in question 10, except that none of the cans on the surface of the display is price marked. However, surveyor finds a shelf sign which states, "Smith's canned peas, $.43 each."

What, if anything, should surveyor record in column 9?

_____

14. Ad states, "Sirloin Steak, $1.37 per pound." Surveyor finds a package containing a three pound sirloin steak with a price label which states "Sirloin Steak, $1.37 per pound. 3 lbs. $4.11"

_____What price, if any, should the surveyor record in column 7?

15.
Transcribe correctly into columns 1, 2 and 3 below the
information contained in the following ads. Correct
information is filled in on corresponding answer sheet
which follows.

Column 1 Description of brand name of item	Column 2 Size and/ or amount	Column 3 Advertised price (note conditional offers)
1.		
2.		
3.		
4.		
5.		

1. a) Yes
    b) Yes
    c) Manager stated that ad as appeared in paper was a misprint. Item does not come in size offered on sale. Item is counted as unavailable.

2. a) Yes
    b) Yes
    c) Manager claimed item sold out, offered substitute. Item is counted as unavailable.

3. a) Yes
    b) Yes
    c) Yes
    d) Item advertised for sale at 3 for $2.70. Only one item left in case. Manager offered it for sale at ninety cents, the sale price.

4. a) 2. - Col. 4 and Col. 6(x)
        3. - Col. 4 and Col. 6(x)
    b) Yes
    c) Of three varieties of item offered for sale in ad, only one was available. Manager claimed that warehouse made the effort and sent only one type.

5. a) No
    b) No

6. a) No
    b) No

7. Circle c).

8. "No price on items." (Surveyors should ask store representative what price is, record price on back of Survey Form, and, if item is overpriced, so mark in column 10.)

9. 1. Smith's canned peas - 43¢ and 46¢

10. 38¢ per can

11. 10 overpriced, 20 inspected

12. Nothing

13. 20 overpriced, 20 inspected

14. $1.37 per lb.

Column 1

	Description & brand name of item	size and/or amount	advertised price (note condition offers)
1.	Ground beef	packages of 5 lbs or more	$.85/lb (in pkgs of 5 lbs or more)
2.	U.S.D.A. choice beef roast, boneless crossrib		$1.19 per lb
3.	Miller High Life Beer	Pony size 7-oz bottles	$1.10 for 6 bottles
4.	Soft drinks - Cragmont	5 1 pt, 12 oz bottles	$1.00
5.	Bel-air, crook neck squash	4 10 oz pkgs	$1.00

ATLANTA
730 Peachtree St., N.E.
Room 800
Atlanta, Ga. 30308
(404) 526-5836

BOSTON
John Fitzgerald Kennedy
Federal Bldg., Rm. 2200-C
Government Center
Boston, Ma. 02203
(617) 223-6621

CHICAGO
55 East Monroe St.
Suite 1437
Chicago, Ill. 60603
(312) 353-4423

CLEVELAND
Federal Office Bldg.
1240 E. 9th St.
Room 1339
Cleveland, Ohio 44199
(216) 522-4207

DALLAS
500 South Ervay St.
Room 452-B
Dallas, Tx. 75201
(214) 749-3056

KANSAS CITY
2806 Federal Office Bldg.
911 Walnut St.
Kansas City, Mo. 64105
(816) 374-5256

LOS ANGELES
11000 Wilshire Blvd.
Room 13209
Los Angeles, Ca. 90024
(213) 824-7575

NEW YORK
22nd Floor Federal Bldg.
26 Federal Plaza
New York, N.Y. 10007
(212) 264-1200

SAN FRANCISCO
450 Golden Gate Ave.
Box 36005
San Francisco, Ca. 94102
(415) 555-1270

SEATTLE
Suite 908 Republic Bldg.
1511 Third Ave.
Seattle, Wash. 98101
(206) 442-4655

WASHINGTON, D.C.
Gellman Bldg. 6th Floor
2120 L St., N.W.
Washington, D.C. 20037
(202) 254-7700

Part 319 - Definitions and Standards of Identity or Composition
    Subpart B - Raw Meat Products
§ 319.15 Miscellaneous beef products.

(a) Chopped beef, ground beef. "Chopped Beef" or "Ground Beef" shall consist of chopped fresh and/or frozen beef with or without seasoning and without the addition of beef fat as such, shall not contain more than 30 percent fat, and shall not contain added water, binders, or extenders . . . . When beef cheek meat (trimmed beef cheek) is used in the preparation of chopped or ground beef, the amount of such cheek meat shall be limited to 25 percent; and if in excess of natural proportions, its presence shall be declared on the label, in the ingredient statement required by § 317.2 of this subchapter, if any, and otherwise contiguous to the name of the product.

(b) Hamburger. "Hamburger" shall consist of chopped fresh and/or frozen beef with or without the addition of beef fat as such and/or seasoning, shall not contain more than 30 percent fat, and shall not contain added water, binder, or extenders . . . . Beef cheek meat (trimmed beef cheeks) may be used in the preparation of hamburger only in accordance with the conditions prescribed in paragraph (a) of this section.

```
ALABAMA----------Division of Gins and Warehouses, Weights
                and Measures, Department of Agriculture
                and Industries, P.O. Box 3336, Mont-
                gomery 36109.
                    Telephone: Area Code 205: 832-6766
                    Incumbent: J.L. Slaughter, Chief

ALASKA-----------Section of Weights and Measures, De-
                partment of Commerce, 2263 Spenard Road,
                Anchorage 99503.
                    Telephone: Area Code 907: 279-0508
                    Incumbent: Frank J. Adkins, Chief
                              Inspector

ARIZONA---------Weights and Measures Division, Depart-
                ment of Administration, 10202 North 19th
                Avenue, Phoenix 85021.
                    Telephone: Area Code 602: 271-5211
                    Incumbent: Richard F. Harris
                              Assistant Director

ARKANSAS--------Division of Weights and Measures,
                Department of Commerce, 4608 West 61st
                Street, Little Rock 72209.
                    Telephone: Area Code 501: 371-1759
                    Incumbent: Sam F. Hindsman, Director

CALIFORNIA-------Division of Measurement Standards, De-
                partment of Food and Agriculture, 8500
                Fruitridge Road, Sacramento 95826.
                    Telephone: Area Code 916: 445-7001
                    Incumbent: Walter S. Watson, Chief

COLORADO--------Weights and Measures Section, Division
                of Inspection and Consumer Services,
                Department of Agriculture, 3125 Wyandot,
                Denver 80211.
                    Telephone: Area Code 303: 892-2845
                    Incumbent: Earl Prideaux, Chief
```

```
 * List prepared by:
    Office of Weights and Measures, National Bureau
    of Standards, Washington, D.C. 20234  301-921-2401
    Revised May 1975
    Harold F. Wollin, Chief and Executive Secretary,
    National Conference on Weights and Measures
                                        301-921-3677
```

Division of Labor, Oil Inspection Section,
Department of Labor and Employment, 1024
Speer Boulevard, Denver 80204. (Supervises
devices for measurement of petroleum pro-
ducts and promulgates specifications, toler-
ances, and codes.)
Telephone: Area Code 303: 892-2096
Incumbent: Milton D. Schneider, Chief
Oil Inspection Section

CONNECTICUT---Weights and Measures Division, Department
of Consumer Protection, State Office
Building, Room G-17, Hartford 06115.
Telephone: Area Code 203: 566-4778 and
566-5230
Incumbent: John T. Bennett, Chief

DELAWARE------Division of Standards and Inspections,
Department of Agriculture, Drawer D, Dover
19901.
Telephone: Area Code 302: 678-4824
Incumbent: Eugene Keeley, Supervisor
Office of Weights and Measures

DISTRICT OF
COLUMBIA-----Division of Weights and Measures, Bureau of
Building, Housing, and Zoning, Department
of Economic Development, 1110 U Street, S.E.
Washington, D.C. 20020.
Telephone: Area Code 202: 629-4661
Incumbent: Kenneth G. Hayden, Chief

FLORIDA-------Division of Standards, Department of Agri-
culture and Consumer Services, Mayo Building
Laboratory Complex, Tallahassee 32304.
Telephone: Area Code 904: 977-8161(ext.146)
Incumbent: Sydney D. Andrews, Director

GEORGIA-------Fuel and Measures Division, Department of
Agriculture, Agriculture Building, Capitol
Square, Atlanta 30334.
Telephone: Area Code 404: 656-3605
Incumbent: O.D. Mullinax, Director

HAWAII-------Division of Weights and Measures, Depart-
ment of Agriculture, 1428 South King Street,
P.O. Box 5425, Honolulu 96814.
Telephone: Area Code 808: 941-3071
Incumbent: George E. Mattimoe, Deputy
Director

IDAHO---------Bureau of Weights and Measures, Department of Agriculture, 2126 Warm Springs Avenue, Boise 93702.
    Telephone: Area Code 208: 384-2345
    Incumbent: Lyman D. Holloway, Chief

ILLINOIS------Bureau of Product Inspection and Standards, Department of Agriculture, Emmerson Building, State Fairgrounds, Springfield 62706.
    Telephone: Area Code 217: 782-3817
    Incumbent: Murvil D. Harpster, Chief

INDIANA-------Division of Weights and Measures, State Board of Health, 1330 West Michigan Street, Indianapolis 46206.
    Telephone: Area Code 317: 633-6860
    Incumbent: Lorenzo A. Gredy, Director

IOWA----------Weights and Measures Division, Consumer Protection Services, Department of Agriculture, Capitol Building, Des Moines 50319.
    Telephone: Area Code 515:281-5716
    Incumbent: J. Clair Boyd, Supervisor
            Standards Control

KANSAS--------Weights and Measures Division, State Board of Agriculture, State Office Building, 10th Floor, Topeka 66612. (Tests weighing and measuring devices except as noted below.)
    Telephone: Area Code 913: 296-3846
    Incumbent: John L. O'Neill, State Sealer

    Motor Fuel Tax Section, Department of Revenue, State Office Building, Topeka 66625. (Tests devices used for the measurement of motor fuels.)
    Telephone: Area Code 913: 296-2411
    Incumbent: Warren G. Foster, Supervisor
            of Weights and Measures

    State Grain Inspection Department, 801 Harrison, Topeka 66612. (Tests hopper scales over which grain is officially weighed.)
    Telephone: Area Code 913: 296-3451
    Incumbent: Nicholas Fabac, Assistant
            Director

KENTUCKY------Division of Weights and Measures, Department of Agriculture, 106 West Second Street, Frankfort 40601.

                    Telephone: Area Code 502: 564-4870
                    Incumbent: George L. Johnson, Director

MISSISSIPPI---Consumer Protection Division, Department of
              Agriculture and Commerce, State Office Bldg.
              P.O. Box 1609, Jackson 39205.
              Telephone: Area Code 601: 354-6258
              Incumbent: Joe B. Hardy, Jr., Director

              Office of State Motor Vehicle Comptroller,
              P.O.Box 1140, Jackson 39205. (Exercises
              supervision over gasoline-measuring devices)
              Telephone: Area Code 601: 354-7430
              Incumbent: Adlia Morgan, Director of
                         Petroleum Tax Division

MISSOURI------Weights and Measures Division, Department
              of Agriculture, P.O. Box 630, 2632 Indus-
              trial Drive, Jefferson City 65101.
              Telephone: Area Code 314: 751:4278 or
                                          751-4982
              Incumbent: J.W. Abbott, Director

MONTANA-------Division of Weights and Measures, Depart-
              ment of Business Regulation, 805 North Main,
              Helena 59601.
              Telephone: Area Code 406: 449-3163
              Incumbent: Gary L. Delano, Administrator

NEBRASKA------Division of Weights and Measures, Depart-
              ment of Agriculture, P.O.Box 4757, 1420 P
              Street, Lincoln 68509.
              Telephone: Area Code: 402: 471-2875
              Incumbent: Steve Malone, Administrator
                         Division of Weights and Mea-
                         sures

NEVADA--------Bureau of Weights and Measures, Department
              of Agriculture, P.O. Box 1209, Reno 89504.
              Telephone: Area Code 702: 784-6413
              Incumbent: Knute D. Pennington
                         Chief Deputy State Sealer

NEW HAMPSHIRE-Bureau of Weights and Measures, Division
              of Markets and Standards, Department of
              Agriculture, State House Annex, Room 201
              Concord 03301.
              Telephone: Area Code 603: 271-3700
              Incumbent: Walter J. Tusen, Chief
                         Inspector

NEW JERSEY----Office of Weights and Measures, Division of
Consumer Affairs, Department of Law and
Public Safety, 187 West Hanover Street,
Trenton 08625.
Telephone: Area Code 609: 292-4615
Incumbent: William J. Wolfe, Sr.
State Superintendent

NEW MEXICO----Division of Markets, Weights, and Measures,
Department of Agriculture, P.O. Box 3170,
Las Cruces 88003.
Telephone: Area Code 505: 646-1616 or 1617
Incumbent: Charles H. Greene, Chief

NEW YORK------Bureau of Weights and Measures, Department
of Agriculture and Markets, State Campus
1220 Washington Avenue, Albany 12235.
Telephone: Area Code 518: 457-3452
Incumbent: J. Fred Tucker, Director

NORTH CAROLINA-Consumer Standards Division, Department
of Agriculture, P.O. Box 27647, Raleigh
27611.
Telephone: Area Code 919: 829-3313
Incumbent: Marion L. Kinlaw, Director

NORTH DAKOTA--Department of Weights and Measures, Public
Service Commission, State Capitol,
Bismarck 58501.
Telephone: Area Code 701: 224-2412
Incumbent: Adin Helgeson, Director

OHIO----------Division of Weights and Measures, Depart-
ment of Agriculture, Reynoldsburg 43068.
Telephone: Area Code 614: 866-6361
Incumbent: Kenneth R. Adcock, Chief

OKLAHOMA------Marketing Division, State Department of
Agriculture, 122 Capitol, Oklahoma City
73105.
Telephone: Area Code 405: 521-3861
Incumbent: R.W. Powell, Director

Fuel Inspection Division, Oklahoma Corpora-
tion Commission, Jim Thorpe Building,
Capitol Complex, Oklahoma City 73105.
Telephone: Area Code 405: 521-2487
Incumbent: Roy A. Stafford, Director

Motor Fuel Division, Oklahoma Tax Commission, 2501 Lincoln Boulevard, Oklahoma City 73194
(Tests vehicle tanks.)
Telephone: Area Code 405: 521-3241
Incumbent: Herman H. Rice, Director

OREGON----------Office of Weights and Measures, Department of Agriculture, Agriculture Building, Salem 97310.
Telephone: Area Code 503: 378-3792

PENNSYLVANIA----Bureau of Standard Weights and Measures, Department of Agriculture, 2301 North Cameron Street, Harrisburg 17120.
Telephone: Area Code 717: 787-9089
Incumbent: Walter F. Junkins, Director

PUERTO RICO-----Department of Consumer Affairs, Edison 306 St., Jardines Metropolitanos, Rio Piedras   00927.
Telephone: Area Code 809: 726-7585
Incumbent: Maximiliano Trujillo,
          Assistant Secretary,
          Bureau of Enforcement

RHODE ISLAND----Department of Labor, 235 Promenade St., Providence 02908.
Telephone: Area Code 401: 277-2756
Incumbent: Edward R. Fisher, Administrator, Mercantile-Weights and Measures Division

SOUTH CAROLINA--Consumer Protection Division, Department of Agriculture, P.O. Box 11280, Columbia 29211.
Telephone: Area Code 803: 758-2426
Incumbent: Charles T. Smith, Director

South Dakota----Division of Consumer Protection, Department of Commerce and Consumer Affairs, State Capitol Building, Pierre 57501.
Telephone: Area Code 605: 224-3241
Incumbent: Tom Maher, Director

State Chemical Laboratory, Vermillion 57069. (Promulgates specifications and tolerances and has custody of standards.)
Telephone: Area Code 605: 624-3281
Incumbent: D.J. Mitchell, State Chemist

TENNESSEE-------Division of Marketing, Department of
Agriculture, Box 40627, Melrose Station,
Nashville 37204.
Telephone: Area Code 615: 741-1561, 1539
Incumbent: Dale Wilkinson, Director,
and Deputy Director of
Weights and Measures

TEXAS-----------Consumer Services Division, Texas Depart-
ment of Agriculture, John Reagan Building,
Box 12847, Capitol Station, Austin 78711.
Telephone: Area Code 512: 475-4304
Incumbent: Ed Whitesides, Director

Minerals Tax Division, Motor Fuels,
608 LBJ Office Building, 17th and North
Congress Austin 78774.
Telephone: Area Code 512: 475-4334
Incumbent: Jose R. Alcorta
Assistant Director

UTAH------------Weights and Measures Section, Department
of Agriculture, Room 412, State Capitol
Building, Salt Lake City 84114.
Telephone: Area Code 801: 328-5421
Incumbent: Fred D. Morgan, Supervisor

VERMONT---------Division of Weights and Measures, Depart-
ment of Agriculture, 116 State Street,
State Office Building, Montpelier 05602.
Telephone: Area Code 802: 828-2436
Incumbent: Trafford F. Brink, Director

VIRGIN ISLANDS--Consumer Services Administration, Golden
Rock, Christiansted, St. Croix 00820.
Telephone: Area Code 809: 773-2226
Incumbent: Joanna P. Lindquist, Director

VIRGINIA--------Weights and Measures Section, Division of
Product and Industry Regulation, Depart-
ment of Agriculture and Commerce, 1 North
14th Street, Room 032, Richmond 23219.
Telephone: Area Code 804: 770-2476, 2477
Incumbent: James F. Lyles, Supervisor

WASHINGTON------Weights and Measures Section, Dairy and
Food Division, Department of Agriculture,
406 General Administration Building,
Olympia 98504.
Telephone: Area Code 206: 753-5042
Incumbent: John H. Lewis, Chief

WEST VIRGINIA---Division of Consumer Protection, Depart-
ment of Labor, 1900 Washington Street,
East, Charleston 25305.
Telephone: Area Code 304: 348-7890
Incumbent: David L. Griffith, Director

WISCONSIN-------Division of Food and Standards, Department
of Agriculture, 801 West Badger Road,
Madison 53713.
Telephone: Area Code 608: 266-7241
Incumbent: Robert W. Probst, Director
Bureau of Standards

WYOMING---------Division of Markets, Wyoming Department
of Agriculture, 2219 Carey Avenue,
Cheyenne 82002.
Telephone: Area Code 307: 777-7321
Incumbent: William W. Hovey, Director

Alaska	Article XI	Section 1
Arizona	Article IV, Part 1	Section 1
Arkansas	Article VII	Section 1
California	Article IV	Section 1
Colorado	Article V	Section 1
Idaho	Article III	Section 1
Illinois	Article XIV	Section 3
Maine	Article IV, Part 3	Section 18
Massachusetts	Article XLVIII	
Michigan	Article II	Section 9
Missouri	Article III	Section 49
Montana	Article III	Section 4
Nebraska	Article III	Section 2
Nevada	Article XIX	Section 2, 1
North Dakota	Article II	Section 25
Ohio	Article II	Section 1
Oklahoma	Article V	Section 2
Oregon	Article IV	Section 1,(2)(a)
South Dakota	Article III	
Washington	Article II	Section 1(a)
Wyoming	Article III	Section 52(a)
Utah	Article V	Section 1, Statute 20-11-1

general resource

STATE/LOCAL	_PRIVATE_

ALABAMA

Governor's Office of Consumer
Protection
138 Adams Avenue
Montgomery, AL 36104
(205) 269-7477
*1-800-392-5658

Alabama Consumer Association
P.O. Box 1372
Birmingham, AL 35201

Office of Attorney General
669 S. Lawrence Street
Montgomery, AL 36107
(205) 269–7001

Elmore Community Action
   Committee
P.O. Drawer H
Wetumpka, AL 36092
Vera Cole
(205) 567-4361

ALASKA

Office of Attorney General
Consumer Protection Agency
3600 K Street
Anchorage, Alaska 99501
(907) 279-1567

Alaska Consumer Council
833 13th Avenue, West
Anchorage, Alaska 99501

Branch Offices:
Pouch K, State Capitol
Juneau, AK 99801
(907) 586-5931
604 Barnette, Box 1309
Fairbanks, AK 99701
(907) 452-1567

Fairbanks Consumer Group
Edward T. Moonan, Chr.
P.O. Box 483
Fairbanks, AK 99707

Kenai Peninsular Consumer Council
P.O. Box 2940
Kenai, Alaska 99611
Johnston Jeffries
(907) 283-7838

AK PIRG
James Love, Dir.
Box 1093
630 West 4th Ave.
Anchorage, AK 99510
907-278-3661

*Toll-free telephone number.

ARIZONA

Consumer Protection/Antitrust
    Division
Department of Law
159 State Capitol Building
Phoenix, AZ 85007
(602) 271-4266

Cochise County Attorney's Office
Bisbee, AZ 85603
(602) 432-2291

Pima County Attorney's Office
199 North Stone Ave., Suite 208
Tucson, AZ 85701
(602) 792-8668

Consumer Affairs Division
Tucson City Attorney's Office
P.O. Box 5547, 180 N. Meyer
Tucson, AZ 85703
(602) 791-4886

Arizona Consumers Council
Dr. Currin V. Shields, President
6840 Camino De Michael Str.
Tucson, Arizona 85718
(602) 884-2945

Tucson Consumers Council
P.O. Box 12471
Tucson, AZ 85711

Arizona Consumers Council
6480 Camino De Michael
Tucson, AZ 85718
Currin V. Shields, President
(602) 297-3825

Tucson Public Power
1043 E. 6th Street
Tucson, AZ 85719
(602) 622-9409

CALIFORNIA

Department of Consumer Affairs
1020 N Street
Sacramento, CA 95814
(916) 445-1254
*1-800-952-5210 (auto repair
complaints only)

Branch Offices:
107 South Broadway, Rm. 8020
Los Angeles, CA 90012
(213) 620-4360

30 Van Ness Avenue, Rm. 2100
San Francisco, CA 94102
(415) 557-2046

Environment/Consumer Protection
    Section
Office of Attorney General
600 State Building
Los Angeles, CA 90012
(213) 620-2494

*Toll-free telephone number.

Association of California Consumers
Mrs. Sylvia Seigel, Exec. Dir.
3030 Bridgeway Building
Sausalito, California 94965

Consumer Federation of California
Los Angeles, & Orange Cty. Chapt.
621 South Virgil Avenue
Los Angeles, CA 90005
Shirley Goldinger, President
(213) 388-7676

Cal PIRG - L.A.R.
KH 311: U of California
308 Westwood Plaza
Los Angeles, CA 90024
(213) 825-2530

Cal CAG
2315 Westwood Blvd.
Los Angeles, CA 90064
Roy Alper, Dir.
(213) 475-0417

County Offices:
Del Norte County Division of
Consumer Affairs
2650 Washington Boulevard
Crescent City, CA 95531
(707) 464-2716 or 3756

Fresno County Department of
Weights and Measures and
Consumer Protection
1730 South Maple Avenue
Fresno, CA 93702
(209) 488-3027

Consumer Services Deputy
Marin County Human Relations
Deparment
Civic Center, Rm 336
San Rafael, CA 94903
(415) 479-1100, Ext. 2971

Monterey County Department of
Weights & Measures and
Consumer Affairs
1220 Natividad Road
Salinas, CA 93901
(408) 758-3859

Orange County Office of Consumer
Affairs
511 N. Sycamore Street
Santa Ana, CA 92701
(714) 834-6100

Consumer Fraud Division
District Attorney's Office for
Sacramento County
816 H Street, Suite 202
Sacramento, CA 95814
(916) 454-2113 or 2417

Cal PIRG
334 Kalmia
San Diego, CA 92101
Miles Frieden, Dir.

CAL PIRG
214 Eshlenmen
U. of Cal.
Berkeley, CA 94720
(415) 642-4018

Accountants for the Public Int.
351 California Street 16th Fl.
San Francisco, CA 94104
(415) 956-7131

Bay CAL
593 Market Street
San Francisco, CA 94105
Mike Barnes
(415) 543-5632

Organize, Inc.
593 Market Street
San Francisco, CA 94105
Mike Miller
(415) 543-5632

San Francisco Consumer Action
312 Sutter Street
San Francisco, CA 94108
Kay Pachtner, Director
(415) 982-4660

Public Media Center
2751 Hyde Street
San Francisco, CA 94108
Roger Hickey
(415) 885-0200

Consumers United
P.O. Box 311
Palo Alto, CA 94302
Cherrie Bolling, Chairwoman
(415) 328-7269

San Bernardino County Department
of Weights & Measures and
Consumer Affairs
160 E. 6th Street
San Bernardino, CA 92415
(714) 383-1134

Consumer Fraud Unit
District Attorney's Office for
Santa Barbara County
118 E. Figueroa Street
Santa Barbara, CA 93101
(805) 963-1441

Santa Clara County Department of
Weights & Measures and
Consumer Affairs
1555 Berger Drive
San Jose, CA 95112
(408) 299-2105

Santa Cruz County Department of
Weights and Measures and
Consumer Affairs
640 Capitola Road
Santa Cruz, CA 95062
(408) 425-2054

Consumer Affairs Coordinator
Stanislaus County Office of Consumer
Affairs
P.O. Box 3404
Modesto, CA 95353
(209) 526-6211

Ventura County Department of
Weights and Measures and
Consumer Affairs
608 El Rio Drive
Oxnard, CA 93030
(805) 487-5511 Ext. 4377

NorCAL PIRG
Box 702
Santa Clara, CA 95953
Patricia Marrone, Dir.
(408) 984-2777

Consumer Federation of California
911 13th Street
Modesto, CA 95354
Frank Damrell, President
(209) 526-3500

American Consumers Council
Bernard F. Kamins, Ex. Sec.
9720 Wilshire Boulevard, Suite 208
Beverly Hills, California 90212

Citizens for Consumer Action
Mrs. F.G. Snyder, President
4230 De Costa Avenue
Sacramento, California 95821

Consumer Action
26 7th Street
San Francisco, CA 94103
(415) 626-4030

People's Lobby
Joyce Koupal, Dir.
3456 West Olympic Blvd.
Los Angeles, CA 90019
(213) 731-8321

Consumer Federation of Cali.
2200 L Street
Sacramento, CA 95816
Frank Darrell, Jr.

CONNECTICUT

Commissioner
Department of Consumer Protection
State Office Building
Hartford, CT 06115
(203) 566-4999
*800-842-2649

Office of Attorney General
Capitol Annex, 30 Trinity Street
Hartford, CT 06115
(203) 566-2203

Office of Consumer Protection
City Hall
Middletown, CT 06457
(203) 347-4671

Connecticut Consumers
Association, Inc.
Thomas Brooks, President
P.O. Box 404
Storrs, Connecticut 06268

Conn PIRG
P.O. Box 1571
Hartford, CT 06101
Jack Hale, Dir.
(203) 525-8312

CCAG
130 Washington St.
Hartford, CT 06106
Marc Caplan, Director
(203) 527-7191

Connecticut Consumer Assn.
8 Ellsworth Road
W. Hartford, CT 06107

Connecticut Consumer's Group
25 Spindrift Lane
Milford CT 06460
Mike Aulenti
(203) 878-0414

Consumer Information Service
Shirley Haner, Ad.
1 Landmark Square #100
Stamford, CT 06901
(203) 359-2112

*Toll-free telephone number.

COLORADO

Office of Consumer Affairs
Office of Attorney General
104 State Capitol
Denver, CO 80203
(303) 897-2542

County Offices:
Adams, Arapahoe, Boulder, Denver,
   Jefferson Counties:
Metropolitan District Attorney's
   Consumer Office
655 South Broadway
Denver, CO 80209
(303) 777-3072

CoPIRG
Un. Center Activities Area
Un. of Northern Colorado
Greeley, CO
(303) 351-4504

Colorado League for Consumer
   Protection
8230 W. 16th Place
Lakewood, CO 80215
John Van Vranken
(303) 233-5891

El Paso and Teller Counties:
El Paso County Office of District
   Attorney
303 South Cascade, Suite B
Colorado Springs, CO 80902
(303) 473-3801

Pueblo County Office of District
   Attorney
County Courthouse, RM 344
Pueblo, CO 81003
(303) 543-3550

Colorado Consumers Association
P.O. Box 471
Boulder, CO 80302
(303) 441-3700

DELAWARE

Consumer Affairs Division
Department of Community Affairs
and Economic Development
201 West 14th Street
Wilmington, DE 19801
(302) 571-3250
New Castle County: 658-9251
Kent County: 678-4000
Sussex County: 856-2571

Consumer Protection Division
Department of Justice
Public Building
Wilmington, DE 19801
(302) 571-2450

DISTRICT OF COLUMBIA

District of Columbia Office of
   Consumer Affairs
1407 L Street, N.W.
Washington, D.C. 20005
(202) 629-2617

Public Citizen
P.O. Box 19404
Don Sodo, Dir.
DC 20036

D.C. Citywide Consumer Council
M. Paul Smith, President
4547 Lee Street, N.W.
Washington, D.C. 20019

Consumer Federation of America
Carol Foreman, Dir.
1012 14th Street, NW Suite #901
Washington, D.C. 20005

Center for Science in the Public
   Interest
1757 S Street, NW
Washington, D.C. 20009

Consumer Assn. of DC
915 D Street, N.E.
Washington, D.C. 20002
Janie Boyd, Chairwoman
(202) 547-6496

Neighborhood Legal Services
1344 H Street, N.E.
Washington, D.C. 20002
Paula Heickel
(202) 399-6431

Neighborhood Consumer Info Center
3005 Georgia Avenue, N.W.
Washington, D.C. 20001
(202) 723-1540

Auto Owners Action Council
733 15th Street, N.W.
Washington, D.C. 20005
(202) 638-5550

DCPIRG
800 21st Street, N.W.
Washington, D.C. 20006
Randy Swisher, Dir.
(202) 676-7388

Anacostia Consumer Help Center
2906 Martin Luther King Ave., S.E.
Washington, D.C. 20032
(202) 562-3261

FLORIDA

Fair Trade Practice Office
Department of Legal Affairs
The Capitol
Tallahassee, FL 32304
(904) 488-4481

Consumer Fraud Division
State Attorney's Office for
Brevard County
County Courthouse
Titusville, FL 32780
(305) 269-8421

Florida Consumers Assn., Inc.
John S. Rippandelli, President
Box 3552
Tallahassee, Florida 32303

FPIRG
334 University Union, FSU
Tallahassee, FL 32306
(904) 644-1811

County Department of Consumer
  Affairs
200 S.E. 6th Street, Rm 202
Fort Lauderdale, FL 33301
(305) 765-5307

Consumer Protection Division
Metropolitan Dade County
1399 N.W. 17th Avenue, RM 200
Miami, FL 33125
(305) 377-5111

Office for DeSota, Manatee, and
  Sarasota Counties
2078 Main Street
Sarasota, FL 33577
(813) 955-0918

Palm Beach County Office of
  Consumer Affairs
301 North Olice Avenue
West Palm Beach, FL 33401
(305) 655-5200, Ext. 566-7-8-9

Pinellas County Office of Consumer
  Affairs
150 Fifth Street, North, Rm 167
St. Petersburg, FL 33701
(813) 441-8976

Division of Consumer Affairs
City Department of Human
  Resources
220 East Bay Street
Jacksonville, FL 32202
(904) 355-0411, Ext. 531

Director, City Division of Consumer
  Affairs
175 Fifth Street, North
St. Petersburg, FL 33701
(813) 893-7395

Florida Consumer Federation
P.O. Box 1191
220 East College
Tallahassee, FL 32302

American Consumer Association
P.O. Box 24141
Fort Lauderdale, FL 33307
Margaret Kent, President
(305) 772-5198

Dade County Consumers Council
Mrs. Lillian Gheer, Chairman
1741 S.W. 4th Street
Fort Lauderdale, Florida 33312

Florida Consumers Federation
Rod Tennyson
Clematis Street
West Palm Beach, Fla. 33401
(305) 659-5133

GEORGIA

Georgia Consumer Services
Department of Human Resources
Ponce De Leon Office Park, 13
618 Ponce De Leon Avenue, N.E.
Atlanta, GA 30308
(404) 894-5845
*1-800-282-4900

GPIRG
201 Washington Street, SW
Atlanta, GA 30303
Larry Katzman, Dir.
(404) 659-7082

*Toll-free telephone number.

Assistant Attorney General for
   Deceptive Practices
Office of Attorney General
132 State Judicial Building
Atlanta, GA 30334
(404) 656-3343

Atlanta Office of Consumer Affairs
City Hall Memorial Drive Annex
121 Memorial Drive, S.W.
Atlanta, Georgia 30303
(404) 658-6310

Georgia Consumer Council
Mrs. Mattie Waymer, President
Box 311
Morris Brown College
Atlanta, Georgia 30314

Georgia Power Project
P.O. Box 1856
Atlanta, GA 30301
(404) 523-6078

Southern Regional Council
52 Fairlie Street
Atlanta, GA 30303
Peter Petkus
(404) 522-8764

Georgia Conservancy
Virginia R. Harbin
3376 Peachtree Road #414
Atlanta, GA 30326
(404) 262-1967

HAWAII

Director of Consumer Protection
Office of Governor
250 S. King Street, 602
Kamamalu Building
P.O. Box 3767
Honolulu, HI 96811
(808) 548-2560 (Administration)
(808) 548-2540 (Complaints)

Life of the Land
Debbie Bodden
404 Piikoi Street, Rm 209
Honolulu, HI 96814
(808) 521-1300

IDAHO

Consumer Protection Division
Office of Attorney General
State Capitol, Rm 225
Boise, ID 83720
(208) 384-2400

Consumer-Business Association
428 Park Avenue
Idaho Falls, ID 83401
Chris Cavanaugh, President

Idaho Consumer Affairs
P.O. Box 1006
Boise, ID 83701
Helen-Kay Kreizenbeck
(208) 376-6510

ILLINOIS

Consumer Advocate's Office
Office of Governor
State of Illinois Building, RM. 2000
160 North LaSalle
Chicago, IL 60601
(312) 793-2754

Consumer Fraud Section
Office of Attorney General
134 N. LaSalle Street, RM. 204
Chicago, IL 60602
(312) 641-1988

Consumer Complaint Division
Cook County Office of State's
    Attorney
Civic Center Suite 303
Randolph at Clark
Chicago, IL 60602
(312) 443-8425

Chicago Department of Consumer
    Sales, Weights & Measures
City Hall, 121 N. LaSalle Street
Chicago, IL 60602
(312) 744-4092

Consumer Protection Commission
Village Hall, 200 Forest Boulevard
Park Forest, IL 60466
(312) 748-1112

Illinois Federation of Consumers
Mrs. Eve Galanter, President
5420 S.E. View Park
Chicago, Illinois 60615
        or
Mrs. Helen Nelson, Exec. V. Pres.
53 West Jackson Blvd.
Chicago, Illinois 60604

National Consumers United
1043 Chicago Avenue
Evanston, IL 60202
Jackie Kendall
(312) 475-2260

Rev. Jesse Jackson's PUSH
930 E. 50th Street
Chicago, IL 60604
Gilbert Cornfield, President
(312) 373-3366

Midwest Academy
600 W. Fullerton
Chicago, IL 60605
Heather Booth
(312) 935-6525

Illinois Public Action Council
59 E. Van Buren
Chicago, Ill. 60605
Bob Creamer

Businessmen in the Public Interest
109 N. Dearborn St.
Chicago, IL 60602

IPIRG
Student Government Office
Southern Illinois University
Carbondale, IL 62901
(618) 536-2140

INDIANA

Consumer Protection Division
Office of Attorney General
215 State House
Indianapolis, IN 46204
(317) 633-6496 or 6276
*1-800-382-5516

Division of Consumer Credit
Department of Financial Institutions
1024 Indiana State Office Bldg.
Indianapolis, IN 46204
(317) 633-6297 (Credit Only)

Lake County Office of Prosecuting
   Attorney
232 Russell Street
Hammond, IN 46320
(219) 931-3440

City Office of Consumer Affairs
City of Gary—Annex East
1100 Massachusetts
Gary, IN 46402
(219) 883-8532-33-34

Indiana Consumer Center
Alan Classen
730 East Washington Blvd.
Ft. Wayne, Ind. 46802
(219) 422-7630

Consumer Association of Indiana
Mrs. Eve Purvis, President
910 North Delaware Street
Indianapolis, Indiana 46202

INPIRG
703 E. 7th Street
Bloomington, IN 47401
Charles Glick, Dir.
(812) 337-7575

IOWA

Office of Attorney General
220 E. 13th Court
Des Moines, IA 50319
(515) 281-5926

Iowa Consumers League
Box 189
Corydon, IA 50060
Bob Muma, President
(515) 872-2329

Iowa PIRG
Roger Colton, Dir.
Iowa PIRG State Office
Oakdale, IA 52319
(319) 353-7049

Iowa Consumers League
Peter Westergaard, President
P.O. Box 1076
Des Moines, Iowa 50311
(515) 987-1372

KANSAS

Office of Attorney General
State Capitol
Topeka, KS 66612
(913) 296-3751

Kansas City Consumer Assn.
7720 W. 61 Street
Shawnee Mission, KS 66202
Ernest Salvas, President
(913) 432-0485

*Toll-free telephone number.

Johnson County Office of
  District Attorney
County Courthouse, Box 728
Olathe, KS 66061
(913) 782-5000, Ext. 318

Sedgwick County Office of
  District Attorney
County Courthouse, 5th Floor
Wichita, KS 67203
(316) 268-7405

Wyandotte County Office of
  District Attorney
710 North 7th Street
Kansas City, KS 66102
(913) 371-1600, Ext. 231-234

Municipal Office Building
One Civic Plaza
701 N. 7th Street, RM. 350
Kansas City, KS 66101
(913) 371-2000, Ext. 230-231

City Attorney's Office
215 East 7th Street
Topeka, KS 66603
(913) 235-9261, Ext. 205

Consumer United Program
Max H. Evans
8410 West Highway 54
Wichita, Kansas 67209

Consumer Assistance Center
Cathy Butts
North Central Kansas Libraries
Juilette & Poyntz
Manhattan, KN 66502
(913) 776-7776

CAN HELP
P.O. Box 4253
Topeka, KN 66616
(913) 235-3434

KENTUCKY

Office of Attorney General
The Capitol, Rm. 34
Frankfort, KY 40601
(502) 564-6607
*1-800-372-2960

Jefferson County Department of
  Consumer Protection
5th and Market, Rm. 401
Louisville, KY 40202
(502) 581-6280

City Department of Consumer Affairs
MSD Building, 400 S. 6th Street
Louisville, KY 40203
(502) 582-2206

Consumer Association of
  Kentucky, Inc.
Glenda Lewis/Frank Yudkin
P.O. Box 111
Frankfort, KY 40601
(502) 875-2207/587-0772

KYSPIRG
Rm. 31 Student Center
University of Louisville
Louisville, KY 40299
(502) 588-5809

Community Incorporation
Anita Phillips
222 No. 17th Street
Louisville, KY 40203
(502) 583-8385

*Toll-free telephone number.

LOUISIANA

Governor's Office of Consumer
  Protection
1885 Wooddale Boulevard, 1218
P.O. Box 44091, Capitol Station
Baton Rouge, LA 70804
(504) 389-7483
*800-272-9868

Office of Attorney General
234 Loyola Avenue, 7th Floor
New Orleans, LA 70112
(504) 529-1636

East Baton Rouge Parish
  Consumer Protection Center
1779 Government Street
Baton Rouge, LA 70802
(504) 344-8506

Jefferson Parish Office of
  District Attorney
1820 Franklin Avenue, Suite 23
Gretna, LA 70053
(504) 366-6611, Ext. 441

Monroe Office of Consumer Affairs
City Plaza, Monroe City Hall
Monroe, LA 71201
(504) 387-3521

City Office of Consumer Affairs
City-1W12
New Orleans, LA 70112
(504) 586-4441

Louisiana Consumer League
James L. Gray
P.O. Box 14301
Baton Rouge, LA 70808
(504) 581-9322

LA Center for the Public Interest
700 Maison Blanche Bldg.
New Orleans, LA 70112
David A. Marcello

MAINE

Office of Attorney General
State House
Augusta, ME 04330
(207) 289-3716

MainePIRG
68 High Street
Portland, ME 04101
(207) 622-9411/774-3066

Consumers Affairs Program
Task Force on Human Needs
Bruce Szal
240 Main Street
Lewiston, ME 04240
(207) 783-0720

*Toll-free telephone number.

MARYLAND

Office of Attorney General
One South Calvert Street
Baltimore, MD 21202
(301) 383-3713

Anne Arundel County Office/
  Board of Consumer Affairs
Arundel Center, Rm. 403
Annapolis, MD 21404
(301) 268-4300, Ext. 346

State's Attorney's Office
316 Equitable Building
Baltimore, MD 21202
(301) 396-4997

Montgomery County Office of
  Consumer Affairs
24 Maryland Avenue
Rockville, MD 20850
(301) 340-1010

Prince George's County Consumer
  Protection Commission
Courthouse
Upper Marlboro, MD 20870
(301) 627-3000, Ext. 561 or 589

Maryland Consumers Association,
  Inc.
Walter M. Falck, President
P.O. Box 143
Annapolis, MD 21404

Maryland Citizens Consumer Council
P.O. Box 5767
Bethesda, MD 20014
Iris Schneider, Pres.
(301) 530-6362

MaryPIRG
Rm 3110 New Main Dining Hall
University of Maryland
College Park, MD 20742
(301) 454-5601

Neighborhoods Uniting Project
3706 Rhode Island Avenue
Mr. Rainier, MD 20822
Rich Fowler
(301) 277-7085

CEPA
400 N. Linwood Avenue
Baltimore, MD 21224
Jim Hammond

Southeast Community Organization
10 S. Wolfe Street
Baltimore, MD 21231
Stan Holt
(301) 327-1626

Maryland Action Coalition, Inc.
8120 Fenton Street
Silver Spring, MD 20910
(301) 585-4482

MASSACHUSETTS

Executive Office of Consumer Affairs
State Office Building
100 Cambridge Street
Boston, Ma 02202
(617) 727-7755

Department of Attorney General
State House, Rm. 167
Boston, Ma 02133
(617) 727-8406

Franklin County Office of District
   Attorney
Courthouse
Northampton, MA 01060
(413) 584-1597

Boston Consumer's Council
City Hall, Rm. 721
Boston, MA 02201
(617) 722-4100, Ext. 236-7-8

Fitchburg Consumer Protection
   Service
455 Main Street
Fitchburg, MA 01420
(617) 345-1946

Lowell Consumer Advisory
   Council
City Hall
Lowell, MA 01852
(617) 454-8821

City Consumer Assistance Center
Adams Building, Rm. 306
1354 Hancock Street
Quincy, MA 02169
(617) 773-1380 Ext. 246-7

Town Office of Consumer Affairs
Town Hall, 75 Middle Street
Weymouth, MA 02189
(617) 335-2000, Ext. 46

Massachusetts Consumer Assn.
Miss Velia T. DiCesare, President
69 Readville Street
Hyde Park, Massachusetts 02136

Mass PIRG
120 Boylston Street Rm 320
Boston, MA 02216
Steve Morgan, Dir.
(617) 423-1796

233 N. Pleasant Street
Amherst, MA 01002
(413) 256-6434

Massachusetts Community School
107 South Street
Boston, MA 02111
Mark Dyen
(617) 542-5352

Massachusetts Fair Share
739 Broadway
Chelsea, MA 02150
Mark & Barbara Splain
(617) 884-1368

National Consumer Law Center
1 Court Street
Boston, MA 02108

Association of Massachusetts
   Consumers
Boston College
140 Commonwealth Avenue
Chestnut Hill, MA 02167
Rev. Robert McEwen
(617) 969-0100

Peoples Bicentennial Commission
490 Beacon Street
Boston, MA 02115
Randy Barber
(617) 259-0226

MICHIGAN

Office of Attorney General
670 Law Building
Lansing, MI 48913
(517) 373-1140

Michigan Consumer Council
414 Hollister Building
Lansing, MI 48933
(517) 373-0947

Michigan Association for
   Consumer Protection
P.O. Box 71
Madison Heights, MI 48071
Walter Benkert, President
(313) 399-2251

Consumer Protection Unit
Bay County Office of
  Prosecuting Attorney
515 Center Avenue
Bay City, MI 48706
(517) 893-3594

Genessee County Office of
  Prosecuting Attorney
105 Courthouse
Flint, MI 48502
(313) 766-8768

Jackson County Office of
  Prosecuting Attorney
464 County Building
Jackson, MI 49201
(517) 787-3800

Saginaw County Office of
  Prosecuting Attorney
115 S. Michigan Avenue
Saginaw County Courthouse
Saginaw, MI 48602
(517) 793-9100

Consumer Protection Division
Washtenaw County Office of
  Prosecuting Attorney
200 County Building
Main & Huron Streets
Ann Arbor, MI 48108
(313) 994-2420

Wayne County Consumer Protection
  Agency
356 E. Congress
Detroit, MI 48226
(313) 224-2150

City Consumer Affairs Department
809 City-County Building
2 Woodward Avenue
Detroit, MI 48226
(313) 224-3508

Consumer Alliance of Michigan
1811 N. Connecticut Avenue
Royal Oak, MI 48073

Consumer Action Center
115 1/2 E. Liberty Street
Ann Arbor, MI 48107
John Knapp, Director
(313) 665-4451

Michigan Citizens Lobby
Barbara Grossman
105 Fairfax Office Plaza
15660 West 10 Mile Road
Southfield, MI 48075
(313) 559-9260

PIRGIM
615 E. Michigan
Lansing, MI 48933
Joe Tuchinsky, Director
(517) 487-6001

Detroit Consumers Association
Gerald R. Amster, President
29207 Ford Road
Garden City, Michigan 48135

Consumer Research Advisory
  Council
Alreda Riley
51 West Warren Ave #310
Detroit, MI 48201
(313) 831-2290

Consumer Alliance of Michigan
14382 Glastonbury Road
Detroit, MI 48223
(313) 868-5400

Citizens for Beter Care
960 East Jefferson Ave.
Detroit, MI 48207

MINNESOTA

Office of Attorney General
102 State Capitol
St. Paul, MN 55155
(612) 296-4512

Minnesota Consumers League
Mrs. Tobey Lapakko, President
1671 South Victoria Road
St. Paul, Minnesota 55118

Hennepin County Attorney's Office
248 Hennepin County Courthouse
Minneapolis, MN 55415
(612) 348-4528

City Department of Licenses
& Consumer Services
101A City Hall
Third Avenue & 4th Street
Minneapolis, MN 55415
(612) 348-2080

City Office of Consumer Affairs
179 City Hall
St. Paul, MN 55415
(612) 298-4567

MPIRG
3036 University Ave, S.E.
Minneapolis, MN 55414
Jonathan Motl, Dir.
(612) 376-7554

Center for Urban Encounter
3410 University Avenue, S.E.
Minneapolis, MN 55414
(612) 331-6210

Northeast Minnesota Consumers
League
206 W. 4th Street
Duluth, MN 55806
Ray Allen
(218) 727-8973 X5

Minnesota Consumer Alliance
Jim Glaser
3410 University Ave, SE
Minnesota, MN 55414
(612) 331-7770

MISSISSIPPI

Office of Attorney General
Justice Building, P.O. Box 220
Jackson, MS 39205
(601) 354-7130

Department of Agriculture and
Commerce
High and President Streets
P.O. Box 1609
Jackson, MS 39205
(601) 354-6586

Mississippi Consumers Assn.
375 Culley Drive
Jackson, MS 39206
(601) 362-6643

MISSOURI

Office of Attorney General
Supreme Court Building
P.O. Box 899
Jefferson City, MO 65101
(314) 751-3321

Department of Consumer Affairs,
Regulation and Licensing
P.O. Box 1157
Jefferson City, MO 65101
(314) 751-4996

Missouri Association of
Consumers
John J. Weisen
Box 514
Columbia MO 65201
(816) 454-6333

MoPIRG
Box 8276
St. Louis, MO 63136
Herb Gross, Director
(314) 361-5200

Greene County Prosecutor's Office
County Courthouse, Rm. 206
Springfield, MO 65802
(417) 869-2465

City Office of Consumer Affairs
City Hall, 11th Floor
Kansas City, MO 64106
(816) 274-1638

Greater Kansas City Consumer
  Association
Denver Cook
320 East 10th Street
Kansas City, MO 64106
(816) 471-8030 X49

American Council on Consumer
  Interests
238 Stanley Hall
University of Missouri
Columbia, MO 65201

MONTANA

Consumer Affairs Division
Department of Business Regulation
805 North Main Street
Helena, MT 59601
(406) 449-3163

Lewis and Clark County
  Attorney's Office
County Courthouse
Helena, MT 59601
(406) 442-4550

Missoula County Attorney
County Courthouse
Missoula, MT 58901
(406) 543-3111

Consumer Affairs Council
P.O. Box 414
Helena, MT 59601

Center for Public Interest
P.O. Box 931
Bozeman, MT 59715
(406) 587-0906
Rick Applegate

Student Action Center
Joseph Brown, Dir.
University Center
University of Montana 59801
(406) 243-2451

NEBRASKA

Department of Justice
State Capitol, Rm 2119
Lincoln, NB 68509
(402) 471-2341

Consumer Fraud Division
Douglas County Attorney's Office
Omaha-Douglas Civic Center
18th and Farnam Streets, Rm. 909
Omaha, NB 68102
(402) 444-7625

Consumer Alliance of Nebraska
Chuck Havlicek
Nebraska Center
33rd & Holdrege
Lincoln, NB 68483
(402) 472-2844

NEVADA

Office of Attorney General
Supreme Court Building
Carson City, NV 89701
(702) 885-4170

Department of Commerce
Collet Building, Suite 219
1111 Las Vegas Boulevard, South
Las Vegas, NV 89104
(702) 385-0344
(800) 992-0900

Clark County District Attorney's
  Office
County Courthouse, 200 E. Carson
Las Vegas, NV 89101
(702) 386-4011

Washoe County District Attorney's
  Office
County Courthouse
South Virginia & Court Streets
Reno, NV 89501
(702) 785-4253

Consumers League of Nevada
Charles Levinson
3031 Garnet Court
Las Vegas, NV 89121
(702) 457-1953

Citizen Alert
Susan Orr/Katherine Hale
Box 5731
Reno, NV 89513
(702) 747-5053

Poor People Pulling Together
1285 W. Miller
Las Vegas, NV 89106
(702) 648-4645
Emma O'Neil, Dir.

NEW HAMPSHIRE

Office of Attorney General
Statehouse Annex
Concord, NH 03301
(603) 271-3641

NHPIRG
University of NH
Box 200
Durham, NH

Newmarket Health Center, Inc.
Robert G. Peck, Dir.
84 Main Street
Newmarket, NH 03857
(603) 659-3106

NEW JERSEY

Division of Adminstration
Department of Public Advocate
P.O. Box 141
Trenton, NJ 08625
(609) 292-7087
(800) 792-8600

Department of Law & Public Safety
State Office Building
Newark, NJ 07102
(201) 648-4010

Consumers League of New Jersey
20 Church Street
Montclair, NJ 07042
(201) 744-6449

Consumer Affairs Project
449 Central Avenue
Newark, NJ 07107
Dennis Cherot
(201) 481-5000

Atlantic County Office of
Consumer Affairs
25 Dolphin Avenue & Shore Road
Northfield NJ 08232
(609) 646-6626

Bergen County Office of Consumer
Affairs
355 Main Street
Hackensack, NJ 07601
(201) 646-2650

NJPIRG
32 W. Lafayette Street
Trenton, NJ 08608
Steve DeMicco, Dir.
(609) 393-7474

Burlington County Office of
Consumer Affairs
Grant Building, Rm. 101
54 Grant Street
Mount Holly, NJ 08060
(609) 267-3300

Camden County Office of Consumer
Affairs
Commerce Building, Rm. 606
No. 1 Broadway
Camden, NJ 08103
(609) 964-8700, Ext. 277

Cumberland County Department of
Weights & Measures and
Consumer Protection
800 East Commerce Street
Bridgeton, NJ 08302
(609) 451-8000 Ext. 296

Somerset County Department of
Consumer Affairs
County Administration Building
Somerville, NJ 08876
(201) 725-4700

Community Union Project
Donald Clark
116 No. Oraton Pkwy
East Orange, NJ 07017
(201) 675-8600

National Consumer Advisory Council
Bill Shepard
217 13th Ave.
Belmar, NJ 07719
(201) 681-7494

NEW MEXICO

Office of Attorney General
Lamy Building, P.O. Box 2246
Santa Fe, NM 87501
(505) 827-2844 or 5237

Albuquerque Consumers Assn.
Dr. David Hamilton, Jr., Chairman
4844 Southern Avenue, S.E.
Albuquerque, NM 87108

Bernalillo County District Attorney's
Office
Courthouse, 415 Tijeras, N.W.
Albuquerque, NM 87101
(515) 766-4340

Eddy County District Attorney's Office
P.O. Box 1240
Carlsbad, NM 88220
(505) 887-3121

District Attorney for Valencia
County
Los Lunas, NM 87031
(505) 865-9643

New Mexico PIRG
P.O. Box 4564
Albuquerque, NM 87106
Mike Huston, Dir.
(505) 277-2758

Southwest Research & Information
Center
Katherine Montague
Box 3524
Albuquerque, NM 87106
(505) 265-0451

NEW YORK

State Consumer Protection Board
99 Washington Avenue, Rm. 1000
Albany, NY 12210
(518) 474-8583

Consumer Frauds & Protection
Bureau
Office of Attorney General
Two World Trade Center
New York, NY 10047
(212) 488-7530

Erie County District Attorney's
Office
25 Delaware Avenue
Buffalo, NY 14202
(716) 855-2424

Nassau County Office of Consumer
Affairs
160 Old County Road
Mineola, NY 11501
(516) 535-3282

Oneida County Consumer Advocate
County Office Building
800 Park Avenue
Utica, NY 13501
(315) 798-5076

Onondaga County Office of
Consumer Affairs
635 James Street
Syracuse, NY 13203
(315) 477-7911

New York Consumer Assembly
465 Grand Street
New York, NY 10002
Eileen Hoats, Director
(212) 674-5990

NYPIRG
5 Beekman Street
New York, NY 10038
Donald Ross, Director
(212) 349-6460

Irate Consumers of Ulster County
Box 419
Saugerites, NY 12477
Jack Walters, President
(914) 246-4021

ACT SHARP
15 Durham Avenue
Buffalo, NY 14215
Lee Smith
(716) 895-9314

Consumer Council of Genessee Valley
99 Penfield Road
Rochester, NY 14610

Consumer Association of Greater
New York
109 Heather Drive
Rochester, NY 14625
Judy Braiman, President
(716) 381-5958

Orange County Department of
Weights and Measure and
Consumer Affairs
99 Main Street
Goshen, NY 10924
(914) 294-5822

Rockland County Office of Consumer
Protection
County Office Building
New Hempsted Road
New City, NY 10956
(914) 638-0500, Ext. 395

Steuben County Department of
Weights & Measures and Consumer
Affairs
19 East Morris Street
Bath, NY 14810
(607) 776-4949

Suffolk County Department of
Consumer Affairs
Suffolk County Center
Veterans Highway
Hauppauge, Long Island, NY 11787
(516) 979-3100

Westchester County Office of
Consumer Affairs
Office of County Executive
White Plains, NY 10601
(914) 949-1300

Colonie Consumer Protection Agency
Memorial Town Hall
Newtonville, NY 12128
(518) 783-2700

Town Consumer Protection Board
Town Hall, 227 Main Street
Huntington, NY 11743
(516) 421-1000

City Department of Weights and
Measures and Consumer Affairs
Police Headquarters
Roosevelt Square
Mt. Vernon, NY 10050
(914) 558-6000, Ext. 27

Human Affairs Program
410 College Avenue
Ithaca, NY 14850

Metropolitan New York Consumer
Council
Dr. Ralph R. Reuter, Chairman
1710 Broadway
New York, New York 10002

Consumer Action Now, Inc.
49 East 53rd Street
New York, New York 10022
(212) 752-1220

Empire State Consumer Assoc., Inc.
Judy Braiman
109 Heather Drive
Rochester, NY 14625
(716) 381-2758

Consumer Action Program
Adolfo G. Alayon
270 Pulaski Street
Brooklyn, N.Y. 11206
(212) 453-7602

Oswego Consumer Protection League
Joanne Burman
Rt 8
Oswego, NY 13126
(315) 342-3850

Institute for Consumer Education
300 Dun Bldg.
110 Pearl Street
Buffalo, NY 14202
(716) 834-4236/834-0300

Store Front
140 West State Street
Ithaca, NY 14850
(607) 273-9012

City Consumer Affairs Committee
City Hall
New Rochelle, NY 10801
(914) 632-2021, Ext. 218

City Department of Consumer
  Affairs
80 Lafayette Street
New York, NY 10013
(212) 566-5456

City Consumer Protection Board
Ramapo Town Hall, Route 59
Suffern, NY 10901
(914) 357-5100, Ext. 57 or 58

City Bureau of Consumer Protection
City Hall, Rm. 206
Jay Street
Schenectady, NY 12305
(518) 377-3381, Ext. 314 or 357

Yonkers Office of Consumer
  Protection, Weights and Measures
City Hall, Rm. 316
Nepperhan Avenue
Yonkers, NY 10701
(914) 965-0707, 963-3980, Ext. 359

NORTH CAROLINA

Office of Attorney General
Justice Building, P.O. Box 629
Raleigh, NC 27602
(919) 829-7741
*1-800-662-7925

Department of Agriculture
P.O. Box 27647
Raleigh, NC 27611
(919) 829-4216

Charlotte Police Department
Law Enforcement Center
825 East Fourth Street
Charlotte, NC 28205
(704) 374-2311

North Carolina Consumers Council
Honorable Richard S. Clark,
  President
108 E. Jefferson Street
Monroe, North Carolina 28110

North Carolina Consumers Council
Route 5, Box 50 1/2
Henderson, NC 27536
Lillian Woo, President
(919) 876-4575

NCPIRG
P.O. Box 2901
Durham, NC 27705
Peter Brown, Dir.
(919) 286-2275

---

*Toll-free telephone call

Carolina Action
Box 2842
Durham, NC 27705
(919) 682-6076

Institute for Southern Studies
17 Davie Circle
Chapel Hill, NC 27514
Bob Hall
(919) 942-1218

I CARE, Inc.
P.O. Box 349
Statesville, NC 28677
Nell Clevenger
(704) 872-8141

NORTH DAKOTA

Office of Attorney General
State Capitol
Bismarck, ND 58501
(701) 224-2485

Bismarck-Mandan Consumers
League
Mr. Bernard Graff, President
1105 Sunset Drive
Mandan, ND 58554

Area Low Income Council
1219 College Drive
Devils Lake, ND 58301
(701) 662-5388

OHIO

Office of Attorney General
State Office Tower, Suite 1541
30 East Broad Street
Columbus, OH 43215
(614) 466-8831

Department of Commerce
33 North Grant Avenue
Columbus, OH 43215
(614) 466-3491
*800-282-1960

Franklin County Office of
  Prosecuting Attorney
Hall of Justice; S. High Street
Columbus, OH 43210
(614) 462-3520

Consumers League of Ohio
Mrs. Dorothy M. Austin, Ex. Sec.
940 Engineers Building
Cleveland, OH 44114

Ohio Consumers Association
Dr. Jean Bower
P.O. Box 1559
Columbus, OH 43216
(614) 422-0321

Consumer Action Movement
13540 Superior
East Cleveland, OH 44102
Steve Brobeck
(216) 451-6112

---

*Toll-free telephone call

Lake County Consumer Protection
  Council
Prosecuting Attorney's Office
Lake County Courthouse
Painesville, OH 44077
(216) 352-6281, Ext. 281

Montgomery County Office of
  Prosecuting Attorney
County Courts Building
41 North Perry Street
Suite 308
Dayton, OH 45402
(513) 228-5162 (Criminal Fraud only)

City Division of Weight and
  Measures, Consumer Protection
69 North Union Street
Akron, OH 44314
(216) 375-2612

City Office of Consumer Affairs
City Hall, Rm. 119
601 Lakeside Avenue
Cleveland, OH 44114
(216) 694-3200

City Consumer Protection
  Commission
919 Walnut Avenue, N.E.
Canton, OH 44704
(216) 455-8951, Ext. 249

City Department of Community
  Services
220 Greenlawn Avenue
Columbus, OH 43223
(614) 461-7397

City Bureau of Consumer Affairs
101 West Third Street
Dayton, OH 45402
(513) 225-5048 or 5574

City Consumer Protection Agency
565 North Erie Street
Toledo, OH 43624
(419) 244-6897

City Department of Health
City Hall
Youngstown, OH 44503
(216) 744-0270, 0279, 5960

Citizen Action
1241 Terminal Tower
Cleveland, OH 44113
Jay Seaton
(216) 687-0525

Consumer Protection Association
118 St. Clair Avenue
Cleveland, OH 44114
Solomon Harge, Director
(216) 241-0186

Active Clevelanders Together
Rev. Kenneth E. Jones
11628 Madison
Cleveland, OH 44102
(216) 221-8300

OhioPIRG
65 South 4th Street
Columbus, OH 43215
Rick Parker, Director

Humanity House
475 W. Market Street
Akron, OH 44303
John Looney
(216) 253-7151

Consumer Conference of Greater
  Cincinnati
Henrietta C. Tasmus
7432 Clovernook Avenue
Cincinnati, OH 45231
(513) 521-3498

OKLAHOMA

Department of Consumer Affairs
Jim Thorpe Building, Rm. 460
Oklahoma City, OK 73105
(405) 521-3921

Office of Attorney General
State Capitol Building, Rm. 112
Oklahoma City, OK 73105
(405) 521-3921

Delta Community Action Found.
  Inc.
Jacob Civis, Dir.
1024 Main Street
Duncan, OK 73533
(405) 255-3222

OREGON

Office of Attorney General
1133 S.W. Market Street
Portland, OR 97201
(503) 229-5522

Department of Commerce
Salem, OR 97310
(503) 378-4320

Jackson County Office of District
  Attorney
County Courthouse
Medford, OR 97501
(503) 779-1379

Multnomah County Office of District
  Attorney
600 County Courthouse
Portland, OR 97204
(503) 248-3974

Oregon Consumer League
3131 Northwest Luray Terrace
Portland, OR 97210
Jan Rathe
(503) 228-8787

OSPIRG
Pythiam Building, 2nd floor
918 S.W. Yamhill Street
Portland, OR 97205
Bill Van Dyck, Director
(503) 222-9641

Rain
Steve Johnson
2270 N.W. Irving
Portland, OR 97210
(503) 227-5110

PENNSYLVANIA

Bureau of Consumer Protection
Office of Attorney General
23A South Third Street
Harrisburg, PA 17101
(717) 787-9714

Allegheny County Bureau of
  Consumer Affairs
Jones Law Building, 12th Floor
4th and Ross Street
Pittsburgh, PA 15219
(412) 355-5402

Alliance for Consumer Protection
P.O. Box 1354
Pittsburgh, PA 15230
Suzanne Stadl
(412) 243-0163

Pennsylvania League for Consumer
  Protection
127 Locust Street
Harrisburg, PA 17101
William Matson
(717) 233-5704

Bucks County Department of
Consumer Protection
Administration Annex
Broad and Union Streets
Doylestown, PA 18901
(215) 348-2911

Delaware County Office of Public
Information
Toal Building
2nd and Orange Streets
Media, PA 19063
(215) 891-2288

Lackawanna County Department of
Transportation, Environmental,
Consumer Affairs
News Building, 8th Floor
Scranton, PA 18503
(717) 342-8366

Lancaster County District Attorney
Consumer Protection Commission
County Courthouse
Lancaster, PA 17602
(717) 299-4222

Montgomery County Consumer
Affairs
County Courthouse
Norristown, PA 19404
(215) 274-5000, Ext. 228

Mayor's Office of Consumer Services
City Hall, Rm. 143
Philadelphia, PA 19107
(215) MU6-2798

City Office of Consumer Advocate
City-County Building, Rm. 517
Pittsburgh, PA 15219
(412) 281-3900

Bucks County Consumer
Organization
30 Spice Bush Road
Levittown, PA 19056
(215) 945-3373
Albert H. Reef

South Wilkes Barre Citizens
Wilma Burt
Wilkes Barre, PA 18702
(717) 822-5173

Philadelphia Area Consumer
Organization
1410 Chestnut Street
Philadelphia, PA 19102
Carl Dahlgren
(215) 763-1744

Grey Panthers
3700 Chestnut
Philadelphia, PA 19104

Citizens United Together
1022 Burch Street
Scranton, PA 18505
(717) 346-5642

Consumer Education and Protective
Association
6048 Ogontz Avenue
Philadelphia, PA 19141
(215) 424-1441

United Consumers of the Alleghenies
William A. Dickert
P.O. Box 997
Johnstown, PA 15907
(814) 535-8608

RHODE ISLAND

Rhode Island Consumers' Council
365 Broadway
Providence, RI 02902
(401) 277-2764

Rhode Island Workers Assn.
212 Union Street
Providence, RI 02903
George Nee, Ray Lemoine
(401) 751-2008

Office of Attorney General
250 Benefit Street
Providence, RI 02903
(401) 831-6850

RIPIRG
Memorial Union
University of Rhode Island
Kingston, RI 02881
(401) 792-2585

RIPIRG
Box 1930
Brown University
Providence, RI 02912
(401) 274-6238

Rhode Island Consumers League
Urban League of Rhode Island
131 Washington Street
Providence, RI 02903

Rhode Island Statewide Coalition of
  Community Organizations
726 Dexter Street
Central Falls, RI 02911
Bill Droel
(401) 723-3147

Rhode Island Consumers' League
Mrs. Juanita Handy, President
2 Progress Avenue
East Providence, RI 02914

Coalition for Consumer Justice
Henry Shelton
428 Dexter Street
Central Falls, RI 02863
(401) 723-3147

SOUTH CAROLINA

Department of Consumer Affairs
Columbia Building, 6th Floor
1200 Main, P.O. Box 11739
Columbia, SC 29211
(803) 758-2040
800-922-1594

Hampton Office Building
Office of Attorney General
P.O. Box 11549
Columbia, SC 29211
(803) 758-2553 or 2313

SCPIRG
Box 28384 Furman University
Greenville, SC 29613
Pat Patten, Chr.
(803) 294-2174

Midlands Community Action Agency
2000 Washington Street
Columbia, SC 29204
(803) 779-7250 X68
William Scott

SOUTH DAKOTA

Division of Consumer Protection
Department of Commerce and
  Consumer Affairs
State Capitol
Pierre, SD 57501
(605) 224-3177

Consumers League
Harold Mortimer
Rapid City, SD 57701
(605) 343-6836

South Dakota Consumers League
P.O. Box 106
Madison, SD 57042
(605) 256-4536
J. Gene Hexon

SDACORN
611 South 2nd Ave.
Sioux Falls, SD 57104
(605) 332-2328
Dewey Armstrong

TENNESSEE

Department of Agriculture
Lab and Office Building
Ellington Agricultural Center
Hogan Road, Box 40627
Melrose Station
Nashville, TN 37204
(615) 741-1461
*800-342-8385

Office of Attorney General
Supreme Court Building, RM. 419
Nashville, TN 37219
(615) 741-1671

Tennessee Consumer Alliance
821 17th Avenue, S.
Nashville, TN 37203
D. Denty Cheatham, President
(615) 242-0386

The Highlander Center
Rt. 3 Box 370
New Market, TN 37820
(615) 933-3443
Mike Clark, Dir.

Elk & Duck Rivers Community
   Assoc.
701 So. Lincoln Ave.
Fayetteville, TN 37334
(615) 433-7182

TEXAS

Office of Attorney General
P.O. Box 12548, Capitol Station
Austin, TX 78711
(512) 475-3288

Bexar County Office of Criminal
   District Attorney
San Antonio, TX 78205
(512) 220-2323

Consumer Fraud Division
El Paso County Office of District
   Attorney
City-County Building, RM. 401
El Paso, TX 79901
(915) 543-2860

TexPIRG
Shelia Cheaney, Dir.
Box 237 UC
University of Houston
Houston, TX 77004
(713) 749-3130

Texas Consumers Association
906 Nueces
Austin, TX 78701
James Boyle, President
(512) 477-5791

Texas Consumers Association
Paul Cardwell, Jr., President
2633 Greenland
Mesquite, Texas 75149

---

*Toll-free telephone call

Harris County Office of District
Attorney
301 San Jacinto
Houston, TX 77002
(713) 228-8311, Ext. 7493

Tarrant County Office of District
Attorney
New Criminal Courts Building
300 West Belknap Street
Forth Worth,TX 76102
(817) 334-1603 (Criminal Consumer
Fraud)

County Office of District Attorney
County Courthouse, Box 171
Hempstead, TX 77423
(713) 826-3335

City Department of Consumer
Affairs
City Hall, Rm. 108
Dallas, TX 75201
(214) 744-1133

Texas Consumer Associated
P.O. Box 12542
Houston, TX 77017
(713) 228-1521
Stephen M. Vaughan

Dallas Community Action
Consumer Education Department
2208 Main
Dallas, TX 75201
(214) 742-2500
Calvin McCoy

Low Income Consumer Club
1510 Plum Street
Texarkana, TX 75701
(214) 794-3386
(501) 774-5259
Thelma Williams

UTAH

Office of Attorney General
236 State Capitol
Salt Lake City, UT 84114
(801) 328-5261

Trade Commission
Department of Business Regulation
330 East Fourth South
Salt Lake City, UT 84111
(801) 328-6441

League of Utah Consumers
180 East First South
Salt Lake City, UT 84111
Glen Hatch, President

UPIRG
P.O. Box 8752
Salt Lake City, UT 84108
Larry Bench
(801) 966-4747

Utah Consumers Organization
203 East 7th So.
Salt Lake City, UT 84111
Bonnie L. Lee

Salt Lake Community Action Agency
Tim Funk
2033 So. State
Salt Lake City, UT 84115
(801) 487-3641

League of Utah Consumers
2096 No. 220 East
Provo, UT 84601
(801) 375-6726
Dr. Virginia Cutler

VERMONT

Office of Attorney General
200 Main Street, P.O. Box 981
Burlington, VT 05401
(802) 864-0111 or 862-6730

Deputy State's Attorney
Economic Crime Division
Chittenden County State's
    Attorney's Office
39 Pearl Street, P.O. Box 27
Burlington, VT 05401
(802) 863-2865

VPIRG
26 State Street
Montpelier, VT 05601
Whitey Bluestein, Dir.
(802) 223-5221

Vermont Alliance
5 State Street
Montpelier, VT 05602
Steve Hedger
(802) 229-9104

Vermont Consumers' Association
Mrs. Thomas Kleh, President
72 Lakewood Parkway
Burlington, Vermont 05401

Consumer Assoc. for the Betterment
    of Living
Anne Jones Haas
Box 77
Danby, VT 05739
(802) 293-5462

VIRGINIA

Office of Attorney General
Supreme Court Building
1101 East Broad Street
Richmond, VA 23219
(804) 770-2071

Arlington County Office of Consumer
    Affairs
2049 15th Street, North
Arlington, VA 22201
(703) 558-2142

Fairfax County Department of
    Consumer Affairs
Erlich Building, Suite 402
4031 University Drive
Fairfax, VA 22030
(703) 691-3214

Prince William County Office of
    Consumer Affairs
Garfield Administration Building
15920 Jefferson Davis Highway
Woodbridge, VA 22191
(703) 221-1101, Ext. 14

Virginia Citizens Consumer Council
Mrs. Doris Behre, President
3408 Cameron Mills Road
Alexandria, VA 22305

Virginia Citizens Consumer Council
Box 777
Springfield, VA 22150
Judy Kory, President
(703) 560-9228

North Anna Environmental Coalition
P.O. Box 3951
Charlottesville, VA 22903
June Allen
(804) 293-6039

Concerned Citizens for Justice, Inc.
Douglas E. Caston
P.O. Box 1409
Wise, VA 24293
(703) 328-9239

Tidewater Citizens Coalition 4801
Peachtree Lane
Virginia Beach, VA 23455
(804) 499-0845

VAPIRG
Campus Center
College of William & Mary
Williamsburg, VA 23185

WASHINGTON

Office of Attorney General
1266 Dexter Horton Building
710 Second Avenue
Seattle, WA 98104
(206) 464-7744
*800-552-0700

King County Prosecutor's Office
C517 King County Courthouse
516 Third Avenue
Seattle, WA 98104
(206) 344-7350

WASHPIRG
Box 225 FK-10
University of Washington
Seattle, WA 98195
Don Clockson, Director
(206) 543-0434

Washington Committee on Consumer
   Interest
2701 First Avenue
Seattle, WA 98121
Christine Whitney
(206) 682-1174

Central Seattle Community
   Council Federation
2410 E. Cherry Street
Seattle, WA 98122
Jim Metz
(206) 322-7100

Community Action Council
P.O. Box 553
Port Townsend, WA 98368
Harold S. Buck
(206) 385-0776

Blue Mountain Action Council
19 East Popular Street
Walla Walla, WA 99362
(509) 529-4980
Peter M. Frisvold

WEST VIRGINIA

Office of Attorney General
State Capitol Building
Charleston, WV 25305
(304) 348-8986

West Virginia Citizen Action Group
1324 Virginia Street East
Charleston, WV 25301
(304) 346-5891

West Virginia Consumer Association
Mrs. Jack N. Sizemore, President
410-12th Avenue
Huntington, WV 25701

*Toll-free telephone call

Council of Southern Mountains
125 McDowell Street
Welch, WV 24801
(304) 436-2185

WVPIRG
Mountainlair SOW
West Virginia University
Morgantown, WV 26506
(304) 293-2108

WISCONSIN

Governor's Council for Consumer
  Affairs
16 North Carroll Street, Rm. 415
Madison, WI 53702
(608) 266-7340

Trade Division
Department of Agriculture
801 West Badger Road
Madison, WI 53713
(608) 266-7228

Department of Justice
State Capitol
Madison, WI 53702
(608) 266-7340

Racine County Community Action
  Committee, Inc.
Thomas E. White
Memorial Hall
72 7th Street
Racine, WI 53402
(414) 633-1883

Concerned Consumers League
524 W. National Avenue
Milwaukee, WI 53204
David Matz, Director
(414) 645-1808

Wisconsin Consumers League
Box 1531
Madison WI 53701
(608) 238-8153
Louise Young

Center for Public Representation
520 University Avenue
Madison, WI 53703
Louise Trubeck, Director
(608) 251-4008

Wisconsin People's Rights Org.
152 W. Johnson
Madison, WI 53703
Pat Raymond
(608) 256-2794

WYOMING

Office of Attorney General
Capitol Building
Cheyenne, WY 82002
(307) 777-7775

Wyoming Consumers United
  Program
864 S. Spruce
Casper, WY 82601
Frank Spillane, President
(307) 234-6060

REFERENCES

Part 1, Introduction
1. Soaring costs of medical care. *U.S. News & World Report,* Washington, D.C., June 16, 1975.

Chapter 1
1. *Fortune, 500 Edition,* May 1965–1975.
2. *Annual Survey Report,* Pharmaceutical Manufacturers Association, Washington, D.C., November, 1976, p. 1.
3. *Ibid.,* p. 3.
4. *Ibid.*
5. Milton Silverman and Philip R. Lee 1975. *Pills, profits, and politics.* Berkeley, Calif.: University of California Press, p. 29.
6. Brand vs. generic drugs—it's only a matter of time. Henry E. Simmons, M.C., M.P.H., Director, Bureau of Drugs, Food and Drug Administration, FDA Consumer, March 1973, p. 6.
7. Drug bioequivalence. Office of Science and Technology, United States Congress, July, 1974.
8. Prescription drugs: retail price disclosures, staff report to the commission. Federal Trade Commission, Washington, D.C., January, 1975, p. 19.

Chapter 2
1. *Newsletter,* Massachusetts Medical Society, Boston, Mass., May 1974.

Chapter 3
1. Robert Kastenbaum. *Aging and Human Development.* New York: Knopf, 1974, pp. 36–37.
2. *Nursing home care in the United States: failure in public policy, introductory report.* Subcommittee on Long-Term Care of the Special Committee on Aging, U.S. Senate, U.S. Government Printing Office, Washington, D.C., December 1974, p. 22.
3. *Ibid.,* p. 25.
4. *Nursing home care in the United States: failure in public policy, supporting paper No. 1. The litany of nursing home abuses and an examination of the roots of the controversy.* Prepared by the Subcommittee on Long-Term Care of the Special Committee on Aging, U.S. Senate, December, 1974, p. XI.
5. *Ibid.,* p. 167.
6. *The Nursing Home.* Connecticut Public Interest Research Group, November, 1974, p. 3.
7. *Would you call this home? Maine nursing homes: a consumer's perspective.* John G. Melrose, Maine Public Interest Research Group, November 1974, p. 2.
8. *Ibid.*
9. *Ibid.,* pp. 3–4.

Part 2, Introduction
1. *Energy alternatives: a comparative analysis.* Sciences and Public Policy Program, University of Oklahoma, Norman, Oklahoma, 1973, p. 13.

2. *Exploring energy choices.* Energy Policy Project of the Ford Foundation, Washington, D.C., 1974, p. 1.

Chapter 4
1. *A nation of energy-efficient buildings by 1990.* The American Institute of Architects, Washington, D.C., 1974, p. 3.
2. Energy conservation: its nature, hidden benefits, and hidden barriers. Lee Schipper, Energy and Resources Group, University of California, Berkeley, California, p. 31.
3. *A Time to choose,* (A Report to the Energy Policy Project of the Ford Foundation), Ballinger Publishing Company, Cambridge, Massachusetts, 1974, pp. 45-111.

   Amory B. Lovins. Energy strategy: the road not taken? *Foreign Affairs,* October, 1976, p. 65.
4. *Ibid.,* p. 22.
5. *Patterns of energy consumption.* The Stanford Institute for the Office of Science and Technology, Washington, D.C., 1973, p. 24.
6. *Energy and the built enviornment: a gap in current strategies.* The American Institute of Architects, Washington, D.C., 1974, pp. 11-13.
7. *Lighting and thermal operations: energy management action program for commercial, public, industrial buildings.* Federal Energy Administration, Office of Conservation and Environment, Washington, D.C., 1974, p. 7.
8. *Ibid.,* pp. 7, 9.
9. *Energy conservation through effective utilization.* Charles A. Berg, Institute for Applied Technology, National Bureau of Standards, Washington, D.C., 1973, p. 9.
10. *Ibid.,* p. 6.

Chapter 5
1. The lifeline rate concept. Report by the Office of Consumer Affairs/Special Impact, Federal Energy Administration, January, 31, 1975, p. 1.

Part 3, Introduction
1. *Consumer price index.* Bureau of Labor Statistics, U.S. Department of Labor.
2. Bureau of Economic Analysis, U.S. Department of Commerce.
3. *Ibid.*
4. On food chain profits. Staff Report to the Federal Trade Commission, July, 1975, p. 5.
5. *Ibid.,* p. 10.
6. *Ibid.,* p. 3.
7. *Ibid.,* pp. 11-16; *Food from market to consumer.* Final report of the National Commission on Food Marketing, 1966; *Fortune, 500 Edition,* 1965 through 1974.

Chapter 7
1. Food dating: shoppers' reactions and the impact on retail food stores. USDA Economic Research Service, Market Research Report #984, Washington, D.C., January, 1973, p. 2.
2. *Ibid.,* p. 8.

3. Food labeling, goals, shortcomings, and proposed changes. General Accounting Office, Report to Congress, January 29, 1975, p. 44.

4. *Ibid.*

5. Cost aspects of open dating and unit pricing. N.V. Lawson, Vice President of Accounting and Date Processing of Safeway Stores, in a speech to the 21st National Association of Food Chains Controllers Conference, San Francisco, May 23–26, 1971.

6. Food labeling: goals, shortcomings, and proposed changes. General Accounting Office, Washington, D.C. Jan. 1, 1975, pp. 48–49.

Chapter 8
1. Unit pricing in perspective. Theodore W. Leed, Professor of Food Marketing, University of Massachusetts. From remarks made at opening of the Northeast Conference on Unit Pricing, March 13, 1972.

2. Esther Peterson, Unit pricing—a giant step for consumers. From a speech delivered at the Conference of Weights and Measures Officials, July 14, 1971.

Chapter 9
1. Retail food store advertising and marketing practices trade regulation rule including statement of its basis and purpose. Federal Trade Commission, Washington, D.C., 1971. p. 5.